Made in Japan

Made in Japan

Revitalizing
Japanese Manufacturing
for Economic Growth

Japan Commission on
Industrial Performance

The MIT Press
Cambridge, Massachusetts
London, England

This work originally appeared in 1994 under the title *Meido in Japan: Nihon Seizōgyō Henkaku e no Shishin* published by Daiyamondo Sha, Tokyo.
© 1994 JCIP

This book was set in Palatino on a PC in Ventura Publisher by Wellington Graphics.
Printed and bound in the United States of America

Library of Congress Cataloging-in-Publication Data

Meido in Japan. English
   Made in Japan : revitalizing Japanese manufacturing for economic
growth / Japan Commission on Industrial Performance.
     p. cm.
   Includes bibliographical references and index.
   ISBN 0-262-10060-6 (hardcover : alk. paper)
   1. Industries—Japan. 2. Manufacturing industries—Japan.
3. Japan—Economic policy—1989– I. Nihon Indasutoriaru Pafōmansu
Iinkai. II. Title.
HC462.95.M4513 1997
338.4'767'0952—dc21   97-26637
                                                          CIP

Contents

Foreword   ix
Shoichi Saba

Prologue: In Search of a Global-Scale Manufacturing
Mechanism   xiii
Hiroyuki Yoshikawa

I   **General Outlook for the Growth of Japanese
Manufacturing Industries**   1
Kei Takeuchi, Haruo Shimada, and Hiroyuki Itami

II   **Manufacturing Industries**   17

1   Development of the Electronics Industry   19
Haruo Shimada

2   Home Electric Appliance Industry   51
Kei Takeuchi

3   Automobile Industry   71
Takahiro Fujimoto and Akira Takeishi

4   Metallic Materials Industry   97
Yasunori Baba and Shinji Takai

5   Factory Automation Equipment and Industrial Machinery
Industry   123
Hiroyuki Itami

6   Chemical Industry   141
    Konomu Matsui and Shin-ichi Kobayashi

7   Fiber, Textile, and Apparel Industries   171
    Kei Takeuchi

III Common Problems   191

8   Paradigm Shift   193
    Haruo Shimada, Hiroyuki Itami, and Kei Takeuchi

9   Manufacturing Technologies   209
    Yasunori Baba

10 Management of Research and Development   225
    Konomu Matsui

11 Structural Distinctions within Japanese Manufacturing   253
    Yukio Watanabe

12 Educational System in Raising Human Capital   273
    Shin-ichi Kobayashi

13 Changing Circumstances of Employment: From Homogeneous
    to Heterogeneous Work Force   291
    Atsushi Seike

14 Fixed Investments and Finance Sources: From a National to a
    Global Perspective   311
    Hisashi Yaginuma

15 International Development of Manufacturing   335
    Hiroyuki Itami

16 Role of Government (Industrial Policy)   359
    Toshihiro Kodama

Afterword   391
Koji Kobayashi

Appendix: Members of the Japan Commission on Industrial
Performance   393

Index   407

Foreword

Shoichi Saba

This book gathers together in a final report by the Japan Commission on Industrial Performance (JCIP) the results of three years of investigation and study on the state of Japanese manufacturing industries and the problems that they face.

The concern of our Commission was not with the short term, nor with attempts to find solutions to passing problems. Instead, we have sought to look at fundamentals: to anticipate the demands that the twenty-first century will make on manufacturing and to examine several key structural concerns from a wide perspective. We have used a somewhat experimental approach to understanding these issues. The Commission's membership is drawn from the two worlds of academe and industry, and a distinguishing feature of this report is an innovative approach that draws on the expertise of both groups to investigate and clarify issues.

As this study neared completion toward the end of 1993, the Japanese economy found itself in unprecedented difficulties. There was animated debate on the causes and on what the future may hold. One conclusion was a general recognition among experts that there is no simple one-dimensional explanation; what is happening in Japan today is more than another swing in the business cycle, much more than an adjustment to the bursting of a bubble economy.

Since the end of World War II, the Japanese economy has been supported by three distinct systems: the Japanese economic system, the Japanese market system, and the Japanese management system.

The general characteristics of the so-called Japanese system have included limited salary differentials and a progressive tax system with high marginal rates, lifetime employment, and promotion and increases in salary with seniority. It is a system that has proved successful in allowing some 125 million people to live within a limited territory without producing significant unemployment or unsettling disparities in wealth. It has maintained relatively high economic growth while raising living standards. Yet the restructuring demands confronting Japan today all carry the same message, that the system and its attributes are on the verge of collapse.

Serious issues now challenge some Japanese industries—particularly those in manufacturing. Over the last twenty to thirty years, the Japanese system had motivated the nation's manufacturers to develop diverse strengths. The manufacturing industries were able to supply the world with high-quality products at low prices by honing international competitiveness while improving quality and productivity and building up technological capabilities.

However, in time these efforts no longer enjoyed positive results. Increased competitiveness produced trade imbalances, especially with the United States, and Japan's growing trade surplus led to strained relations between the two nations. Competitiveness also fueled a high yen that distorted purchasing power parity, preventing the Japanese from enjoying a lifestyle commensurate with the yen's exchange rate. When these trends became coupled with a stagnation in the world economy, Japanese companies, particularly those in manufacturing, were hit hard.

Now yet another challenge is rearing. The cumulative effects of concerted rationalization and attempts to increase productivity have begun to show themselves in the operations of U.S. companies. Improvements are also being seen in product quality. In short, the performance of American companies is getting better, throwing some long shadows over the very competitiveness Japanese manufacturers had long taken pride in.

In 1989 the Massachusetts Institute of Technology published its landmark study of productivity in American companies, *Made in America*. MIT's analysis of the decline of U.S. international competitiveness came as a jolt to American complacency and also caused quite a stir here when it was translated into Japanese.

Made in America brought it home to Japanese business leaders that well-organized research could provide useful insights into what might be expected by industry in coming years. Senior management in manufacturing was persuaded of the value of a similar analysis of their own operations. These sentiments led to the establishment of JCIP by the Japan Techno-Economics Society (JATES) in 1990, and eventually to this report.

Unlike MIT, JCIP did not limit the focus of its investigation to productivity. It set the wider goal of examining how Japanese manufacturing companies can maintain the effectiveness of the systems they have formed over time, notwithstanding the vast changes that are remaking the world and the position of Japanese companies in it. Put another way, can the traditional virtues of Japanese industry be carried into the future as strengths? Or is there a danger, similar to that detailed in *Made in America,* that present strengths, left unchanged, may become future weakness?

The exploration of these questions involved 17 university researchers working with almost 200 people from 34 companies. Hiroyuki Yoshikawa, president of the University of Tokyo, represented the academics working on the project, while Michiyuki Uenohara, special adviser to NEC, and I were asked to take on the responsibilities of corporate representatives. JCIP proposed the basic division of work that was followed: The contributing companies identified and presented the vast volumes of data required, and the academics carried out a comprehensive, objective analysis and evaluation.

For the purposes of study, the 34 contributing companies were divided into seven categories:

• Industrial electronics (computers, semiconductors, communications equipment, etc.)

• Consumer electronics (home electric appliances, audiovisual equipment, etc.)

• Metal products (steel, nonferrous metals, etc.)

• Automobiles

• Chemicals

• Fibers, textile, and apparel

• Factory automation equipment and industrial machinery

The progress took time. The process of organizing the researchers to work together lasted over a year, from spring 1990 to early summer 1991. Then came two years of substantial analysis and debate. Naturally enough, some of the evaluations and the advice offered proved painful to the companies. However, while everything was subject to thorough discussion and review by all involved, the work proceeded on the understanding that the views and value judgments of the academic side would prevail in the final analysis and evaluation.

Some of the dramatic changes that hit Japan's politics and economy as this work was under way prompted several last minute revisions and additions to the report, but they are few in number. As I have already noted, we are not concerned with the immediate term but in focusing on what manufacturing industries should be like in the twenty-first century. I hope that we have succeeded, and that this report will become a useful source for readers wanting to understand the future of Japanese manufacturing.

I cannot close this introduction without extending my deepest gratitude and thanks to the many people from universities, companies, and think tanks throughout the country who have contributed to this report. While sheer numbers prevent me from naming individuals, the evidence of their contributions—their research, participation in surveys, their analyses and explications—is to be found on every page of this book. This report is a record of all their effort.

I also wish to express my appreciation to JATES for providing both the overall concept and the means to its realization. JATES served with distinction as the secretariat for planning, organizing, and conducting the research that produced this report.

Tokyo, March 1994

Prologue: In Search of a Global-Scale Manufacturing Mechanism

Hiroyuki Yoshikawa

Future of the Manufacturing Industries

Now that Japan holds an important position within the world economy, I feel that it is important that we analyze the problems and make a forecast for our nation's manufacturing industries. The problems facing manufacturing are not unique to the Japanese economy; they inevitably extend to issues concerning the free trade system itself such as has led to trade friction.

Japan has become an economic giant accounting for 15 percent of the world's production. Its high economic growth has allowed a long-time goal of catching up with the United States to be fulfilled on the tail of this success.

The development of the manufacturing industries looks back to the opening of Japan to the outside world in the Meiji period (1868–1912), which came also at a time of great social change in the United States and Europe. It was an age when scholarship, technology, and industry succeeded conspicuously, and wealthy societies were being born. Indeed Japan's opening may have been stimulated and brought to fruition by the gap between its wealth and that of the West.

The opening of Japan proceeded by transplanting Western methods into this country in diverse fields. The incentive to catch up with the United States remained the same even during World War II and the period of confusion after its end. Japan's present economic development seems to have been born because this incentive operated properly in the new postwar environment. If asked what Japan did to catch up during this period, the most succinct reply may be that it joined the industrialized nations of the West. Its process of entering the industrialized group might be summarized in the following way:

The prosperity of the United States and Europe had depended on the development of their manufacturing industries since the time of the Industrial Revolution. Seen from the stance of the development of manufacturing and the wealthy society that it produced, the Industrial Revolution may very well have been due to the discovery of manufacturing industries that had developed autonomously.

People worked in manufacturing companies and produced goods that made them wealthy. By earning an income, they became consumers who could purchase goods. Companies were able to offer many goods through a social division of labor. The fact that individuals could be employed in different types of manufacturing made it possible for many kinds of goods to be produced at the same time which enriched all of society.

This fundamental mechanism behind a people's wealth became a powerful cycle based on consumer income acquired in the manufacturing industries. Japan's industrialization was no different.

As Japan's initial goal of catching up was attained after World War II, the imported Ford-style mass-production methods from the Industrial Revolution steadily raised production efficiency. Japan rejoined the industrial age as a truly faithful latecomer, and continued on its way, by means of this wealth-producing mechanism, toward becoming an industrially rich society. As a cooperative participant in the world's industrial system, Japan's goal then was to bring about further development by advancing its production systems. In reality Japan succeeded by producing high-quality goods more cheaply. Moreover the benefits it gave purchasers contributed to the country's industrial progress.

Shouldn't this fact have been widely welcomed by the rest of the world? After all Japan was a rookie in the world of making things. Also should Japan not have been applauded around the world for adding to and advancing the wealth-producing mechanism that had been built by the United States and Europe?

Reality hit hard as this mechanism, the boon of the Industrial Revolution, gradually began producing contradictions. One cause of those contradictions was the intensity of demand on Japanese industries. Those contradictions have consisted of trade friction arising from imbalances in trade income, structural unemployment in the advanced industrialized nations, the paradox of non-profit-making investments in research and development, and so on, and they have cast doubts on the merit of a free market economy. Additional circumstances, such as restrictions on trade exports, appear to call for rewriting the free trade system too.

Rather than viewed as a territorial matter of complications in the trade between two countries, these contradictions could perhaps be considered from a more basic standpoint. Although over 200 years have passed since the onset of the Industrial Revolution and the industrial system continues to progress, three-quarters of all the people on this earth have yet to be included.

Indeed the costs of industrialization have been rising to the point where it is now difficult to enter the system at will. Long latent global environmental problems have also begun to surface as further contradictions of the benefits of Industrial Revolution alert us to limitations of the earth's resources. While these environmental problems have been developing, three-quarters of earth's people are still behind, and that clearly indicates the limits to this wealth pursued by Japan and the West for the past 200 years.

By this understanding we ought to realize that Japan's entry was a factor that caused the contradictions of global industrialization to manifest. We should see that it is our obligation, as a people both affected by and affecting the situation, to seek solutions to the arising contradictions.

However, the problems are not so simple that they can be solved by just partially revising our nation's policies. They are problems experienced on a global scale and by all industries. In other words, they need to be approached via reforms in the world economy, and with a reorganizing mechanism that may entail a second Industrial Revolution.

By analyzing the Japanese manufacturing industry, we might be able to find this mechanism that will lead to a revolutionary growth in the world's manufacturing industries. This was the impetus for the planning and publication of this book.

Some Suggestions for Policy Changes

The Japanese manufacturing industries have made great strides toward solving the many contradictions they currently face. Among their efforts have been the transfer of manufacturing sites overseas, the release of technological patents and expertise to the public, and cooperative research and development in technology. In addition government policy has taken diverse steps in lowering tariffs, opening up government procurements to worldwide bidders, and internationalizing research and development projects, for example.

Yet, at present, not even one of the imbalances in trade revenues shows any sign of being improved, and structural factors seem to be responsible for that. It is likely that the contradictions centered around trade revenues will not be resolved by the combined effort presently exerted by corporations and the government were it even to be carried far into the future. The trade revenue problems will not go away simply by a people's dynamic adaptability to change in circumstances either—a notable feature of the Japanese economy in the past. Nor will the capacity to cut costs made possible by that sacrifice do the trick.

In other words, on the one hand, we should not be complacent about the existing ways of doing things but should seek a basis for change commensurate with the individuality of Japanese manufacturing. On the other, we should not hesitate to provide leadership in seeking a mechanism that has also implications for manufacturing industries worldwide.

Our research approach was undertaken on the idea that perhaps we have not the adequate knowledge about our industries to make viable proposals. While it is generally recognized that Japan's high economic growth was conducted around manufacturing and its formidable international competitive strength, we must question whether the Japanese competitive power was really so strong. And if it was strong, then what was the source of that power and how can it be maintained? We must be familiar with the following points: What are the basic contradictions in the free market economic system that places absolute value on the pursuit of competitiveness? Do these contradictions manifest strictly accidentally such that our country has no responsibility for and control over them? Or do the causes of the contradictions lie within Japan and, consequently, can only be solved from within this country?

Knowledge of the history of Japan's manufacturing, its present management environment and managerial strategies within the industries, for example, is needed for gaining an understanding of these points. After all that information is analyzed and put in perspective, we will have the basis for making some adequate proposals for change.

To begin our work toward this end, we brought together leading members of industry who possess abundant experience, and are active managers, and scholars from academic institutions who are deeply versed in the manufacturing industry to examine these concerns. We set up seven industrial section meetings that included, besides several members of industry in the relevant fields, two members from academic institutions serving as coordinators. Much off-the-cuff information/data were presented by the industrial side, and more details emerged via energetic debates between industry and academe. The results of these exchanges are presented in the chapters in part II.

Common issues to all of manufacturing were brought out in the discussions. The members of the academic committee share these issues with us in the writing of part III. Every aspect of manufacturing is analyzed, starting from the common attributes of Japanese manufacturing industries and proceeding to their very individual structures. The general remarks of part I are written with these final analyses in mind. Presented in part I are also a number of proposals for the immediate and long term, and there is some speculation about what can be expected of Japan within the world economy in terms of its economic growth. There is much new material provided by these authors. From my position as an executive director of this project, I would like to give an outline of the central issues in the following section. I hope that readers will take it as a starting point for reading the rest of the book.

A Challenge of Revitalizing Manufacturing

It is well known that worldwide wealth was made possible by manufacturing industries. But there are fundamental contradictions in the traditional mechanism for this wealth. For this reason not all peoples have been included in that mechanism, and that presents a number of problems for the Japanese manufacturing industries.

The first problem has to do with the policy taken by the Japanese manufacturing companies to proceed with a de facto expansion of its share of the product market, a policy that may not work so well in the future, anyway. The idea behind expanding the market share was that as the production of the same good increases, so do improvements in its manufacturing technology, leading to both an improvement in product quality and a decrease in production costs, and thus to competitive strength. But increase of competitive power has a cyclic effect as it further expands market share. A win-win situation is created among competitors when the world market is growing faster than the increase in production, and that was the experience of the Japanese manufacturing industries. A win-lose situation is created when market expansion is slower than production.

There is much anxiety nowadays that the world economy may plunge into a win-lose state. The danger is that the circumstances that have enabled the accumulation of wealth will collapse from a decline in effective demand and structural unemployment as the competitive war produces losers. That is to say, with the creation of losers, the competitive costs of the world economy as a whole will end up larger. If by the concept of global productivity we express concern for long-term productivity by all peoples—such that is manifest by the free market system—we are, in contradistinction, moving toward lowering productivity.

Market expansion seems to be a way to avoid this problem, but the contributions that Japan can make toward expanding the market are limited at present. Japan rather needs to expand its market by stimulating domestic demand, to create employment by moving jobs overseas, and to set up local vendors as well as service policies, which means export of technology and of education by accepting foreign students, and so on.

Then, again, the services suggested do not seem to be qualitatively adequate. A qualitatively new market may need to be formed to make the venture overseas practical and new products created that require training in basic research. Japan must take the initiative and show other industrialized nations that industry can be revitalized such as by the manufacture of a new line of goods. Mostly those manufacturing industries that have reached maturity and no longer require research investments can be transferred to nonindustrialized nations where the knowledge inherent in these industries can be shared with a fresh group of producers and consumers.

The pursuit of competitive strength by high productivity is no longer a sufficient manufacturing strategy. Manufacturing industries worldwide must rather take up the challenge of increasing global productivity over the long term. While no such system yet exists to take this new perspective on reality, Japan might strive to be a leading player.

More than technology a new system needs creative personnel with a vision of the future economy. However, among the younger generations in Japan the trends are away from both the sciences and the manufacturing industry, and this has cast a long, dark shadow on this matter. The Japanese manufacturing industry basically has to get involved and put forth the incentive for young people to turn to the engineering sciences.

With a persuasive scenario on global environmental problems, and global productivity viewed from this benign perspective, we might take the burden on the earth as the denominator and the amount of welfare that might be offered to the peoples of this earth as the numerator. Naturally the recycling of resources to keep the burden on the environment low will be an important task in expanding global productivity.

We need ideas on manufactured goods that have completed their life-spans physically or functionally and can be recycled. Manufacturing industries must be made more efficient, for an industry's continuity may eventually depend on not using additional natural resources at all, and risk their depletion, but on recycling discarded goods. To this end, we need industries that convert goods that have exhausted their lives back to their resource states.

This means manufacturing industries ought to start thinking about building "reverse" factories that process waste products and turn them over for reuse. Unlike the traditional-style factory that carries the arteries of industry, a reverse factory might be seen to be using the artifacts of industry as resources. One more factory may thus be made to accompany each traditional factory.

Strictly speaking, a technological system that reverts products back to their resource state has yet to be pioneered. Ideas that are even more high-tech than anything existing today will be needed to put together a reverse factory. At present, hardly any effort is being made in Japan toward using recycled products in the manufacturing industries. Lamentable, too, are signs that Japan is falling behind the United States in both the technological development attending such an advancement and attempts to sweep away equipment investment costs.

The reverse factory is merely one measure for revitalizing the manufacturing industries of industrialized countries. If the Japanese manufacturing industries now only adopt results achieved in the United States without being challenged to advance their own system, they may plunge themselves—and thus the country—into an intractable state of decline.

The new challenges for the Japanese manufacturing industries call for a clear design enabling a rebirth from within and a new system from without that buttresses the free market economy. Japan should expect to step forth to pay the proper costs of responding to both its internal and external challenges. It must learn anew to say good-bye to superficial wealth.

Made in Japan

I

General Outlook for the Growth of Japanese Manufacturing Industries

Kei Takeuchi, Haruo Shimada, and Hiroyuki Itami

Problems and Perspectives

Fundamentally at issue in this book is a searching of ways for the Japanese manufacturing industries to exist in the twenty-first century. It means recognizing the conditions that allow for continual development through a self-analysis of industry performance. The manufacturing industries stand at the foundation of Japan's economic strength; their importance will not decline even in the twenty-first century. Japan clearly has no future if it fails to maintain the conditions for development of its manufacturing industries.

We feel a need to search for the direction to be taken by Japanese manufacturing in the twenty-first century, while holding always before us the development of manufacturing within the history of Japan and how these industries can be properly positioned within the global environment.

Basically in every country the development of manufacturing industries has never been an independent process. Japan is no exception. The development of the Japanese manufacturing industries after World War II has been deeply connected with the process of growth and change in this country's society and economy overall. The development of manufacturing industries has been a driving force, ushering in changes in the entire economic system.

On the other hand, the growth of manufacturing has been influenced by changes in Japanese society as the meaning and position held by the manufacturing industries within Japanese society began to change considerably. A perspective on manufacturing industries within this history is necessary for both understanding the postwar development of the Japanese manufacturing and taking a view toward the future.

A second perspective on an international scale may show how Japan and the Japanese manufacturing industries can participate in a global society. It is also a perspective on each industry's contribution to the outside world.

Japanese manufacturing, which has come to assume much weight internationally, has the responsibility to be heedful of the rest of the world. While in an increasingly smaller world the idea of contributing to the world economy is linked to restraining the development of manufacturing industries, the world and Japan can hardly partake in a zero-sum game.

Development of Japanese Manufacturing

Three distinguishing features can be found in the historical background of Japanese manufacturing. One is a zigzag pattern, for from the beginning Japanese manufacturing has not proceeded in the same direction nor even developed uniformly. To this day manufacturing industries change directions frequently. This zigzag tendency is important to keep in mind for discussions of Japanese manufacturing industries. As will be seen later, the changes in Japanese manufacturing have been helped by both historic disturbances and opportunities from other fields in Japan and overseas.

Another distinguishing feature is the gradual development of an industrial plan. Japan has had an industrial structure matching the level of development of the economy at each stage, and has furthermore steadily altered it. Japan did not suddenly undertake advanced industry, nor did it try to specialize only in light industry. That is to say, while aiming for a broad-ranging industrial structure within its borders, Japan has gradually been able to alter its industrial base and its industrial presence. Such incremental development is evident in every industry structure.

In the obsession with manufacturing autonomy, the tendency was to include almost every type of manufacture within the country—to acquire a full set of industries, or what might be dubbed "full set-ism." Yet there are precious few examples in Japan of unprofitable industries, or of those that have gradually undergone extinction. This has been advantageous from the macroeconomic view.

A final point on the distinctive history of the Japanese manufacturing is that it has been shaped by foreign socioeconomic systems whose influence has been retained. The fact that the Japanese manufacturing did not develop strictly on its own underscores the importance of outside factors in its future.

Good Fortune and Conformity

Japanese industry has been continually carrying out structural reforms since the end of World War II. The success of almost all of the reforms so far can be attributed in great part to the maintenance of peace both in Japan and abroad, auspicious economic circumstances and technological trends, and conformity between national policies and management strategies.

When Japan began reaccumulating capital after World War II, by chance it was able to ride smoothly the waves of technological reform. Its proficiency in grappling steadily with the latest technology of the times was more a stroke of good luck. Then in the 1970s when the first oil crisis caused a shift in the industrial structure, it additionally strengthened Japan's capacity to deal with challenging circumstances.

While the appreciation of the merits of adversity varies considerably among industries in Japan, there are some industries that benefited from the oil crises and some that did not. Performance then in terms of management does not always depend on the actual strength and merits of the industry alone.

For example, in terms of international competitiveness, the first oil crisis was advantageous for the automobile industry, which successfully developed low-energy-consuming and low-pollution-producing vehicles. On the other hand, it was unfavorable to the chemical industry which faced escalating materials costs. There were also differences in an industry's or corporation's ability to confront the crisis by turning it to an advantage. All that had to do with performance, but individual management abilities were far from uniform.

On the macroeconomic level, there were no examples of the Japanese government and its people cooperating thoroughly to carry out major long-term policies, although national policies and corporate management strategies appear to have been coordinated on the whole. Japan received a very large shock from the first oil crisis. But the second oil crisis was completely absorbed so that it had hardly any effect in terms of macroeconomic figures; the congruity between government policy and management strategy enabled Japan to cope extremely well.

State of Development in the Present-day

On the whole Japanese manufacturing has demonstrated strong competitive power. It has maintained this power through high product quality (not simply in the sense of a physical product but also including the manufacturing industries' adaptability to market factors in extending their range of goods, prompt delivery, service contracts, etc.), high productivity at the plant sites, and low production costs. Nevertheless, some doubt exists whether high productivity is representative of Japanese society overall if admitted is its value-added or manufacturing productivity.

A high level of technological accumulation supports manufacturing's competitive power. An outgrowth of "full set-ism" has been a very strong industrial base with superior technology in a wide range of industries. Automation has proceeded along with improvements in product quality and diversification.

The accumulation of internal corporate reserves, though once quite low compared to those in the United States and Europe, has now become robust in Japan. Likely the investment standards—particularly, internal capital—will continue to be maintained at the same high level.

Most important, economic growth has raised the level of people's income. With improvements in income, the Japanese market has grown enormously. That has further benefited Japanese manufacturing which depends heavily on domestic demand.

Problems Lurking in the Shadow of Development

There are two sides to every coin, and the development of Japanese manufacturing is no exception.

The main problem is not limited to the manufacturing industries. It is that the various social systems that are the foundation of Japanese industrial development, and that have supported the paradigm of mass production at its very core, have begun to change significantly. These systemic changes have affected stable employment relations based on lifetime employment and wages according to seniority, intra-company unions, a large well-educated male labor force, workplace morale, and so on, all of which functioned quite effectively up to now in an economy that experienced expanding markets and successively the appearance of new markets. High income and stable employment were achieved but at the price of changes in the social system, employment relations, and the social awareness of the people.

Next, with the increase in the Japanese income level, there have been conspicuous increases in production costs internationally in many industrial fields that were comparatively late to improve their productivity. The relative rise in such costs is more striking in nonmanufacturing areas than in manufacturing and in capital commodities than in commodities associated with so-called consumer wealth. In manufacturing, because of the general increase in production costs, domestic production is now facing severe cutbacks, except in areas showing certain technological strengths, distinctive product lines, or else marked improvements in productivity.

Then there is the matter of value-added productivity which is not all that remarkable despite the high physical productivity at production sites. The value added is the amount retained by the company after it subtracts external payments from the price of a sale. Unlike output indexes, such as the amount of physical production, the number will be larger if a product's market price is high—that is, if the same product is sold at a higher price. On the other hand, if the cost of purchasing externally is high, the added value will be low. That is to say, value-added productivity is influenced by price, and considered in terms of added value per worker, it is value-added productivity. Now, measured by worker, the value-added productivity of the Japanese manufacturing industries is not so high.

In the Japanese market there compete a great many models and brands of the same good, and there have been some dramatic innovations to meet certain consumer needs. But all this has diminished the merit of mass production and raised per unit production costs, which in turn has lowered added value. Excessive services, another feature of the intense competition among corporations, have indirectly brought about cost increases too.

To complicate the matter even further, the distribution structure in Japan has a large influence on value formation, which puts the manufacturing industries at a disadvantage. In the way it distributes added value few improvements of productivity in an industry return to it.

A final problem is international friction. The Japanese manufacturing industry has managed to capture markets in the United States and

Europe, but not without encountering political friction. As a result overseas activities of Japanese corporations, especially exports, are now facing restraints.

Basic Directions at Present

The problems facing Japanese manufacturing industries suggest a need for clarifying some basic measures that will allow their continued development. We need to consider the current direction of Japanese manufacturing before we can make a shift in the standard paradigm. From the point of view of both products/technology and international development, there are three basic directions:

1. Continue high-level technology in each corporation.
2. Adhere to market needs in the development of products.
3. Make direct global investments.

Note that measure 2 has elements both conforming and in contradiction with measure 1. While technology has to be high in order for it to have a high added value, the danger remains that traditionally cited problems, like overdesigned products and overproduction of a small number of different goods due to competition, will become more serious. Two questions must be considered for the future of the Japanese manufacturing industry. One is whether the efforts to raise technology and make direct overseas investments are adequate. The other is whether these policies are myopic in focusing only on the Japanese point of view and overlooking other ways for correcting the imbalance in the Japanese manufacturing industry's large presence in the world.

An awareness of these points will help us in planning the future of Japanese manufacturing.

Future Tasks

Ideological Shift

Ideological shifts have already begun in the management structures of manufacturing industries as well as in the social system that is the backbone of industry. Indeed the very management principles and structural adjustments within manufacturing that have been enabling Japan's growth and development so far are now, in some cases, instead hampering industrial development. Included are the long series of investments made during the bubble economy.

Additionally affecting manufacturing industries are the unsettling demands of the times. A general malaise has been plaguing the institutions of government and the universities that have supported the manufacturing industries, and they can no longer fully back their further development.

Clearly there are critical changes to be made in the paradigm on which manufacturing has been traditionally based. The following are some areas where to start reforms:

1. The rules of competition and Japanese market imperfections.
2. The parallel competition paradigm.
3. Japanese employment practices.
4. The top management structure.

Involved are problems not so shallowly rooted that they can be solved by the manufacturing industries alone. The government, companies, and universities must work together to usher in the changes and reform the organizational structure of manufacturing industries.

Three Proposals

Present-day Japan is established enough to be in a position to contribute to the international discussion on the future of its manufacturing industries.

Among the various ideas that might be set forth are contributions to the advancement of world technology, to the distribution of economic activity worldwide, and to the protection of the global environment. These contributions are not meant to be just altruistic; they will help maintain the development of Japanese manufacturing and Japan's prosperity as a whole.

Contributions to the Advancement of World Technology

The Japanese manufacturing industry should consider raising the level of the world's technology by transferring its advanced industrial technology abroad, and it can also do this by improving basic research and advancing technological knowledge within Japan.

The development of industrial technology has been a history of transfers in technology and economic opportunities from advanced nations to developing ones. This perspective on the dissemination of technology might be called "technoglobalism." Technoglobalism is a way of thinking that stands in opposition to "technonationalism." Technonationalism is when each country strives to maintain dominance in industrial development, international competitiveness, military power, and so on, by monopolizing advanced technology. In addition to not developing technology reciprocally, each country asserts its ownership of technology and knowledge. Then each turns protectionist about technology in order to prevent its flow and spread elsewhere, in contrast to technoglobalism which emphasizes the promotion, transfer, and sharing of technology.

While technoglobalism may be challenged by corporations concerned about intellectual property and by national interest groups in the countries that possess advanced technology and knowledge, our thought is that the weight in the transfer of technology should be given to intellectual ownership. We need a system whose compensations for intellectual property do not limit the use and application of advanced technology and knowledge by others.

Contributions to the Distribution of Economic Activity
Japan maintains trade relationships with both industrialized and developing countries. In its trade with the United States and the EC, Japan has occasionally encountered friction, since its manufactured products are highly competitive and have led to trade imbalances in other countries. In principle, nevertheless, Japan has been adhering to the idea of free trade.

But one cannot deny the tendency to dominate the market among Japanese companies overseas. This tendency may be seen too as a way to compensate for the lack of domestic demand. With its low-priced exports Japan has to avoid a "deluge" of exports, which has caused considerable confusion in the industrial orders of other countries.

Japan has both aided the economies of developing countries and been confronted by competition for their abundant low-cost labor supply. Of course it is essential for Japan, which is lacking in natural resources, to maintain friendly relations with all regions of the world, if only for the reason that our prosperity and welfare are interdependent.

Direct investments abroad may be the most powerful way to build a mutually beneficial relationship with developing countries. These investments could take the form of transferred technology and management training in order to cultivate human resources and technical skills in particular regions. We ought to consider improving the procurement of goods locally and moving into developing products for local markets.

Direct investments overseas expanded rapidly throughout the 1980s. In the 1990s, while investments in the financial field have grown sluggish, investments in manufacturing have, after a short dormant period, returned considerable profits. The success of this investment in manufacturing suggests some strategies for future investments:

1. Aim production toward local markets. There is no denying that overseas Japanese companies are inclined to serve as bases for development and for exports aimed at Japan or other developed countries. Recently there has been a trend toward meeting the needs of local markets, as seen by the examples of the electronics and the automobile industries.

2. Emphasize the importance of the plant sites. The emphasis on ideas at the plant sites can be also applied in overseas manufacturing. It contributes to productivity, product quality, and on time delivery.

3. Be responsive to innovations in technology occurring at the locality. Japanese corporations are periodically criticized as having control over the transfer of the latest technology. But a vast amount of technology has actually been transferred via operations at overseas production sites. Technological transfer, which is important to economic development, tends much more nowadays to consist in improving product quality and efficiency at the production site rather than in any secret documents on the latest high technology. Economic gains are larger because training can be carried out locally. There is also improvement in the quality of work, so maintaining a locale's autonomy in technology is a simple strategy.

The politics of global investment can be effective in contributing to the distribution of the world economy. Direct investments by Japanese companies tend very much to run parallel among corporations and to be geographically clustered. When one company in the same business begins investing, an avalanche of other companies starts investing too.

Likewise investments have tended to be concentrated in regions or countries where the risk is believed to be low; not many investments go to unfamiliar areas which might present high risks. This sort of attitude toward investments makes Japan appear somewhat selfish and calculating. Companies should give thought to reforming these practices and make an effort to support the outside world.

The same could be said for foreign access to Japanese markets. Japanese corporations ought to refrain from doggedly defending their markets to the bitter end. Many Japanese companies up to now have expanded production based on the notion that an increase in market share or a large expansion will lead to corporate profits. Their reasoning has been that the goods will get absorbed in the international market no matter how great the volume produced.

But this logic is no longer valid. The balance in the world economic system is not being considered when there is a one-way flow of goods. Japan must aim for free trade whereby something can be purchased from a country that can produce the item at a better price than it takes Japan to make the same thing.

Contributions to the Protection of the Global Environment
The global environment and the world's resources are finite. Japanese manufacturing must begin to show an awareness of the global environment in its industrial activities. A good place to start is by considering the impact of its productivity on the future of world resources.

The wealth that has resulted from the expansion of manufacturing industries has also inundated the globe with mass-produced objects. This deluge has upset the once secure stability of nature. In other words, manufacturing industries are disturbing the earth's natural systems as they are creating their aggregate of goods. Global productivity can be maximized by taking the ratio of those costs and output to the ecosystem on a global scale. Namely

$$\text{Global productivity} = \frac{\text{Aggregate function of an industry's product}}{\text{Amount of disturbance to ecosystem in producing it}}$$

The extent of global disturbance is the aggregate amount of materials and energy consumed in a product's life cycle from the time it is planned, developed, produced, and used until it is thrown away. This includes as well ecological changes due to the accumulation of abandoned materials and the like.

If the global productivity ratio is low, then the disturbance in delivering a fixed abundance of goods will be large, so the idea of manufacturing the good should be abandoned. The aggregate function (numerator) gives the fundamental value of the good to the ecosystem, and the amount of disturbance (denominator) gives an indication of the environment's durability.

Such a perspective on maximizing global productivity is likely to become important to manufacturing industries in their continued development. But additionally Japanese manufacturing industries should step back and reflect on whether there has been something in their activities up to now that has been hard to support from the standpoint of the global environment, but the Japanese corporations should not have to undergo this introspection alone.

The latest discrepancy in global productivity is the fierce rivalry among Japanese companies. The obvious examples include rapidly outdating products, obsessive emphasis on product quality, excess product variety, excess advertising, excess research and development investments, and the list goes on. Some of this activity may be due to corporations caught in a flow of circumstances beyond their control, but the time has come to give serious thought to corrective measures.

Further, if Japanese manufacturing industries are to consider helping raise global productivity through a transfer of their technology to developing countries, it might be good to start within Japan by improving the environment by using low-energy fuels, for example.

Suggestions: Keywords for Corporate Activity

How to Change Attitudes toward Competition

Competition is the keyword in changing long-held attitudes toward the marketplace. Although it is both the nucleus of the market economy and the wellspring of industrial energy, when competition goes too far, it ventures way beyond the negative effects of merely oppressing corporate profits. Herein lies the heart of the issue for Japan's strong manufacturing industries which are now pressed to reconsider their attitude toward competition.

Of course, bringing in ideas that will somehow restrict competition, if only partly, can be dangerous. However, Japanese manufacturing industries, with their intrinsic parallel and excessive competition, probably cannot help but turn to constructive cooperation in some form. Expressed another way, these industries must effect a balance between competition and cooperation. On the one hand, cooperation may mean unity in product standards such as might lead to healthy competition rather than to circumstances akin to a cartel. Coordination of basic research and development is one form of desirable cooperation.

There is no real need to limit industry cooperation to a circle of Japanese companies. Today, though assuming the lead at the international level, Japan is carrying out projects relating to intelligent manufacturing systems in a move toward cooperating with world rivals to raise global productivity.

How to Deal with Creative Technology

The second keyword for the Japanese manufacturing industry in the twenty-first century is *creative technology.* It is true that Japan up to now has mainly improved and further developed technology created in other countries. However, now that it has lined up with the front-runners of the world, there are demands on Japan to be technologically more creative. Although some creativity is entailed in improving and further developing technology itself, a far greater level of activity is now expected of Japan.

In particular, two things may be important in moving toward that aim. One is the fostering of creativity among technicians and workers. The second is more emphasis placed on the technological field—especially soft technology.

The cultivation of creativity should be seen as desirable by Japanese people of all classes working in every kind of job, since human creativity is at the root of all technological and strategic progress. As is shown in this book, the custom in Japanese corporations has traditionally been to emphasize organized learning and the acquisition of skills centered around teams, habitual reforms, and compensations leaning strongly toward equality. In this environment, corporations have generally not nurtured creativity.

However, currently the Japanese management and employment philosophy that once stressed teamwork is starting to undergo change. The emphasis has shifted to making better use of workers who have developed specialized knowledge. From this standpoint there will be great demand for personnel and management structures that know how to evaluate creativity.

Furthermore, in view of the present state of Japanese manufacturing industries, improvements in soft technology are especially urgent. Soft technology, which includes design and computer software, is becoming the focus in various manufacturing areas that have so far stressed making things and were not inclined to recognize and invest resources in areas without readily visible results. That inadequacy has been clearly recognized, and the weight is being shifted to research and development in soft technology.

How to Maintain Adaptability

Adaptability is characteristic of a country like Japan which developed industrially to an abnormally rapid degree in a short span of time. It first of all involves positioning one's past experiences within a large— or international—framework. Second, it means being aware of the extent of one's influence in the world. Japanese companies have generally not been responsive to either of these requisites.

The Japanese experience is relative to the development process of its economy as well as to a unique corporate management style. Japanese industries therefore need to understand the different experiences of other countries as well as of other eras. Similarities must be understood too. For that reason Japan needs to take part in an exchange of information with other countries.

Adaptability also means recognizing the extent of one's influence. Japan is not a minor country. Nevertheless, Japan tends to efface itself on the international scene as if trying to hide itself like a small country. To be sure, political problems have been caused by the Japanese manufacturing's deluge of products into foreign markets, and this is precisely because Japanese companies have grown so large. As in the case of an adolescent boy who has suddenly realized his physical strength, it takes learning to recognize the extent and limitations of one's power.

The Japanese manufacturing industries must be more political in their international activities. For example, in serving the idea of global productivity, they should consider the impact of a company's behavior and any political implications for the host country. This ought to be a part of corporate strategy. Many Japanese companies are already in positions where, willingly or not, they cannot ignore the political aspect of their actions.

Essential Long-Term Tendencies within a Short-Term Favorable Economy

After a brief recession brought on by a high yen in 1986, Japan entered a bubble economy. It was a favorable time for manufacturing industries. Some companies neglected their real work and became entangled in money games, but they were the exceptions. Efforts unfolded to become globalized and to raise labor productivity despite the high yen and high costs involved, as will be discussed in subsequent chapters. Some manufacturing industries took an overoptimistic view of market trends and, lured by extremely low cost equity financing, built extravagant facilities.

But in late 1992 the situation changed. The bubble burst, and the purchasing power of the "high yen" dropped dramatically. Japanese manufacturing industries suffered a severe blow. Now these industries must grapple with essential structural alterations in taking a long-term view; they cannot just concentrate on short-term prospects. If they do so, their technological foundation, which has been developed over a long period of time, may end up falling right out, leaving them structurally without a core like a donut. This could, for instance, happen if, in dealing with a 100 yen to one dollar exchange rate, industries try to maintain their competitiveness in world markets by reducing staff, cutting subcontractors' costs, and moving production bases completely overseas.

Clearly an exchange rate nearly twice the purchasing power parity is "unnatural." We must work to obtain policies that correct the excessively high yen. But the manufacturing industries must also avoid continuing with unreasonable levels of exports and accumulating a trade surplus—a situation that only leads to higher yen. Under the high yen, manufacturing ought to be particularly cautious that any necessary price increases on exports are not obstructed by domestic business competitors. Although much of the current recession is not the fault of manufacturing, these industries did overvaluate themselves during the bubble economy. Now they must be careful not to underrate themselves and lose confidence because of poor corporate management results.

Many things need to be rectified and changed in Japanese industries, especially in manufacturing. Such matters are discussed in every chapter of this book. Here we want to stress that what ought to be protected must be upheld even during adverse times.

Japanese manufacturing's most valuable asset is the worker. Worker morale must take priority. That is to say, workers' satisfaction, the innovations they develop as a result, and workers' abilities to absorb new technology are all built on trust between employees and their corporations, among companies, and among people belonging to different companies. Relationships of trust must be upheld even during a recession. The industry must make every effort to avoid measures like employment adjustments that damage this trust such as closing plants and abandoning long-term business relations. Success can be expected of structural changes with a long-term outlook only if they are premised in a relationship of trust.

Having such a perspective onto themselves, manufacturing industries, though facing a major shift in their activities, will still be capable of responding to traditional systems, customs, and values that are undergoing change as well. Grappling with adaptability and new principles of competition in order to enact this shift and move forward with creative development indeed appears to be the direction of Japanese manufacturing industries in the future.

II

Manufacturing Industries

1 Development of the Electronics Industry

Haruo Shimada

The electronics industry referred to in this chapter include the following four industrial fields: semiconductors, computer software, computer hardware, and communications equipment. These fields of industry mainly consist of electronic components and equipment for industrial use. Their importance is rising not only in the Japanese industrial structure but also worldwide.

This chapter will emphasize the following points:

1. The Japanese electronics industry has achieved amazingly rapid development over the past twenty to thirty years. It has caught up with the U.S. lead in a number of areas and is now even more competitive in semiconductors and some other areas.

2. The Japanese electronics industry has manifest remarkable strength in productivity due to the Japanese corporate management and employment style.

3. In the immediate term, new strategies are needed to raise creativity and product quality despite changing circumstances such as the decline in labor force since 1992.

4. Great expectations have been placed on the development of multimedia to serve as the foundation of the high-information society in the twenty-first century. However, Japan still lags far behind in multimedia technology, which is being developed quite actively in the United States, and little progress has been seen at present.

5. International cooperation is an important issue for the electronics industry. This could be achieved by corporate mergers, multinational cooperative ventures, shared technology, partnerships in the development of new technology, as well as by transfers abroad of corporate functions.

1.1 Development of the Semiconductor, Computer Hardware, Software, and Communications Equipment Industries

The semiconductor, computer hardware, software, and communications equipment industries stand out among the growth fields within the Japanese manufacturing industry. Their rate of growth in the manufacturing industry's overall productivity index has increased fourfold over the past thirty years from 1.7 to 7.0 percent.[1]

In particular, in the past decade (1981–1990) output in the electronics industry increased from ¥10.8 trillion to ¥23.9 trillion.[2] During this decade exports saw a more than twofold increase, though the yen base decreased slightly in the late 1980s due to the significantly high yen.[3] About 40 percent of exports went to the United States, so there was conspicuous concentration of Japanese products in American markets.[4] On the other hand, imports were only at one-sixth the level of exports as of 1989, and they had experienced a rapid growth of nearly 2.4 times in the most recent decade.

This rapid development of the electronics industry stems from the fact that productivity per unit of labor rose by leaps and bounds, with dramatic technological reforms in products ranging from vacuum tubes to transistors, ICs, LSIs, and super-LSIs. The innovations in semiconductor technology stimulated product development in other fields of industry, providing computers and communications equipment, for starters. The large-scale technological, economic, and social changes brought on by the electronics industry may be said to have herald a third Industrial Revolution.

In recent years there has been a clear shift in the development of electronics equipment from hardware to software. That may reflect the qualitative social changes taking place by the vast information made available in the advancement of information technology.[5]

Semiconductors

The semiconductors field experienced the most rapid growth in recent years. Although output fluctuated in the last decade, the field grew tremendously from ¥1 trillion to nearly ¥4 trillion.[6] The proportion occupied by semiconductors in the electronics industry's total output doubled from 7 percent in 1970 to 15 percent in 1990.[7]

Such rapid growth has been due primarily to a remarkable increase in productivity per unit of manufacture and economies of scale in the wake of the development of more highly integrated semiconductors. An additional factor was a sharp decrease in the cost per bit of memory.[8] Then came amazing improvements in production capacities, so many industrial products came to incorporate ever more electronic parts, and the output coefficient of semiconductors in industrial products rose conspicuously[9] along with dramatic developments in semiconductor technology. The Japanese semiconductor industry's development was helped by the fact that the transistor industry in its initial period strongly tended toward labor intensity in the assembly process, for example. In this respect it was fortunate that Japan had a large, capable female labor force.

Integrated circuits were first developed in the early 1960s. ICs are suitable for many systems, and they are a critical component of electronic computers and information-processing equipment for industrial use. Back in the 1960s the United States was strong in this technology, and the percentage of parts exported from Japan was low. In fact Japan mostly imported. Much of the imported application equipment was also American made. In Japan, efforts to develop technology to produce comparable ICs and highly reliable telephone switchboards were carried out as a public interest project by the government, mainly at the research center of the Nippon Telegraph and Telephone Public Corporation (later privatized as NTT).

In 1966 the Ministry of International Trade and Industry (MITI) launched its first large-scale project, the development of high-performance electronic computers. As a result the development of Japan's semiconductor technology was accelerated around large-scale integrated circuits.

While it was in the United States that initially the idea of using semiconductor memory in the computer memory device was published, it was a Japanese manufacturer that first developed semiconductor memory in 1968, as a task of MITI's large-scale project. In 1970 an American manufacturer released dynamic memory chips which made the induction of IC memory into a computer's main memory device possible. Because of this the United States secured a position of superiority until around 1975. Up to this time Japanese makers were still enthusiastically adopting technology from American manufacturers.

Then, after Japan launched the Super-LSI Research Union in 1976, it took the lead in MOS memory technology, and the American industry's competitive power declined. At present Japan is the main developer and producer of semiconductor memory, but South Korea is catching up. South Korea's pace in this pursuit has been quite rapid, and it seems to be moving faster than had been the experience of Japan, which nevertheless has been able to maintain its edge in both production and development.[10]

The United States developed the microcomputer with semiconductors in 1971. Thereafter it developed and marketed a succession of new models with further improved capabilities to meet the world's demands. The United States managed to achieve a position of superiority in these microcomputer markets, not so much because of high-quality labor power and the dispositions of the technicians supporting semiconductor technology but rather because it was able to block other companies' entry by patents on its architecture. As of this writing (1991), Japanese manufacturers still have not had much success in entering this market except with microcomputer components that do not require the architecture.

While the Japanese semiconductor industry was accomplishing rapid growth and catching up, the share of the American industry, which had been the main force of the world in terms of development and production of semiconductors up to then, started undergoing a sharp decline. Until the first half of the 1980s, the world was led by American firms like Texas Instruments, Motorola, and Fairchild. However, since the latter part of the 1980s, their lead has been replaced by companies like NEC, Hitachi, and Toshiba.

Beginning in the late 1980s, many Japanese semiconductor manufacturers have come to occupy the upper ranks in the world[11] (but in 1993 Intel, an American company, held the top position). Already Japanese companies' share of the world's semiconductor market had expanded dramatically starting in the mid-1970s, while the American share dropped, falling well below Japan's since the late 1980s. Under such circumstances friction between Japan and the United States over the semiconductor trade grew steadily harsher in the 1980s.

In the United States, besides a handful of giant firms like IBM, AT&T, and Motorola, semiconductor production is handled on a small-scale by many highly specialized companies. Japan's semiconductor production is led only by giant vertically integrated electronic manufacturers.[12] The Japanese structure has made it easy for Japanese companies to carry out the necessary large-scale investments with a long-term view and to develop the system and devices en bloc through vertical integration. Another important aspect is the emphasis on higher-quality products to meet the demands of both industrial and personal use, and this has enabled Japanese semiconductor products to earn a reputation for high reliability at home and abroad. All the while, from a fairly early period, Japanese-made transistors and ICs have been in great demand for their high reliability.

As with the manufacture of other industrial products, Japan's unique method of quality control, in which all employees participate (through QC [quality control] circle activities and TQC [total quality control]), has contributed considerably to the success of the electronics industry. Another major factor behind this success was the early involvement of Japan's public telegraph and telephone corporation which, in its efforts to transistorize, introduced ICs into their apparatuses and thus improved the reliability of the communications equipment. As a result it set up a strict system for checking the reliability of semiconductors for communications and enforced strict quality control in the manufacturing process.

Computer Hardware

It may be convenient to discuss the development of the hardware field by dividing it into stages. The period from the end of World War II to the 1950s was the time when Japan's supreme mission was to catch up somehow with the United States. Japanese universities, national research centers, and manufacturers joined forces to proceed with development. As a result MITI's transistor computer ETL Mark III and NTT's parametron computer Musashino-I were completed, respectively, in 1956 and 1957. Then, in 1959, NEC and Hitachi, respectively, displayed the transistor NEAC 2201 and the parametron HIPAC 101 at the first International Information Conference in Paris. In addition Fujitsu completed its parametron FACOM 201 and 202.

The 1960s were a time of technological cooperation. Domestic equipment was manufactured that copied the parent machines of foreign partner companies. In 1961 seven domestic manufacturers concluded contracts on the basic use of patents with IBM and founded the Japan Electronic Computer Company (JECC), as IBM began production in Japan. In 1964 IBM released the 360-series and established the concept of mainframe computers. From about 1965 each Japanese company began domestic production of their foreign partner company's computers.[13] In 1970 IBM released the formidable IBM370 whose new technology challenged domestic manufacturers even further.

The 1970s were an age of cultivating domestic technology. In 1970 to 1972 each Japanese company continued with and began developing new equipment using domestic technology that reflected the results of major MITI projects, the public telegraph and telephone corporation's DIPS project, and so on.[14]

Six computer manufacturers in 1972 formed the Union for Research into Technology for the New Computer Series. In 1973 the government decided to liberalize computers. In 1976 NEC and Toshiba released the new ACOS 77 series, and Hitachi and Fujitsu put out the M series. From that time a pattern was formed whereby once IBM released equipment carrying new architecture, each domestic company would respond by putting out machinery with superior capacities at the same price as IBM's. From about 1978 each domestic maker got a lead on IBM with the induction of 16-kilobit MOS memory. This was roughly the time when Japanese companies reached a position of superiority over IBM in semiconductor technology.[15]

It was in the 1980s when the Japanese computer industry made its greatest progress. Each domestic manufacturer supplied OEM and technology to its former partner company but also exported actively overseas. Japanese companies started shipping out supercomputers, which IBM had not yet among its product line.[16] IBM responded by loading a vector structure onto the mainframe IBM 3090. Nevertheless, the Japanese manufacturers often led partially even in architecture.

In 1990 each domestic firm released new machinery ahead of IBM, which reversed the former pattern where IBM put out new machinery in the mainframe equipment area, and each Japanese manufacturer responded by following through with its own machines.[17]

Japanese computer manufacturers were matched effort by effort by IBM, their major world competitor. Domestic manufacturers have recently surpassed IBM Japan, a leading player within Japan.[18] The trends now are for office computers, which have seen a very rapid increase in the past ten years or so, and minicomputer work stations, which is another area that has grown dramatically over these past several years.[19] Felt in these trends is the effect of computer user companies' now downsizing amid the economy's current fluctuations.

Along with the domestic computer industry's development, the international competitiveness of Japanese computer manufacturers rose remarkably. Exports started increasing dramatically in the 1980s and came to surpass imports by far. During the 1980s imports of computers increased 2.2 times while exports expanded by 2.6 times.

Tariffs on computers and related equipment were abolished in Japan in the latter half of the 1980s.

Given such circumstances, trade friction concerning computers arose between Japan and the United States, as well as between Japan and Europe. Through the MOSS deliberations and other negotiations, a policy on the procedures for adopting supercomputers was formulated, and a series of measures for dealing with the situation has been taken. Attention is now being paid to the role of the government's industrial policies as one condition for encouraging the computer industry's development. Large-scale development projects and a subsidy system to support development of basic technology seem above all to have fulfilled crucial roles. In addition development projects centered around NTT and work being done at large-scale computer centers at universities appear to have stimulated development among computer makers to a certain degree.

Computer Software

The software industry has grown along with the computer industry. The tide of the market in recent years has been the tendency toward downsizing in computers against the backdrop of semiconductor technology's dramatic development. We are moreover seeing a rapid development of software that has transportability, making it easier to operate various software packages on different types of equipment. This makes integrated applications and distribution simpler.

The construction of data bases has increased along with the increase in information processing in society. As a result software has acquired greater importance in recent years. The software industry in Japan has grown under the system of confederate companies (*keiretsu*). The trend in recent years has been for software companies to go independent, and entry into this field has been extremely hectic as of late.

In an attempt to promote the software industry, the government has actively grappled with ways to promote the information-processing industry. Laws on business associations, and the like, concerning information processing, were established back in 1970. Also in that year the Information-technology Promotion Association (IPA) was set up.

The trouble between Fujitsu and IBM is an example of friction over software rights. This problem is connected in the broad sense to the protection of intellectual property rights. The issue of intellectual property rights is likely to get more attention in the future when theoretically both industry and the economy are expected to become further integrated.

Communications Equipment

Communications technology in prewar Japan may have been sporadic, but it was not entirely backward.[20] On the other hand, the state of electric communications business was truly weak. The launching of the public telegraph and telephone corporation and the opening of the airwaves became the cornerstones of the development of Japan's post-war electric communications business.

In 1950 new airwave laws were promulgated. So the use of airwaves, which had been monopolized by the government until then, was opened up to the general public. As radio broadcasting was expanded and television broadcasting launched, broadcasting equipment, radio receiver, picture tube, and related industries followed.

In 1952 the public telegraph and telephone corporation was restructured as a public corporate body, establishing business operations with a long-term view in response to the restoration of communications equipment and the rapid increase in demand for telegraphs and telephones. The next year its first five-year plan was formulated. Besides actively adopting the advanced technology of various foreign countries, the corporation highly motivated the development of Japan's own technology, and Japanese communications equipment manufacturers responded in full force to its demands.

First of all, the setup of the long-distance calls network began to undergo expansion. This network was employed simultaneously in television relays between major cities nationwide. In 1954 microwave transmissions were launched between Tokyo, Nagoya, and Osaka. Then in 1956 coaxial cable transmission was adopted between Tokyo and Yokohama, and in that year the first domestically produced cross-bar switchboard was placed into operation.

Nevertheless, as the orders for telephones accumulated, the majority of long-distance service remained in-a-waiting-for-operator-assistance form. For this reason the public telegraph and telephone corporation in 1958 produced its second five-year plan aimed at dissolving the queuing of orders and making direct long-distance dialing possible throughout the nation. To reach this objective, the corporation speeded up technological development. This included the miniaturization of all communications equipment by semiconductor technology, improvements in reliability, lowering electric power consumption of machinery, and making wireless, unmanned relay stations. Moreover high-capacity microwave transmissions and coaxial cable transmissions were put into practice, bringing transmission technology to world levels.

In 1963, as telephones were disseminated throughout Japan, improvements were demanded in system reliability. Various measures were instituted, such as improving the routes for long-distance transmission. In 1965 PCM transmission, the forerunner of Japan's digital transmissions, began its nationwide service. Then in 1966 a new crossbar-style switchboard went into operation.

Around that time the objective of the fourth five-year plan, which aimed at instantaneous long-distance dialing, was almost completed, and attempts were being made to establish digital technology and integrated program control technology in order to offer new diversified services (facsimile, data, etc.) more effectively. A precedent was set not only with coaxial cable methods and microwave relays but also with coaxial PCM, wireless PCM, integrated program control electronic switchboard (analog), and so on.

The development of telephone technology led to the development of digital electronic switchboards and optical fiber transmission equipment. As a result, by 1970, Japanese transmission technology ranked with that of Europe. By 1980 it had reached the technological level of the United States.

With these efforts expended toward technological development, the world competitiveness of Japanese communications equipment rose. As exports greatly expanded, so did trade friction.

The communications equipment industry has been continuing its rapid growth. Total production for 1970 came to approximately ¥469 billion (of which wire communications equipment accounted for about ¥342 billion, and wireless communications equipment for about ¥127 billion). In 1980 the total record went up to ¥1.06 trillion, of which wire communications equipment accounted for about ¥670 billion, and wireless equipment for about ¥390 billion. Thus in a mere ten years these areas increased at the extremely rapid rates of 2.3 and 2.5, respectively.

As of this writing in 1990, the total output is worth approximately ¥2.6 trillion. Wire communications equipment such as conveyor instruments and switchboards have reached nearly ¥2 trillion, and wireless communications equipment about ¥640 billion.

Again as of 1990, exports have totaled ¥814.7 billion and imports ¥117.4 billion. About 40 percent of exports and over 70 percent of imports were carried on with North America. The ratio of exports to imports in trade with the United States at that time was regaining some balance compared to what has been the case in recent years. Yet exports still amounted to more than triple that of imports.

The communications equipment industry in Japan was perfected in 1978, when the problem of backlog orders for telephones was resolved and direct, instantaneous long-distance dialing spread throughout the nation. With 1981 as the point of inflexion, along with the decline in growth of orders from NTT (then the public telegraph and telephone corporation), the industry switched to a line of growth dependent on foreign demand.

Orders came primarily from the United States, Europe, and Asia. In addition to on-site switchboards, the products for export have included mass-produced system terminals such as push-button tele-phones, facsimiles, and car telephones. The result has been an on-slaught of exports from Japan met by tension and trade friction with the United States.[21]

The communications industry can be run smoothly, even in the face of differences in forms of business and trade, as long as the standards of both communication protocol and interface are maintained. In this sense the international standardization of communication protocol and interfaces is extremely crucial.

1.2 Market Structure and Corporate Competitiveness

Market Share

Semiconductors

Today most Japanese makers are among the top semiconductor manu-facturers in the world. In terms of the yield of shipments in 1991, NEC had an 8.5 percent share, Toshiba 8.2 percent, Hitachi 6.7 percent, Intel 6.3 percent, Motorola 6.0 percent, and Fujitsu 4.8 percent. As for sales in 1990, NEC accounted for 8.5 percent, Toshiba for 8.4 percent, Hitachi for 6.7 percent, Motorola for 6.3 percent, Intel for 5.4 percent, and Fujitsu for 5.2 percent.[22]

Japanese corporations have come to dominate the upper ranks in this way since the late 1980s. In 1975 NEC had just managed to reach the number six spot.

Japan and the United States monopolize the world's semiconductor market. As far as European companies go, Philips, which has a very large share of the European market, barely manages to appear in the number ten slot.

Computers

Although the growth of Japanese corporations has been remarkable in the computer market, American manufacturers—notably IBM—still maintain a large share. A look at world share by computer type (as of 1989) shows that in the mainframe computer field, IBM dominates at 31.1 percent, followed by DEC at 7.4 percent, and Fujitsu at 6.5 percent. Fujitsu heads the Japanese market (as of 1990) with a slight lead at 24.5 percent over IBM Japan's 24.2 percent.

Number one in the personal computer world market (as of 1989) is again IBM at 13.9 percent, followed by Apple at 9.7 percent, COMPAQ at 5.9 percent, and NEC at 5.2 percent. NEC holds an overwhelming 51 percent of the domestic market (as of 1990).

The order of the recent (1990) top-ten rankings for Japanese manufacturers goes as follows: Fujitsu, NEC, IBM Japan, Hitachi, Toshiba, Nihon Unisys, Oki Electric Industry, Mitsubishi Electric, NCR Japan, and DEC Japan.

Communications Equipment

The number of public telephone lines is one way to view the scale and structure of the communications equipment market, and in 1991 the figure reached 550 million worldwide. In terms of number per location, Europe had 182 million public telephone lines, Asia 163 million, and North America 158 million—meaning that three regions account for over 90 percent of the total. The number of such telephone lines in the world is expected to grow by an average of 5.1 percent annually from to 1990 to 1994, to reach a projected total of 640 million by 1994. On the ranking by the number of lines retained in each country, Japan places number two in the world. (The United States is number one.)

On the other hand, the list of the share of the world's communications equipment market by manufacturer as of 1988 goes in the following order: AT&T (14.8 percent), Alcatel (11.6 percent), Siemens (9.8 percent), NEC (8.1 percent), Northern Telecom (7.0 percent), Ericson (4.8 percent), Motorola (3.9 percent), IBM (3.6 percent), and Fujitsu (3.2 percent). Two Japanese companies are among the top ten. In addition, in terms of sales by public electric communications businesses, NTT is tops, followed by AT&T.

Corporate Characteristics

Semiconductors

If Japanese manufacturers are to be compared with their counterparts from Europe and the United States, great differences will be found primarily in production, supply, and the fields of goods sold, all of which reflect historic differences in the domestic market for semiconductors. European and American manufacturers definitely stress semiconductors for industrial use, while their Japanese counterparts, needless to say, are relatively oriented toward mass-market demand. As for corporate form there are many giant, vertically integrated manufacturers in Japan and Europe. The majority in the United States tends to be specialized.

The corporate managements of European and American manufacturers—especially those in the United States—emphasize short-term profits to a striking degree, since constant research and development activities and long-term equipment investments present drawbacks. The American social structure creates considerable discrepancy between an elite minority and a widely ranging working class, with strong labor unions presenting a force of resistance to management. Japanese manufacturers function within a somewhat different social structure.

Manufacturers from the Asian NIES countries offering low wages have fulfilled the role of subcontractors for European, American, and Japanese makers. In recent years they have aggressively brought in advanced technology—especially South Korea—have made large-scale investments, and have achieved rapid growth. These countries are in the process of switching from labor-intensive to capital-intensive systems.

Computer Hardware

The computer hardware business has been getting progressively worse because of the time spent on coping with changes in recent product environments, particularly relating to downsizing and the rapid development of open systems.

In the personal computer field, Microsoft has a monopoly on OSs. Microsoft has joined with IBM to monopolize the supply. Yet its future position is not clear; there is some indication that it will work on developing various cooperative ties.

Much of the hardware from Japanese manufacturers is competitive in terms of function, capacity, reliability, and price. Supercomputers and high-end mainframes, in particular, are highly competitive. However, when included is the competitiveness of their software systems, which have limited application and development strength, they compare unfavorably with American manufacturers.

The price competition among mass-marketed computer hardware is intense. Naturally the Japanese brands are weak in the United States in terms of marketing, support system, and so on, compared to those of American makers. Let us consider the example of mainframe computers made by major Japanese manufacturers. A number of these manufacturers have developed outstanding practical technology in manufacturing computers for compatible use, and they supply a uniform group of parts that have built-in the latest technology. For that reason they enjoy a large share of the Japanese market, which is among the most competitive in the world, and thus Japanese products can be said to be in a superior position internationally in terms of product quality, capacities/price, durability, and so on.

However, computer marketing is not just selling hardware. Services like using a computer to decide how to solve a client's work problems are important too. Moreover computers are employed in key organizational operations, so a maintenance system is necessary. In marketing, a lot of specialized business knowledge is required in each field, and even once established, it may be adequate domestically but not internationally. Weak international marketing is a concern for Japanese manufacturers.

Japanese hardware, with compatibility as its marketing feature, is competitive in the ratio of price to capacity, but shipments tend to be late because of the time lag to follow the de facto standard of computer architecture. Therefore efforts are being made to shorten the delay with on-demand fulfillment of orders.

The operating systems (OSs) of Japanese manufacturers are proceeding with plans to handle backlogs, but they are dependent on the industry's structure which tends to lag behind world standards. While this is not a problem with UNIX, which conforms to world standards, ideas are needed on how to set up standardized systems. Application software also depends in some respects on differences in the computer culture, so it is difficult to make qualitative comparisons. Packaged business software has not been well regarded mainly because of differences in the volume marketed internationally.

Computer Software

The biggest rival of Japanese companies in the mainframe market—a market that cannot be separated from software and hardware—is IBM. The world's largest computer manufacturer (including hardware and software), IBM possesses abundant human, technological, and capital resources. It has always been ahead in the market with ambitious product designs and clever marketing strategies. Nevertheless, in recent years technological gaps in hardware with Japanese makers have all but disappeared. Moreover, because of the exorbitant costs of software development, troubles such as copyright disputes have arisen with Japanese manufacturers.

Comments on the personal computer market—a market where its software and hardware are independently formed—will pertain to OSs and universal or specialized applications. In the OS field the major rival of Japanese corporations is Microsoft. Microsoft got its start as a venture company and with outstanding foresight and sharp strategies (in collaboration with IBM) grew into the world's largest company specializing in personal computer software. Its products have become the de facto standard (DFS) in the global marketplace.

In the universal applications field, Lotus is a major rival of Japanese companies. Many such companies got their start as venture capital groups. With the success of their products, they grew rapidly by buying up and/or merging with other companies. The technological gaps between Japan and the United States in this field are so large that the problem of friction does not even arise.

A comparison of Japanese software companies with their American counterparts reveals the following characteristics:

As far as basic software is concerned, Japanese manufacturers are good with functions that have already taken root, but they still are a step behind in pioneering new concepts. Their operational application software used at government offices and public institutions compares well with their American counterparts.

Outstanding software is being supplied to financial organizations. Advanced systems have been developed, and a world financial network is under construction. Client (financial) institutions are leading the strong trend toward sophistication and uniqueness.

While software designed and tailor-made for different large companies in the manufacturing, financial, and distribution industries is highly sophisticated, packaged software for the mass-market is much less developed. The trend toward customized software opens up a wide gap between the United States and Japan in the physical capacities of software companies. The United States is far ahead in scientific technology because of the extensive cooperation between academe and industry found there. Also in the United States there are educational/research systems and organizations like NASA (National Aeronautics and Space Administration) and DOD (Department of Defense) that stress innovation.

The presence of NTT looms large in information and communications in Japan. But, while the fundamental technology related to the infrastructure is good, it lacks strength in pioneering applications. In the field of office automation, new concepts for personal computers and LAN are always coming from the United States. This has to do with differences in the social outlook and marketing strength. In the hobby field Japan leads due to the rapid growth of the family computer, which has been towed along by hardware. However, in view of DOD's tremendous power, the gap existing between Japan and the United States in defense technology is such that it is not even worthwhile to attempt a comparison.

Communications Equipment

The companies mentioned in the following paragraphs are fierce competitors in the field of communications equipment.

AT&T has come to run the world's largest communications business by developing operations like communications network services and the manufacturing/marketing of communications equipment. For many years it held the overwhelming lead in the volume of communications equipment production. But in 1984 not only were some of its communications network services dismantled and partitioned into seven RHCs (regional holding companies), but also the purchase of such communications equipment was completely deregulated, causing AT&T's market share to drop.

However, on the occasion of the divestiture, AT&T attempted to shift its corporate structure from that of a monopoly public service corporation to a strategically competitive company, and it proceeded with a thorough rationalization of management. With an eye to the unification of the EC market, it also promoted collaboration with European firms to develop markets and operations. It is planning as well global development by proceeding into the pan-Pacific region, including Japan.

Alcatel, which was established as a joint company between CGE (France) and ITT (USA), has grown while maintaining a close relationship with the French Electric and Communications Administration. Also through aggressive M&As such as of Telettra (Italy), it has become a more globally competitive corporation. With marketing routes acquired via M&As and production bases spread about like a net throughout the globe, Alcatel in 1989 surpassed AT&T to become number one in the world.

Siemens, Northern Telecom, and Ericson are also planning to unfold global operations and could be formidable rivals.

Two Japanese manufacturers, NEC and Fujitsu, are ranked among the top ten. Japanese makers have been lucky, too, with the national communications policies and industrial policies. They have benefited by working with advanced clients. As a result they have been able to fortify product plans, develop technologies, and advance their technological strengths. They supply not only Japanese markets but also those of North America, Asia, Latin America—indeed the whole world— with products that are outstanding in terms of price, delivery, quality, and so on.

A Subjective Comparison of International Competitiveness

In this section, based on the aforementioned considerations, I will select three or four representative products from each field (semiconductors, computer hardware, software, and communications equipment) of the electronics equipment industry. I will then introduce the subjective evaluations of experts from Japanese industry on how the competitiveness of Japanese companies in each field differs from their counterparts in the United States and Europe. The following appraisals are based on the opinions of randomly chosen business people who participated in our research project. The evaluations were designed to include areas like capacities (functions), product quality, price, productivity, delivery, and creativity.

Semiconductors

Memory With respect to capabilities and functions, Japanese semiconductors are stronger than those of the United States, Europe, and South Korea. Japan holds an especially wide lead in nanotechnology. It is superior to the United States and Europe in product quality too. An emphasis on the idea of high intrinsic quality contributes to this.

Japanese productivity is higher than that in the United States with Europe, but South Korea is catching up quickly. With respect to deliveries, Japan is good in handling fluctuations in demand. Its creativity has strength, but the United States has powerful high-speed processing. The United States also holds a superior position in design software.

Microprocessors The United States leads Japan in capabilities and functions, particularly the latter. However, there are no differences in product quality. Japan is ahead in price and productivity. The United States has unassailable strength in creativity; it leads, above all, with microprocessor architecture. The design software of the United States is superior as well, followed in rank by that of Japan and Europe.

ICs and ASICs for Industrial Use In terms of capabilities, the United States leads with semiconductors for computer use, and the European countries in semiconductors for communications. Japan has extended its fields of superiority from consumer use to industrial use. It leads in quality, price, and productivity. Japan excels in creativity, but the United States takes the lead in system technology. The United States also stands in a position of superiority with design software and is followed by Japan and Europe.

ICs and ASICs for Mass-Market Use Japan is strong in the integrated technology needed for making small, lightweight electronic items. These components have demonstrated superiority in capability, quality, cost, and above all productivity; however, the United States still maintains the lead in design software.

Computer Hardware

Mainframes Japan is ahead in product quality, productivity, and cost. As for price, in the wake of IBM's recent low-price marketing, discrepancies no longer exist between the United States and Japan. With regard to deliveries, the United States generally can deliver on short-term notice, and it is superior in creativity too. Furthermore in OSs, American corporations are ahead in terms of functions.

UNIX Base Machines This is an important field, and an expansion of the market can be expected in the computer industry of the future. While Japan excels in product quality, the United States is superior in terms of price and cost. The United States also leads in creativity. Moreover developments in the UNIX OS are centered around American firms to give the United States an indisputable monopoly on the top position.

Office Computers In small-sized equipment systems with proprietary OSs that can be easily used, Japan excels in quality, cost, and creativity.

PCs At present the PC world is centered on IBM and Macintosh. When IBM compatibility is considered, Japan is superior in the quality of hardware, but the United States leads in matters like price, cost, and creativity. American makers have conquered the world in particular in OS and have an overwhelming lead. In respect to the next generation equipment, OSs are diversifying, and fluctuations will occur in the share of major hardware.

Computer Software

Operating Systems (OSs) Japan can be said to excel in quality, productivity, and cost. But it is generally difficult to appraise price. Japan is fast on deliveries; however, American firms such as IBM and AT&T (in the UNIX field) stand in a superior position in creative power.

Packaged Software American corporations lead on the whole in quality, price, productivity, cost, creativity, and so on. European companies follow in rank, leaving Japan in a subordinate position. But Japan has displayed a certain amount of creativity in game software.

Communications Equipment

Ultra High-Speed Optical Transmission Equipment Japan shows strength in hardware capabilities and quality. Japan is particularly strong in items like optical devices, gate alleys, and ultra high-speed ICs. It even supplies optical devices to the United States. In terms of productivity, the United States leads in design, and Japan in manufacturing. With respect to creativity, the United States leads in basic technology, followed by Japan and Europe. In addition, as far as devices go, Japan shows special strength in optical devices, gate alleys, and ultra high-speed ICs, for example. However, the United States overtakes Japan in functionality—human-machine interfaces, documents, and the like—followed in order by Europe and Japan.

Switchboards for N-ISDN Stations The quality of Japanese hardware is high, and no major problems with software are found. There is no reason to compare prices among countries, since the United States has maintained a narrow lead over the markets of other countries, with an effective pricing strategy. The United States and Europe can take advantage of economies of scale to lower cost, whereas Japan falls behind. In terms of creativity, the United States leads, followed by Europe and then Japan. However, in the wake of the privatization of NTT, service functions have been improved considerably in Japan too.

Cellular Telephone Terminals The breakdown rate is low for Japanese equipment, and the quality is higher than the American and European counterparts. Hardly any differences in prices exist between Japan and the United States, but European companies are at a disadvantage because they produce in Asia and the United States. Japan has a slight lead in productivity and cost, since it has been proceeding with automation, and the like. That is reflected in the delivery periods. In creativity the United States is fundamentally superior, but Japan also has shown some ingenuity in applications and miniaturization.

Characteristic Facts First, the Japanese electronics industry underwent very rapid development for several decades since the end of World War II. Its growth was particularly impressive in the 1980s. The recession since 1990 has had a strong impact on this industry. For this reason it may not be feasible to map out a future that includes the continued rapid growth familiar up to now.

Second, the Japanese electronics industry has been characterized not merely by its speed of development. Japan is a prominent nation in the quality of its semiconductor, computer, and communications equipment. It has either caught up with or surpassed the industries of the United States which used to supply both technology and knowledge to Japan and which were once the greatest challenge to Japanese companies. In other aspects too the technological disparities between the United States and Japan and in their competitive strengths have been narrowing. Such circumstances have sharpened the economic friction between the Japanese and the American electronics companies over intellectual ownership and the like.

Third, the competitiveness within Japan's electronics industry has been intense. This shows up in the quality, price, and delivery (QPD) of electronic equipment. Considerable ingenuity and administrative effort goes into improving QPD by fostering a sense of solidarity among the operational teams and workers on the shop floor.

Fourth, as mentioned in the previous section, many technicians working on the frontline of international competitiveness in the Japanese electronics industry have subjectively judged Japanese products in various fields to excel over their American and European counterparts in terms of QPD. In particular, in their self-evaluation, they consider their high competitiveness internationally to be due to their superior manufacturing methods.

Nevertheless, many of the same self-evaluations by Japanese technicians note that in various major products the Americans excel in creativity. The competitiveness of American software and system products is highly praised. Expressed another way, the Japanese electronics industry is highly competitive in manufacturing, but in ideas and imagination they trail their American counterparts.

Fifth, with regard to international standards, the Japanese electronics industry has greatly contributed to the establishment of de jure standards. However, they noticeably lag behind the United States in de facto standards, which are often known to exist in the computer and software fields.

Finally, in dealing with market fluctuations, a review of the progress so far of the electronics industry indicates that its remarkable growth was achieved by adapting to changing circumstances. Although the outlook given the changing environment in recent years remains unknown, we can expect many different adaptations to changes in market conditions. Since in addition advanced technology has rapidly become more complex, sizable investments are needed for technological innovation. Meanwhile limitations are starting to become obvious in the resources—especially human labor—that can be mobilized by a corporation. Thus, to an increasingly conspicuous degree, companies are being pressed to develop new strategies.

1.3 Outlook for the Electronics Industry

Market's Future

The megatrend of increasing availability of information that has characterized today's social economy is expected to continue growing. The trend toward having more information available in the social economy is the likely lever in the continued development of information-processing and communications technology. Information-processing technology is expected to prosper dynamically by way of progress in semiconductors, computers, and software. The same may be said about communications technology that is allied with the development of software and data bases. That is because new industries and lifestyles creating new demand will likely be generated in future society.

According to the *Vision of the Electronics Industry in the 1990s* compiled by MITI, the electronics industry's market will experience consistent growth worldwide from 1987 to 2000; the forecast for semiconductors is an average growth rate of 13.6 percent annually, for electronic computers 11.9 percent, and for communications equipment 8.7 percent. The market scale thus in 2000 should come to ¥27 trillion, ¥116 trillion, and ¥33 trillion, respectively.

Until 2000 domestic demand for semiconductors is expected to expand by 14.8 percent, for electronic computers by 13.3 percent, and for communications equipment by 8.3 percent. The increase for each is expected to reach ¥12 trillion, ¥16 trillion, and ¥4.5 trillion, respectively.[23]

As far as individual fields go, more highly integrated, high-capacity semiconductors are expected to be developed. Along this line, the cost of semiconductors will probably become lower, so demand for them will increase by leaps and bounds. As semiconductors become introduced in all industrial products, their use is expected to increase remarkably in computer manufacturing.

Nanotechnology is necessary in manufacturing highly integrated, high-capacity items. The magnitude of equipment investments will necessarily increase, so there is no denying that worries whether individual corporations will be able to recoup those investments are growing. The resources of a number of companies are now being consolidated to make such large-scale investments. Cooperation among companies in recent years is also a sign that they are pooling their resources in order to be able to recover their costs. We cannot assume so simply that the growth will be linear in the future.

The software industry is linked with the computer industry. Since it is also integral with several fields, independent estimations are not always easy. However, according to the MITI's *Vision of the Electronics Industry in the 1990s*, demand for semiconductors should expand greatly from ¥1.6 trillion in 1990 to ¥7.8 trillion in 2000. Moreover, during the same period, information-processing services and information supply services can be expected to grow, from ¥1.2 trillion to ¥4.5 trillion and from ¥0.3 trillion to ¥3.3 trillion, respectively.[24]

In the communications equipment field, the outlook is that B-ISDN services will be disseminated to households throughout Japan with more speed and a wider range of networks based on digital technology, optical technology, and the like. In the coming age of multimedia, the communications equipment industry is expected to achieve astounding growth too.[25]

The Communications Equipment Industry Society forecasts an expansion in the industry's output during the five-year period from 1991 to 1996 from ¥2.7 trillion to ¥3.5 trillion. The average rate of growth for wire communications equipment during this period will be around 2 percent annually. But, considering the aforementioned technological progress, wireless communications equipment could be expected to accomplish higher growth, likely in the 9 percent range.[26]

In this way the electronics industry can be seen to continue growing over a long period of time based on a megatrend for readily available information in today's economic society. The forecasts of demand quoted here were made in the late 1980s or around 1990 when the Japanese economy was still expanding rapidly, so perhaps we ought to have some reservations about the pattern that growth may now take.

Thereafter, right after the bubble burst, the Japanese economy quickly became sluggish. In 1991 to 1992 the electronics industry experienced immediate effects as business conditions declined rapidly worldwide. The stagnation in demand is expected to continue for quite a while. Even if long-term growth is maintained in this industry, its pattern of growth will never ever again be in a straight upward line.

Downsized and Open Systems

Lately downsized and open systems are being advanced in the semiconductor, computer, and communications equipment industries. Downsizing became widespread in the last decade because of changes in information processing. The vertical information-processing system, which was the mainstream up to the 1970s, could not keep up with the expansion of the commercial market in both volume and complexity. Downsizing accompanied the construction of a distributed information-processing system in the 1980s. As a result smaller size equipment could be made with higher capability and at lower cost.

Through technological innovations in semiconductors and memory, improvements were made in the capabilities of CPUs and memory devices, enabling further miniaturization. For example, by the end of the decade, the processing speed of the microprocessors used in the CPUs of small-sized computers was accelerated over 100 times. RISC-style CPUs, which operate at even greater speed, have been appearing since the late 1980s.

Meanwhile, the construction of high-speed, mass-transmission communications lines is proceeding rapidly in each industrialized nation. Communications are also being digitalized. The development of ISDN networks is a good example. Other advances in communications software have enabled different machinery types to be connected into local area networks (LANs). Because of technological innovations that have made available low-priced, high-capability, small-sized computers, since the 1980s businesses can be linked by a number of small- and medium-sized high-capability machines set up in networks as distributed information-processing systems.

Advances in connecting electronic machinery made by different manufacturers in order to create such open systems sharing application software and data transmission are currently receiving much attention. In an open system, different equipment can be assembled together (creating a multiple facility) regardless of manufacturer. The distributed processing system is especially appropriate to the business operations of small companies.

The expectations are that distributed processing systems will proceed hand-in-glove with the spread of UNIX, OSI will become standardized, smaller lower-priced high-capability electronic equipment will be constructed through technological innovations, and LANs will become widespread. In the computer market the trend is toward personal computers and small workstations, replacing the demand for large computer equipment.

Currently the dissemination of UNIX systems and the opening of systems are dependent on downsizing, and there is some talk that the direction of the computer industry may change as the availability of information grows. Likely users will construct their own systems with equipment configurations according to their own needs rather than depend on systems designed by large manufacturers, such as is now the domain of IBM. There is also the possibility that as the new collaboration and rearrangements of the computer and information-processing industry will give rise to issues of leadership rights over new joint business operations, such as is now the domain of UNIX.[27] We can say that the construction of distributed information-processing systems through a open system has just begun, but business standards for OSs and CPUs have yet to be established.

Many manufacturers has been adapting UNIX to their product lines as an open system. Every manufacturer of hardware, software, and MPUs with an axis in UNIX has been actively moving to make the OSs and MPUs adopted by them into a business standard. This has engendered the formation of various leagues by corporations.

These corporate leagues have encouraged cooperation and purchasing within their leagues, collaboration among companies that do not belong to their leagues, and the formation of new leagues. Open systems on a world scale will likely speed up this reorganization of businesses into corporate leagues of different manufacturers of semiconductors, computers, and communications equipment.

Thus the future picture of the industry shows alliances among corporate groups and equipment manufacturers. Along with such changes, we should expect an increase of demand for intelligent and high value-added operations, in particular, information networks and software.

Multimedia

The volume of information in Japan has been rising dramatically in line with technological progress in the information and communications fields. Now the ready availability of information has permeated not only the activities of industry and institutions but also the lives of ordinary people in their private homes.

Most striking is recent rapid progress in digital technology which has enabled a broad range of image information to reach people in all walks of life. This technology is expected to become the foundation for new information technology known as multimedia.

In multimedia letters, sounds, and pictures are digitized and processed together so that they form a unified expression. Multimedia might be considered a Digital Revolution. Multimedia will enable memory, processing, and transmission to be used more conveniently, since every kind of information—text, sounds, still images, and animation—will be available in the same framework all at once in digital form. All these are things that cannot be treated by analog processors. For example, with satellite broadcasting digitalized, the number of channels will be several times that existing under analog broadcasting. Far more subscribers will be able to use cellular digital telephones, and it is believed that the methods of using not only texts but also sound and animation will enlarge significantly the market for personal computers that handle multimedia.

Entirely new information equipment could appear as computers become integrated with home electric appliances. And that is not all. Likely industrial-level innovations will occur via cooperation and integration with the computer industry of mass media such as films, broadcasting, newspapers, and publishing. We can fully expect the creation of an industrial model that is fundamentally different from what has been traditionally known.

In the information equipment industry, computers, televisions, and telephones have been considered so far as different machines. But they will become merged as the barriers among computer manufacturers, home electric appliance makers, and communications equipment manufacturers are removed. Already in the information service industry the barriers among broadcasting, telephones, CATV, and publishing are disappearing as their technologies converge.

Most important in producing a multimedia market are the market activities that promote collaboration between the information equipment industry centered around research and development and the information service industry centered around the use of technology. This bespeaks of a collaboration among multiple and diverse corporations in the multimedia business. In other words, the typical industrial model known up to now will change, for it is now becoming impossible for one industry to develop everything.

Clearly, as we approach the twenty-first century, multimedia will become an important strategic industry. At present the United States holds the central position in attempts at creating a multimedia market. There the multimedia industry has benefited from an outstanding communications infrastructure and service industry and has been fueled by venture capital and renewed competition due to relaxed regulations. It may be some years from now before the fruits of its development are put to full use in the Japanese market.

The greatest problem right now lies in the disparities between Japanese and U.S. multimedia technology. Because of insufficient information about multimedia, Japanese corporations tend to put off dealing with the issue. However, the past model of success whereby Japanese firms joined the market after its creation and then raised the share more by manufacturing good, cheap products will not work in the multimedia field. At present the future remains uncertain; there will be risks and pain. But searching for a way to participate in the American multimedia market should be moved to the head of Japanese corporations' objectives.

Cultivating Creativity

The preceding discussion suggests the need for better personnel training strategies to nurture intellectual capabilities and creativity vis-à-vis
the human resources supporting the electronics industry. At the root
of this issue are the changes reached in the educational and the corporate environments which contribute critically to the cultivation of
creativity.

Improvements in Elementary and Middle-Level Education
There is no need to stress anew the merits of bringing standard knowledge to students in elementary and middle schools, but creative talent
can be suppressed by an overemphasis on a standardized education.
The Ministry of Education, Science, and Culture's points of guidance
ought to be broadened and strengthened within a framework that
allows outstanding students to develop their abilities. There should be
provisions for elective courses and grade skipping in the straight track
to college entrance.

Higher Education
Besides a fixed curriculum, higher education (college, graduate school,
etc.) ought to provide opportunities for discovering and solving practical problems. The fundamental educational program should be one
in which conceptual power, creativity, and imagination are fostered
through application to research problems and work experience.

Moreover the present weaknesses in research facilities and the curriculum structure in colleges are a serious problem. While it may be
difficult to improve college research facilities and curricula uniformly
throughout Japan, the government should consider supporting programs in colleges that have comparatively outstanding records in
research and education. One way may be to institute a system of
discounts and amortization in the administration of university facilities
or even make available reciprocal privileges so that scholars have free
access to research facilities.

Administration of Research at Corporations
There is much in the administration of company research that can use
reform. The merits and strength of the administration of R&D at
Japanese firms lie in the fact that the goal is attained in an orderly way
by teamwork among researchers who closely and mutually exchange

and share information in accordance with their strictly managed schedules. Nevertheless, it is hard to cultivate unique and creative R&D under this system.

An emphasis on market needs in R&D, profits, and organizational hierarchy make it hard for creative research to flourish. That psychology has permeated the work of researchers too, for many prefer producing results with fixed evaluations quickly within a group rather than to proceed in splendid isolation with unique and creative research. The system needs to be reformed in order to give administrators of research funding wide discretionary powers. They should be encouraging creative research contributions that go beyond parallel and formal statistics.

International Coexistence and the International Role

In closing, we would like to discuss Japan's international role. In recent years Japan has built up a big presence in the world's markets. Japanese products have been welcomed by consumers around the world, and that has presented a threat to rival producers and prompted trade friction.

However, rivalry and change are indispensable to economic activity, so the resistance to Japanese exports cannot be fully eradicated. In fact, while Japan has received great benefits from the world's free trade system, it is also in a relationship of mutual dependence with its trading partner countries around the globe. Therefore it is essential for Japan to maintain its relationship of trust vis-à-vis cooperation with other nations of the world.

If Japan does not, then in the long term its economic prosperity will be endangered. With this in mind, we would like to discuss five ways in which Japan, and especially the electronics industry, can improve trade relations with other countries.

Corporate Collaboration and Networks

Technology, information, capital, and human resources can be exchanged and shared through collaborative affiliations to form close cooperative networks. A solid foundation for international coexistence could be formed via industry relationships. What is more, in advanced fields like the electronics industry such exchange is essential as technological development becomes more sophisticated, increasing the burden of large investments. Sharing corporate management may become a legitimate strategy too.

Mixtures and Cooperation
Through international cooperation and networking, corporate activity cannot avoid becoming globalized. People of different ethnic groups or from countries with different cultural and historical backgrounds will inevitably be mixed together and employed in R&D, production, and marketing. Up to now, people have manufactured products within the framework of their own country, culture, and corporate behavior, and competed in world markets. But from now on we can expect a demand for strategies that combine the merits of such diversity and heterogeneity and take advantage of multicultural strengths.

Direct External Investments and Technology Transfers
So far Japanese industries have made progress in globalization by direct investments overseas that have transferred or spread technology. As the people in different regions of the world work with our technology and practice our management style, the transfer of technological knowledge will progress naturally.

Today the Japanese electronics industry is developing production and R&D bases throughout the world. Very intense and effective technology transfers are occurring via experiences at these local sites. Mainly the technology being transferred is manufacturing technology, which is a particular strength of Japanese corporations. Such knowledge also happens to be the most profitable for the recipient nations. But Japanese corporations have much to learn in their alliances with local firms, especially the ways in which these partners think.

Creative Technology and Specialization
As technology transfers are advanced, it is to be expected that the disparities in competitive power will shrink and technological and competitive power will arise in the recipient site, likely in a boomerang effect. While that may appear unfavorable to the source of the transfer, it is only in a short-sighted view. The rise in competitive power, and correspondingly the rise in both production and income in the site receiving the transfer, will cause the market to expand so that in the long run the source of the transfer will fundamentally benefit from the expansion of exports. In order to secure this benefit, the source of

the transfer must continue to develop technology and competitiveness in uncharted fields. The history of the world's economic development is said to be one of ceaseless transfers of technology from advanced countries to developing countries and of further technological innovations in the advanced nations.

This relationship is not simply between advanced nations and developing ones. It is the way of the world. Economic growth is a global affair, whereby advanced countries bring technology to a high level and, through interdependent relationships, spread that technology via a lateral spread of labor to other nations. Expressed differently, creative technological development has a way of finding suitable niches.

International Cooperation

Frequent and intensive exchanges of information help countries recognize each other's merits and, in the competition among their industries, enable innovation. If anything, Japanese industry and society have traditionally received more information on an international basis than they have transmitted. Now that a sophisticated level of technology has been attained in several fields, ways of dispatching that technology must be strengthened in order to build a framework for mutual understanding and international cooperation.

Notes

In putting together this manuscript, I was greatly helped by comments and information supplied by Koji Maeda, advisor to the board of NEC, and members of the semiconductor, computer, and communications equipment industries' working group. I would like to take this opportunity to express my gratitude.

1. The data are from 1957 to 1987.

2. The total output of industrial electronic equipment, consumer electronic equipment, and electronic products are based on MITI's annual publication *Seisan Dotai Tokei* (Figures on Production Movements).

3. Import and export data are from the Ministry of Finance's *Yushutu-nyu Tokei* (Figures on Imports and Exports).

4. Based on 1989 data.

5. For example, the ratio of that output computer-related production held in Japan's GNP increased from 1.8 to 2.4 percent between 1985 and 1989. The ratio of information services increased much more rapidly during the same period, from 0.5 to 1.13 percent.

6. This is according to MITI's figures. Shimura, Y., *2000—Nen no Handotai Sangyo* (The Semiconductor Industry in 2000), Management Center, Japan Management Association, Tokyo, 1992, p. 42.

7. Shimura, Y., ibid., p. 42.

8. Kobayashi, K., *C&C Modern Communication* (in Japanese), Simul Press, Tokyo, 1985, pp. 114–17.

9. Shimura, Y., ibid., p. 206.

10. Shimura, Y., ibid., pp. 186–90.

11. The Data Quest company provides detailed information on semiconductor makers' share of the world market to its subscribers but does not allow their release to a third party.

12. Shimura, Y., ibid., pp. 82–84.

13. Hitachi linked up with RCA to begin producing the HITAC-5020 and HITAC-8000 series, NEC with Honeywell to produce the NEAC-2200 series, and Toshiba with GE to produce the TOSBAC-5400, 5600 series. Fujitsu began producing the FACOM-230–50, 60 on its own.

14. NEC's NEAC-2200/1700, Hitachi's HITAC-8700/8800, Fujitsu's FACOM 230–75, etc.

15. Fujitsu's M-200 (1978), Hitachi's M-180 (1979), NEC's ACOS-900 (1978), etc.

16. Hitachi's S-810/10, 20 (1983), Fujitsu's VP-100, 200 (1983), and NEC's SX-1, 2 (1985).

17. Hitachi's release in June 1990 of M-880; NEC's of ACOS-3800 in July; and Fujitsu's of M-1800 in September. IBM's release of its ES 9021 came one day after Fujitsu's.

18. Sales by major computer makers such as Fujitsu, NEC, and Hitachi have undergone a rapid, nearly fourfold increase in recent years. In the Japanese domestic market, Fujitsu's and NEC's sales have surpassed those of IBM Japan by far.

19. Basically computer sales have begun to decline rapidly in the wake of the recession since 1991.

20. Kobayashi, K., ibid. pp. 31–33, 50–52. Kitahara, Y., *INS Yutaka na Mirai o Kizuku* (INS Will Build a Rich Future), Diamondo, Tokyo, 1981, pp. 102–106.

21. Amid all that, Japan was charged by the United States for dumping car telephones in 1984 and 1985, and for push-button telephones/small-sized PBXs in 1988. By contrast, directly after the Caterfone Decision (1968), the market for switchboard equipment stagnated—due to the equipment outdatedness, the high yen, and the oil crises—before its local production could reach maturity. Facsimile machines have a world supply rate of nearly 100 percent, but that did not become an issue because no other country was affected. On the other hand, the fact that company F from Japan withdrew for political reasons even after becoming the lowest bidder in a major project for optical transmission of mainstay communications on the U.S. East Coast bespeaks of the impossibility of separating communications from issues of security maintenance.

22. These data are based on *JECC Computer Notes* (in Japanese), published by Japan Electronic Computer Co., Tokyo, and the aforementioned book by Shimura. Since the original source of those materials was Data Quest, I have refrained from quoting more detail here.

23. *90-Nendai no Denshi Sangyo Vision* (A Vision of the Electronic Industry in the 1990s), edited by the Electronic Equipment Department, Machinery and Information Bureau, MITI; MITI Industrial Survey Committee, 1989.

24. Ibid.

25. *Joho Tsushin Nenkan '92* (1992 Information Communications Annual), Information Communications Research Center, p. 633.

26. *Tsushin Kiki Chuki Juyo Yosoku* (Mid-Term Forecasts of Demand for Communications Equipment), Communications Industry Association of Japan, 1991.

27. Since each existing version must be unified and standardized in order for UNIX to become the "business standard," two standardization organizations, UI (Unix International) and OSF (Open Software Foundation), were formed in 1984. Also in that year, in Europe, X/open was founded as a UNIX standards organization. In addition to the participation of firms in UI and OSF, UI and OSF themselves have each made investments.

UI and OSF operations have not yet been unified, but recently both sides have cooperated in developing application software made by their leading manufacturers (Sun and HP). Moreover an increasing number of manufacturers has been developing products incorporating the technology of both organizations, so the standardization/unification of UNIX is essentially still progressing.

2   Home Electric Appliance Industry

Kei Takeuchi

The home electric appliance industry discussed in this chapter includes electronic appliances. It is formed from the following three sectors: electric machinery for home use, audiovisual equipment, and information-processing machinery for use at home.

These three sectors saw tremendous development in Japan after World War II. Amid the growth and development of the postwar Japanese economy, the "electrification of the home"—by the spread of television and audio equipment, as well as by the spread of information processing into the home—advanced so that this area became, along with the automobile industry, a durable consumer goods industrial sector. At the same time the growth and development in this field served as a driving force behind Japan's economic growth.

This industry contains all-around electric/electronic makers including some that have existed before World War II (Hitachi, Toshiba, and Mitsubishi), makers of a whole range of household electric/electronic equipment that developed rapidly after World War II (Matsushita, Sharp, and Sanyo), makers of AV and information machinery (Sony, etc.), as well as makers that have specialized in certain other products. Among the companies noted are many that are representative of the postwar Japanese industry.

The home electric appliance industry in Japan is characterized by the fact that each large corporation produces a considerably diverse range of goods. Moreover a great many types and models of the same item are offered by several different makers.

The competition among corporations is very stiff. Endless improvements are carried out in product type and efficiency, and the prices of goods undergo substantial lowering. Despite all that, corporations in this field have continued developing up to now, thanks to advancements in technology, improved productivity, and expansions of the market. Furthermore the corporations have worked out product cycles whereby the industry's main goods appear, are disseminated, and mature, while at the same time the goods themselves create a succession of intertwined demands.

Now with the prolonged recession and the high value of the yen, each company in the home electric appliance industry has been forced to proceed with restructuring. Up to now the home electric appliance industry had carried out continual expansion, while passing through product cycles of major goods. This has led to considerable difficulties in halting the inclination toward expanding the industry. Viewed from a midterm perspective, any more expansion of the domestic market cannot be anticipated. In addition, because of the rapid growth of industries in China and the NIES countries and the anchoring of the high yen in the international marketplace, not only is an expansion of exports unlikely, but an increase of imports from abroad can be expected as well.

Under such circumstances home electric appliance corporations have proceeded with policies that expand overseas production and partially scale down domestic production. Furthermore they are now revising their rules of rivalry in order to alter their excessive competitiveness and promote strategic cooperation, including partnerships with foreign corporations.

The current (as of 1993) recession has presented a difficult situation for the Japanese consumer electric appliance industry, yet it has also provided an opportunity to make substantial changes. In the long run it opens up possibilities for developing more information-processing equipment for the home and related electronic products. Home automation in the true sense could be built as a system integrating home electric appliances, AV equipment, and information-processing machinery. It is a task for the future.

2.1 Postwar Development

After World War II rapid changes took place in the production indexes for "electric machinery including those for industrial use, as shown in table 2.1 (which takes the year 1980 as the 100 index). Though not indicated in the table, production jumped suddenly to 60.1 in 1973. Afterward, in the wake of the 1973 oil crisis, it declined but began rising after 1975.

Table 2.1
Production indexes for electric machinery

1940	1950	1955	1960	1965	1970	1975	1980	1985	1990
0.5	0.4	1.2	7.2	13.3	42.9	49.2	100.0	215.0	321.5

Table 2.2
Production indexes for the entire manufacturing sector

1940	1950	1960	1970	1980	1990
8.1	3.7	18.2	66.5	100.0	149.0

During this period, the integrated indexes for the manufacturing industry changed, as indicated in table 2.2. By comparing these tables, we can understand that the growth of the electric machinery industry was especially remarkable even within the manufacturing industry.

The electric machinery industry includes both the electric and the electronic industries. The electric industry has two subsections: heavy electric apparatuses and consumer electric equipment. The electronic industry is divided into three: consumer electronic equipment, industrial electronic equipment, and electronic parts. We will consider here the following three areas: (1) consumer electric equipment, which includes electric motor appliances like washing machines and refrigerators and electric motor/heating appliances like electric braziers and air conditioners, (2) consumer electronic equipment such as televisions, VTRs, and tape recorders, and (3) information-processing equipment like personal computers and world processors which have only recently been promoted for home use.

Altogether the yield of consumer electric equipment and consumer electronic equipment, according to MITI's figures on production trends, reached ¥6.7 trillion and ¥7.2 trillion, respectively, in 1987 and 1990. In 1987 it acquired a 24 percent share of the total world production of $112.4 billion. If the portion of production overseas by Japanese companies and that of joint corporations are included, Japanese companies' would share in the broad sense will most likely come to 30–35 percent.

With respect to information-processing equipment for the home, the output of personal computers, word processors, telephones, facsimiles, and the like, in 1989 was about ¥2 trillion. Consumer equipment is

Table 2.3
Fluctuations in production and exports (%)

	Consumer electric equipment		Consumer electronic equipment	
	Production	Exports	Production	Exports
1960–65	13.4	23.9	7.2	21.6
1965–70	18.5	35.7	34.1	30.8
1970–75	11.5	15.1	1.6	8.7
1975–80	10.8	23.9	13.1	18.5
1980–85	6.8	14.0	10.9	13.2
1985–90	3.3	−8.7	−2.0	−7.2

estimated to account for one-quarter of that. For that reason the annual output of the Japanese home electric/electronic appliance industry to be taken up here is estimated to be worth ¥8 trillion. Up to now it has corresponded to about 3 percent of the manufacturing industry's output and approximately 25 percent of electric machinery.

Exports occupy a large position in the home electric appliance industry. The proportion of exports to production in 1965 was 28 percent, but in 1975 it was 38 percent and in 1985, 60 percent. Thereafter the figure declined in the wake of the high yen. In 1990 it was 37 percent, with a monetary value of ¥3.8 trillion. By contrast, imports were at the 4 percent level at the end of the 1980s, and they were primarily imports from the NIES nations. Thereafter imports of products made by subsidiaries of Japanese corporations in other countries have been on the increase.

The changes by time periods in the growth of output and exports are depicted in table 2.3. As the table shows, the fluctuations in consumer electronic equipment have been great. Exports grew dramatically in the 1960s, but then they became sluggish due to the oil crisis in 1973–74. After 1975 exports expanded considerably again. However, they started declining because of the high yen in the latter half of the 1980s; output dropped along with exports.

The output of electronic parts for household electric products came to ¥10.8 trillion in 1981, ¥18.5 trillion in 1985, and ¥23.9 trillion in 1990. Of that, the output for consumer equipment was, respectively, in those years about ¥3.5 trillion, ¥5.2 trillion, and ¥4.5 trillion. Thus the output did not grow all that much and declined considerably. Since more than half of the electronic industry's products are exported, estimations are

Table 2.4
Labor productivity in Japan and Germany (USA = 100)

	1975	1977	1979	1981	1983	1985	1987	1989
Japan	23	29	39	49	60	68	67	83
Former West Germany	81	79	75	79	83	83	73	74

Table 2.5
Changes in labor productivity (1975 = 100)

	1975	1977	1979	1981	1983	1985	1987	1989
United States	100	121	136	145	152	162	196	220
Japan	100	153	229	303	395	475	563	781

that about just ¥2 trillion worth of the Japanese electronic industry's products are supplied to the Japanese home electric appliance industry.

Viewed in terms of employment, the number of people working in the consumer electric equipment and electronic industries increased rapidly from 186,000 in 1965 to 337,000 in 1970. The figure stagnated in the first half of the 1970s, only to begin increasing again from 1975 and to reach a peak of just under 400,000 in 1984. Afterward, because of the rising yen, sharp employment adjustments were carried out so that the number of employees decreased to 305,000 in 1989.

The output of added value per person in 1990 was ¥12.77 million in the entire manufacturing industry, while the figure for electric machinery as a whole came to ¥11.45 million. Of that the amount for consumer electric equipment was ¥15.56 million, and that for radios and televisions was a high ¥18.56 million. But the respective figures for electric audio equipment and video equipment were quite low at ¥8.83 million and ¥7.82 million. By contrast, the respective figures for chemicals and steel were ¥29.68 million and ¥19.83 million, indicating that these are more capital-intensive industries.

The changes in the value of labor productivity in Japan and Germany, taking the U.S. standard as 100, are indicated in table 2.4. The data come from the Japan Productivity Center. The value, taking the year 1975 as 100, is shown in table 2.5. We can thus see that the Japanese electric machinery industry's productivity has grown enormously both relatively and absolutely.

In addition, since the aforementioned figures measure value-added productivity through purchasing power parity, they will be different if calculated under the present exchange rate. They show that Japan is still lower than the United States in absolute value.

2.2 Product Characteristics

A distinct feature of the electrical machinery industry is that the mainline items have passed through a typical product cycle and undergone successive change. Until about 1950 radios had the highest output figures. However, starting about 1955, electric refrigerators and washing machines became popular, only to be replaced around 1960 by black-and-white televisions. In the latter half of the 1960s, color televisions came into production and managed to surpass black-and-white televisions by 1968. Televisions continued to dominate for a long while until the 1980s when video tape recorders caught up with them. For ten years thereafter videos held the top position, only to be overtaken in 1990 by room air conditioners, whose growth began in the 1980s.

With respect to exports, radios were the main export through the first half of the 1960s. However, from about 1965, the sales of televisions took over; then from about 1980 video tape recorders increased dramatically.

Domestically information-processing equipment is just starting to be acquired by households, and recently purchases of facsimiles have spread. Portable telephones are becoming popular too. However, their dissemination has been slower here than in the Asian NIES countries, perhaps because there is little need for portable telephones in Japan, where public telephones are widely available. Besides, portable telephones have come on the Japanese market rather late.

Already widely disseminated as office equipment, Japanese-language word processors are now entering households. Nevertheless, it will be some time before personal computers come to be widely used in homes.

The Japanese home electric appliance industry is characterized by the fact that several companies produce similar products and compete with each other. There are about ten major makers alone that produce virtually every type of machine. Add companies specializing in certain products, and that figure jumps to fifteen to twenty corporations in competition with each other.

The rivalry is fierce among all the corporations, and it serves both to keep down cost and to improve the merchandise. But that strategy also produces a kind of glut in the market caused by a ceaseless stream of new equipment. As of 1991, 348 types of refrigerators are said to have been sold. In addition a survey of the ten major manufacturers showed that altogether they produce 211 types of televisions, 97 types of videos, and even 103 types of vacuum cleaners.

The Japanese home electric industry's competitiveness in the domestic market indeed seems to be excessive. Temporarily South Korea once increased its share in Japan but was unable to secure a share of the Japanese market, which has been the case with products from the Asian NIES nations and large-sized goods from the United States. Imports may likely increase in the future in the form of products made by Japanese companies overseas flowing into Japan. Yet competition with foreign corporations in Japan is not liable to become much of an issue. Foreign countries will probably demand that Japan open its electronic components market, including semiconductors; they will try to increase their share too. But they are unlikely to launch an offensive for their final products in the Japanese market.

The situation is different for home information-processing equipment. In this field there is a growing tendency for concentration by a comparatively small number of firms. Because of linguistic circumstances, foreign companies were virtually excluded from the competition until quite recently. In 1992 an American company developed basic software that can use Japanese-language software. With the further development of an inexpensive personal computer that is less than half the price of the same type of Japanese-made machinery, Japanese corporations could be swept into extremely fierce competition. Here the fundamental weakness of Japanese software technology will prove critical.

2.3 Industry Structure

A look at the major Japanese home electric appliance manufacturers reveals a great variety of names including words like *denki* (written with the characters meaning electric, electric machinery, or electric apparatus) and *seisakusho* (factory). These distinctions indicate differences in their origins.

Corporations producing home electric and electronic appliances are divided into integrated electric machinery makers, integrated home electric appliance makers, and integrated electronic equipment makers, and some specialize in the manufacture of audio equipment. In addition there are related companies that make parts and special mechanisms. Sales for the large corporations among them come to ¥4 trillion to ¥5 trillion. There are also companies that make over ¥7 trillion in interconnected accounts; included here are a number of firms representative of the Japanese manufacturing industry.

Integrated electric machinery makers, represented by Hitachi, Toshiba, and Mitsubishi Electric, manufacture all kinds of electric and electronic equipment for industrial and home use. Before World War II they focused more on heavy electric machinery than on home electric items. But around 1955, faced with stagnation in the heavy electric machinery field, they turned to the home electric appliance industry, where the market had begun expanding rapidly.

However, the home electric appliance field is now on the decline. Of the ¥3.9 trillion in sales in Hitachi's March 1992 closing accounts (from an independent audit), the home electric appliance field could claim ¥490 billion, or only about 12.5 percent. In the same year this field accounted for 21 percent of sales at Toshiba and 21 percent at Mitsubishi Electric. These figures represent a drop over a five-year period from 20 percent at Hitachi, 26 percent at Toshiba, and 26 percent at Mitsubishi Electric.

Integrated home electric appliance manufacturers are represented by Matsushita, Sanyo, and Sharp. All three are companies that grew rapidly after World War II in response to the great expansion of the Japanese electric appliance market, and they developed into major world corporations. However, recently these companies have been increasing their proportions of electric machinery and electronic equipment for industrial use as well. For example, sales of information industry equipment and electronic components have come to account for 42 percent of the total at Matsushita. At Sharp the figure is more than 50 percent, and it is close to 40 percent at Sanyo.

Integrated electronic equipment manufacturers include Sony, Victor of Japan, and Nippon Columbia. Sony, in particular, is often mentioned, along with Matsushita, as a representative high-growth corporation of postwar Japan. Mainly videos, audios, and televisions are produced by these manufacturers. They also manufacture a few related products for industries such as broadcasting.

These three integrated electronics manufacturers have different origins, technological bases, and corporate cultures; they have also shown individuality as companies. Yet their activities have been approaching each other along with their expanded growth. This discernible tendency for corporate cultures to approach each other is causing the striking individuality of their products to fade away.

Specialized manufacturers of sound equipment that are centered around audios include Pioneer, Kenwood, and Aiwa. The sales at these companies are at most approximately ¥400 billion annually. However, more than a few similar companies have their own unique components and technology and thus have a solid established base.

A characteristic of the Japanese home electric appliance industry is that large manufacturers produce a diverse machinery for a great variety of products. Furthermore a considerable number of them are making not only end products but also their own components and materials. While it is quite common for companies to order parts from subcontractor companies, a large percentage is produced within their plants. Nevertheless, even among large corporations, a vast number of subcontractor transactions occur. The situation is strikingly different from that with large corporations in the automobile industry, which order almost all their parts and materials from the outside and specialize only in assembling.

The percentage of external orders by Japanese electric machinery manufacturers is said to be low compared to that of foreign companies. That situation is converse to that of the automobile industry, which is why even gigantic home appliance companies have many different kinds of plants, or else several plants that produce many different products within the same factory grounds. This has led some observers to suggest that they are more an aggregate body of a large number of small- and medium-sized corporations rather than one giant corporation. On this point, home electric appliances are different from the automobile industry, which has large assembly line facilities, or industries like steel or chemicals, which are equipped with refineries. That is likewise attributable to the fact that the establishment of flexible production methods has made it possible to carry out continual changes in the main line of products. This stands in contrast with industries with large facilities and equipment whose products do not change fundamentally for a long time.

2.4 Basis for Success

Until recently the home electric appliance field had experienced extraordinary success, even with relation to all the Japanese manufacturing industries. Despite the oil crisis of 1973–74 and the high yen starting its rise in 1986, it was able to continue growth.

The explanation for this growth lies fundamentally in the existence of a large domestic market that has kept on enlarging. The industry was also able to develop and continue its high competitiveness in both domestic and foreign markets because of ceaseless technological innovations. According to the government's survey on research and development expenditures by all industries, those by the electric machinery field have accounted for one-third of the total. In terms of the proportion of sales, it has placed second only after the pharmaceutical industry.

We can list several reasons for these results. First is improved labor productivity, as was mentioned earlier. From the rise in the productivity of all factors, technological advances can be inferred, so the rate of advancement by electric machinery must be much higher than that of other industries. This is why the prices of products have been coming down, as shown in the comparison of wholesale price indexes in table 2.6. Over the long term the prices of electric appliances have dropped conspicuously more than the prices of other industrial products. That is evidence alone that technological progress benefits the consumer.

There is of course improved product quality to consider. As new models and types of machinery were developed in the Japanese home electric appliance industry, various small improvements were made in product quality. The accumulative effect of such practice has, over the long term, enabled Japanese products to have their own unique quality. These improvements took advantage of ME technology and incorporated microcomputers. But the gradual improvement is not adequately reflected in the price indexes, for in real prices the decline has actually been much greater than what is shown in table 2.6.

Even in bringing elements of basic technology from overseas, the industry has demonstrated originality and connected new product concepts to them. It has greatly lowered the cost of technology developed in the United States; in particular, it has succeeded in the market by adapting military or industrial technology to consumer products. Pocket computers, tape recorders, Walkmans, VTRs, and so on, are just some examples. In home information-processing equipment, there have been developed word processors capable of handling the characteristics of the Japanese language that once were primarily intended for office usage (the monopoly position of Japanese companies in this field is now being threatened by the gradual increase of word-processing software for home personal computers). Likewise the facsimile machine has been made capable of handling the Japanese language as

Table 2.6
Comparison of wholesale price indexes

	1960	1965	1970	1973	1975	1980	1985	1990
Overall average	42.8	43.7	48.6	58.0	76.2	100.5	100.0	90.6
Industrial goods	48.1	47.7	52.4	61.5	79.0	100.7	100.0	93.1
Electric machinery	105.2	93.2	91.9	90.0	108.4	106.8	100.0	75.3

images and thus has replaced the telex, its predecessor, which was not successful in the Japanese domestic market because it was not adequate in transcribing the language.

In addition the Japanese home appliance industry has been able to create products suitable to the Japanese people's life style and culture. Consistently this industry has proceeded boldly to develop new products and to pioneer markets. On this point the spirit of entrepreneurship has played a crucial role. A number of outstanding entrepreneurs representing postwar Japan, such as Konosuke Matsushita, were born out of the home electric appliance industry.

2.5 Distribution Problems

Many electric appliance stores exist in Japan. In the business census of 1988, there were 66,000 such specialized stores. This number decreased somewhat in 1991 to 63,000 stores. When to the 1988 number are added general retail stores handling home electric appliances, the total comes to a staggering 85,400. In comparison, the number of retail stores specializing in electric equipment for use at home in the United States is 47,000—one-third the number per person in Japan. The large majority of retail stores in Japan are really very small. Half of these stores are family run with only one or two workers.

Most of the Japanese electric stores, called *keiretsu* shops, are affiliated with certain manufacturers. When the electric industry grew rapidly after the war, there were few distributors knowledgeable enough about products to handle them. Consumers did not have the technological knowledge either. Then, since the products of this early period also had functional problems, it was necessary to provide services like assistance in the selection and installation of goods, or maintenance and repairs. For that reason electric manufacturers themselves had to organize and maintain stores that handled their products. Thus in the 1960s most retail stores became affiliate stores. Those belonging to the big six makers alone reached 55,000, including Matsushita's 24,000. This figure accounts for 90 percent of electric shops, excluding the so-called super stores.

Because such affiliate stores formed long-term relationships with customers and responded to ordinary requests like repairs, they also helped manufacturers acquire a stable market share. But they were pressed by the need to carry a full range of products in order to meet customer demand. As a result their affiliate companies started to produce a large variety of appliances for every conceivable use.

Recently, however, many affiliate stores have been closing. Startling advances are being made both by home electric appliances super stores that do not get into affiliations with manufacturers and by so-called discount stores that sell a great volume of things besides home electric appliances at low prices. These two factors have contributed to a dip in sales of affiliate stores to below 40 percent.

2.6 Price Structure

The prices of home electric appliances have been dropping for a long time. In the 1980s the decline was particularly conspicuous in consumer price indexes. The prices of televisions, pocket calculators, and tape recorders have fallen to less than half their 1980 prices, and electric fans and washing machines to less than 70 percent. This can be partly explained by the competition with foreign products and the recession due to the high yen, but fierce rivalry at the retail level is an even bigger reason. It is said that if a new product, such as appears every year, of higher capability and quality can be sold at the same price or even lower than the previous year's model, the old product's price goes down in an instant.

This practice does not really benefit consumers. It can render manufacturers incapable of both acquiring a proper value-added price and recouping development expenses adequately.

The recent drop in prices has been largely due to confusion in the distribution structure caused by the rapid growth of volume marketing through super stores. There is no denying that so-called price-fixing has been encouraged by excessive rivalry among manufacturers in order to secure a market share.

Nevertheless, the actual market prices at the super stores, discount shops, and affiliate stores vary. On average they are said to be approximately 80 to 85 percent of the retail price suggested by the maker. Since the manufacturer's shipment price is said to be about 75 percent of the suggested retail price, retailers' profits are rather small. Then there are rebates and discounts carried out in various forms, so the manufacturers' actual shipment prices have been getting even lower. Therefore price structure can be very complicated and not very clear.

Some structure to the market must be established and the rules of value-added distribution defined for the sake of this industry's future. It is essential that excess competition be controlled and that price standards be reinstated, but this must be done without infringing on consumers' interests or the Antimonopoly Act. And that presents difficulties.

2.7 Technological Structure

The Japanese electric appliances industry has spent considerable moneys on R&D and has invested heavily in technological development. As a result it has attained extremely high productivity, product quality, and capabilities, making it a strong rival internationally. But, at the same time, that has very much benefited the consumer.

Nowadays there is not so much room to improve the technology in assembly processes of home electric appliance manufacturing. Because of automation the industry has surged ahead. Nevertheless, along with the diversification of products has come a return to products being made manually.

The development of a principal line of merchandise has important meaning now. The product concepts of black-and-white and color televisions, refrigerators, and washing machines, for example, were developed overseas. The concepts behind word processors, VTRs, video cameras, and pocket calculators—at least those for the general consumer—were developed in Japan. There are further some products like Japanese-language word processors, quilt warmers, and—from quite a while back—rice cookers that were developed for the Japanese market. No doubt, in the near future new ideas will lead to other successful new merchandise for both the domestic and overseas markets, but at moment no sign of this is evident.

Successful products do not always involve high technology. Television games are a good example; they are not technologically sophisticated in either their hardware or their software. They have enjoyed success mostly in being offered at low prices to children; their high profits come from marketing game software, and not the hardware.

A good candidate for the principal product of the next generation is the HDTV (high-definition television). If this comes within the reach of ordinary households, a market will appear with an accumulated worth of more than ¥10 trillion for receiver equipment alone. The technological problems have been fundamentally solved, and if mass production takes off, the prices of HDTVs may be lowered to a point where they could be afforded by most people. The problem really lies in standardization, including international dimensions, and in its soft aspects concerning the content of the programs to be broadcasted. Much of this will depend on government policy.

In the home electric information equipment field, personalized program equipment and sophisticated telecommunications equipment (including portable telephones) are becoming the leading products. Their future development depends on features such as whether telecommunications systems using optical fiber cables, and the like, will reach ordinary households and whether the information transmitted on them will be welcomed in homes. CATV networks, which are being employed experimentally in certain regions, have not yet been regarded highly because of the questionable quality of their programs.

At present the gradual advances of technology have improved many electric household appliances and lowered their costs, mostly due to semiconductor technology. However, the merits of mass production have been lost, and the recovery of development investments is becoming difficult. To remedy this situation, some attempts are being made to reduce the number of machine parts by making standard modules. By modules that can be used in many different machines, manufacturers are hoping to reduce the costs involved in machine switchovers. As important are the improvements in efficiency, since some of the production process can be computerized. Clearly the burden of development costs can be lowered by lengthening the period for developing new products and by cutting down on the number of different machines. But the competition among corporations is making that hard to put into practice.

2.8 Globalization

Since 1985 overseas investments by home electric appliance corporations have grown considerably. Many companies have also moved their production facilities overseas because of the rising yen, and they are in the process of switching over from exports to local production.

The most obvious reason for globalization is that in the assembly stage it is more profitable to produce at sites overseas where personnel costs are low than to manufacture domestically in Japan and then transport the goods abroad. It is even good business sense to develop and produce goods at the site of a market where they can be fit to a people's lifestyle. But the main reason is production costs in Japan, both in terms of swelling personnel costs and a dearth of labor power. Second, production abroad ensures against changes in domestic economic conditions and fluctuations in the exchange rate, with the added bonus that trade friction is avoided because exports are low.

The proportion of overseas production carried out by Japanese corporations is already over 10 percent. At some large firms foreign employees account for more than 30 percent of the staff, including those at affiliate companies. The greatest number of sites is found in Asia—particularly Southeast Asia. The products made there head not only to the local domestic market but are also for export. Some of the exports go back to Japan as well.

Recently some large Japanese corporations have been establishing research centers in the United States and Europe in order to take advantage of the R&D capacities of scientists and technicians there. This move came as a result of the high yen which has virtually eliminated any difference of salaries for researchers in Japan and the western countries, and in some cases salaries in Japan have been higher.

However, to proceed with true globalization, management itself must become internationalized, and this includes hiring foreigners for administrative positions in company headquarters—which presents many difficulties, starting with the question of language. Nevertheless, it is clear that a number of large corporations in the home electric appliance industry are starting to become multinational corporations.

2.9 Current Direction

The home electric appliance industry, which has continued to develop since the end of World War II, has reached its maturation stage. To continue its growth, it must carry out structural reforms. The serious economic recession since 1992 has strongly affected this industry. Company profits have declined considerably, so the necessity for change has become all the more clear.

In 1992 an essay published by Akio Morita of Sony in the February issue of the monthly magazine, *Bungei Shunju,* created quite a stir. In it Morita expressed some doubts about the industry's full success. He wrote: "The Japanese manufacturing industry has achieved high labor productivity and high product quality through excellent technology. While having strong international competitive power, its workers spend the longest hours on the job of all industrialized nations. Nevertheless, its level of capital is not necessarily so high, and the income of its managers is much lower than that in the United States. Moreover, the dividends paid to stockholders are extremely low. Why is it that no one seems to be earning adequate profits?"

Morita looked for causes in activities like immoderate model changes due to excessive rivalry among corporations, the pursuit of distinctiveness, and price lowering. Morita warned companies to stop their irrational extreme competitiveness. He suggested that they should rather offer high-quality goods at steady prices over the long term, maintain adequate profit margins, and give adequate shares of profits to both workers and stockholders.

Morita's ideas roused many reactions. He was most severely criticized for implying that corporations should aim for profits at the expense of consumers. However, for the consumer it is really more profitable to have high-quality goods that last a long time, though they may have to be obtained at a slightly higher price, given the alternative which is to be constantly pressed to purchase new machines as the old ones start to break down. Moreover from the perspective of maintaining natural resources and the natural environment, reducing waste, and promoting recycling, a "throw-away" society with its deluge of merchandise is no longer politically correct.

Morita's claims are fundamentally on target at least in regard to the home electric appliance industry. The industry for the time being must make a solid effort to improve itself, taking note of the following points:

• *Avoid overdiversification of products, frequent model changes, and useless versatility.* This will reduce the burden of development investment costs and bring profits by virtue of economies of scale. Useful products mean value-added pricing, and just that fact alone should effect reform and stop the tendency for all other companies to jump immediately into a new product market developed by some company A.

• *Reorganize the market so that a logical and simple pricing mechanism can be established.* Fair competition among companies means that the industry should avoid dramatically cutting prices. The distribution structure can be made efficient by lower distribution costs in order to secure an appropriate share of value-added prices.

• *Push ahead with automation and low-energy-consuming products.* The shortage of labor power, reduction of working hours, and rise in wage costs will be fundamental trends for quite a while. Corporations should also consider consolidating their production activities.

• *Continue with globalization, taking a long-term view.* Overseas activities should advance employment guarantees and transfers of technology that contribute to the economic well-being of the other country. Besides competition, there can be collaboration and cooperation with foreign companies.

In the latter half of 1993, with the recession in the Japanese economy particularly severe, the home electric appliance industry fell into the most adverse straits it has known since the immediate postwar period. Each corporation was forced to cut back the scale of production and rationalize personnel. Since the home electric appliance industry had continued expanding up to then, it was not accustomed to a recession. It must now grapple with full-fledged restructuring. Each company must face breaking away from conformist attitudes and set up its own corporate strategies. With bold entrepreneurship the home electric appliance industry took off from practically zero after the war and by its corporate strategies grew into the greatest industry in the world. The time has come again to show that innovative spirit of entrepreneurship.

Among the new corporate strategies to meet the changes in circumstances that many companies have developed is one worthy of attention here concerning moves toward strategic collaboration on an international scale. While carrying out competition, on the one hand, large world-class firms are forming networks of cooperation with each other. We cannot say at the present time how that will affect not just Japan but also the rest of the world. However, it is certain that international relationships in industry are going to become even closer.

2.10 Long-Term Trends

Even though the home electric appliance industry has entered its mature period, long-term prospects are opening in diverse directions. Some promising trends are discussed below.

Among home electric appliances there will likely be more dissemination of room air conditioners, but nothing seems to be a big success for the time being. There may be some new products introduced, but successes are hard to predict, since some new products like quilt warmers have been hits up to now and others like the home bread-maker have been flops.

Taking a long perspective, the most promising are modularized products. Modular kitchen systems have already been merchandised but not widely disseminated. Their market is closely connected with housing and the construction of homes, or even home renovations. The cooperation of architects and builders is necessary in developing the technology and planning merchandise for that purpose. Therefore the industry must proceed in cooperation with the construction industry or work to diversify corporate activities.

We might also consider the the concept of the intelligent house, whereby the functions of an entire house are unified by computer control. Developments here will proceed with the availability of such programming. Then there is the concept of the intelligent town that unites everything regionally. Both concepts have still not gone beyond the drawing board.

Primarily we should concern ourselves with the fact that up to now home electric appliances have only mechanized or automated a few household chores once performed by human beings. Taking one leap further, we might even imagine changing the idea of housework itself. For instance, houses might be built that do not produce any waste that requires vacuum cleaning.

With respect to audiovisual equipment, the most promising in the very near future is the high-definition television. If high-definition television receivers come into mass production, the price will drop to several hundred thousands of yen. Then the HDTV will spread rapidly to ordinary households.

However, improved program broadcasting is essential for HDTV to be widely disseminated. Just continuing the current television broad-casts with high definition will not suffice to make the most of that technology. It certainly will not entice people to spend several hundred thousand yen. That is a problem that will interest the industrial world. Likely there will arise government policies on the increase and distri-bution of satellite broadcasting channels, for example.

There are some international complications concerning HDTVs. The Japanese high-definition television, also called high vision, was devel-oped ahead of the world. However, the EC and the United States, fearing a Japanese monopoly, have been working to develop a different type. Negotiations and rivalry, including political deals, are likely to continue in the future over the establishment of a globally standardized type. Since the HDTV market is expected to be enormous, reaching out to the entire world in the twenty-first century, it is important for the Japanese electric industry to secure a fixed hold on this market. Therefore the Japanese should not set themselves up as a daring rival, such as might exacerbate international friction. What is needed is a global system of cooperation among not only the industrialized nations but also with the NIES countries and China, where production of television sets has been increasing dramatically as of late.

Finally, with respect to household information systems, office automation (OA) equipment is likely to become accepted for home use. People who are used to operating equipment like word processors and personal computers in their place of work will naturally bring them into their homes. So the equipment may end up disseminated in this way.

The fact that American corporations have recently begun selling in Japan personal computers that are much cheaper than any known so far has threatened Japanese companies for the time being. However, at a price of about ¥100,000 per machine, there is an impetus for purchasing a personal computer for strictly private use (rather than bringing equipment from the workplace home). In line with that would be required easier-to-use software. In many ways Japan's software still is not up to that of the United States.

Along with the dissemination of information equipment for home use, the form of information transmission, which has mainly been carried out so far through letters and printed text on screen, will probably undergo change. "Electronic publishing" of dictionaries and academic conference bulletins is already being carried out experimentally. Encyclopedia publishing will probably move in that direction in the future too.

In addition information transmission that unifies print, images, and sound—in other words, multimedia—will develop. As this occurs, information equipment and AV equipment will be employed integratedly and likely open up a new field for the home electric appliance industry. However, software technology must be developed at various levels for these fields to take off and grow. There is not much meaning in putting just printed matter into an electronic and compact mode when available are distinctive AV features of electronic technology to put into full use in order to bring information technology to a high level.

Information networks will likely reach the home via this information technology. But at present still much has to be done toward fully outfitting both the software and hardware technologies in order to adapt the home personal computer for use as an information network terminal. First of all, the hardware system for an information network has to be built as a social infrastructure; servicing is all the more important in its soft aspects. The information network services executed experimentally so far through regional CATVs can still hardly be called sufficiently useful. While some of that cannot be helped because of regional limitations, an even bigger reason is that not enough ingenuity has been used in the soft aspects of information supply services.

A wide range of soft technology, from basic software to the content of programs for broadcasting, must be developed in the future. Furthermore there is the matter of system maintenance, from codes and unified protocol to legal relationships. Some of the larger aspects of use will thus require strategic directions from the government.

As we approach the twenty-first century, we are seeing true electrification and true electronification of home life. Home automation will bring to fruition a higher level of home electrification that will unite all home electric appliances, AV equipment, and information equipment systematically. The future of the home electric appliance industry will surely be in that direction.

3   Automobile Industry

Takahiro Fujimoto and
Akira Takeishi

The Japanese automobile industry is internationally recognized to have developed a highly competitive manufacturing system with a low level of waste and nonessential activities. It is known as a lean production system. However, the industry will have difficulties in heading into the twenty-first century under the present system alone. In a short period of time, the industry has come to face stagnation in domestic sales and a decline in profits because of the high yen, while the gap in its competitiveness with American makers has been closing. Moreover the middle- and long-term forecasts are that a continual increase in the amount of production, as has been seen up to 1990, cannot be expected in the future, that the amount of labor power provided by the younger generation will decrease, and that there will be changes in people's values in regard to life-long commitment to corporations.

The Japanese automobile industry will have to deal with these changing circumstances by maintaining its existing strength of a lean production system while redesigning practices that have lacked balance. This will mean a shift from an emphasis on lean continual growth to an emphasis on total performance that considers the people who have a stake in the automobile industry—not just the consumer but also the labor market, stockholders, parts makers, dealers, and so on.

Worldwide competition, cooperation, and conflict have progressed simultaneously in the automobile industry. Cooperative relations are in the process of being formed among rival companies. In the future the question is likely to be how to use competition, cooperation, and conflict in a timely way to define corporate goals. Important here too will be to strike a "balance" among competition, cooperation, and conflict.

The Japanese automobile industry is now at a turning point. If emphasis is placed only on strengthening competitiveness (through

lower costs and improvements in quality) and extreme measures are
enacted for maintaining and fortifying the present system, there is a
danger of its collapsing. However, if a balanced lean system is put into
effect, the industry may very well more capably endure the ongoing
domestic recession in the 1990s. In addition, in maintaining competitiveness but accomplishing industrial performance of a higher order,
the Japanese automobile industry will more likely be respected both
at home and abroad.

3.1 Japanese Automobile Industry's Performance

From a Lean on Growth to a Lean on Balance

Quite some time has passed since the Japanese automobile industry
was first internationally recognized for its high industrial performance.
But is this entirely true? That conclusion will vary according to how a
person defines industrial performance. We will consider performance
in two fundamentally different ways: internal performance (the business record based on objective indexes that can be measured within
the company—productivity, yield, the rate of defects in the production
lines, the inventory turnover rate, etc.) and external performance (the
business record evaluated by stakeholders of the firm).

Certainly internal indexes show that Japanese automobile manufacturers have generally tended to manifest high performance both individually as corporations and as an industry. However, external
performance is as important, since it indicates how the company is
contributing to its stakeholders.

An evaluation of an industry's or company's external performance
depends on which of the stakeholders is doing the appraisal. The main
stakeholder groups are consumers (both present and potential customers), employees (the labor market), manufacturers who supply parts
and materials, stockholders, worker organizations, and ordinary citizens. Performance vis-à-vis the product market (consumers) is called
competitiveness. Performance in the narrow sense means this competitiveness, but in the large sense, the industry's or corporation's performance entails contributions to all stakeholders and not just consumers.

From such a perspective, because of the high yen in recent years,
Japanese manufacturers in the narrow sense of performance (competitiveness) have lost their lead in the rivalry over costs, though they have
maintained competitiveness overall in Japan and overseas. For this

reason MIT's International Motor Vehicle Program (IMVP) has extolled the lean production system[1]—literally a production program trimmed of excess fat.

When we turn to performance on a broader scale, that of the Japanese automobile industry has not been high from the perspective of all stakeholders. Rather the Japanese automobile industry has been trailing in terms of competitiveness. The issue is will the Japanese automobile industry be able to continue to give top priority to market considerations (competitiveness) in a lean production system tending toward growth? Will it be able in the future to strike a good balance with its achievements in high industrial performance and maintain its traditional competitiveness? Clearly a shift in objective from lean growth to lean balance will be necessary.

Competitiveness

Domestic Trends

In 1992 the Japanese automobile industry came face to face with the problems of a sluggish economy. In 1993 and 1994 came a big decline in sales caused by the high yen. Overseas, however, Japanese automobiles were continuing to raise their market share and generally maintain strong international competitiveness (see figure 3.1). In fact the share of Japanese-produced automobiles in world markets has increased. Some Japanese manufacturers are in the top ranks in both revenue and the number of motor vehicles produced (see table 3.1).

Behind that success is a complete system that simultaneously reduces costs, improves quality, and ensures product differentiation. Much is accomplished by the early detection of problems in cutting down on waste, maintaining a short production and development cycles, soliciting companywide participation in problem-solving and improvement activities, using the parts manufacturers' technological strength and capacities for improvements, and providing flexible, versatile operational organizations and production facilities for a multi-skilled work force.

As the outstanding international competitive power of Japanese automobiles became clear in the 1980s, Western—especially American—manufacturers strove to catch up. The gap between Japan and the United States narrowed in a number of important indexes of competitiveness such as assembly productivity, quality of the manufactured product, and development lead time. Because of the

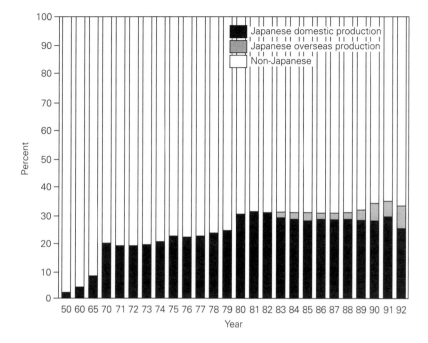

Figure 3.1
Japanese automobile production share in the world. Data on the number of vehicles produced overseas are not complete but vary somewhat according to demographics. Source: Data adapted from Nissan's *Automobile Industry Handbook* and the Japan Automobile Industry Association's *Statistics on Automobiles in Major Countries.*

progressive appreciation of the yen, in 1993 and 1994 the cost of a Japanese automobile rose considerably more than that of an American automobile of the same class. However, the average level of Japanese automobiles in terms of overall product competitiveness still remained high. At present American manufacturers do not yet appear to have caught up entirely.

Although this competitiveness of Japanese automobiles remains strong at the assembly level, it is not unreasonable to be apprehensive about Japan's position when the whole supply chain from parts manufacturers to sales dealers is included. Because of the limited data on suppliers and dealers, it is difficult to make broad international comparisons. However, we did consider several indexes.

For example, the disparities between Japan and the United States in labor productivity of the automobile manufacturing industry, including parts manufacturers, are small compared to those of assembly

Table 3.1
International rankings of automobile manufacturers (for 1992)

Rank	Company	Nation	Number of vehicles produced/shipped	Reference	Sales ($million)
1	GM	United States	7,156,000	World shipments	132,775
2	Ford	United States	5,764,000	World shipments	100,786
3	Toyota	Japan	4,895,000	World production	80,622
4	VW	Germany	3,499,000	World production	56,734
5	Nissan	Japan	3,015,000	World production	48,935
6	Chrysler	United States	2,175,000	World shipments	36,897
7	Renault	France	2,045,000	World shipments	33,885
8	PSA	France	2,023,000	World sales	29,387
9	Honda	Japan	1,860,000	World production	32,629
10	Mitsubishi	Japan	1,821,000	World production	25,112
11	Fiat	Italy	1,617,000	Italian production	47,929
12	Mazda	Japan	1,487,000	World production	20,477
13	Suzuki	Japan	1,153,000	World production	9,942
14	Hyundai	Korea	859,000	Korean production	8,606
15	D. Benz	Germany	688,000	World production	63,340
16	Isuzu	Japan	668,000	World production	12,476
17	Daihatsu	Japan	634,000	World production	6,909
18	FHI (Subaru)	Japan	587,000	World production	8,273
19	BMW	Germany	580,000	German production	20,611
20	Volvo	Sweden	410,000	World production	14,921

Souce: Data on number of vehicles produced by overseas manufacturers based on *Daily Automobile Journal*'s "Automobile Industry Handbook." Information about the number of vehicles produced by Japanese manufacturers came from FOURIN materials, and that about connected proceeds from each company's report on negotiable stocks.
Note: Based on worldwide shipments. The count may vary from company to company depending on production, shipments, sales, etc. Some companies are excluded in the count because their rankings fluctuate. Sales are based on connected settlements of accounts, and fields other than automobiles are included, too. The connected proceeds of Japanese manufacturers in the 1992 period were calculated at the average exchange rate of $1 = ¥127.

workers alone. Nevertheless, Japanese makers do appear on the average to be in a better position. Whether Japan or the United States has higher value-added productivity in its automobile industry depends on the dollar-yen exchange rate. But when the market rate is used, Japan has the lead.

The United States is generally said to have higher sales productivity. And it is clear that the United States is ahead if we compare productivity at the per-salesperson index. Yet there is virtually no difference between the United States and Japan in the index for all employees at dealers. This appears to be because the Japanese dealerships on the average are larger than those in the United States, with relatively high efficiency in remote areas.

On the whole, the disparities between Japan and the United States are smaller when the comparison is extended from just automakers to the whole supply chain, ranging from parts manufacturing to distribution. Nevertheless, nothing definitive has taken place to change the general opinion that the Japanese were stronger competitively in the 1980s.

A point that should not be overlooked in connection with competitiveness is that in recent years the pace of Japanese improvements has been slowing down. For instance, the labor productivity index (amount of work per vehicle) of the automobile industry (parts and assembly) enjoyed an annual growth rate of 6.3 percent in the 1970s. But in the 1980s it hardly changed at all, with annual rates centering about 0.3 percent.

The same trend can be observed in the indexes of productivity for individual assembly plants. A continued growth can still be observed for productivity at the value-added base. This indicates that the added value of Japanese automobiles rose because of improved technological levels and more luxurious appointments. However, the slowdown in growth of productivity, which is a fundamental index of manufacturing, suggests that the Japanese automobile industry's productivity level has reached a plateau.

Imbalance of Performance
In the eyes of all stakeholders the Japanese automobile industry has not performed well. These have been a great many imbalances between the product market (toward consumers) and the labor market (toward employees) that in the larger picture have serious implications for the future of the industry. The issue of the imminently long-lasting

labor shortage, particularly of young male workers, has given rise, for example, to concerns about disparities between the industry's reputation in the product market and in the labor market, between consumer satisfaction and employee satisfaction, and between diverse product lines and the homogeneity of the work force—especially at the production site.

Up to the present time everything had somehow worked, even with the heavy emphasis on the consumer and the product market. Continual growth resulted from strong competitiveness. The 1960s saw quantitative growth of the domestic market (motorization), the 1970s export growth, the first half of the 1980s overseas earnings (especially from the United States), the latter half of the 1980s a growth in the domestic market—particularly in the luxury products. The driving force has changed, but opportunities for growth that stakeholders other than consumers can agree with have always existed.

Other factors contributing to the industry's growth were eager and generally flexible workers, stockholders, local organizations, and parts suppliers. For example, in the labor market, after the widespread labor conflicts of around 1950, a stable labor-management system was formed. Labor relations were generally handled by intracompany unions that offered negotiations between labor and management, a regular supply of young male workers, permanent employment, training in job skills, and so on. Unlike the unions at American and European automobile manufacturers which led to unstable relations between labor and management and tended to hinder productivity and improvements in quality, Japanese unions have contributed importantly in raising their industry's competitiveness.

Of course the contingent of temporary workers to supplement this system cannot be ignored, and we cannot deny that individual workers were sometimes dissatisfied. But at least such problems did not undermine, nor affect in any significant way, the automobile industry's competitiveness.

As success in the product market led to high company's sales and profits, the stakeholders received their share, and workers received pay raises. In responding to demand by auto manufacturers for strict cost reductions, suppliers enjoyed expanding orders, which in turn allowed them to reduce costs through economies of scale. The price of stocks went up. In fact during this period the system could be maintained as long as the manufacturers concentrated on customer satisfaction and strengthening competitiveness, mainly on improvements in quality, cost, and delivery (QCD). They could get by without thinking much about internationalization of stakeholders other than the consumers. However, as will be discussed in the next section, this oversight in policy has started to penalize the industry internationally.

3.2 Intermediate- to Long-Term Outlook: Limits to Competition Model

As we head toward the twenty-first century, we can expect the automobile industry to change its course and concentrate less on competitiveness.

First, the slowdown in domestic production has brought down the number of exports to the United States and Europe. Another boom in the domestic market that might spark high growth can hardly be imagined. The labor crunch in Japan is expected to continue and also to limit growth, and thus to affect all stakeholders.

Second, the stakeholders' attitudes are changing, with workers becoming less tolerant of the long hours on the job, the workplace's environment, and the work load. No longer can management rely heavily on a massive labor force of dedicated young men who devote their lives to the company working two factory shifts. Along with internationalization has come pressure on Japanese automakers to expand their corporate practices into areas having to do with a heterogeneous composition of labor, especially in North America where they are watched strictly by the local community.

Moreover the demand for parts abroad and the leveling off in the volume of domestic production has made it difficult to increase the domestic production of parts. Therefore it is not reasonable to expect the cooperation from parts manufacturers known up to now to continue in the near future.

Finally consumers as a whole have become sensitive to the wider impact of corporate practices on stakeholders other than consumers (what critic Katsuhito Uchihashi calls the "socially responsible consumer"). This new breed of consumer does not buy the products of a company that fails to treat its employees well or is not popular with the local community, even if the products are good. For example, Volvo users tend to have a high regard for the entire Volvo company's ethic, and they loyally buy the firm's products. Such consumers look at a company's consistent societal concerns—namely at its corporate sense of duty—and make purchase decisions accordingly.

The era is gone when a Japanese automobile company could focus just on competitiveness and customer satisfaction and still satisfy all stakeholders and maintain productivity. We have reached an age in which improving performance internationally must be made a primary consideration.

As of this update in 1996, the Japanese automobile industry is facing a slump in profits. Investments in balancing industry practices while maintaining competitiveness have hit a plateau, and that presents a heavy burden for the future.

How should the system of Japanese automobile manufacturers be overhauled in order to achieve a balance? Multilevel global networks have been evolving since the 1980s (see figure 3.2). Japanese automakers will be pressed to reconsider their whole performance system, including production, development, and distribution, in order to construct a framework that brings the components of competition, cooperation, and conflict into perspective.

We think that on the domestic side the idea of a lean production system should be expanded and balanced to include assessments by the labor market, suppliers, and other shareholders. Again, this means a shift from an emphasis on growth in pursuit of traditional competitiveness to an emphasis on balance.

Multilevel Global Networks

Networks are being formed internationally by the exchange of information between companies and plants at various levels concerning management strategy, product planning, product engineering, process engineering, production, marketing, and so on; they are loose multinational cooperative networks. On the one hand, competition among the automakers has intensified but has not resulted in drastic retrenchments. When competition seems about to force a firm out of business, the government, viewing automobiles as a flagship industry, may intervene to keep it going. But unilaterally protected trade and the formation of regional blocks are not a reality, and that would go against the flow of the times. In terms of a balance between the two extremes (i.e., global oligopoly and regional protectionism), an intermediate scenario—that is to say, the formation of multilevel, international

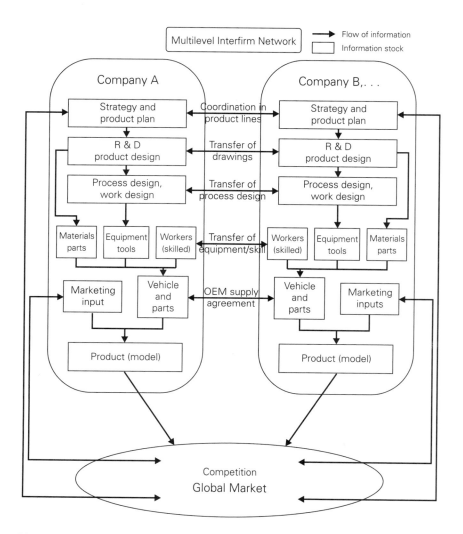

Figure 3.2
Global multilevel interfirm network. Several competing companies are loosely connected at each stage of development, production preparation, and production. Companies collect information on their products and compete in advertising them. Yet, in having exchanged some of the information beforehand via cooperative relations, they can complement each other in the competition.

networks within companies and between companies—appears to be the logical direction for the industry to take.

The international networks comprising the automobile industries of Japan, Europe, and the United States that are now being formed at various levels are designed to deal with international rivalry by a built-in mechanism for rectifying disparities in competitiveness. This mechanism has actually caused international competition among different companies to get fiercer. But just when it seems that a retrenchment of the less competent companies will occur as a result, trade friction arise, bringing in government involvement for a while. If prolonged, the management resources of other companies will be distributed through loose cooperative networks (financial participation, technological cooperation, joint ventures, providing OEM, production commissions, etc.). This serves as a brake on further irreversible disparities in competitiveness. That way the affected company does not need to downsize right away and can continue its level of production.

No doubt the 1980s were unprecedented in that competition, cooperation, and conflict proceeded in parallel in the world's automobile industries. Trade conflict continued over automobiles as companies both cooperated and competed with each other for their market share. However, as a result the automobile industry evolved on the whole as an integrated system. That trend has continued into the 1990s.

Consequently it is no longer appropriate to analyze the international competitiveness of automobiles from the single perspective of Japan compared with the United States and Europe. Needed is a perspective that brings the Three Cs (competition, cooperation, and conflict) into the picture. Consideration should also be given to differences within the levels of output by country, by company, and the like. Since the Three Cs are integral to any overall game plan, Japanese firms should not try to deal separately with competition, cooperation, and conflict. Instead, they ought to consider all three sides of the international picture in setting corporate strategy.

Labor Market

The ongoing shortage of labor power, largely caused by the low birth rate and by the demand for shorter working hours, has become a more important issue in the automobile industry than in other industries. This is a structural problem that will persist unless the present assembly production system, which relies largely on a young male labor force, is considerably redefined. At this juncture the prediction is that many large Japanese factories will successively make the necessary structural changes during this century. Their success will depend on retaining the present system's strengths while transforming it into something that will work thirty years into the future. If the current system is left alone, there is the danger of it gradually collapsing onto itself in the future.

One alternative is to supplement the present system with the spot labor market (temporary workers, foreign workers, subcontracting workers, etc.). In fact there have been many cases of automobile and parts manufacturers employing large numbers of temporary workers at high wages at times of increased production. However, this can have a spiraling effect, whereby regularly employed multiskilled workers become lax and a great many quit (high job turnover), exacerbating the labor crunch and further dependency on temporary workers. Under this scenario the multiskilled worker system, which has long supported Japanese manufacturers' competitiveness, would be in a state of crisis well before the twenty-first century. While promoting shorter hours encourages a dependency on temporary workers, it is a natural future course. However, we should not let the panacea of shorter hours take flight on its own. Shorter work hours may have a remedial effect on the problem of internal collapse, but also discussions on how to reform the total system are necessary.

Up to now the so-called lean production system which has depended on a homogeneous young male labor force and the cultivation of multiple skills has had built-in processes for organizational problem-solving and improvements through participation on the shop floor. It was through that system that the present high state of competitiveness and growth was accomplished, raising productivity, quality, and flexibility simultaneously. Nevertheless, as we have seen, that system cannot be maintained into the twenty-first century. So far senior citizens and women have been in the minority among Japanese auto workers. Assembly plants will additionally have to bring older female workers into their labor force. These will be calls for improvements in the work environment and facilities, reforms in work methods, automation to reduce physical strain, more flexible work schedules, and enhanced social benefits such as pensions, maternity leaves, and day-care facilities. In other words, wide-ranging reforms and equipment investments are very much needed. Present-day structural problems in the shortage of engineers and sales personnel must be solved in a similar manner.

There is much to learn from North America and Europe. In the past, for example, companies in Germany and Sweden have dealt successfully with labor crunches. Building a mechanism for mutual learning by corporations in Japan, the United States, and Europe should be an international agendum.

One of the measures for dealing with the domestic labor shortage has been to disperse assembly bases to other provinces of Japan and construct automobile-production capacity in developing regions in Asia. But still much remains to be done in the way of fixed investment, personnel investment, maintaining competitiveness, and securing local supply resources for parts in remote areas. Developing networks of parts manufacturers in such areas is a problem, since making overseas investments places an additional burden on Japanese suppliers constrained by reductions in domestic volume.

Already direct investments in the United States have become a personnel and capital burden to many parts manufacturers. The question here is, Will there be any surplus capacity for direct investment in other regions like Asia? There are naturally limits to rapid transfer overseas of production capacities. Therefore the scenario of massively reducing the present amount of domestic production (which has been 11 million to 13 million vehicles annually), because of a labor crunch and shorter working hours, and shifting the production bases overseas will also largely affect domestic parts manufacturers. This is too risky an operation to be carried out quickly. Thus we do not see this scenario rapidly taking place in the near future.

Impact of Technological Changes

In the 1990s regulations are being advanced on automobile safety, emission gas, fuel economy, and recycling with existent technology, and the like. Radically new parts technology is needed. It is such innovation that encourages the growth of more fundamental research and development, for example, on engines, while the outlay to design new automobile models may drop.

Consider the alternative of a global oligopoly if the companies cannot keep up with the high pace of technological development. To avoid such an extreme, firms ought to cooperate in fundamental technology that raises the technological level of products, perhaps by

furnishing technology by contract and granting OEM. The point is that
intense competition in the development of products is beneficial, again
supported by a multilevel network strategy for cooperation and
competition.

Parts Procurement and Distribution System

Assembly manufacturer is only one side of the automobile industry.
Even if just the assembly manufacturers' problems were solved, that
would account for only 30 percent of the manufacturing cost and 15
percent of employment (parts, assembly, sales).

In the procurement of parts, the Japanese supplier system up to now
has received much attention from abroad. European and American
manufacturers have started to build long-term relations with a small
number of parts manufacturers and to include them in the development of products.

However, the existing Japanese system has to balance the demand
for lower prices and improved quality by assembly manufacturers
with competition among parts manufacturers, on the one hand, and
increases in the volume of orders, maintenance of stable transactions,
and technological support from automakers, on the other hand. In the
future a ceiling must be reached on the expanding domestic production. Otherwise long-term stable relationships will collapse if domestically parts cannot be obtained because of parts manufacturers
expanding their operations overseas in order to facilitate local procurement of parts at these distant factories. Dissatisfaction over the distribution of profits will no doubt rise between suppliers and assembly
manufacturers.

Under those circumstances, as the relationship between parts makers
and assembly manufacturers deteriorates, the fine balance between
quality and cost will fall apart. Currently there is much pressure from
other countries to open up the procurement arrangements in Japan
and overseas. But parts makers are contending with a shortage of labor,
increased burdens of development and overseas investments, and the
like just as are the assembly manufacturers.

The problems in the parts industry are not simply limited to first-tier
suppliers. They are more serious for small- and medium-sized, second-
tier and third-tier parts manufacturers. To investigate the extent of this
crisis, we questionnaired automobile parts manufacturers, mostly in
Kanagawa Prefecture, in 1992. A comparison of the first-, second-, and

third-tier suppliers' answers shows greater pessimism about the future among the smaller-scale secondary and tertiary manufacturers.

For example, more second-tier than first-tier and more third-tier than second-tier parts makers are planning to curtail their automobile-related business in some form, such as shifting to a nonvehicle business, reducing automobile work, or retiring from the business. This will mean a gradual erosion of the automobile industry's foundation from the bottom up. The fact that small-scale, third-tier makers are considering a switch to other industries should make us realize that the second-tier manufacturers are experiencing particularly rough times too. Their survival will depend on strengthening the existing supplier system with a suitable labor system that includes the small- and medium-sized, second-tier and third-tier makers.

Meanwhile the Japanese distribution system does not have a good reputation. Its door-to-door sales method has been pointed out to be inefficient even by MIT's IMVP standard. As was mentioned earlier, while there are no disparities in productivity between Japan and the United States, at the distribution end the Japanese side has no clear superiority akin to that in manufacturing. One look at profits confirms that the distribution sector is weak compared to parts and assembly. There is further the shortage of labor problem, since it is difficult to hire a sufficient sales force willing to work long hours. Unlike Japanese automobile sales which are established as a separate distribution industry, with dealers receiving financial and management support from the automobile manufacturer, the distribution and retailing of parts has no solid framework for its activity. Since the sale of automobiles can fluctuate dramatically, experiencing cycles of rising and declining sales, an efficient and profitable parts distribution system must be strong even during recessions.

3.3 Shift to Balanced System and a Multilevel International Network

Production System

By hiring senior citizens and women, the automobile industry could reduce disparities in the work performed by men and women, both young and old, with the same years of experience. The trends in the labor market have been for some time now eradicating gender and age discrepancies by reforms in plant operations and automation. Once this work is fully completed, all Japanese companies will respond to that challenge, just as they have all adapted continually to improvements in their shop-floor participation style of operation.

The production assembly method in use today was established in the first half of the twentieth century by the American car manufacturer Henry Ford. Since then, although many firms made some modifications, the basic system did not change. Primarily this is because automation in the automobile assembly process has been more difficult to install than in other fields. Complete automation of the assembly process will be out of the question for at least another twenty to thirty years. In other words, the final assembling of automobiles will continue to be labor intensive. In particular, that final stage presents several problems, since the work tends to be tiring and monotonous, which can alienate workers further from the job and cannot keep up with diversification in product types.

The lean production system and the Volvo system, both of which are currently getting much attention have reached a crossroad. The former is not accepted by the labor market, and the latter faces a lack of competitiveness. (In November 1992 Volvo announced the closures of some of its plants, including one in Uddevalla which had in use the so-called Volvo production style. Still this cannot be said to be a decision caused by problems inherent in this style, for Volvo has continued its system at other plants.) Indeed the mass assembly process in the twenty-first century may end up a mix of competitive nonconveyor production with people-friendly assembly lines.

In response to the gravity of the labor shortage in automobile plants, the creation of pleasant shop-floor conditions for employees is becoming a priority in the redesigning of factories, though the bedrock of competitiveness like improvements in productivity and quality is not entirely ignored. Plant design is an issue not only from the ergonomic point of view but also because it can transmit a "caring" corporate message to both employees and the local community. The age may come when industrial designers—so-called human behavioral specialists—will become more involved in the design of factories and other work facilities.

Automation will also require conceptual changes in the shift to a balanced lean system, particularly in the automation of the labor-intensive final assembly process. In assembly operations, not only does automation reduce cost, but it can improve the working environment by easing the work load which is a factor in enabling a people-friendly shop floor.

Product Strategies and Research and Development

Excessive product variety, model changes, specifications, and price discounts have been viewed as undermining the automobile industry. Better product strategies are needed. For instance, the model change cycle could be extended without slowing the pace of adopting new technology when it is feasible. Such a strategy would give the automobile industry some leeway in allocating resource investments for new technology.

The product development process of Japanese automobile manufacturers has generally been lean; yet the product designs tend to be fat. By new product designs that drop such extravagance, cost reductions might be realized without lowering customer satisfaction. In the 1990s, while it may be hard to improve productivity, only through earnest effort at the shop floor (*kaizen*) will cost reductions by way of design simplification be possible. Value engineering (VE) may be the needed production concept. Implicit in it is cooperation in every detail between the project leader, who holds full responsibility for product concepts, and the value engineering staff. The main point is to maintain a strong sense of priorities in the planning and concept stages in order to put together a cost-effective product design. Here the imagination and capabilities of the project leader are critical.

Making interchangeable parts among models is a related issue. The percentage of parts common in design and used among models has been lower among Japanese automobile manufacturers than at their Western counterparts. The advantage this presents is a model's total quality, integrity, and differentiation from other models. However, this is not an optimal way for Japanese manufacturers to continue. There is no denying that a proliferation of differently designed parts with similarities in function has tended to raise costs beyond what is necessary.

The presently sluggish domestic production forebodes a reduction in the volume of orders for individual parts and in engineering work. Therefore the manufacturer of certain common parts that do not sacrifice product competitiveness would reduce costs. In the near future, distinguishing between the parts that must be customized for certain models and those that can be made the same for all other models would be the responsibility of the project leader.

Manufacturers such as Toyota and Nissan already have plans to reduce the total number of parts by at least 30 percent. As such plans for design simplification are advanced, subcontracting makers and secondary parts makers that have traditionally specialized in small-lot production of parts will be hit hard by a reduction in orders. For this reason the system of common parts should be introduced gradually.

Since balancing the identity of a firm's product line with diversity in individual products will no longer be the case, solid product strategies that unify models and provide a corporate identity will be decided by each company. To be sure, high among such considerations will be the company's design philosophy, such as which relates to variety in surface and structural designs.

Japanese automobile manufacturers should anticipate resistance from project managers and divisions that plan companywide technology and product strategies. Or else bad feelings may arise between individual product leaders and the functional divisions. The task of coordinating interproject mechanisms without lowering a project leader's morale or a project organization's vitality will indeed be formidable.

The consensus on project management techniques suggests an effective way to introduce such reform, namely to strengthen the role of project leaders, use small development teams, and synchronize development with production. Automakers are now at the trial-and-error stage in managing multiple projects; this is an important challenge for the future.

Parts Suppliers and the Distribution System

Cooperation among automobile parts manufacturers and dealers in reforming the parts distribution systems is obviously necessary. Also important are the procurement and sales strategies of the automobile manufacturers; they set the initiative for change.

On parts procurement strategies, the automobile industry ought to retain factors that have contributed to competitiveness so far. Points to be considered toward that goal are improvements in making orders and coping with networks.

1. *Changes in orders.* The industry could increase the common parts ratio by setting restrictions on the number of variations for each part, for example. When production reaches a ceiling rate, there are limits on how far suppliers can reduce costs. Conditions for raising economies of scale as well as conditions for product rationalization and

improving productivity should be established. Further, as stated earlier, variations among parts can be reduced by standardizing them and by restricting orders to a small number of parts manufacturers. However, careful consideration must be given toward supporting the industrial base of small- and medium-sized manufacturers that produce parts in small lots.

2. *Diversifying networks.* Rising procurements from abroad and new transaction relationships established in factories that have been moved overseas can be a catalyst in seeking other suppliers and loosening supplier networks. Parts manufacturers that have moved overseas and cannot adjust to the new environment will likely be consolidated through mergers and the like, resulting in fierce competition among surviving parts manufacturers within a loose network of suppliers. Competition will likely stiffen too among the parts suppliers that have been the backbone of the Japanese supplier system up to now.

On sales strategies, the path to the dealers' independence lies in their shift of emphasis from number of vehicles sold to dealers' profits. Particularly important will be their capacity to cope in periods of market decline. Debates on the switching from door-to-door to showroom sales have become one point of this discussion. Incidentally MIT's IMVP report advocates the highly effective lean system for sales, while pointing out that the Japanese system of door-to-door sales has yet to reach that level.

Door-to-door sales may not seem particularly efficient, yet they have had a relatively stabilizing effect on sales during recessions. Switching to showroom sales could damage this stability in times of market recession. Since this concerns leveling the volume of production (*heijunka*), the problem extends to assembly and parts manufacturers. We must not forget that door-to-door sales are viewed within the total system of distribution and manufacturing. Essentially both showroom sales and door-to-door sales have their positive and negative aspects, so they cannot be used against each other. A system should be considered that flexibly includes both types of sales according to customer preferences.

There is then the issue of profits lost through discount sales. Japanese automobiles have been criticized for having retail market prices that are too low. Here we must distinguish between low prices and discounted prices at the dealers. "High quality at low cost" is the basic idea behind our marketing philosophy now. For this reason we cannot easily accept the thought of setting high prices or raising prices to raise profits; that would make light of the dynamics found in competition. At the same time there is something fundamentally wrong with allowing chronic discounted price wars to continue among dealers as a means of bringing about low prices.

To be sure, discounted prices in the sales outlets are a major weapon that dealers and, in turn, the manufacturer use in their race for market share. Then we as consumers who generally welcome discounts cannot rid ourselves of the anxiety that maybe someone out there is buying an automobile under more advantageous terms, since we are not familiar with what the real price should be. Inevitably wildly ranging discounts lower the motivation of manufacturers and suppliers to make incremental cost reductions in manufacturing and product development, and inevitably dissatisfaction and anxiety over prices affect consumers. Of course manufacturers and customers will respond differently depending on whether the custom of discounted prices abates while there are ongoing efforts to cut costs and set low standard prices, or on whether large-scale discounts are carried out after relatively high prices are established.

The Japanese automobile industry is characterized by the fact that parts makers, assemblers, and dealers conduct their businesses in a comparatively uniform way. Parts manufacturers—at least the first-tier parts manufacturers—and assembly manufacturers have organized cooperative associations (*kyoryokukai*) and maintain long-lasting business relationships. Long-standing steady relationships likewise characterize the distribution sector. The large degree of capital invested by the manufacturers in parts suppliers and dealers is a phenomenon not found often in the United States and Europe.

History so far has seen the assembly manufacturer as the pivotal figure that moves this total framework along. However, now that growth in domestic production cannot, in general, be expected, automobile manufacturers must grapple with a new system that will enable the parts makers and sales dealers to become less dependent on manufacturers in their business affairs. That system will also open Japan's procurement and sales system to foreign manufacturers.

Once again, we need to point out that practices that are efficient locally may not necessarily be the most appropriate in global terms. In the United States, parts, assembly, and sales function rather autonomously. When a dealer's sales drop, the number of sales people is promptly cut. In time the volume of automobiles produced by the manufacturer will drop as well, and layoffs will occur frequently, even at the supplier companies.

The American experience bespeaks the fact that optimizing a part alone is accompanied by a price. Recently American manufacturers have come to recognize that problem and are trying to build cooperative relationships with parts makers and to support their dealers. Conversely, since Japan can no longer provide a basis for growth, the challenge in the 1990s for Japanese automobile manufacturers will be to seek locally optimal solutions that are innovative and yet retain a balanced view.

Global Management

Management on the international scale has been becoming ever more complex. Japanese automobile manufacturers rapidly increased their overseas production plants in the 1980s, with the number rising nearly threefold, from 78 in 1980 to 224 in 1991. But that does not necessarily mean these plants are being operated efficiently. The huge outlays on capital and maintenance at these plants are factors bearing down heavily on automobile companies' earnings.

How to make one's own company more efficient within the global network is an important issue for the future. It will be equally crucial for companies to form efficient and effective networks that keep them informed on areas where they should cooperate and where they should compete. The construction of such a focused system for global operations must be made a top priority.

It should nevertheless not be ignored that aggressive direct investments overseas have contributed to improving the technological power and competitiveness of automobile makers and created jobs in many other countries. Production in these countries has benefited many more overseas stakeholders—local employers, suppliers, the local economy and community, and so on—than just consumers. Consideration ought to be given also toward attaining a balance in this regard instead of centering on efficiency alone. There are multiple aspects to globalization, and it all depends on effective management of international networks. The skill with which globalization is handled will greatly influence corporate competitiveness and international friction.

Already problems are arising in company management of automobiles jointly developed through international business alliances, namely between American and Japanese makers or European and

Japanese makers, in that composite models are getting blended into a company's own product line. Although this may help diversify a company's product line, it can damage its identity. How to uphold consistency in the company's product line while taking advantage of an international network will be an issue closely watched in the future.

Investment Costs for Reforming the System

Funds are needed for carrying out large reforms in production and development systems. Opinions vary, however, on whether this is a matter to be discussed in terms of the current operating profit rate or whether it is a matter of cash flow (net profits). Others question concern whether profits should be made mostly from sales within Japan or whether the trail left by the era of the low yen exchange rate (a time when Japan earned money abroad) can be retraced. To be sure, deliberation must begin over what is the best profit arrangement for the global market, but with the consumer in mind. Although the notion of optimal profit level is not acceptable in our product market, we need some discussion on what amount of cash flow will accommodate rising production costs.

That is to say, as mentioned previously, both investment capital and new technology will be required in shifting to a lean balanced system in Japan or in transferring such a system to the United States and Europe. The capital burden will be high for Japanese manufacturers, who will further need to invest in research and development on vehicle safety, fuel economy, and environmental matters like emission control in response to foreign pressure. Then there are the investments needed to maintain product competitiveness, for the tempo of improvements in Japanese productivity has grown sluggish and the United States and Europe have been catching up in some ways.

Those smaller manufacturers that are incapable of keeping up with this pace of change will close their operations, which is something that can happen in Japan, the United States, or Europe. Left in that state, such conditions inevitably lead to a global oligopoly. To prevent this occurrence, cooperation among companies via global networks must be promoted, along with efforts to raise the technological level of the entire industry in basic technologies for environment-oriented engines and fuel economy, for example. Another way to avoid oligopoly is to support lower-ranking companies. In the end diverse competition at each product level does benefit consumers.

3.4 Reform in the Twenty-first Century

Looking back, we see that the Japanese automobile industry's international competitiveness reached its peak in the first half of the 1980s. That was a time when, aside from the low yen rate, the industry developed significant advantages over the average European and American automobile industries in both quality and productivity. In the late 1980s Japanese manufacturers' position of relative competitive superiority began to shrink as American makers started to catch up, as Japanese manufacturers transferred management resources to firms in the United States and Europe, as the improvement rate stagnated among Japanese manufacturers, and as the yen rose.

Nevertheless, Japanese automobile companies have maintained a relative lead in competition in total product quality, and they accept lower profits than their American counterparts. For these reasons the share of Japanese automobiles in major markets in the West have progressed steadily, and 1990 was a year in which the overall strength of Japanese cars was ultimately recognized abroad.

However, after that year, the Japanese automobile industry came to face for a short period various problems of a different nature. There was a labor force shortage in 1991; then a full-fledged domestic recession, degenerating corporate earnings, and a deficient cash flow in 1992; followed by a decline in export competitiveness in 1993 and 1994, due to the high yen. In the background was the issue of trade surplus with the United States, and trade friction continued to smolder. Given that Japanese firms were pressed to cope with so much during a short time span, it is not surprising that some pessimism has arisen.

Yet dare we go on. The industry's present worries about the recession, declining profits, and a drop in competitiveness may in fact present the perfect time to rebuild a vision starting with short-term measures but with a long-term range and actively convey that vision to other countries. Taking a long view, the true challenge of a lean corporate system is not the way it responds in the immediate term to a drop in the market but the way it anticipates what lies ahead. This means preparing the system for fluctuations in the volume of production due to cyclical replacement demand, for low growth over the long term, and for the aging of the labor force.

More precisely, domestic production can be expected to respond to a cyclical pattern of surges and declines based on changes in demand. This is a fact of the automobile market in other industrialized nations.

The concern here is whether that cycle will be broken as shortages of labor occur at peak times and as shortages of cash flow, or restraints on investments, occur at low times.

This is a matter of great concern for the existing system which is lean on growth. Consequently the position of this author is that the true challenge will be in moving to a lean but balanced system that can deal with fluctuations in demand and changes in the population structure. The mechanisms for collective learning, problem solving, and continual improvements, which are the basis of the lean production system, must be preserved.

Primarily the necessary cash flow and competitiveness must be secured by lowering costs through lean product design and eliminating discount wars. Then there should be a consistent investment effort to improve the workplace and to create jobs overseas. Workplace and environmental considerations are important in maintaining the system internally and in establishing international trust. Finally new concepts might be attempted for the distribution system in terms of meeting customer demands and for a modification of the Ford-style assembly line with automation that is people friendly. In that sense, what should be aimed for is a lean, completely balanced system capable of dealing with trial and error. Now is also the time to try different approaches at various sites of production, sales, and product development.

In international relations it is important not to view competition, cooperation, and conflict as separate games and overreact to another party's actions. The Japanese ought also to try and break the traditional pattern of being good at competition but bad at coping with conflict. They should rather consider both as integral elements of one game. The key idea is to use the international cooperation network to the best advantage. The Japanese automobile industry also cannot put on a passive front in circumstances of aggravated trade friction. An international cooperation program must be proposed and initiated by the Japanese side. Here, too, the key idea is to break away from an emphasis on competition and move to balance the system by a long-term perspective.

Contrary to many opinions expressed recently, we cannot be pessimistic about how the Japanese automobile industry will handle a short-term crisis in 1993 and 1994. We foresee a midterm recovery in demand in the mid- to late 1990s. However, since measures to deal with fluctuations, including a recovery, have yet to be fully prepared, we have adopted a rather cautious view. The true telling point may very well be the advent of increased production despite the shortage of labor power, which may come as the recession eases in 1992 to 1994. If a company manages to solve such immediate problems, it may well end up maintaining competitiveness over the long term both internally and externally and, moreover, remain respected both at home and abroad. In other words, this author has taken a conditionally optimistic view for the long haul.

Note

1. No precise definition of "lean production system" exists, but it is a concept that is based on the Toyota production method, though considerably simplified. Its structural features include the reduction of activities such as inventory that do not provide added value, operations that allow problems on the shop floor to surface, continual review of activities that respond to these problems, on-the-spot improvements in productivity, quality, delivery, and flexibility and a flexible mass-production system enabling workers to develop multiple skills as well as produce small lots of goods. Although there has not been much reference to companywide total quality control (TQC) in the MIT report, it is an essential feature of the lean production system.

4   Metallic Materials Industry

Yasunori Baba and
Shinji Takai

Ever since the Meiji Period (1868–1912) the Japanese metallic materials industry (hereafter sometimes called the metals industry) has been modernizing by adopting technology from the West. During the era of high economic growth after World War II, it established new facilities and began its own original technological development. Thus, with the steel industry in the forefront, it has put on the greatest show on earth in fabricating commodities.

However, the metals industry, which basically supplies materials to other industries, is very much affected by economic trends. In recent years the stagnating condition of exports caused by the rapid appreciation of the yen has dealt a direct blow to the industry. Faced by the rising yen, technology cannot be easily managed, and international competitiveness has declined. Amid this economic crisis each metal firm has had to make white-collar worker employment adjustments and to diversify operations in their struggle for survival.

The dividing line between eventual success or failure depends on how metals companies creatively expand and manage to set up a new industrial concept. They can only strengthen the industry by taking up new challenges. Among these are the technological possibilities of introducing flexible small-volume production and meeting new societal objectives arising out of global environment problems. By redefining itself, the industry can look forward to innovations in technology, markets, organizations, and institutions that will permit an escape from the present state of industrial maturity.

How to make an effective use of the dynamics of adaptability for overcoming maturation must be the main consideration in the metallic materials industry's strategies. More precisely, the issue is how to retain and utilize the skills that have been built up over many years with energetic investments in technology, facilities, and human resources. While it is true that the metals industry's development up to now has depended on a symbiotic social system comprised of a wide-ranging industrial membership, investments must be made in assets from a long-term perspective to ensure that this system does not reach functional paralysis or a point of serious fatigue.

Primarily, at the corporation level, Japan's reputation for high manual skills must not be sacrificed, for in the long term that is the core of its industrial competitiveness. Diversification must, in principle, proceed from this concept of its strength. To revitalize the growth of companies, diversification objectives must include programs aimed at cultivating the human resources needed to manage the new technological bases. Beginning with R&D, product planning must closely respond to market forces; by this means new product concepts should be developed. Now that we cannot avoid industrial change, it is incumbent on top management to take charge of the direction of industrial development.

4.1 Formation of a Paradigm for Diverse Volume Production

General View

Some clarification of the metals industry's performance is necessary before we attempt to analyze and review that industry's future. Some discussion is also necessary concerning the basis for the methods of production currently used by the industry.[1]

A survey of the steel industry's production shows crude steel remaining at about 100 million tons for several years. In 1993 sales came to just under ¥12 trillion, and its 14 percent of the world's share positioned it number one globally. The number of employees, which marked a record of just under 380,000 at the industry's peak in 1970, has now been more than halved at 180,000. The export base of Japanese rolled steel accounts for 12 percent of the world's share—a figure only second to Germany's. However, the export environment has been steadily deteriorating, and imports are on a slight increase.

As for the market structure, the blast furnace manufacturers' share of crude steel production is approximately 70 percent. The electric furnace manufacturers saw an increase in proportion, so their share now comes to 30 percent. Although the two formerly had clear, separate specializations, that structure is in the process of collapsing due to both the construction of electric furnaces by blast furnace makers and the introduction of hot coils by electric furnace manufacturers in recent years.

Because of the demand for electric wire, the Japanese wire rod industry's sales rose to ¥2.3 trillion in 1991, making it number two in world production. It employed just under 80,000 workers. We can analyze the industry's structure by separating the large companies that manufacture optical fibers, for example, from the small- to medium-sized companies, which account for about 90 percent of the 460 companies comprising this industry. Among the nonferrous metal industries the volume of copper production, which grew rapidly after World War II, fluctuated greatly with the closure of copper mines after the oil crises. Now the industry produces roughly 10 percent of the world's share of copper ground metal.

Aluminum refining became a 1.46-million-ton industry in the 1970s. But because of the hikes in electric power rates due to the oil crises, the field lost international competitiveness and sharply dropped to an annual production of 35,000 tons in 1988. The domestic demand for aluminum rose dramatically to 3.71 million tons in 1991 with the rapid expansion of demand by beverage can and automobile makers. However, to meet this demand 99 percent of new ground metal is imported.

The steel industry's strength in manufacturing should be considered from the standpoint of productivity internationally. In comparing Japan, the United States, and the former West Germany in a time series based on labor productivity in 1975, we can see that Japanese productivity underwent considerable growth from 1978 to 1979. Except for 1986, when it was hit by the high-yen-induced recession, it has progressed favorably. If we compare each country, taking American labor productivity as 100, Japanese productivity was only at the 70 level until 1978. However, since 1979 it has stayed at a level of 110 to 130, which is above the U.S. level.

Similarly the basic unit of energy per unit production has measured up impressively in international comparisons. For example, if the basic unit of energy consumption by the Japanese steel industry in 1990 is taken as 100, the indexes for the United States come to 135; even the relatively sound former West Germany had 107. How was this strong position in manufacturing achieved? This will become clear in the rest of this section as we summarize the Japanese steel industry's postwar history.

Demise of Mass Production

The production track of this country's steel industry can be roughly divided into three phases. Each phase is characterized by a new technological paradigm relating to a dominant technology and meets the needs of the economy.

The first phase was the initial period from 1950 to the early 1970s when coastal ironworks using the vertical method of making steel were constructed. Technologically speaking, the industry concentrated on importing the most advanced equipment in the world and improving it for mass production. Huge blast furnaces were constructed, and LD (long-distance) converters were introduced. These early decades corresponded to Japan's period of high economic growth, and the fundamental strategies at that time were to pursue economies of scale and raise the production rate after acquiring the latest large-scale equipment. The industry also aimed to lower the unit costs of production by eliminating the burden of fixed costs.

Alliances among major steelmakers in the purchasing of natural resources and marketing of closely resembling products leveled the competition.[2] Fierce rivalry for shares existed through the weapon of lowering costs by constructing new ironworks. This mass-production strategy reached a peak in the output of crude steel in 1973 but fell dramatically into a slump that same year because of the oil crisis. That is to say, the Japanese steel industry had reached its maturation level and so was limited in its growth-oriented strategies. The construction of new blast furnaces was deferred, and some operations suspended. The steel industry plunged itself into a fierce competition based on cost reductions.

In the second phase, which dates to the oil crises of 1973, attempts were made to establish a systems technology that both lowered costs and conserved energy. Continuous casting methods were widely introduced for this reason. To cut costs further and reduce the volume of production, a smaller basic unit of production that improved the yield was needed. At the same time policies to curtail production costs amid the rising prices of energy were aligned with policies to conserve energy. As it turned out, the cost-cutting efforts in operations required hardly any investments, since improvements in operational efficiency were considered energy-saving policies.[3]

Positive Impact of Computers

Computers solved many of the problems that had emerged from the energy crises. By actively bringing computers onto the shop floor, Japanese companies succeeded in rapidly raising productivity.

Major steel corporations first brought in mainframes around 1955. Thereafter each company made their computer systems on-line and at real time, and also systemized sales, production administration, and the supervision of management. Thus computers came to be used more strategically from the time of the oil crises and were applied to continuous casting. In the 1980s the rate of equipment operation improved dramatically thanks to the dissemination of continuous casting methods.[4] This, in turn, did very much toward raising productivity during the same period.

In product marketing, customers' needs steadily came to tilt toward diverse small lots and shortened delivery periods; in other words, a demand arose for just-in-time deliveries.[5] To respond adequately, all information about sales, production, and distribution had to be both accurate and timely. The flow of information speeded up with the use of computers.

Since the mid-1980s every major steel manufacturer has begun to grapple with reconstructing the corporate information system. If we take the example of the production operation systems at steel mills, design plans for each separate traditional product were formulated so as to unify all products in order to achieve synchronized and continuous operations. Moreover a production planning system uniting all processes from upstream to downstream was drawn up. Even quality control was unified by a reorganization of the information system. By introducing and upgrading computers in all processes at steel mills, improvements were made in the production automation rate, and a system backup was ensured as well.

As of 1990 the number of process computers set up in steel mills has reached 1,249.[6] In international terms this figure is extremely high, as figure 4.1 shows by a comparison, in megabytes, of computer systems per 1,000 employees; the Japanese steel industry comes out ahead at 1,120 megabytes. Also, as is shown in figure 4.2, along with the adoption of process computers, the number of employees dropped dramatically, while the adoption of computer systems brought about a rise in labor productivity.

Formation of Diverse High-Volume Production

The technological premise for the steel industry's move into the third phase was the construction of a huge production system that depends on CIM (computer integrated manufacturing), whereby computer

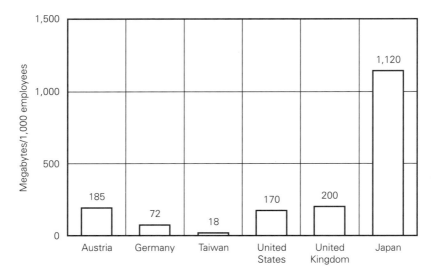

Figure 4.1
Use of computers at major steel mills in 1990. Source: Japan Steel Federation *Wagakuni Tekkogyo no Gijutsuryoku* (The Technological Strength of Our Nation's Steel Industry), 1992.

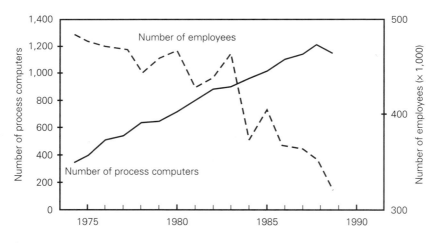

Figure 4.2
Number of computers systems introduced and the changes in number of employees. Source: Japan Steel Federation, *Wagakuni Tekkogyo no Gijutsuryoku* (The Technological Strength of Our Nation's Steel Industry), 1992.

control was expected to unite the upstream and downstream combined with batch processing of diverse product types in continuous production. However, with the realization of this third phase, Japanese steel companies had to initiate reforms in their marketing strategies. Comprehensive changes in both manufacturing and marketing were necessary. Marketing networks were established for forward contracts as well as for on-order production.

Generally speaking, steel companies found that in order to run high-volume production effectively for a complex variety of goods, they had to make[7] (1) adjustments in the supply and demand of the various products, (2) redesign production processes for standardized equipment loads, and (3) define more precisely the terms of service work. These difficulties have been surmounted by long-term purchasing agreements that specify the transfer of goods under conditions fixed some months ahead. This way the demands for a wide-range of products were met, on the one hand, while enabling the effective management of a huge system that required high-level control.

As a sales method, the forward contract has enabled steel manufacturers to maintain a large stable volume of production and sales. Manufacturers who were directly connected with customers could depend on long-term sales transactions, and marketing networks stabilized both price and quantity.

Such a unified, high-level manufacturing and marketing system could be constructed because of the existence of CIM. It should be noted that the steel industry in Japan additionally produces a high volume of different products for the assembly industries.

4.2 Profit Reinvestment Strategies as a Source of Corporate Dynamics

Golden Path of Steel

The source of corporate vitality that has supported the Japanese metal companies' growth can be found in the investment strategies that have historically shaped this industry. The motivation for a steel industry has defined the very features of the metallic materials industry.

Steel is primarily an industry that produces basic materials for manufacturers, so it has a social responsibility to ensure a stable supply to all industries. Since this industry depends on enormous capital investment often exceeding ¥10 billion per facility unit, the fixed costs are high. With thirty-year depreciation conditions, it is difficult to renew equipment. Conversely, since steel constitutes the material of most products, the price elasticity of demand is usually high.

Naturally, then, stability in the production/competitive environment is necessary to business. It is further desirable for companies to conduct business by planning ahead. Steel firms have to anticipate and control their market conditions as much as possible. Cooperative gamelike behavior has therefore characterized the steel industry, with the following features:

First, the steel industry has maintained stable sales by lowering its dependence on spot transactions in the market and rather concluding long-term contracts with customers.

Second, each manufacturer has refrained from using short-term competitive strategies that endanger the stability of the market for steel, and they have particularly refrained from acquiring a market share by lowering prices strategically. Over the years the leadership that industry has sustained in manufacturing technologies can be regarded as the key to its continued success.

Third, cooperative relationships are maintained among manufacturing companies as well as with their customers. Also a stable correlation exists between production volume and price.

Fourth, investment strategies provide for regular advancements in technology.

In fact each company monitors information from customers on prices and new directions affecting demand. Short-term production and sales plans are then made based on that information. At the same time long-term plans are adjusted to provide for future capital investments.

Strategic Investment Performance

Let us look back on the trends in investment. Steel manufacturers' basic costs showed a decline as manufacturing technology became computerized. By fixed price standards, steel secured a profit of 4 to 6 percent, which was equivalent to that of other industries (e.g., automobile and electric machinery manufacturers). During the slump from 1983 to 1986, when profits fell to −0.4 percent, long-term capital procurements became viewed as a means of stabilizing profits. Long-term capital investments rose from 6.9 percent in 1986 to 9.4 percent in 1987.

In this way active investments were maintained in order to stay competitive, with fixed investment fluctuating at around ¥500 billion. Even in 1987, when earnings fell into the red from the previous year, investments reached ¥490 billion. By international standards, such capital investments are high. A comparison of the investment levels of Japan and the United States from the 1970s on shows that the Japanese consistently exceed the American record. In the 1980s that disparity became even larger.

Research and development investments by the steel industry have increased rapidly in recent years. They more than doubled from ¥120 billion in 1980 to ¥257.2 billion in 1990.[8] Compared with other industries, the R&D expenses per researcher in this field averaged ¥45.4 million, which greatly surpasses the ¥27.9 million average for all industries. From an international standpoint, the average R&D investment expenses by each leading Japanese steel company in 1990 came to more than six times those of the United States and about twice those of European countries. Even its ratio against sales is 1.75 percent, which is more than double the European figure of 0.82 percent.

On the whole it is clear that through active investment strategies, the Japanese steel industry has had an outstanding record in capital and R&D procurement compared to its counterparts in other nations.

4.3 Shop Floor and Versatile Personnel Training Policies

The Japanese steel industry has been distinguished for its productivity and has excelled both in manufacturing technologies and in system engineering by combining adopted technologies. This contrasts with its tendency not to pioneer markets with new merchandise concepts. In this regard notice should be given to the facts that manufacturing knowledge is created on the shop floor and that companies are well versed in measures for putting such knowledge into effective use. In reality, many technicians at steel mills engage in R&D activities right on the shop floor, although they are not members of an R&D staff. In fact, we could say that only through collective efforts on the shop floor is advanced technology sufficiently being manifested.

Expert Systems Introduced on Site: The Case of ALIS

We will discuss the creative aspect of on-the-job learning in manufacturing by presenting the example of the ALIS (artificial and logical intelligence system) introduced into blast furnace operations at Nippon Steel Corporation's Kimitsu Steel Mill.[9]

An understanding of the blast furnace method is required in order to see the significance of the ALIS's innovation. In the blast furnace method, iron stones and coke are injected into the upper part of the furnace while hot air is blown in from a hole called *haguchi* (literally, "mouth of the wing") below the kiln. The combustion of hot air and fuel produces a high-temperature gas consisting of carbon monoxide and nitrogen. As that gas passes over the iron stones and coke to the upper part of the kiln, the iron stones deoxidize and molten iron is obtained.

The mechanism behind this manufacturing process has yet to be explained scientifically. Although there is a small window in the *haguchi,* only the flames are visible; thus the actual state of the kiln cannot be observed accurately. For that reason even today blast furnace operations have greatly relied on the "sixth sense" of an experienced worker. The experienced worker deduces the state of combustion by looking through the window at the color of the flames and the surrounding conditions. Then based on that, he adjusts the proportion of hot air to coke and operates the blast furnace. The ALIS is an expert system developed to standardize such blast furnace operations. The Kimitsu Steel Mill at present time has three blast furnaces, two of which have been using the ALIS since 1988.

How was the ALIS developed? The system was put together by the cooperation of selected experienced workers knowledgeable about blast furnace operations and software engineers who elicited their advice. Then everything was codified and put into a program.

One reporter described the situation in the following way:

Each and every decision that supports operations is backed by a high level of expertise. Nevertheless, experienced employees are not aware of how much expertise they actually have, so it is hard for them to express what they do verbally. Exchanges like the following went on time after time:

"We'll add 50 kilograms of coke here."
"Why?"
"Because the level of heat has dropped."
"How do you know that?"
"You can tell by looking at the sensor."
"Do you look only at this sensor?"
"No, I look at one more."
"Are two sensors enough?"
"No, three."

This conversation resulted in a document about ten centimeters thick.[10]

The factors directly responsible for the ALIS's success can be summarized as follows:

1. Available were blast furnace operators with much experience and sophisticated skills.

2. These experts had developed analytical abilities that enabled them to act intuitively in running the blast furnaces.

3. The software engineers were well-versed in blast furnace operations and thus could sufficiently draw out the workers' expertise.

An important point is that both the experienced workers and the software engineers had multiple track careers. For example, the worker interviewed above came to be in charge of blast furnace operations nine years after joining the company and being a laborer. Then, after training as a foreman of operations and approximately one year of work in the staff field, he returned to running the furnace for another ten years. Working in the staff area, which entails duties like recording changes in the process in an operations diary, is said to provide valuable experiences for mastering analytical capabilities concerning the blast furnace. What kind of personnel-training policies led to the creation of human resources equipped with such wide-ranging skills and knowledge?

Policies for Training Versatile Personnel

Let us move to look at company policies for training personnel and developing capabilities.

As is customary in Japanese firms, the foundation of personnel-training policies lies in a wide-ranging job rotation system that was devised in consideration of developing employee abilities. Providing employees with the opportunity of continual on-the-job-training (OJT) is expected to create versatile staff within the firm. In addition job versatility is encouraged by exchanges outside the firm.

For instance, when a joint development project is being considered between the manufacturer and an industry customer, the director in charge at the maker company does not simply carry out R&D but must use his skill in understanding the customer's needs. Such marketing skills by the manufacturer are indispensable to the success of a joint project, and the person in charge of R&D is expected to acquire these skills.

On the one hand, detailed plans for developing capabilities have been adopted for the shop floor as well. These provide for specialized study and training, including courses for attaining different levels like that of director of operations and mechanic foreman, and for learning newly introduced technologies and system setups like IE and QC. Recently a policy has been adopted of sending selected mid-level technicians to industrial technology junior colleges—those on a promotion track. Small-group interaction is important in OJT on the shop floor in order to keep in balance off-the-job-training (Off-JT).

Let us consider the example of Nippon Steel Corporation's JK (*Jishu Kanri*—"autonomous initiative") activities. JK activities are based on the idea of autonomous employee groups:

Each employee belongs to a small group that selects a leader. The group may have a leader, but everyone in it has a position of equality, can carry on discussions about problems on the shop floor, and set objectives. Then everyone participates in the efforts to attain those objectives.

Emphasis is also placed on personnel-training policies in order to motivate workers to take pride in their work. The number of different objectives that the JK activity groups undertook kept increasing until 1982. Thereafter there was a decline, but in 1989 the number was 17,204. A look at their overall content indicates that the proportion given to "lowering costs" was very high.

4.4 Formation of Symbiotic/Resonant Systems

The Japanese steel companies have formed cooperative relationships both among themselves and supportive relationships with other industries to meet changing industry needs. Symbiotic relationships have been formed with the government, universities, and foreign steel corporations as well. However, a number of problems have appeared in these relationships (figure 4.3).

Development of Corporate Alliances

As far as relations among domestic companies go, joint basic research and development is encouraged by the Japan Steel Association Joint Research Society (prior to 1963, the Steel Technology Joint Research Society). It is thanks to this organization that sophisticated domestic technology has successively appeared since the late 1960s in labor-intensive divisions such as strip mills. Additionally there exists a

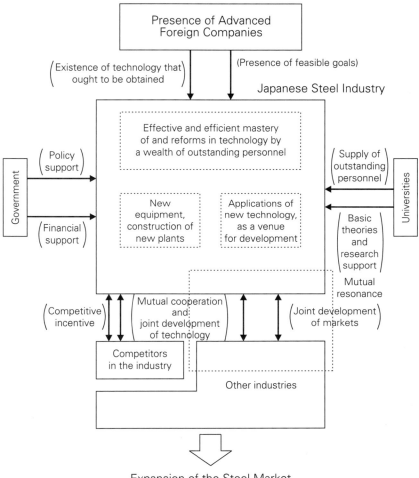

Figure 4.3
Symbiotic systems in the Japanese steel industry from the time of technological introduction to the time of high growth, 1960–1980.

tradition of unofficial information exchanges within the steel industry's community.

In the relationship between the steel industry and academe, universities have primarily functioned as a source of outstanding graduates for the industry. The steel industry has offered favorable employment opportunities to university graduates. Since about the 1870s, during the early years of the Meiji period, Japanese universities have continually focused on education in steel-forging and general steel technology. During the steel industry's high growth from 1960 to 1970, the metallurgy programs at universities more than doubled.

Another benefit accruing from academe is that universities have carried out research in fundamental theories. A major contributor has been the Japan Steel Association, an engineering society specializing in steel, which was founded in 1915 and has developed basic research related to steel and metals in general. In turn the steel industry has continually offered schools information on manufacturing that has contributed to academic research.

Alliances with foreign steel corporations arose mainly as a measure of dealing with trade friction. Japanese steel exports increased rapidly in the second half of the 1960s. But, with the first oil crisis, in the United States and Europe the steel industries fell into a slump, and import restrictions were intensified. Japan has to restrain exports in response to protectionist measures like the enactment of the American trigger price system in 1978, followed by the EC's basic price system. As a result, since the late 1970s, Japanese steel exports have stagnated.

A more positive relationship has resulted from exports of technology to other countries, technological guidance for developing countries, and—in recent years—industrial cooperation with the industrialized countries. For example, the cooperative relationship with the United States began with linkups between Japanese steel companies and American franchises of Japanese automobile manufacturers. Joint ventures have now been entered by Nippon Steel and Inland Steel, NKK and National Steel, and Kawasaki Steel and Armco, for example.

As a result investments made by Japanese steel corporations in the American steel industry has totaled between $5 billion and $6 billion over the past ten years. The entire amount of fixed investments made by American steel firms during this period is believed to come to approximately $22 billion, which amounts to the Japanese steel industry having furnished one-quarter of that sum.[11] These enormous investments are expected to be recovered by the introduction of the blast furnace from the United States in the Japanese steel industry. Since the end of 1991 major Japanese corporations have been forming joint venture companies. This trend suggests that Japanese steel manufacturers are replacing trade friction by cooperative arrangements.

Phenomenon of Interindustry Support

The development of rolled steel for automobiles is a case in point of how supportive relationships between materials manufacturers and user companies work. In the wake of the oil crisis, making lightweight car bodies in order to conserve fuel was an important challenge for automobile manufacturers. To meet this challenge, steel manufacturers developed low-relief planking using highly resilient steel plates. As the relationship between steel and auto manufacturers was further cultivated, there emerged products such as steel plates laminated with plastic in order to be lightweight as well as vibration-proof and double-layered surface-processed, rust-proof steel plates. Also every year the planks of steel sheets used in automobiles became thinner. Close rapport between Nippon Telegraph and Telephone (NTT) and various wire rod manufacturers has likewise led to the development of optical fiber in the wire rod industry. NTT has independently assessed the capacity results of the experimental work.

Mention also ought to be made about the support that arose between steel manufacturers and manufacturers of steelmaking machinery. The engineering capacities within the steel industry are intimately connected with the work of steel manufacturers, and sharing that expertise cuts down on the time spent in reaching investment decisions right up to equipment start-up. It also reduces the capital outlays for constructing steel mills, and that has enabled the steel industry to ride the tide of the market in a timely way.

Let us turn our attention to the close rapport occurring at the level of industry. For instance, when lightweight steel materials for the Japanese shipbuilding industry became necessary, the industry rose to the task. These improvements sustained its international competitiveness, and the shipbuilding industry flattened its rapidly expanding demand for steel. Seen from this standpoint, we can understand that the advancement of CIM in the steel industry has been crucial for the just-in-time system in the Japanese automobile industry.

Problems in the Symbiotic/Interindustry Relationships

Interfirm symbiotic relationships within the industry raise the issue of collusion among rivals. In addition traditionally corporate strategies have been rendered alike by the industry's dependence on the same group of suppliers and materials manufacturers. Certainly friendly relations among rivals have contributed to raising the Japanese steel industry's technological level by leaps and bounds.

The flip side of such congenial competition may be likened to staying the course assiduously in a bicycle race. By this analogy one might inquire, Is it appropriate for just one bicycle to have the highest gears? Or more generally, Can one go farther by riding a bicycle or by driving a car, which also does not totter while being steered?[12] Of course congenial competition undermines competitive strategies, but electric furnace products as well as various steel products from South Korea, Taiwan, and Eastern Europe have consistently been more competitive in price.[13] In Japan, on the other hand, even manufacturers of comparatively low-cost electric furnaces have had problems with the rising cost of scrap iron. Although they now have a slight advantage under the high yen, the outlook is not good.

There is further the matter of an imminent functional breakdown in the interindustry support system. Again let us look at the example of improved steel plates for automobiles. In response to the automobile industry's needs, the steel industry advanced the development of high value-added products but not without creating a number of problems for itself.

In particular, enormous R&D investments were made to meet the demand for surface-processed steel plates. Because of circumstances of cooperation among competitors, the price was not established at a level adequate for recovering the capital invested, especially considering that these were said to be high value-added steel plates. To this day a profit structure by product type in the steel industry has not been set up so that prices can be based on product quality.

Moreover the average unit cost of steel materials since 1982 has stayed at a low level because of the automobile manufacturers' demand for low-cost materials. The rise in demand for surface-processed steel plates with low profitability compared to hot/cold hammered-out plates has ended up forcing the burden all the more on the steel manufacturers. Meanwhile the added value arising from the phenomenon of interindustry support seems to have mainly accrued to the users' side. As a result of negotiations between steel manufacturers and automobile manufacturers in 1991, for the first time in nine years, an agreement was reached to raise prices of thin plates for automobiles. Nevertheless, the danger of system paralysis still exists, such that could hinder investments in technology, facilities, and human resources.

Basically the problem is presented by the very fact that product concepts for materials are born out of the close relationships between materials manufacturers and users. The resonance between these two areas indeed contributes considerably to the advancement of custom designed products. However, in this scheme of things it is difficult for the materials manufacturer to create new product concepts independently. Radical reforms in the R&D system, such as a shift to product development emphasizing self-supporting marketing, are necessary for materials manufacturers to attain competitiveness on their own.

Finally the supportive relationship of this industry with universities and the government has recently begun to weaken. Although the metallic engineering programs at universities have more than doubled from 1960 to 1970, the number of students in this field has undergone a major decline since the 1980s. The steel industry has now become selective about how to apply industrial strategies in view of the need to stress international cooperation despite the Japanese government's intervention in the form of adjustments in production, price, and capital investments during the period of development.[14]

4.5 Industrial Maturity and Corporate Strategies

Maturation and Stagnation of Corporate Dynamics

The steel market is already saturated, but steel export opportunities are severely restricted. Since industrial cooperation overseas cannot be expected to develop rapidly, there is a danger that the industry's dynamics will degenerate.

In the past fresh engineering graduates swarmed to the steel industry. Especially during the period of high economic growth, vast numbers of talented youth found employment with major steel manufacturers. However, the industry is now mature, and rationalization trends have resulted in an excess of personnel. In particular, there will be a shortage of posts for experienced middle-aged and older people (raising the issue of what to do with highly capable personnel).

If these circumstances are coupled with a decline in the volition to work, there is fear that corporate dynamics will stagnate overall.

Let us consider the question of how the steel industry can secure talented personnel in the future. Surveys on the employment preferences of young graduates indicate a drop in the steel industry's popularity, so there is not much optimism in the forecast here.[15]

The progressively higher ascent of yen is rendering the problem all the more grave. In other words, the rising yen in recent years has surpassed the point where competition can be dealt with through technologically driven cost reductions. Also the Japanese steel industry's price competitiveness has definitely begun a path of decline. If the price rise is left alone, domestic users will have no choice but to turn away from the products. That will in time upset the stable relationships built between domestic manufacturers and users.

Should there be policies allowing fixed costs such as white-collar employment to be adjusted in order to improve short-term competitiveness under the high yen exchange rate? Here we must consider the historical circumstances of the Japanese steel industry which was built up through long-term investments in technology, facilities, and human resources. Certainly some deep thought needs to be given to how far to go in curbing the spreading malaise among large corporations, where uninspired work by management and the work force has been on the rise.

We need also to consider what is truly necessary technology when it is purely a matter of industrial philosophy to pursue superiority at the cost of profits. Cutting down on skilled technicians will raise the costs of successive technologies and repair services. That can only result in technological decline and thus a collapse in the foundation of the steel industry's competitiveness.

Strategies for Revitalizing the Industry: Technological Possibilities

Today the world's steel industries are riding the tide of technological innovation. The blast furnace method, which was originated in Europe and developed in the United States, is now in wide use in Japan. Recently a lightly equipped low-volume production technology has begun to appear as an alternate system to the high-volume system centered around the blast furnace.

There has been worldwide interest in this new smelting reduction technology, which suggests that the blast furnace's converters may well be replaced with electric furnaces. Further the conventional large-scale continuous casting method and the continuous casting of thin slabs, as well as the simple rolling method, are likely to be replaced by high-speed, high-volume rolling. The new technology still has knots in it that must be untangled before high-quality production can begin. If we take into account the cost-effective equipment, the flexibility it ensures for meeting local market needs, and future improvements in product quality as a result, we have a good indication of what the mainstream activity of steel manufacturing may be like in the twenty-first century.

Until all that happens, the blast furnace method will maintain its position of superiority in cost and product quality as long as it continues its flow of productivity. But steel-downsizing technology systems are appealing for a number of reasons:

1. In Japan's mature market the demand for steel has shifted from mass production of a single product to diverse, low-volume production, and thus the blast furnace method cannot be used to its full advantage.

2. Inexpensive, low-volume simple production processes like mini-mills have lowered the barriers to entry in steel production and thus have lowered prices.

3. The large number of new entries has brought about a drop in blast furnace production and thus led to a decline in its productivity.

Amid these changes in the market and the economy, the steel industry has now launched a technological survival war. As it approaches the twenty-first century, the industry is being pressed to heed these emerging circumstances and to construct a new production system that will be suitable for the next generation.

Fortunately the Japanese steel industry has a large stock of technological skill, so it is in little danger of being late with technological innovation. But Japanese blast furnace manufacturers have invested heavily in their existing production equipment, and many have still not recovered their costs.

Whenever a new technological level is reached in the world, it nevertheless gives rise to an economic rationality of not disposing of existing investments, and that works as a brake against the introduction of the latest technology. Attention should be given to the fact that such economic logic not only deters change but also works against recouping earlier investments.

Mature technology can easily deteriorate. On the other hand, a nation whose industry possesses only immature technology will drop out of competition. Of course the demand for steel will not subside entirely. But it is a matter of who will supply the cheaper and better products. For that reason the cost of technological development has become a necessary burden, forcing the industry to search for cheaper methods of production. Cooperative research is being carried out in Japan on developing a new smelting reduction process and some way to recycle scrap steel.

Diversification Strategies: A Lesson from the Wire Rod Industry

Major steel manufacturers have reinvested profits in order to maintain growth in a mature market. They have jumped into diversifying their operations by developing related areas like electronics, information communications, new materials, and regional economies. However, these gigantic steel corporations have no guarantee of business in the fields to which they newly advance. Considerable energy is required to be at the helm of a large enterprise. Here we will consider the wire rod industry which has promptly diversified and has been turning out steady results.

A wide-ranging technological foundation consisting not only of metallurgy but also of inorganic and organic chemistry, electrical engineering, and mechanical engineering is necessary for manufacturing electric wires and cables. Open communication among technicians of different specialties is indispensable as well. Under circumstances calling for accumulated knowledge and experience related to other fields, the wire rod industry designed diversification strategies that would respond to the maturation of the market. The proportion of nonwire rod business (at six major companies) gradually increased from 37 percent in 1981 to 49 percent in 1986, and it has thereafter fluctuated at around 50 percent. The proportion of the same at 91 principal companies was 38 percent in 1990. Optical fiber communications and related electronic parts, system equipment, new materials, and energy-related areas comprise the primary areas of diversification. As an example let us briefly consider the case of diversification and the R&D management at Sumitomo Electric Industries, a company that has experienced the most advanced diversification in the industry.

The history of Sumitomo Electric Industries' diversification strategy got its start in 1960, when long-term goals were established that included switching its business focus to information-processing industry and equalizing the sales of wire rod and nonwire rod products. Since wire rods are a product made through a confluence of technologies, recognition of their possibilities for wide-ranging diversification took root around 1970, along with diversification activities that proceeded to be carried out steadily into related production areas.

Sumitomo Electric Industries has continued up to this day with its multifaceted operations based on electric wire and cable-manufacturing technology. This can be seen in the fact that ultrahard alloys, a prewar example of successful diversification, materialized with the foundation of manufacturing technology for making ultrahard dice for stretching electric wires (figure 4.4). In recent years Sumitomo Electric Industries has developed several products employing unrelated derivative technologies and has emphasized generic technologies with broad applications.

Since Sumitomo Electric Industries' R&D management system has refined its diversification strategies, we will next focus on its program for new products, from research and development to commercialization. The research and development objectives at Sumitomo Electric Industries come from autonomous studies by researchers affiliated either with the R&D department or one of the company's business sections. Basically they concentrate on improving existing products and manufacturing technology within the various business sections.

Each research project is then turned over to teams of about ten people. At the point where a change becomes feasible and is approved by the company, a sample number of the new product is launched in the marketplace. When annual sales for that product reach about ¥100 million, it is moved from the research and development section to a production office, and then after ¥300 million to ¥500 million to a production department. When sales reach the ¥2 billion level, the product gets established as an independent line of the department or acquires a department of its own. If it results in a new department, it will become a self-supporting budget system.

For this reason a director not only must have knowledge and experience in technological development but also management skills combined with a sales sense. The supervisors of research continually encourage creative ideas and give the researchers full autonomy; they contribute ideas for R&D projects with a long-range perspective of over twenty years. In the past fifteen years no research program has been forcefully ended. Of the 300 current programs, around 80 percent were conceived by the researchers themselves.

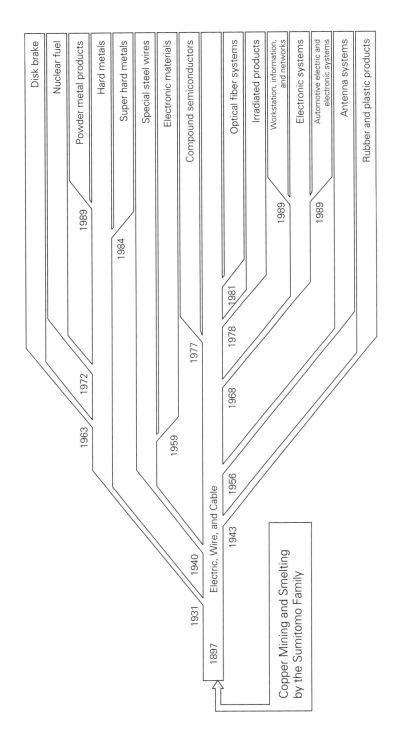

Figure 4.4
Diversification through technological innovation at Sumitomo Electric Industries, Ltd. Source: Sumitomo Electric Industries, Ltd.

What sort of lessons can be learned about metallic materials companies in general from the experiences of Sumitomo Electric Industries?

First of all, reliance on outside human resources was kept to a minimum; the company nurtured its own personnel and as a result entered new markets, though the lead time for entry could be longer than the company had anticipated.

Second, diversification from core technology can be a shortcut to success. In the steel industry, business can be improved by externalizing the software development capacities accumulated within a firm.

Third, the marketing of materials as finished products depends on training and developing personnel who have the creative intelligence for research as well as a business acumen.

Necessity of the Leadership at the Top

Each Japanese metallic materials company has built up an industrial adjustment system for growth that goes beyond the corporate frame. The phenomenon of interindustry cooperation plainly shows that manufacturers have need for open communication with users who can be directly connected to their product development programs. The middle-level manager on the shop floor must be capable of encouraging any needed incremental innovation. That has certainly contributed to diversified, high-volume production in Japan.

However, now that dark shadows are being cast on the myth of economic growth, corporate management too has cause to transform itself. The Japanese approach entails sharing information based on a relationship of trust and continual adjustments to circumstantial changes. But this style of management is only suitable in a stable management environment where it is possible to predict change. Then, in times of great instability, management efficiency drops.[16] In other words, in periods of change, correct and prompt decisions by top management are essential in order to rally a market and break away from industrial stagnation. Success is a matter of rationalization accompanied by a strong business survival sense.

Notes

1. See the Working Group (WG), Japan Commission on Industrial Performance, *Kinzokukei Sozai Sangyo WG Hokokusho* (Report on the Metallics Materials Industry), February 1993, for information about the metallic materials industry as a whole.

2. For details, Okamoto, H., *Gendai Tekko Kigyo no Ruikei Bunseki* (A Taxonomical Analysis of Current Steel Firms), Minerva Shobo, Tokyo, 1984, pp. 318–38.

3. For details, *Tetsu no Wadai* (Steel Topics) 28 (October 1979), Nippon Steel Corporation, p. 5.

4. Monthly statistical reports on steel show that the rate of equipment operation, which is obtained by comparing the amount of production with nominal capacity, for continuous casting went from 50 percent at the beginning of the 1970s to 100 percent in 1980. This rate gradually increased, despite cyclical fluctuations, to 125 percent in 1990. So the industry can pride itself on its high productivity which compares favorably with electric furnace operation.

5. At the present time wholesale stock adjustments are difficult to foresee, and production according to forecasted trends in demand is impossible. For this reason production is based on fulfilling orders within forty days of an order's placement.

6. Data on the introduction of process computers since 1991 are provided in the Japan Steel Federation's publication *Nihon no Tekkogyo* (The Japanese Steel Industry). For example, the figures are rolling 50.8 percent, sheeting 11.0 percent, steelmaking 9.9 percent, and pig iron-making 4.6 percent.

7. For details, see Okamoto, H., ibid., pp. 130–36.

8. When looking at these figures, we should pay attention to the fact that the proportion of investments for the field of steel products in the R&D expenses of the Japanese steel industry has steadily declined, averaging around 50 percent in recent years. Along with the progress of the business diversification, R&D investments in areas other than primary products have become active too.

9. Data are based on the authors' field work at the Kimitsu Steel Mill. For information on ALIS, see Katsuhiko Yui et al., Koro Process no Sogyo Kanshi Shien ni okeru Chishiki System no Tekiyo (The Application of Intelligence Systems in Operational Administration Support of Blast Furnace Processes), *Keisoku to Seigyo*, August 1987, and Masakazu Iwai, *Tetsu ni Kakeru* (Betting on Steel), Diamond, Inc., Tokyo, 1992.

10. *Nihon Keizai Shimbun*, July 5, 1987.

11. *Nihon Keizai Shimbun*, January 22, 1993.

12. Comments by Tokio Mitamura (then executive director of Nippon Steel Corporation) at the third meeting (May 10, 1991) of JCIP's working group on the metallic materials industry.

13. "The production costs of hot coils—a basic steel material—at Pohang Iron & Steel Co., the largest steel manufacturer in South Korea, are about 30 percent lower than the Japanese level" (quote from Kim Dong Han, chief researcher at the Daiwoo Economic Research Center), *Nihon Keizai Shimbun*, January 23, 1993.

14. In regard to the Japanese steel industry's industrial policies, refer to Ryutaro Komiya, Masatora Okuno, and Kotaro Suzuki, eds., *Nihon no Sangyo Seisaku* (Japan's Industrial Policies), University of Tokyo Press, Tokyo, 1984, chapter 10, pp. 255–276; and Yoshiro Miwa, *Nihon no Kigyo to Sangyo Soshiki* (Japanese Corporate and Industrial Organization), University of Tokyo Press, Tokyo, 1990, chapters 9 and 10, pp. 237–303.

15. We looked at the fluctuations in the rankings of Nippon Steel Corporation's popularity among recent engineering and science graduates, based on data from Recruit

Research Inc., Nippon Steel Corporation may have then placed fourth because it had recaptured the top position in corporate rankings for sales with its merger in 1971. Thereafter, its popularity with recent graduates declined. This decline continued conspicuously, for a long period, accompanied by a decline in corporate sales rankings. Since 1988 it has hovered between the 40th and 60th rankings.

16. Marengo, L., *Knowledge Coordination and Learning in an Adaptive Model of Firm*, Elgar, Cheltenham, England 1994.

5   Factory Automation Equipment and Industrial Machinery Industry

Hiroyuki Itami

The factory automation (FA) equipment industry and the industrial machinery industry range from robots to construction machinery, from programmable controllers to machine tools, and included are machines for steel mills and papermaking. Consequently the problems faced by each company are different; for that reason the necessary countermeasures must differ as well. However, here I will dare to treat these two entities—factory automation equipment and industrial machinery—as one FA industry generally because the machinery produced is used at the production site. This industry has enormous importance because it has supported all of Japanese manufacturing. In fact the problems of Japanese manufacturing are generally embedded in it.

I will emphasize in this chapter the following points:

• The international competitiveness of this industry in Japan is quite high overall. But, since its scope encompasses a wide variety of products, there are some areas where, depending on the item, a company's international competitiveness is not so good.

• The R&D of Japanese companies, which differ by product as well as by type of research, is often sporadic. In certain research areas and concepts American and European companies still take the lead. Conversely, there are many consumer products and production technologies where Japan is ahead. Innovations in Japanese technology are cumulative and oriented toward specific production needs. Greater contributions could be had in the future if universities and public institutions support basic R&D.

• The FA industry does not fare well in total value-added productivity—the notion that everything from development to procurement and distribution is connected to productivity on the shop floor. This is because of fierce price competition easily causing prices to plunge.

Another reason is that there are many small- and medium-sized companies with low productivity and the distribution sector's productivity is much lower than that of a large manufacturing corporation.

• The FA industry is partitioned into small markets, and within each market there exists an excessive variety of products to meet the needs of different customers. But the problem here is that the highly competitive conditions that inevitably result cause manufacturers to continually respond in kind. This market characteristic presents the danger of lowering efficiency overall.

• A great many corporations can enter a market because of the existence of subcontractor clusters. In fact a whole production system has been built by this division of labor consisting in subcontractor companies. It has raised dependence on overseas production (outsourcing) by Japanese companies and allowed large corporations' production systems to be flexible.

• Japanese firms have now reached a turning point in technology, demand, and competition. The technological questions now raised are how far to proceed with successive innovations and how to maintain technological growth. The demand question concerns the stagnation of domestic demand and the saturation of foreign markets with exports. The competition question is how to raise corporate profitability given the large number of rival companies.

5.1 Strong International Competitiveness

The international competitiveness of Japanese factory automation equipment is very high on the whole. However, the FA industry spans a number of areas, so it is hard to compile overall indexes. To give just one example, in the latter half of the 1970s, the number of computerized numerical control (CNC) machine tools produced in Japan surpassed that of the United States, and Japan emerged as the world's leader. Then, at the beginning of the 1980s, Japan outranked the United States for output value. Japanese products captured about a 30 percent share of the world's markets also for steel mills, paper-converting machines, and plastic injection-molding machines, for example, to become number 1 in the world. Of course Japanese companies are not strong in all product areas. Nevertheless, it is the opinion of the majority of members who participated in this survey that Japanese firms are among the top in the world or else lead by their most products' competitiveness.

An indicator of that competitiveness is a product's performance against price. (Here the term "performance" means not only a product's fundamental efficiency but also qualities like reliability and durability.) In other words, a Japanese product's relative performance level is expected to be high compared with a similar product made in other countries and sold at the same price. Then, since the price of the Japanese product with high performance is comparable, its international competitiveness goes up.

The relatively superior position of this industry's performance level (or decline in relative price) has developed for the following reasons: Compared to its counterparts in other countries, the higher performance of Japanese FA equipment has been maintained for products of the same quality or function with (1) low costs in manufacturing (rationalization of costs) and (2) low profit margins from large sales.

All these factors have occurred together, and not just one can explain the Japanese advantage. While Japanese firms have been criticized for dumping in markets overseas because their profit margins are very low, it is basic logic that profit-sacrificing cannot last forever. Even though some Japanese companies may have acquired a market share by so-called dumping, which ignores costs and profits, it is impossible to sustain a company on dumping alone.

Market sense holds that it is difficult to pursue cost reduction and the differentiation of products at the same time. Yet Japanese companies have managed to do just that. How has this been possible?

Various reasons have been cited up to now. For instance, among the ones given so far are the lean production systems, efforts to reduce costs by constructing a flexible division of labor, the high level of technology and skill at production sites, the accumulation of thorough reforms (kaizen) at production sites, the demanding Japanese buyers requiring a strong focus on the consumer, continual efforts to improve capacities in response to surveys of customer needs, the product development process in which the production and marketing sections participate from the initial stage, cooperation among the various sections related to the products, fierce domestic competition, efforts to lower costs with a presumed price, the general tendency of management to include long-term personnel in decision-making, and the long-range perspective of managers.

Given such speculation about the source of Japanese companies' competitiveness, it is clear that this strength cannot be explained by one factor alone. The impact of each factor is not that large, so a combination of them will make Japanese products relatively low priced in terms of their capacities and functions in markets overseas.

The FA equipment industry is inclined to be an on-order production industry. Unlike general mass-produced consumer goods, not much in the way of cost reductions can be hoped for through volume production. Consequently the importance of economies-of-scale production as a source of competitiveness is not expected to be as great as in the case of general consumer goods. Moreover this industry's customers are not an anonymous and indefinite number of individuals but a definite number of companies. In general, production engineers on the customer side evaluate the products; this means that the customer is capable of judging the technological aspects of the product accurately. For this reason, in contrast to mass-produced consumer goods, there is little chance that the item's sales will be influenced by elusive factors like the customers' sensitivities or tastes. Furthermore communication between the manufacturer and the user is eased by the fact that the customer is a particular company.

Under such circumstances, while product costs (prices) are one matter, there is a tendency, if anything, in the FA equipment industry for technological superiority to be the focus of rivalry. Relatively speaking, technology tends to be the focus of competition, and these companies steadily accumulate technology while striving to make the shop floor efficient too.

5.2 Competitive Research and Development

Although the competitiveness of Japanese companies is high, it is often said that their products are derivative and that their true technological level and especially the power to carry out new development is weak. Should such a general conclusion really be drawn from a few isolated cases?

In fact Japanese R&D capacity leads the world in some respects, though there are many areas in which foreign firms are notably stronger. Concerning the different applications of technology, Japan has been ahead in production-related R&D, while other countries have developed software and new technological concepts. The distinction is that Japan is strong on development but remains somewhat weak in fundamental research. Such a tendency seems to be present in the product end as well.

The Japanese products that have been highly competitive in the marketplace and supported by outstanding technology were not so technologically impressive in the past. Many of these products or their technology originally came from outside of Japan. They have traversed a time course, starting after World War II when their technology was introduced into Japan, that has involved a stretch of catching up until they could become serious competitors.

The turning point in the catching-up phase appears to have come around 1980. Thus 1980 was the watershed year, although the introduction of technology from abroad became fully absorbed from the mid-1950s to the mid-1960s. Thereafter, as Japan digested the imported technology, it accumulated its own technological power. In the mid-1960s to mid-1970s the fruits of Japan's autonomous developments started to appear. Steadily the technological level was raised, and in the mid-1970s technological introduction contracts were dissolved one by one. By the mid-1980s Japan had its own unique line of goods and technology, and that has remained to the present day.

Two good examples are construction machines and paper-converting machines. In regard to construction machines, Komatsu introduced wheel-loader technology from the American company, International Harvester, in 1964, and dissolved the contract in 1982. It also introduced power shovel technology from the American firm, Bucyrus-Erie Co., in 1963, and dissolved the contract in 1983.

As for paper-converting machines in 1956, Mitsubishi Heavy Industries began production of corrugating machines, which make the corrugated sheets for cardboard boxes from rolled paper, and box-making machines, which print and cut corrugated sheets to produce cardboard boxes. In 1961 Mitsubishi signed a technological cooperation contract with Langston, an American company. But by 1981 Mitsubishi could proceed on its own and thus dissolved the collaboration.

In this way historically research and development began in a number of fields through technological imports and reached a high technological level in Japan. Furthermore, according to a survey by the Japan Industrial Robot Association, over 80 percent of Japan's industrial robots were developed by Japanese companies on their own. When the number of robots developed by domestic firms cooperatively with other Japanese companies is included, this figure comes to about 95 percent. Technological transfers from overseas and sales of imported foreign products have accounted for no more than about 5 percent.

At the present time the supply of technology from Japan in the machinery industry amounts to over 40 percent of technological imports. This marks a dramatic improvement over the figure of less than 20 percent at the beginning of the 1980s. But the reference to *overseas* is frequently used here because, in contrast to technological imports that come from the so-called industrialized nations, the Japanese export of technology is often directed to other Asian countries.

Among technological imports or license contracts from abroad, there are some cases where the Japanese technological standard is low, so Japan must depend on foreign technology. There are also cases where Japanese companies had no other choice but to conclude contracts because they were bound by basic patents, even though, given the present level of technology, those imports would not be necessary. There are finally cases where contracts are signed in view of the foreign firm's name value, and the trust in the brand name. These different motives are obvious. The fact that at the present time Japan is still paying for basic patents developed long ago is an unavoidable aspect of the historic time lag faced by a nation that was late to be industrialized, and it is not related to the current state of its technology.

R&D activities by Japanese companies that have made technological progress possible have a number of distinctive features. One is that companies, by accumulating small innovations, have come to amass technology and raise the competitiveness of their products. Second, since such cumulative innovations were widespread and have become the substantial stock of their competitiveness, R&D hurdles were lowered in many respects.

The low barriers to communication among engineers in Japan is one big reason why innovation is more widely possible than it is for foreign companies. As has been demonstrated in overlapping product development processes—which is an important distinguishing feature of Japanese companies—generally production departments are involved in the early stages of product development. Moreover there is much interaction between the technicians in research centers and scientific research offices and the engineers on the shop floor who are thoroughly familiar with daily production activities; good relations are maintained between these two areas. By contrast, in the United States and Europe, the barriers between designer and manufacturing engineers are high, and it has been pointed out that even within a section high communication and emotional barriers exist between the scientists and the engineers.

The good relations between Japanese engineers are not limited to designers and production engineers but exist among engineers in different areas of specialization such as mechanical engineering and electrical engineering. In the Japanese FA industry electronic machinery was advanced through such collaboration between mechanical and electronic/electrical engineers, which among themselves they refer to as "mechatronics." Also, thanks to the cooperation among mechanical and electronic/electrical engineers, Japanese firms have managed to efficiently introduce automation and numerical control technology in machine tools.

Further low communication barriers exist outside the company, in relationships between engineers at manufacturers and engineers at the user firms. Cooperative working relationships with the user firms— and particularly with engineers at the production site—are especially important in the FA industry. The reason is that FA machinery is fundamentally inclined toward one-off production, so understanding correctly users' needs is directly connected to product competitiveness.

Furthermore, since FA products are utilized on the shop floor, the user firms' shop-floor technicians, who have hands-on experience with these products, may discover new needs that went unnoticed by a manufacturer up to then. Such engineers are an important source of information when technological improvements are being considered. Japanese companies thereby gain knowledge about users' needs out of such close relations with the user firms, and that leads to new R&D. Even though individually the impact may not be great, Japanese companies' competitiveness has been sustained through the accumulation of such small innovations.

Nevertheless, it is well known that Japanese companies have not devoted enough effort toward creating product concepts as, for instance, has the United States, which today is strong in creating software systems and architecture for controlling industrial machinery while Japan remains relatively weak. That is a challenge for Japanese companies to take up in the future.

5.3 Total Productivity

The general international opinion has been that Japanese product competitiveness is high, while its product technology is variable but at a point where it can sufficiently compete. That opinion is based on international performance comparisons directed at Japanese software.

The debates over achievement levels of productivity concern the vast numbers of human and financial resources invested and the effective yield of those investments. High productivity thus means that there is less input than output.

Productivity can be measured by various means: added value (the amount of added value produced by a single worker), physical labor productivity (the amount of physical production per capita), productivity of the equipment (the added value or amount of physical production per unit with relation to the capital invested), and so on. For international comparisons the means of measuring productivity are not always clear. The truth is that past data are rarely available for this wider sphere of activity. However, the general opinion of stakeholders has been that in Japan the shop-floor productivity of large corporations, which make finished products, is high. But some also expect foreign countries to have higher productivity at the value-added level.

Added value indicates what is left after subtracting fixed costs from the firm's sales. In contrast to the output index, which corresponds to the volume of physical labor productivity, this figure becomes large when the market price of a product is high (if the product can be sold at a high price). A good discussion of international competitiveness based on value-added productivity appears in the Japan Productivity Center's survey report, *International Comparisons of Labor Productivity.*

By that survey in 1990 Japan was only eighty-seventh in value-added output per hour of labor in the category of general machinery, which includes FA equipment; the index takes U.S. productivity as 100. This figure places Japan much lower than the general image evoked by its product competitiveness, and it is hard to think that it reflects the actual state of the Japanese machinery industry.

The main problem may be in the exchange-rate conversions instance, the survey uses purchasing power parity as the foreign exchange rate. It calculates the exchange rate as $1 = ¥202.7. So the U.S. value-added output is much larger than if it were calculated at the actual exchange rate. Among some other factors that make the Japanese figures appear lower is the common tendency of Japanese corporations to distribute their products outside, making internal production appear to be low overall in the Japanese manufacturing industry. Even though the added values were compiled for similar activities, these factors have worked to reduce the added-value estimates for each company.

However, while the productivity of Japanese firms may not be as low as that calculated by the Japan Productivity Center, Japanese productivity in terms of product competitiveness may not be as high as it is generally thought. In fact it differs very little from that of the United States and Europe.

Let us consider productivity more fully: First, we will look at all activities in manufacturing, which include small- and medium-sized companies supplying parts and components as well as development, distribution, and outside services of large corporations. Second, we will include factors like profits and values added, or price in addition to the physical labor efficiency. We will use the Productivity Center's value-added estimates for the whole industry.

Overall, it is said that the rate of internal manufacture of parts by Japanese companies is low and that they rely on the small- and medium-sized company sector for the vast majority of their parts and components. Production efficiency in the small- and medium-sized companies is thought to be lower than that of large corporations. Furthermore, as was noted earlier, Japanese companies tend to send distribution outside, and the efficiency of the distribution and service industries in Japan is apparently low compared to that in the United States or Europe. Now, if we combine the manufacturing areas of companies (plants) with the distribution/service areas, and also the manufacturing industry with all Japanese commerce, we may wonder if a more efficient system can be at all possible. But, if we limit this calculation just to manufacturing and combine the large corporations with the small- and medium-sized companies, the productivity does not appear as high as the commonly held image.

On the other hand, the productivity of Japanese firms in product development is said to be high compared to Western counterparts. An example is the low number of engineering worker-hours required for developing a new product in Japan. However, the efficiency of these worker-hours strictly entails the productivity of a single development course. In other words, even though the productivity of a one-time development project may be high, if model changes are carried out too frequently, then the entire efficiency of the development department is lowered. Added to that is the issue of repeated model changes in industrial machines affecting the user company's profits. For instance, investments can be recouped in a short time if industrial production machinery is efficient and produces quantities of goods at high speeds. With every model change equipment must be updated and new investments made, causing a decline in investment efficiency.

Then there are the huge expenses required to maintain the substantial sales/service networks (some people claim they are proportionately too large) of Japanese companies. It is quite common in Japan for product damage and breakdown repairs to be made at the distribution stage. With the idea of free repair service widely accepted in Japan, the cost burdens at the distribution stage are large. Added to that is the fact that since the sales prices of products are relatively low, the profitability for a Japanese company becomes that much lower. For instance, data on this industry show that the purchase price of industrial equipment with roughly the same capacities is 1.3 to 2 times higher in Europe than in Japan. In addition the development cost is about three times higher than in Japan. Therefore, when matters like the price and model life cycles are considered, there is not much disparity in the added value per product.

Total productivity thus depends on both fixed costs and market price. No matter how efficient manufacturing activities are, if a product's price is low, its value added is low, and its value-added productivity drops. In this sense the productivity of Japanese companies can hardly be considered high. Then, if the product's price is lowered, the efficiency of productivity gets even lower. Add a short product cycle that causes an increase in development expenses, and productivity is lowered some more.

This is not an argument that can be easily backed up with data. However, it is not difficult to see that Japanese industry's total productivity is less than perfect in comparison with physical productivity on the shop floors of large companies, and that quite a distinction must be made between two types of productivity. Here a good case can be made for not discussing the strength of Japanese industry on the basis of large firms' production sites alone.

So why then are there gaps between Japanese industry's total productivity and physical labor productivity? The reason has to do with the distinguishing features of demand and competition in this industry as well as with the characteristics of labor divisions within small- and medium-sized subcontractors.

5.4 Market Demand and Competitive Corporate Activities

If we are to describe the present state of the Japanese FA machinery, we might say that there is an excess variety of products in a limited market. The Japanese FA market is not big. For example, the total market sales of industrial machinery in fiscal year 1990 came to approximately ¥23.2 trillion, or about 54 percent of the domestic automobile market. In other words, the domestic market is only about half of that for automobiles, and it is divided among diverse, multifarious industrial machinery areas.

Basically FA machinery tends to be produced one-off/on-order, and not mass-produced like consumer products. Moreover, because of the increasing sophistication (high speed and automation), large-scale size, and systematization of technology, manufacturers are now finding it difficult to carry out development independently without joint arrangements with users. Sales are a large consideration in these arrangements; it is more a matter of making what will sell, and not that of selling what's been made. Factory automation equipment is custom-made; it is not made as an exclusive line directed at specific products.

Although joint development of equipment with the user has brought about an accurate understanding of customer needs, giving it a competitive advantage, the FA industry is pressed also to deal with their customers' future needs in order to stay competitive. The result has often been an excessive number of products. To maintain market share, companies have increased their number of models, and that has entailed high costs. As the number of models increases, the efficiency of production drops because of the low-volume of diverse goods, and many models go out of date quickly. Further contributing to the increase in costs are shortened model cycles and shortened periods for developing new models. In recent years the phenomenon of rising sales with no net profits has been occurring because of this decline in efficiency.

In other words, despite the fact that the FA industry's market share is not particularly large, the variety of products is enormous. Then, since the market is not large, users' demands can be easily accommodated, so product variety has expanded rapidly. To be sure, the responsibility here lies mostly with the users, but the FA industry must take some of the responsibility too, for it should show some interest in competitive behavior.

Japanese companies sometimes compete aggressively for shares in markets where not all that much in the way of future profits can be expected from the view of both outsiders and insiders. The industrial machinery industry does not have a large market share, and its market has hardly a prospect for substantial future growth. Its products tend to be very single-purpose and are individually produced, so it is hard to have expectations about economies of scale and the effects of experience, at least at the production stage.

Nevertheless, many manufacturers have continued to seek a larger share, even at a sacrifice of current profits. Few companies withdraw from competition, so the lineup of rivals does not change much. To complicate the matter further, because the rivals know each other, the competition does not become one in which one side thoroughly smashes the other. Therefore the need to pull out does not arise.

The focus of the rivalry is the standard of relative price over function, and the race is to develop new products based on that idea. However, it is strictly competition in subtle differences, not a full-fledged rivalry to create new products. That phenomenon tends naturally to appear at the technological level, where similar companies compete in the same dimension of differentiation. For this reason they depend on making minute innovations, directly responding to market needs by joint development arrangements with industrial users.

The competition in FA machinery is fierce, so prices are hardly ever raised. That has led to the disparity in sales prices with American and European companies. The rivalry is intensified by the fact that once a certain company releases a new product, it is comparatively simple for others to launch a similar product. The condition that makes this particularly easy is the great likelihood that the same subcontractors can be relied on for parts and units for the new product. Subcontractors with such receptive powers work together as large clusters of small- and medium-sized companies. Viewed just from a company's production system, that is convenient but at the same time it renders specialization into niches difficult.

Thus, in fierce share wars in a quantitatively limited market, almost inevitably every company ends up with a not very profitable profile. Yet seldom do any firms withdraw, since profits do not drop low enough to bring on bankruptcy, and they also do not get completely flattened. Although no particular cartels exist, in the end there seems to be a tacit agreement to end the rivalry.

Indeed, given such circumstances, there is good reason why companies do not secure market niches, do not make much money, and yet do not collapse. Though their profits are very low, it is the users and customers who benefit from the competition. In the end FA machinery has helped Japan's industrial development overall. Such a higher mission seems to be what sustains these companies, which face fierce competition but continue to make contributions responsibly.

5.5 Distribution of Labor

Like other general machinery industries, the FA industry has a wide-ranging distribution of labor among the small- and medium-sized subcontractors. Of course great discrepancies exist among the firms in this industry. Generally speaking, in many of the companies, about 30 percent of the products are produced internally consisting of strategic parts and parts that cannot be produced elsewhere. Then the firm uses subsidiaries, affiliates, or cooperative companies for subcontracting orders or to acquire capital goods. Dependence on outside procurements by manufacturers of completely finished, unique, custom-made products is at the 70 percent level; likewise dependence on outside procurements is often thought to exist at the 70 percent level for many machine tool manufacturers—an area that has its productivity well established in advance.

Such a division of labor exists in every country, though with some small differences. Outside sources often supply parts and materials for standard goods. More characteristic of Japan is that all processing operations are commonly sent at once to subcontractors. Included here are unit subcontracting, whereby an outside company provides all the parts, and processing subcontracting, whereby only certain details of the processing work are given to subcontractors. Also the materials suppliers may be independent subcontractors, a subsidiary company, or even a consignor.

The technology and productivity standards of subcontractor firms are not up to those of large companies. Yet they appear to be adequate, since the companies making the orders have no sense that their subcontractors' product quality and costs are not internationally competitive. This industrial environment, however, contrasts sharply with the inferior technological level of small- and medium-sized parts and assembly firms which was a great impediment to prewar Japanese machinery productivity. In fact modernization posed a major challenge to these companies in Japan's early postwar period of high economic growth. That change in attitude has meant enormous progress.

Thus, compared with foreign subcontractor firms, Japanese subcontractors can be depended on for their excellence in finished product manufacturer. International comparisons of subcontractors may be difficult, but clear differences can be seen between the United States and Japan in the cost of subcontracting in the production of similar parts. For example, it costs 50 percent more to procure parts in the United States than to have the same item manufactured by a Japanese domestic subcontractor.

One explanation may be the high unit cost stemming from the fact that the Japanese company making the subcontracting order has not established a supplier in the United States. Another reason is the large fixed burden due to the fact that a parts-making company with hundreds of employees has a full set of facilities with a conspicuous amount of idle equipment in slow periods. Then also the very expensive time unit costs of large-scale machine tools should be mentioned. It has been pointed out that the introduction of NC machine tools has not progressed much at small-scale companies specializing in processing. Indeed, in general, there are no known cases in the United States of a single person using several NC machines and of NC machines being efficiently used.

There are various reasons why companies make subcontracting orders. One may be that the technology for manufacturing is essentially not present within the firm. However, even when something is technologically feasible within a company, subcontractors may be depended on because of difficult automation, the need to construct a flexible production system, and the priority of other processes better handled by the company plant due to some distinguishing feature with competitive strength. There may further be advantageous personnel costs in using subcontractors. But the fact that using subcontractors tends to mobilize the surrounding low-waged labor force is common to all nations.

An issue for companies taking the subcontracting course is whether just the requisite amount of the necessary level of product quality can be acquired flexibly when needed. Such a flexible supply system exists socially in Japan. Indeed an important characteristic of Japanese FA manufacturers is that they can mobilize the surrounding labor force when needed, and thus they can keep more flexible production arrangements or reserve labor for difficult automation tasks.

A certain kind of supply system must be present for such labor arrangements to be feasible. Since in Japan a large volume of parts and assembly production subcontractors exists within a narrow territory, companies have proceeded to specialize, and they can compensate for areas of deficiency by using subcontractors. That can typically be seen in the cluster of small- and medium-sized companies in the Keihin (Tokyo-Yokohama) industrial belt. The competition among the small- and medium-sized companies there is fierce. The structure of the supply system of such subcontracting companies provides to the finished product manufacturers a convenient base for the division of labor. In particular, the merits of such a labor structure are considerable for industrial machinery goods that require a flexible production system because automation is difficult or because subcontracting production of a single product is involved.

5.6 Future Direction

The FA industry in Japan formed the backbone of the nation's postwar industrial development. Although the output of this industry has been small, it has remained the core area of manufacturing. As was pointed out earlier in this chapter, the fact that there have been few departures despite excessive competition seems to be largely due to major suppliers meeting the needs of this industry with a unique sense of mission and responsibility.

However, the collapse of the bubble economy and the fact that Japanese industry as a whole has slowed its pace have put this industry at a turning point. The FA industry is now groping for new direction in technology, demand, and competition, which makes for especially rough times. Having relied 100 percent on capital investments in the past, this industry is in an economic slump. Indeed the restructuring in all of Japanese industry has been particularly hard on the FA industry.

Technology and Production Systems

The greatest task in making a technological change in direction lies in finding new technology. Fundamentally that is the challenge for Japan. The Japanese must make or find the source of economic revival by themselves.

At present the origins of the technology in almost all industrial fields in which Japan is strong came from the West. Moreover Japan still relies on Europe and the United States for certain products and low-volume goods that cannot acquire a fixed market share within Japan. For example, in the case of large wind tunnels, the big wooden fans are manufactured in the Netherlands and the electric motors are British made. This has led some people to remark that going to Japan is like stepping back in time to the late nineteenth century when the Western world was just starting to become industrialized.

Japanese firms should occasionally aim at small markets and conduct basic R&D on their own. They should also make the capital investments needed to move beyond traditional technology to breakthrough innovations. Japan can be a wellspring of new technology, and become a true technological giant, by embarking on grand-scale concepts that will lead to technological growth.

Japan is in a good position to invent better industrial machinery. The shop floor of its FA industry which produces machines to be used by other industries could be a rich source of innovation. The image of an industry typified by subcontractors and piecemeal assembly work needs to be cast off. Challenging the basic structure of the production site means reexamining the industry's very foundation.

Automation at production sites is progressing dramatically because of a labor power shortage. There are debates about what that can do to the development of sophisticated skills and about whether it will eliminate technological advancements on the shop floor. The technology and skill founded at the production site has been a major contributing factor to machinery improvements that have accumulated so far in this field in Japan.

There are two counterarguments to consider here. One is that important future technology will continue to hardly depend on the sophisticated skills on the shop floor. In other words, engineers are needed at the production site in order to accumulate the know-how related to automation. The other argument claims that the technological development that encourages automation can replace the accumulation of sophisticated skills at the production site. It emphasizes a positive outlook for factory automation and sees it as supplanting the need to develop technology and skill on the shop floor.

No matter which argument we believe, we can say that if the number of engineers on the shop floor is drastically reduced out of sheer eagerness to see the effects of automation, technology at the production site will be adversely affected and accumulated knowledge dissipated.

The FA industry's high international competitiveness was accomplished with the help of small- and medium-sized companies which enabled the manufacturers to thrive on flexible production systems. Amid the ever-widening labor shortage, there are already misgivings about the loss of skills seen in small- and medium-sized firms, since many jobs that are hard to automate and require skilled handwork are still being farmed out to them. There is much doubt that the skills of these workers will be passed along in the future.

Yet, with major structural reforms occurring, the problem of maintaining production systems is not limited to the small- and medium-sized subcontractors. Indeed, while our thoughts may be on retaining the technological level of skilled workers and engineers at large companies, it is really the delicate question of who will take the helm. If production is not kept at a minimal level, there is a risk to the supply system. That consideration should be enough to encourage ideas on how to maintain the production base of Japan.

Issue of Demand

An issue of demand is the product saturation not only of the domestic market but also of the export market. Moreover in other industries whose use of the FA machinery is marked, both the domestic and export markets are likewise saturated. Remedial actions like limiting the variety of products or withdrawing from unprofitable areas of production can be taken, but a fundamental strategy for the industry has yet to be addressed.

There are two possible ways to proceed here. One is to create new technology within Japan, an idea discussed previously here, which calls for developing unprecedented applications or inventing completely new industrial machines. The other way is to globalize production, seeking out regions via direct foreign investments where demand is still present. Such investments should help hold down trade friction and contribute to the economic development of those regions as well. Neither approach will be easy, and in either case considerable investment in technology and international management will be necessary.

Japan is lucky to be located in a corner of East Asia now undergoing development orientated toward the twenty-first century. There are many challenges to be met there, such as manufacturing products suitable to the industrial development of those nations, forming relationships with their governments for supplying the necessary infrastructure as well as aid from the Japanese government to reduce investment risks. But the most important consideration must be the people's potential, and the FA industry can contribute to East Asia's development by utilizing their skills.

Issues in Competition

The main concern in competition is low profits due to a great many rival companies. To be sure, excessive competition is not all that bad. Competition is the mother of invention, and the supply of products at low prices has its merits for industries on the recipient end.

However, the big problem is the energy waste in people and resources created by overlapping investments for technological development among rival companies. A large number of companies are making overlapping investments that ought to be carried out by a small number of companies. From a market standpoint that entails loss, but to the individual firms it lowers productivity in indirectly related sections. Japanese companies' value-added productivity is surprisingly low not only because prices drop due to fierce competition but also because valuable resources are wastefully fueling the on-going rivalries.

The greatest fault here may be said to be the "me-too" syndrome. The perception that if someone is making something, then I must make it too, is unnecessary. Rather the strategic idea needed is, If someone else is making something, I will make yet a different thing. For that reason the mission of each company needs to be not only to secure profits but also to serve society by its products.

This is not just a question of social consciousness. The real fact that too many companies produce the same product is the reason for the excessive competition. The solution cannot avoid reducing the number of companies in the FA industry. The FA industry has come up against the wall of demand. Therefore a reorganization of the industry, which today consists of a wide range of firms, is inevitable.

It is not healthy to rely on government directions along that line. Each company must start paring down and find its special niche. Those companies that manage to succeed the earliest will build the power to absorb other firms. There will inevitably be a call for a justifiable scenario of industrial reorganization. Establishing that leadership will be a priority.

Specialization should not be viewed as limiting but rather as wide-ranging. Simple niche specialization presents the danger of shrinking the industry—not to mention the fact that it can lead to too little competition. The more desirable path is a broad specialization such that encompasses moving into new fields and developing new industrial machinery.

Changes in direction in technology, demand, and competition all require the foresight of management to take calculated leaps. There is no need to deny the past entirely, for imagination builds on the past.

6   Chemical Industry

Konomu Matsui and
Shin-ichi Kobayashi

6.1   Economic Importance of the Chemical Industry

The chemical industry occupies an exalted position in the Japanese economy. The amount of shipments of this industry's products in 1991 came to ¥24.3 trillion, accounting for 5.3 percent of the Japanese GNP. Its large share of GNP matches that of its counterparts in the industrialized nations of the West.

The chemical industry comprises 7.1 percent of the entire Japanese manufacturing industry and ranks fourth after electric apparatus, transport machinery, and general machinery. Furthermore fixed investments in this field account for 11.7 percent of those for the entire manufacturing industry in Japan, and its research and development expenditures for 16.8 percent.

That the chemical industry's R&D expenses are higher than the amount of investments in production equipment may mean that its constitution is more creative than that of the manufacturing industry. In contrast to the tendency toward maturation noticeable in the electric apparatus and transport machinery industries, we can imagine that the economic importance of the chemical industry will rise in the future.

In the meantime the chemical industry is basically a materials-supplying industry, and it tends to get easily into a passive position in relation to the industries to which it sends provisions. It has several other management weak points in price negotiations and value added rate, for example. The chemical industry's management efforts have been devoted to creating products and technology with higher added value in order to break away from such a weak position.

Since the 1980s the proposition of final products in the total amount of the industry's shipments has been growing; in 1992 it came to over 50 percent. In particular, among all final products the percentage accounted for by high-function and high-value-added items like finished pharmaceuticals and cosmetics is now starting to rise.

The chemical industry can be divided into materials supply and processed chemicals. The processed chemical area has continued to grow, from 38.9 percent, to 44.8 percent, and to 50.6 percent in 1980, 1985, and 1990, respectively. A successive shift to processed chemicals in the chemical industry is likely to raise this industry's economic importance further in the future.

International Competitiveness

The Japanese chemical industry's output in 1991 came to $182.4 billion, placing it second in the world for a single nation after the $287.5 billion of the United States. The figure for the EC was $372.9 billion. Viewed in this way, by regional markets, the Japanese chemical industry occupies one end of a triad formed of Japan, the United States, and Europe. As far as trade earnings and expenses go, there was a surplus in the substantial exports for the materials type of chemical product. In the processed type of chemicals, a surplus can be found too in photosensitive materials, dyes, and paints. Only inorganic chemical compounds and chemical fertilizers among chemical materials products are experiencing low international competitiveness and a deficit. Among processed chemical products, the same can be said about the competitiveness of pharmaceuticals; refined oils, spices, and cosmetics; gunpowder, and the like.

Compared with industries such as fibers, steel, electronics, and automobiles, the chemical industry has not had much success in the international marketplace. This is why its international competitiveness does not seem impressive like that of these other industries.

Factors hindering improvements in the international competitiveness of the Japanese chemical industry include the high cost of raw materials stemming from their low domestic supply, the high cost of fixed expenses because of the small business scale, the high cost of distribution due to the severity of customer demands, and so on. Such points inevitably make the Japanese chemical industry's cost competitiveness quite low. However, Japan, on the other hand, ranks very high in the realm of technological innovation and competitiveness. For instance, up to now European chemical firms have dominated the world markets for dyes, but they were recently forced to give up production of intermediate and basic dyestuff chemicals because of their slowness in adopting environmental measures. That has presented a golden opportunity for the Japanese chemical industry, since it has succeeded in the technological development of a pollution-free nitration method that does not utilize mercury and arsenic acid, such as were used in the products of European chemical firms.

Grappling with Environmental Problems

The greatest distinguishing feature of the Japanese chemical industry is that due to the lack of land space and raw materials within the country, it has tackled head-on the two environmental problems of preventing pollution and conserving resources as well as energy.

Like chemical companies elsewhere in the world, Japanese chemical companies have begun to grapple with the development of pollution-preventing technology, technology to remove contaminated elements, as well as technology to conserve resources and energy. In Japan the chemical industry as a whole has managed to meet with some success. Its pollution-preventing technology has allowed environmental measures to be enacted in Japan that surpass by far those in the United States and Europe. Simultaneously it enabled the accumulation of new technology that can benefit other countries.

Of course many environmental problems remain to be solved. The contributions of the Japanese chemical industry will be important in this respect.

Strategic Directions for the Future

We would like to propose the following four strategic directions that should be considered by the Japanese chemical industry in the future: (1) Expand the scale of business to the level where it ranks with chemical firms in the United States and Europe. (2) Strengthen individual products and operations that are appealing for their originality in order to create new demands. (3) Make a pioneering effort at coexistence and coprosperity with Southeast Asian markets, where Japan has a geographical advantage. (4) Boost research and technological development, for innovation is the source of competitive power.

6.2 Historic Changes in the Chemical Industry and Present Circumstances

The Japanese chemical industry is a mainstay industry that supports the nation's economy. However, it has not experienced as much success in the world's markets as the fiber and steel industries in the past, and the electric/electronic and the automobile industries in more recent times. In fact, from an international viewpoint, the corporate scale of the Japanese chemical industry is relatively small compared to the huge chemical companies in the West. It depends on the applied development of technology and offers little unique technology of its own. Among its several troubling features are the undisputed facts that the Japanese chemical companies lack individuality and have low profitability.

Historic Changes in the Japanese Chemical Industry

The history of the development of Japan's chemical industry is comparatively old. As far back as the 1890s, the mid-Meiji period, signs of success could already be seen in its development of smoke-free gunpowder (white gunpowder) which replaced black gunpowder. Thereafter the industry continued to develop by moving its focus from coal to petroleum chemistry. After World War II the industry grew along with the high growth of Japan's economy to become a mainstay industry.

Chemical Industry's Rise to Power

Shattered and exhausted by World War II, the chemical industry began its postwar climb by reconstructing. Starting in 1946, the industry first restored production equipment in crucial areas through a "priority production policy." Rationalization and modernization were the focus of policies from 1948 on. Then in 1950 the Korean conflict stimulated the economy, for it created a demand for modern provisions, and the revitalization of the rest of the business world followed.

The petrochemical industry got its start in the late 1950s. With the resumption of oil refining after the war, the foundation was laid for obtaining raw materials for the petrochemical industry within Japan. Thereupon a cluster of companies drew up plans to industrialize petrochemicals. In February 1956 the Ministry of International Trade and Industry approved the first petrochemical plan of six companies (Maruzen Oil, Nippon Oil, Mitsubishi Oil, Sumitomo Chemical, Mitsui Petrochemical, and Mitsubishi Petrochemical).

In October of the same year, the polyethylene plan conceived by Showa Denko, Furukawa Electric Industries, and Mitsubishi Petrochemical also received supplementary approval. The petrochemical plans, started in this way, were soon brought to fruition as industrial complexes.

Japan's entry into the petrochemical industry took the following form: First of all, for the Japanese chemical industry it was an advancement into a complete unknown, and for this reason it had to rely on technological transfers from abroad. However, those circumstances presented the industry with the opportunity of selectively importing the most advanced technology. Second, the petrochemical industry was fully subjected to government measures to develop it. The government's influence was particularly strong in matters like the sale of land used by the former Japanese Army and approval of the Foreign Investment Regulations that accompanied the introduction of technology from overseas. Such rigid administrative control came to influence the structure of the Japanese chemical industry.

Petrochemicals continued to expand their market invincibly during the period of high economic growth. In the late 1960s, partly due to the effects of high economic growth and the liberalization of trade, the size of production equipment proceeded to be enlarged in the chemical industry—including the petrochemical field, of course—as a means of fortifying competitive power.

Changeover in the Chemical Industry

As the period of high economic growth came to a close, the chemical industry met with severe times. It was greatly affected by the "Nixon shocks" of 1971 and the first oil crisis of 1973.

A recession from 1968 to 1970 had ended up with the industry facing a surplus of ethylene production capacity. From about 1972 there were successive motions for recession cartels in the chemical industry. Similar motions were made for ethylene-related recession cartels. When the first oil crisis occurred in October 1973, the petrochemical industry was directly hit by the rising costs of raw materials, coupled with a drop in demand. The once strong petrochemicals turned into a depressed industry.

In the early 1970s the issue of pollution took on importance. Because the petrochemical industry had formed industrial complexes, it had to increasingly contend with environmentalists' protests over corporate responsibility for the outflow of contaminated matter into the environment. This is why the chemical industry has pursued technological development more aggressively than other industries, and about 1970 it introduced equipment for desulfurization and denitrification of exhaust gas (i.e., NO_x, SO_x). By the mid-1970s desulfurization and denitrification equipment became widespread.

In the case of the caustic soda pollutant, the industry began by closing the traditional mercuric-method caustic soda production processes. It rather switched over to membrane separation processes as well as to the ion-exchange membrane method. Rationalization progressed further by the entire chemical industry turning to closed-system processes, and altering other manufacturing technologies. While the world's strictest environmental regulations and standards were being laid in Japan, the cost burdens on the companies were steep. But so far the chemical industry has been able to weather it all.

After the first oil crisis and the frenzied prices that came in its wake were surmounted, production in the chemical industry steadily recovered until the late 1970s. As the economy plunged into a recession once more during the second oil crisis at the end of 1978, and prices of raw materials swelled, demand stagnated for petrochemicals. The excessive facilities of the industry exacerbated the situation, for competition among firms got increasingly fierce. Then the race by developing countries to catch up dealt the industry another blow. In fact the harsh reality of surplus facilities became a problem recognized by the industrialized world.

In 1982, under guidelines from MITI, an industrial system framework was instituted to help the chemical industry break away from an imminent structural collapse. The measures enacted included a relaxation of regulations on importing naphtha by chemical firms, the partial abandonment or suspension of major product manufacturing equipment, and the establishment of joint sales companies. The economy managed to begin a recovery in 1983. As the prices of raw materials started to decline, production in the chemical industry picked up. Helped by favorable conditions in the automobile and office automation (OA) machinery industries, for example, ethylene production also made a recovery. The drop in raw materials' prices and the economic recovery brought a steady expansion of demand for the chemical industry centered around petrochemicals from 1986 to 1990; the following year Japan's bubble economy would burst.

In the process of overcoming the oil crises, the Japanese chemical industry grappled with technological development and fixed investments for conserving energy and resources. The basic energy consumption unit by this industry's products showed a stunning 45 percent improvement in a period of a little over ten years from 1976.

But now the chemical industry has again taken a turn for the worse due to the current economic recession. There are efforts in some areas to fully restructure and reengineer, so there will likely be much structural change in this industry.

Present State of the Chemical Industry

Positioning in the Manufacturing Industry

By 1991 annual product shipments by the Japanese chemical industry had totaled ¥24.2531 trillion and its added value ¥11.595 trillion (according to the report values for 1991 in MITI's "Industrial Statistics Charts" in Japanese). The chemical industry's shipments accounted for 5.3 percent of the Japanese GNP—a level matching that of the industrialized nations of North America and Europe.

A look at the assorted standard Japanese industrial indexes shows the shipments of the chemical industry's products to rank fourth in the manufacturing sector (accounting for 7.1 percent of the total), after electric equipment, transport machinery, and general machinery. Moreover the chemical industry accounted for 11.7 percent of the fixed equipment investments in the manufacturing sector (as reported for 1991 in the Economy Planning Agency's *Survey on Trends in Incorporated Companies,* in Japanese) and 16.8 percent of the manufacturing industry's total research and development expenses (as reported for 1991 in the Bureau of General Affairs' *Report on the Survey of Research and Development,* in Japanese). Even in international terms, the Japanese chemical industry has a presence that is on a par with the electric/electronic equipment and transport machinery industries, which are generally regarded as representative of this country.

Diversity of the Chemical Industry

In contrast to the rest of the manufacturing sector, where brand names are synonymous with products, the chemical industry alone uses the generic "chemicals" to represent its products. For that reason the chemical industry cannot be easily defined by its product range. If we were to dare an attempt at a description of the chemical industry, it might be "operations that take chemical processing as principal manufacturing processes as well as a business that blends or reprocesses substances obtained thereby." Basically, in a sense, the words "producing goods through chemical processing" can apply to the steel/metallic and food industries as well, though these are regarded as separate industrial fields.

Likewise, on the one hand, the chemical industry is a major materials supplier, since it provides other industries with basic materials. However, on the other hand, it produces processed chemicals and finished consumer goods as well, so paying attention to it just as a materials supplier is a mistake. Then, again, since the chemical industry is so diversified, it is difficult to discuss categorically all the problems it faces.

What is called the chemical industry in Japan is comprised of a chemical materials industry and a processed chemical industry. The former refines raw and intermediate materials (plastics, synthetic rubber, etc.) which are supplied to other industries that manufacture finished products.

Figure 6.1 describes the composition of the chemical industry by product type and its market share. Clearly the materials supplier side tends to be larger and to account for more than half of the chemical industry's shipments. Prominent among processed chemical products are such high-capacity or high-value-added products as pharmaceuticals, photographic film, and cosmetics which have been experiencing continual growth. In fact the percentage accounted for by processed chemicals within the entire chemical industry has been so strong—going from 40.2 percent in 1975, to 38.9 percent in 1980, 44.8 percent in 1985, and 50.6 percent in 1990—that the chemical industry may be on its way to turning into a "processed chemical industry."

As table 6.1 shows, throughout the 1980s the chemical industry's growth came close to the entire manufacturing industry's average, and the processed chemical industry approached the manufacturing industry's level and even exceeded it while the materials chemical industry slowed its growth. That decline was in large part due to a slump in petrochemical-related fundamental products. (Petrochemicals reached a peak in 1979, but thereafter plunged to less than one-third of that level.) Such data show how widely the chemical industry can range.

Pharmaceutical manufacturing has maintained a high rate of growth and high added value such that it occupies an important position within the entire Japanese chemical industry. However, it is structured differently from the rest of the chemical industry and is further subdivided by distinctive markets, so we will not include it in this chapter's discussion.

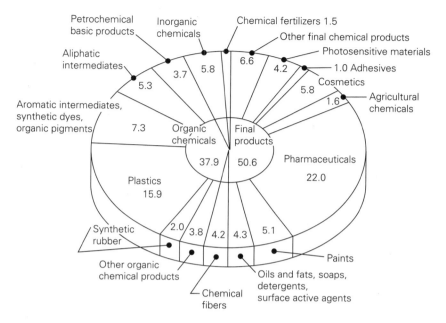

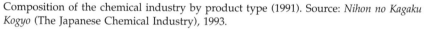

Figure 6.1
Composition of the chemical industry by product type (1991). Source: *Nihon no Kagaku Kogyo* (The Japanese Chemical Industry), 1993.

Japanese Chemical Industry Viewed Internationally

Scale of the Chemical Industry

While overall the Japanese chemical industry has grown nearly as large as all other manufacturing in this country and has a presence nearly that of the chemical industries in the West, at the corporate level there are great differences in scale compared with the top firms in other Japanese manufacturing and the leading chemical corporations in the United States and Europe.

Table 6.2 indicates the scale of operations of the major chemical firms in the West and in Japan. As is clear from these figures, the very top companies in the Japanese chemical industry place only at number ten and below foreign companies. In terms of sales, compared to any top foreign chemical company, the Japanese companies show a threefold to fourfold gap in their net proceeds.

Among manufacturing the chemical industry is generally thought to have good returns to scale, but the chemical industry's small scale has been regarded as indicative of the relative weakness of its cost

Table 6.1
Nominal shipments of the chemical industry's products

	1980	1985	1990	1991
Chemical industry	100.0	114.4	130.8	135.0
Materials type	100.0	103.4	106.4	118.4
Processed type	100.0	131.8	169.9	161.1
Manufacturing sector	100.0	125.1	152.4	160.6

Source: *Kogyo Tokei-hyo* (Industrial Statistic Figures).

Table 6.2
World's major chemical companies (for 1992, in order of proceeds); ($million)

Rank	Company	Country	Sales	Net profits
1	Hoechst	Germany	28,334	730
2	BASF	Germany	27,501	380
3	Bayer	Germany	25,446	965
4	Du Pont	United States	21,734	904
5	Dow Chemical	United States	18,971	496
6	ICI	United Kingdom	18,266	863
7	Ciba-Geigy	Switzerland	15,150	1,037
8	Rhone-Poulenc	France	14,793	274
9	Elf Aquitaine	France	12,649	633
10	Mitsubishi Kasei	Japan	10,282	53
18	Sumitomo Chemical	Japan	8,158	131
24	Takeda Chemical	Japan	6,270	418
33	Showa Denko	Japan	4,526	164
34	Mitsubishi Petrochemical	Japan	4,424	58
35	Mitsui Toatsu Chemicals	Japan	4,322	27

Source: *Chemical Insight*, No. 518, 1993.

competitiveness. There should additionally be consideration given to matters like differences in corporate and marketing structures.

Chemical Products Trade

The Japanese chemical industry's output in 1991 came to $182.4 billion, which placed it in the number two position for a single country in the world after the U.S. $287.5 billion (according to a survey by the European Chemical Industry Federation); at the same time the figure for the EC was $372.9 billion. As a regional market, the Japanese chemical industry can be said to occupy one part of a triad formed by Japan, the United States, and Europe.

Table 6.3 gives the market picture for chemical trade by product area. There can be seen substantial surplus in materials-oriented chemical products, and processed chemical products in 1992 there was a surplus of exports of photosensitive materials, dyes, and paints. There was a substantial trade imbalance in pharmaceuticals; traditionally for Japan this has been the main factor behind an unfavorable trade balance for chemical goods as a whole. Nevertheless, exports of processed chemicals, including pharmaceuticals, have been rapidly rising in recent years, and the range of processed chemical products with foreign markets has tended to expand.

Regionally the Japanese chemical industry enjoys a wide-ranging surplus of exports with Southeast Asia. Its exports to the United States and Europe are less than half of the imports, which leaves Japan with a vast trade deficit, though exports of processed chemicals (excluding pharmaceuticals) to the United States and Europe are starting to increase. The balance of trade with Southeast Asia is attributable partly to the virtual nonexistence of powerful local suppliers. Other factors include the advantageous geographic conditions, Japan's outstanding marketing capacities, and the superior product quality. Consequently the Japanese chemical industry has secured a strong position in the Southeast Asian markets, which includes the domestic Japanese market.

It is true that compared with typical Japanese export industries like automobiles and electronics, the chemical industry does not vigorously engage in exports. However, one could say that since these industries are major recipients of products from the chemical industry, a considerable volume of Japanese chemical products do find their way overseas. In other words, while the Japanese chemical industry may not be directly as strong as that of the United States or Europe, it has nevertheless indirectly maintained certain competitiveness in the world.

6.3   Characteristics of the Chemical Industry and General Outlook

Business Scale and the "Tendency toward Excessive Competition (Kato Kyoso)"

As mentioned previously, the Japanese chemical industry's net profits are small compared with those of U.S. and European leading firms. Moreover the operations of each company tend to be similar, so there are several makers for each product type. Such circumstances have led

Table 6.3
Imports and exports of chemical products (for 1992); ($million)

Product	Exports (a)	Imports (b)	(a) − (b)
Total	24,172	16,958	7,214
Materials type chemical products (subtotals)	15,147	8,882	6,265
Organic chemical compounds	6,714	5,037	1,677
Inorganic chemical compounds, chemical fertilizers	1,322	1,633	−311
Plastics	5,199	1,672	3,527
Synthetic rubber	502	155	347
Synthetic fibers	1,410	385	1,025
Processed type chemical products (subtotals)	9,025	8,076	949
Photosensitive materials	3,174	557	2,617
Dyes, paints	1,541	690	851
Pharmaceuticals	1,366	3,671	−2,305
Refined oil, spices, cosmetics	707	853	−146
Gunpowder, other chemical products	2,237	2,305	−68

Source: Katsumi, Yamamoto, Semarareru Shoraizo to Kokusai Kyosoryoku no Saiko-chiku (The Pressing Future Image and the Reconstruction of International Competitiveness), *Kagaku Keizai,* August 1993, special suppl.

to fierce competition among these companies, who find themselves elbowing each other for small market shares. This is precisely what "excessive competition" entails.

Petrochemicals are a case in point. Japan has twelve ethylene center companies, leaving even the top firm with a share of just about 15 percent, so companies with a 6 percent share can enter the field. The same holds true for polyethylene and polypropylene manufacturers whose number comes to 15 and 14 companies, respectively, which is quite high, resulting in even the leading firm having a share that is under 15 percent.

Such circumstances make economies of scale difficult to pursue. They also invite declines in cost competitiveness, profitability, and international competitiveness, which exacerbate the problem of recouping R&D investments. These industry sore points are becoming issues because international competition is growing fierce and there are no attempts to remedy the situation.

There are four historical reasons for the excessive competition among these similar firms:

1. The Japanese chemical industry was launched with little of its own technological stock. Rather the technology was introduced by the United States and Europe, and as a result each company had to belong to a financial group in order to enter the field. This encouraged a number of company centers to form, such as the twelve for polyethylene, thus determining the scale of the Japanese market.

2. The ethylene centers and their processing plants often form industrial complexes. Since the industries within these complexes are multifaceted, ranging from raw materials processing to finished product, the capital required by a single complex can involve enormous outlays that go beyond the limits of one company's financial resources. Therefore industrial complexes end up as households where several companies combine their resources. It was particularly for the reason of limited capital capacity faced by a single company that the chemical industry was launched, and the proposition of upstream and downstream operations borne by the different firms has been greater than in their counterparts in Europe and the United States. Once an industrial complex comes into being in this form, a vertical integration of upstream and downstream operations, though desirable, presents difficulties. This has posed a major hindrance to restructuring.

3. At the same time when the petrochemicals industry was introduced in Japan, a large number of petrochemical companies have formed. Group management enabled the different company groups to encourage and support their petrochemical members. This is why the decline in short-term earnings for petrochemical companies has not become a factor leading to withdrawal from the business. In fact group management has blocked any reorganization that can undermine its structure.

4. Since no leader company exists in this industry, it has had to rely on the government to solve its problems. While repeated measures such as recession cartels in the industry, cooperative round-table discussions, and joint sales companies may have served a purpose at various times, they have perpetuated the situation, leaving companies lacking competitive power still in business. As a consequence the number of participating companies has remained high.

In the not so distant past when the economy's growth was more lopsided, individual companies could benefit from market expansion. At the same time the competition in technological development among companies in the field had the effect of increasing technological stock. However, today that "me too-ism" has reached an excessiveness that is deterring the chemical industry's future growth.

Cost Competitiveness

As can be seen in figure 6.2, Japanese petrochemicals' profitability largely depends on the rate of operation of ethylene centers. The average rate of operation of about 70 percent in this industry represents the breakeven point for the twelve ethylene centers.

Nevertheless, though the rate of growth reached an all time high of 94 percent in 1992, ethylene experienced a deficit, seemingly due to a couple of factors that had started to surface in 1990. To begin with, there was an imbalance in demand that was being felt in the rate of production. But, in addition to the classic relationship where demand is connected to profits or losses, because of the rapid appreciation of the yen, the domestic market degenerated in tandem with the foreign markets. Then there was an added financial burden that stemmed from increased staff and fixed investments made in the 1980s, during the years of Japan's bubble economy.

Such circumstances amounted to a state of crisis in the Japanese petrochemical industry. As can be seen by the settlements made in the Uruguay Round negotiations, year by year the rivalry with foreign chemical products was getting more fierce both in Japan and abroad. A big issue was the low prices set by Japanese chemical firms which affected international competition.

Taking this issue of the chemical industry's price competitiveness, we need to consider the real state of costs with relation to overseas companies by observing the following contributing factors:

1. *Costs of raw materials and services.* Japan's petrochemical industry relies on imports for most of its raw materials, in contrast with its counterparts in the industrialized nations of North America and Europe. Among these countries the United States is especially rich in raw materials, so the United States has a clear advantage over Japan in terms of costs and the stable supply of raw materials. Moreover, in securing raw materials, regulations on storage of raw naphtha and LPG exist in Japan, and that increases their costs.

2. *Fixed expenses.* Many companies comprise the chemical industry in Japan, but these companies are smaller than those in the United States

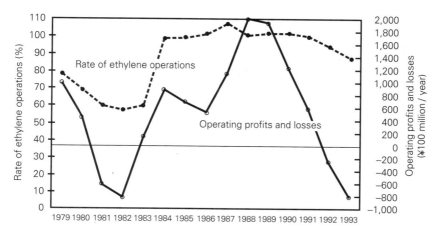

Figure 6.2
Profits and losses at twelve ethylene centers. Source: MITI survey.

and Europe, as can be seen in table 6.4. As a result fixed expenses are higher. In addition, because of the recent appreciated value of the yen, plant construction and personnel costs are higher than in the West. The depreciation fees, interest, taxes, insurance, labor expenses, repair fees, and so on, computed from these costs have led to considerable increases in prices overall. In particular, the expenses incurred by R&D, and related sections at company headquarters and branches, are higher than at U.S. and European manufacturers, and the appreciating yen rate has been raising R&D costs even more. Measures are now being taken to trim R&D expenses.

3. *Distribution costs.* In the production of polyethylene and polypropylene, excessive attention to customer needs has raised the number of grades held by a company into the hundreds, which is about ten times higher than that in the West. Moreover the volume of goods delivered to these customers is small, so the number of lots per round is likewise small and at one-tenth that of the amount in the United States. (The amount utilized is low and the delivery lots are small, even for large manufacturers, because of the *kanban* method.) As a result not only have R&D expenses mushroomed but so have production and distribution costs.

Recently, however, there has been interest in reexamining the traditional ways of doing business, and there are changes being put into practice in some areas. All the aforementioned characteristics of the

Table 6.4
Comparison of the number of chemical manufacturers in Japan, the United States, and Europe and the average production capacity per maker (1,000 tons/yr)

Product	Number of manufacturers			Average production capacity		
	Western Europe	United States	Japan	Western Europe	United States	Japan
Low-density polyethylene	14	11	10	382	336	147
Low-pressurized, low-density polyethylene	10	9	11	120	324	106
High-density polyethylene	16	14	12	198	389	106
Polypropylene	18	13	14	287	349	181

Source: Yano, Yoshihiko, Gosei Jushi no Teishueki Kozo (The Low Profit Structure of Synthetic Resins), *Kagaku Keizai,* November 1993.

chemical industry have raised the costs of Japanese petrochemical products and affected their prices. Nevertheless, we must not forget that these high costs are due to the special circumstances of the Japanese chemical companies, so they cannot easily follow in the practices of foreign firms. Among these are the short time involved in plant construction, the high efficiency of plant operations, the great care given to product quality and safety administration, and the strict observance of delivery periods. Such factors have been critical in establishing intimate cooperative relationships with the assembly-processing industry, which will be discussed later.

Tackling Environmental Problems

While the Japanese chemical industry was experiencing high growth along with Japan's economy, it was confronted by the issue of pollution. However, the industry fought head-on to prevent pollution by observing environmental standards and forming pollution-prevention agreements with local governments.

There were some chemical corporations that protested the regulations because of the effect they would have on their competitive edge, particularly with respect to nitrous oxide (NO_x) and the changes affecting the manufacturing of caustic soda. Nevertheless, efforts were made to transform the manufacturing process for caustic acid by installing equipment that desulfurizes and denitrates exhaust gas. In addition, as rationalization progressed, some processes in chemical industry were closed, manufacturing methods were changed, and so on.

Today the chemical industry's environmental measures far exceed those in the United States and Europe. Manufacturing methods and pollution-prevention technology and recycling technology are part of its technological stock. Some of this pollution-preventing technology was exported at an early stage, so the pollution-preventing technology of Japanese chemical companies has proved to have international value.

Until recent years measures to deal with environmental problems were merely factors that raised costs internationally and caused international competitiveness to decline. However, because of the worsening of environmental pollution in developing countries and an increased interest in global-scale environmental problems, Japanese firms are currently on the ascent in their rivalry with Western chemical companies.

For example, in the production of dyes, European companies have dominated the world's markets up to now. Yet because they have been late in introducing environmental measures, they have been forced to forgo production of intermediate materials for dyes, so a great opportunity exists for Japanese chemical firms to step in. European companies have traditionally employed the method of manufacturing arsenic acid into oxides which depends on mercury as the catalyst. But Sumitomo Chemical Co. has developed a nonpolluting nitro method that utilizes neither mercury nor arsenic acid, and in 1980 it switched to this new manufacturing process.

Moreover, now that close attention is being paid to world-scale environmental problems and global warming, there are likely to be expanding opportunities for chemical firms to make positive contributions toward resolving these issues. Some of these attempts to make chemical technology benefit environmental protection interests are experiments with high molecular gels to revitalize growth in deserts, absorbents to remove oil spills, microorganisms to decompose trash, and chemicals for decomposing environmental contaminants like dioxane. Constructive solutions to global environmental issues can be expected to come from the chemical industry in the future.

Chemical Industry as a Materials-Supplying Industry

Upstream chemical industries such as petrochemicals supply materials to assembly-processing industries such as the automobile and electric/electronic equipment industries. They also provide intermediate and basic chemicals to downstream chemical industries such as pharmaceuticals, detergents, cosmetics, and photographic film. In fact the highly innovative lightweight materials of these industries have raised the international competitiveness of Japanese automobiles and home electric appliances. Other contributions of the chemical industry to the materials used in production processes have brought improvements in the reliability of machine parts as well.

The assembly-processing industries can obtain high-quality goods quickly and cheaply because of the many differentiated materials advanced by chemical firms due to the fierce competition among them. In particular, the increased sales of Japanese automobile and electric/electronic industries in foreign markets have been largely due to the expansion of the chemical industry and the improvement of its capacity for technological development. Further the chemical and assembly-processing industries have helped Japanese manufacturing as a whole develop cluster businesses that mutually benefit each other.

However, the close cooperative relationships among the chemical and the assembly-processing industries do not lack problems. For chemical companies the relationship with assembly-processing firms has presented difficulties with returns on investment due to low pricing and the high yen.

First, the chemical companies are weak in negotiating prices. Because the Japanese assembly-processing industries have high standards in terms of quality of materials, chemical firms are forced into diversified low-volume production. As a result production and development costs are high, and the rivalry among the many firms in the chemical industry does not permit the increased costs to be shifted sufficiently onto prices. Hence the companies' low profits end up constraining their resources for fundamental research, and that has slowed down the development of the technologies necessary to guarantee the chemical industry's future.

Second, overseas advancement by the assembly-processing industry and production commissioned in foreign countries are continual problems because of trade friction and the appreciation of the yen. The chemical industry has further faced a reduction in domestic demand due to a slowdown in the economy's growth. As countermeasures the industry has either to keep supplying materials it has in Japan by exporting products to customers that have moved production overseas or to move abroad with them. However, under the high yen exports cannot easily be increased.

In general, the shift to overseas production has benefited only a few cases. A company has to have its own distinctive technology in order for it to have a competitive edge in overseas areas. Therefore, when the risks of doing business in countries where a company has a weak base are considered, the move abroad cannot be made so simply. For such reasons the chemical industry has been late to join in this trend to produce overseas now actively pursued by Japanese assembly-processing firms.

There is yet the difficulty with the chemical industry's structure. The chemical industry traditionally has embraced multiple downstream industries, such as the plastic processing, that are comparatively small and medium sized. Many in fact are rather tiny, and they lack the strength to develop raw materials on their own. Therefore the structure is such that large chemical companies are forced to shoulder research and development.

Contributions of the Processed Chemicals Industry to Society

The processed chemicals industry, which includes pharmaceuticals, detergents, cosmetics, photographic film, and the like, has a comparatively high demand among the general public. Consequently its structure is quite different from the upstream chemical industry encompassing areas like petrochemicals, which are basically materials suppliers.

Many of the companies in processed chemicals industry have existed since before World War II. During their long history they have seen improvements in the standards of living of ordinary people as well as a diversification of lifestyles in Japan. Over the years they have offered health, beauty, and other products that have raised the Japanese living standards as well.

The sales network reaching the general consumer built up during this long period is something that cannot be constructed by new companies, and it has worked as a barrier to entry into the field. This is why processed chemicals companies have not fallen into a raging competition like the upstream chemical companies. In addition over their long history these firms have accumulated enormous technology, and they have largely relied on their own technology. This too has had the effect of preventing other firms from entering the business.

However, entry into the finished consumer goods field has been bustling with new product markets, and there have been many cases of success. For instance, Kao, a Japanese finished consumer goods manufacturer of detergents, and the like, has developed application products such as an ultra-tiny detergent containing enzymes and high polymer absorbents well ahead of the rest of the world. Moreover, though it was a latecomer as the thirteenth company to enter into the floppy disk business, it managed to branch out into this completely different industrial area. Then it advanced all at once overseas and has now grown into the third largest business operation in the world, after 3M and VerBatim.

Under such circumstances great gaps have been formed between the leading companies and the lower-ranked ones in each downstream chemical area. The earning power of the top companies is generally at a high level even within the entire chemical industry (refer to figure 6.3) and compares well with firms in the United States and Europe.

6.4 Research and Development in the Chemical Industry

The chemical industry, as mentioned previously, is the only Japanese industry whose products do not bear company names. One reason is that the chemical industry freely commands the principles of chemistry and technology and directly creates out of atoms and molecules millions of substances necessary in our daily lives. Its soft technology is also considerably higher than that in other industries. Developing this technology is the role of research and development in the chemical industry.

Special Characteristics of Research and Development

As is clear from the historic changes in the chemical industry, until just a little over a quarter of a century ago, almost all the important technology it needed existed in the United States and Europe. The Japanese chemical industry realized a high-level growth by selectively adopting such technology. In other words, technology was an object to be purchased, and fierce competition took place over how to adopt it ahead of others in a timely way. As a result Japanese chemical firms were late in taking on their own full-fledged research and development. It was only in the 1960s that many of the Japanese chemical companies finally began grappling in earnest with research and development, whereas the history of chemical technology in the West spans over one hundred years.

The "technology" mentioned here means new technology rich in novel substances that were not present in the world until then. Examples include polyethylene, synthetic detergents, and antibiotics. All

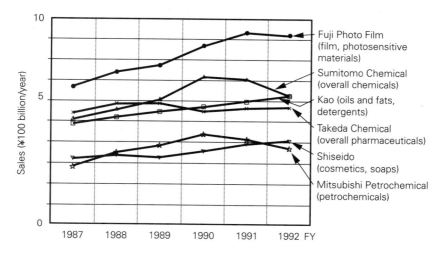

Figure 6.3
Sales in the chemical industry by company type. Note: Sumitomo Chemical's data are for January to December; Fuji Photo Film's are for November to October; the others are for April to March. Source: *Zenkoku Jojo-Kaisha, "Nikkei Keiei Shihyo"* (Nationwide Companies Listed on the Stock Exchange, "Nikkei Business Indexes").

these were developed in the West, but they required various improvements and modifications in order to be used in the market. Economically speaking, technological changes can be also important.

Thus the distinguishing feature of research and development in the Japanese chemical industry has been the many improved and modified technological developments that respond to certain customer needs. As already discussed in the section on cost competitiveness, since orders for materials can be very precise, the Japanese chemical industry has not stinted in efforts to develop multiple grades and products. It has made enormous expenditures on research and development in order to satisfy customers (see figure 6.4).

In addition there are some Japanese chemical firms where 20 to 30 percent of the employees is engaged in research and development. This is a numerical value that is considerably greater than that seen in other industries, and in reality it is a factor behind the high costs.

Distinctive Management Style

The chemical industry handles a great many grades of products, although its companies are smaller than those of other manufacturing

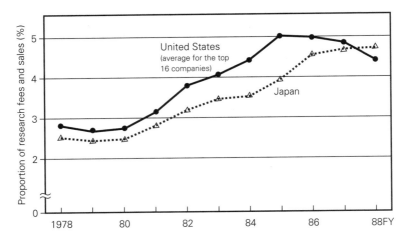

Figure 6.4
Comparison of Japanese and U.S. research expenditures by chemical companies. Sources:
For the United States: *Chemical and Engineering News,* June 19, 1989, p. 59. For Japan:
General Affairs Office Report on the Survey of Research and Development, 1988. For
the 1988 fiscal year average of the top 30 chemical companies: Toyo Keizai, August 1989.
See Hirooka, Masaaki, *Sentan Gijutsu no 90-nendai Tenbo* (The Outlook on Advanced
Technology for the 1990s), Kagaku Keizai, January 1991.

industries. To be sure, the industry will remain thinly dispersed no
matter how vastly R&D is expanded unless these companies diversify.
This is why there tend to be few large-scale, long-term R&D plans
in the Japanese chemical industry but many small-scale, short-term
ones.

Indeed, since managers give priority to customer satisfaction, the
companies are inclined toward doing what everyone else is doing
instead of attempting to be original. They also seldom seem to be
hindered much by their lack of strategy. Therefore, tending to be good
at tact but poor at strategy, they occasionally fall easily into the philosophy of playing to the gallery. Then, when the economy gets bad,
R&D expenses are often reexamined in terms of investment efficiency.
As a result it is no longer possible to carry out consistent activities over
the long term. The planning of technological innovations oriented
toward securing certain future fields of growth somehow ends up
neglected.

However, some interest in individualization and originality has been
rising in these companies in recent years. It is reassuring to see some
visible signs.

Future Direction

The accumulation of creative technological assets in the Japanese chemical industry is presently inadequate. Although the investment in research and development by the Japanese chemical companies has been rising, as can be seen in figure 6.4, for technological development to proceed in step with the West, companies will need to focus on devising technological stock in areas where they can excel. They must abandon parallel research and their "me-too" attitude, or "our company can do what other companies are doing," and make a strategic effort at promoting original R&D.

A strength of the Japanese chemical industry is its capability to adapt merchandise precisely to customer demand—which is a technological skill the industry can pride itself on. The industry also has an outstanding system for maintaining contacts between, research centers and sales departments which facilitates the understanding of customer needs. The industry ceaselessly evaluates and improves its products based their performance in the marketplace. If the Japanese chemical industry were restructured into more distinctive, individualistic clusters of companies, such strengths would be more apparent.

Today the structure of material substances has been clarified at the molecular chain level. In the new millennium the polymers industry will be heading toward advanced structural control at the level of molecules and atoms. The age of new chemistry is on the way.

The technological standards of Japanese chemical firms in their responsiveness to needs have already measured up with their counterparts in Europe and the United States. Unfortunately, in new areas of technology where demand is high, these firms still do not quite meet those of the West in terms of ideas, creativity, challenge, and technological accumulations. Now is the time to break this pattern and take up these issues in research and development. It is also time to devise technologies that do more than respond to demand but create new demand.

We have assembled some ideas on improving R&D in the chemical industry:

1. Set up long-term strategies in areas of strength and maintain core technology through consistent research and development.

2. Withdraw from disadvantageous areas and increase the number of researchers and technicians in strategically important areas.

3. Provide a challenging environment conducive to creative research and development (i.e., original R&D that stimulates demand).

4. Encourage research efforts, and give researchers much freedom. Hire more researchers with higher degrees such as Ph.D.s. Also improve work conditions for the research specialist within the company.

5. Select and discard R&D programs according to their effectiveness.

6.5 Globalization of the Chemical Industry

Globalization has become the primary management objective for Japanese chemical firms. The volume of production by Japanese chemical companies, helped in part by the large size of the domestic market, as was mentioned earlier, places it among the top contenders in the world markets. In terms of trade, except for pharmaceuticals and a few other fields, it has a surplus.

The major chemical companies of the United States and Europe have already established worldwide supply nets, and in recent years they have been globalizing their bases of production and R&D. Thus Japanese chemical companies are quite late in advancing overseas. For example, compared to the 30 to 40 percent sales from overseas accounts of major Western chemical companies, the figure at many Japanese chemical firms is less than 10 percent.

Internationalization of the Japanese Market

The entry of American and European chemical firms into the Japanese market began about 1950, around the time the Foreign Capital Act was instituted. Joint ventures with foreign firms and foreign investments advanced the expansion of the chemical products' market during the period of high economic growth. Though it is often said that there is little presence of foreign capital in the Japanese market, many foreign firms have affiliates in the chemical industry. As of the late 1980s the number of companies locating R&D bases in Japan has been on the rise too. According to MITI's Trends in Foreign-Capitalized Firms, chemicals and pharmaceuticals account for two-thirds of the research centers built in this country with foreign capital. Thus the internationalization of the Japanese market has progressed quite a bit.

As is often pointed out concerning advancements made into Japan by foreign chemical companies, U.S. and European firms believe that a product that does not sell in the Japanese market will not sell elsewhere. They are well aware of the strict demand for quality by Japanese user industries and the critical eyes of Japanese consumers in the finished goods market, so they view the Japanese market as a testing ground of product strength.

Actual State of Overseas Investments

The appreciation of the yen since the late 1980s has been rapidly driving Japanese investments overseas. Between 100 and 200 or so investments are being made annually in chemical industrial fields. However, they account for only about 3 percent of all Japanese direct investments overseas (according to *The Japanese Chemical Industry's Advances Abroad, as Seen in Data*, Kagaku Kogyo Nipposha, 1991). Thus the chemical industry's direct investments abroad lag well behind those of other Japanese industries.

Overseas production bases have existed in Southeast Asia since the 1960s. Efforts to advance technological exports in petrochemical and plastics processing have been helped somewhat by the economic growth in this region. In recent years, along with investments in the United States and Europe by automobile and electric machinery manufacturers, the chemical industry has also invested there mainly by purchasing Western companies. But the big difference is that the operations in Southeast Asia are centered around fundamental chemical products, while those in the United States and Europe are specialty goods oriented.

Internationalization of Technology

The internationalization of technological development, unlike the advancements at the production and sales level, has been moving one pace ahead of other areas. As far as technological trade goes, disparities between technological imports and technological exports have been shrinking since about 1970. Basically the Japanese chemical industry no longer relies much on technological imports. In fact in recent years the yearly contracts for technological exports have climbed to double the number for technological imports. Technological exports to Asia and Southeast Asia have been expanding particularly in order to meet the large needs for local development.

Recently Japanese chemical firms have been among the top companies applying for patents in the United States. The data indicate that in terms of the quality of the patents, they do not take second place to European and American chemical companies. So in terms of technology internationalization is advancing steadily.

Internationalization of the Consumer Product and Specialty Fields

There are a number of Japanese companies that have become world leaders in consumer end products like photographic film and floppy disks, and in specialty fields like agricultural chemicals and dyes. In fact, although internationalization came late to Japanese chemical companies, some product areas had already been competing internationally because of their technology. Furthermore, in being exacting about product quality, the domestic market has forced difficult issues on chemical firms and manufacturers. Their meeting domestic scrutiny has proved to be an asset in internationalizing, for Japanese chemical firms are now in a strong position to internationalize fully.

Future Direction

The delay in Japanese petrochemicals spreading operations overseas so far has been related to its historical start as an importer of technology from the West. However, a fixed market scale ensures returns on both R&D and fixed investments. Management needs to be aggressive in seeking out overseas markets. There are a number of tasks ahead for the chemical industry to consider:

1. World markets for products and technologies can only be approached gradually and only by gradually increasing the number of exports to meet world demand.

2. Southeast Asia and other regions where the living standards are on the rise have the potential of high economic growth. Such regions offer enormous business opportunities for the chemical industry.

3. Research and development promoted overseas must incorporate local resources and the region's market needs.

4. Current overseas development and operations must be reevaluated from a wold perspective and their management activities restructured.

6.6 Four Strategies for Reforming the Chemical Industry

Our analyses of the Japanese chemical industry and interviews with stakeholders have led us in one strategic direction. We can summarize the main points in terms of four Japanese words beginning with "K," or the "four Ks":

1. Stress *kibo* (scale).

2. Promote *koseika* (individualization).

3. Promote *kokusaika* (internationalization).

4. Trust in *kenkyu/gijutsu kaihatsu* (research/technological development).

By "scale" mentioned above, we do not mean the scale of a company overall. We refer to the scale of a single operational unit. It is the same as the practice of management: Rather than consider all at once entire corporate sales, a manager has to focus on each essential unit of operation. Debates about profitability and competitiveness in the marketplace then are more real because they can be related to a singular unit of operation. If a Japanese chemical firm is weak, we should think that it is not because of the size of corporate total sales but because of the weakness caused by limited scale in the units of operation.

Cooperation among businesses and joint ventures should be encouraged to resolve problems of scale. Such collaborations are already beginning, and they seem likely to become a trend in the future. Investments that will benefit in future competition can be considered once a company's identity is ensured in terms of both competitiveness and appropriate profits.

To strengthen identity, in some cases the courage to abandon operations that do not add up to profits will be needed. Naturally companies will want to specialize in the fields in which they excel. But they should recognize the fact that historically the various companies that constitute the Japanese chemical industry were forced into the same product structure out of the necessity to provide services for manufacturers.

In specializing, companies will need to adjust work units, business operations, and strategies. There will as a result probably emerge European- or American-style chemical conglomerates from among these companies. However, it is doubtful that all chemical companies will attempt to consolidate their power in this way. Rather some will rightly aim for a specialized market by concentrating on the products in which they excel, establishing their position in the international market for such goods, securing profits, and promoting investments. Some companies are already proceeding in that direction, and such activities should be reinforced.

The objective of international competitiveness, however, can only be attempted by the chemical industry after it reorganizes its scale of operations and promotes individuality among its companies. International development then becomes a matter of assertively securing more of a market and profits, particularly in Southeast Asia and regions where the standards of living are conspicuously improving.

Research and technological development are areas of strategic importance to company identity and profits, and in the international marketplace the technological power of each firm is the greatest source of competitiveness. This is an essential issue for the chemical industry to consider.

The short history of the Japanese chemical industry, compared to that of the United States and Europe, places it at a slight disadvantage in R&D. Because the Japanese chemical industry has expanded by relying on technological imports, its R&D results have not yet contributed much to forming new businesses. This is an area that holds much promise for enlarging the technological stock and creating new businesses. In the future petrochemicals can be expected to embark on research in biochemicals, new materials, and molecular chains. In this industry thus the road to future growth is nothing other than research and development. For this reason more emphasis should be given to engineering education in the hiring of personnel.

All stakeholders including top management must work together to raise confidence in their company identities, and they must be willing to grapple with management reforms directed at future development. These are the two biggest challenges for the Japanese chemical industry today.

References

Itami, H., and Itami Research Lab, *Nihon no Kagaku Sangyo—Naze Sekai ni Tachiokureta noka* (The Japanese Chemical Industry—Why Has It Been Behind in the World?), NTT Press, Tokyo, 1991.

Data de Miru Kagaku Kogyo no Kaigai Shinshutsu (Data on Advances Overseas by the Chemical Industry), Kagaku Kogyo Nippo-sha, Tokyo, 1991.

Japan Petrochemical Industry Association, *Sekiyu Kagaku Kogyo Sanjunen no Ayumi* (A Thirty-Year History of the Petrochemical Industry), Tokyo, 1989.

Japan Petrochemical Industry Association, *Kiki e no Chosen* (Challenging a Crisis), Tokyo, 1978.

Japan Petrochemical Industry Association, *Nihon Kagaku Kogyo Sengo Sanjunen no Ayumi* (A Thirty-Year Postwar History of the Japanese Chemical Industry), Tokyo, 1979.

Hirooka, M., ed., *Kagaku Kogyo Gairon—Shinjidai o Tsukuru Kagaku Gijutsu* (An Outline of the Chemical Industry—Chemical Technology That Will Create a New Era), Maruzen, Tokyo, 1990.

Hirooka, M., *Sangyo no Gijutsu Suijun to Kokusai Kyosoryoku* (Industry's Technological Levels and International Competitiveness), *Kagaku Keizai* (Chemical Economics), Tokyo, July 1992.

Hirooka, Y., *Wagakuni Kagaku Kigyo no Chukiteki Kadai* (Mid-term Tasks for Japanese Chemical Companies), *Kagaku Keizai*, Tokyo, August 1993 suppl.

Matsuda, S., *Kao no Floppy Disk Jigyo* (Kao's Floppy Disk Business), *Diamond Habado Bijinesu*, Tokyo, January 1994.

Yano, Y., *Gosei Jushi no Teishueki Kozo* (The Low Profit Structure of Synthetic Resins), *Kagaku Keizai*, Tokyo, November 1993.

7   Fiber, Textile, and Apparel Industries

Kei Takeuchi

From the end of World War II until the 1960s, it was the textile industry that brought Japan great renown in exports. Through foreign markets this industry thus fulfilled a historic function of obtaining foreign currency, which was very precious back then.

More recently, along with high economic growth, labor costs in this field have swelled, while the competition with the NIES countries has grown fierce. The Japanese textile industry has lost its competitiveness overseas, and the main force of exports has moved to other industries. Particularly since the late 1980s, when the yen started to steadily appreciate, textile products have been imported into Japan. The imports of fiber products have now started to greatly exceed exports. Moreover some Japanese companies in this field have built production bases or else commissioned processing abroad, and they now are carrying out reverse imports of goods into Japan.

Production in the entire textile industry peaked in the mid-1970s and has declined thereafter. Labor productivity was at an all time high during this period as employment in the fiber industry became drastically reduced.

Fiber products pass through many stages from the production of thread to the point where the finished product reaches the consumer; thus a complicated industrial structure and distribution structure exist. In addition the product's price and the amount sold vary greatly with changes in fashion and in the economy. Enormous risks are entailed. Under severe conditions the Japanese fiber industry has carried out the following structural transformations and managed to survive.

First, the industry has raised labor productivity through technological innovations. Cloth weaving was rapidly automated in the 1970s and 1980s. The high-quality textiles produced as a result have raised the industry's added value. Today, besides textiles with high thread counts, new synthetic fibers are being developed.

Second, the industry has reduced risks by utilizing information directly related to customer needs. Products are being "factory order-made" through the use of information communications and computers.

Third, the industry has developed new areas of growth. New fibers for building interiors as well as for construction and civil engineering work for environmental conservation are being pioneered.

Corporate strategies now include advantageous changes in the distribution of added value by more direct connections with fashion designers and retailers. Their activities have diversified to take advantage of the technology accumulated in the fiber industry's long history.

Particularly since the fiber industry is one of the oldest industries, it expanded well before other industries in Japan. It also matured before Japanese manufacturing as a whole began to experience, blow by blow, the appreciation of the yen starting in 1992. The Japanese fiber industry thus has set about establishing itself as a representative mature industry in a well-industrialized nation. The goal of this enterprise is to find new ways of making high-quality products. As was stated earlier, it is incumbent on corporate management to develop strategies with a clear vision while striving to pioneer diverse directions.

7.1 Japanese Fiber Industry

Prewar Period of Prosperity

The Japanese fiber industry's long history can be traced back well over a thousand years ago when techniques of spinning and fabric weaving were introduced to Japan from China and Korea (see panel A of table 7.1). In the long Edo period, which spanned almost three centuries, from 1603 to 1867, textiles became a market industry. In addition to silk, which was a luxury item, cotton came to be widely produced, replacing hemp cloth in garments for the general population. These textiles were turned out by market-oriented cottage industries that depended on the autonomous production at rural households. In the midnineteenth century plants resembling today's manufactures emerged. Distinct products came to be made in every region of Japan, giving rise to commercial distribution channels. Active distribution centers appeared in Edo (present-day Tokyo), Kyoto, Osaka, and the various castle towns throughout the country.

During the Edo period the techniques of spinning, weaving, dyeing, fitting, and so on, reached a high artistic level. Very sophisticated designs were created that appealed to the samurai and merchant classes as well as to prosperous farmers. Nationwide markets thus could be served by the distinct production of each locality, and the government of each feudal fief encouraged such large-scale production. A system of merchandise distribution developed, thereby stimulating competition in the marketplace which in turn brought on technological progress and improvements in quality.

By the time Japan opened its country to the West in 1868, a system of manufacturing technology was well established as well as systems in soft aspects such as design and commercial distribution. The preparations for modernization that occurred in the Meiji period (1868–1912) advanced this development further. With the opening of Japan, production of raw silk thread rapidly arose for overseas markets, owing to autonomous developments carried out by private citizens ahead of the Meiji reformation.

The Meiji government strove to introduce and cultivate modern technology. The model silk mill built by the government in Tomioka, Gunma Prefecture, as part of a policy to introduce Western technology and promote industries is well known. However, the first to bring in thoroughly modern production methods into the cotton industry was Osaka Boseki, Inc., which introduced ring-spinning machines with 10,500 spindles in 1882. The Japanese cotton industry was developed by private companies and established as Japan's first modern industry in the 1890s. It became the nucleus of Japanese capitalistic growth. The main Japanese fiber export was raw silk thread until around 1920. After the Sino-Japanese War (1895) cotton was largely exported, particularly to Asian countries. Also around that time exports of woven silk increased.

World War I helped Japan raise its international standing, and both its economy and industry developed. The fiber industry then underwent great expansion, and Japan became the world's largest exporter of cotton goods. In the period prior to World War II, cotton goods accounted for 20 percent of the total volume in yen of Japanese exports. From the end of World War II to around the 1960s, fibers formed the very center of the foreign-cash-earning export industries.

Before the war, production in the fiber industry reached a peak from 1935 to 1940. The volume of production was about 30 percent of the maximum after the war.

In the early Meiji period technology was introduced mostly from England. But this industry became technologically independent relatively early and began creating its own technology in the form of automatic looms around 1900. The competitiveness of the labor-intensive fiber industry depended on a low-wage work force consisting mostly of young women. Low-count yarn, cotton thread, and their products comprised the vast majority of exported cotton goods. But, in terms of product quality and labor productivity, Japan still did not measure up to the other industrialized nations.

Postwar Changes

Because of the shift in demand during World War II to wartime production and the damage from air bombings, not to mention the cessation of imports of raw materials from abroad, by 1945 the fiber industry had plunged to less than one-tenth of its prewar level (see panel B of table 7.1 and also table 7.2). However, after the war the fiber industry experienced rapid recovery because of its purely nonmilitary position. By 1955, ten years after the war's end, the volume of production had been restored to its prewar level. The fiber industry recovered to the state where it was once again the top foreign currency earner, just as it had been before the war. In 1955 fiber-related products came to account for 37.2 percent of all exports.

Nevertheless, the postwar fiber industry had to contend with great changes in the structure of fiber materials. Synthetic fibers like nylon which had been invented before the war were being produced in both the United States and Europe, and silk was clearly affected by this development. The position of Japanese raw silk in international trade sharply declined.

In fact production of artificial fibers like rayon and acetate had been carried out in Japan before World War II. Production and export of rayon and acetate continued to grow after the war until the mid-1960s. Thereafter they came to be replaced by synthetic chemical fibers as large growth items.

Japan has since contributed to synthetic fiber technology with unique technology of its own like vinylon. But the industrialization of the big three synthetic fibers, nylon, polyester, and acrylyl was advanced mainly through imported technology. From the mid-1960s synthetic fibers and their woven products became, along with cotton, the crux of Japan's fiber product exports. Later they even replaced cotton.

Table 7.1
Fiber and textile exports

A. Prewar (¥millions)

Year	Total	Cotton yarn	Raw silk	Cotton fabrics	Silk fabrics
1870	17	—	4	—	—
75	23	—	5	—	—
80	28	—	9	—	—
85	37	—	13	—	—
90	57	—	14	—	1
95	136	1	48	2	10
1900	204	21	45	6	19
05	322	33	72	11	30
10	458	45	130	20	33
15	708	66	152	39	43
20	1,948	152	382	335	158
25	2,306	123	879	433	117
29	2,149	27	NA	413	150
30	1,470	15	417	272	66
35	2,499	36	387	496	77
40	3,656	58	446	399	38

B. Postwar (¥billions)

Year	Total	Raw silk and silk fabrics	Cotton yarn and fabrics	Synthetic fibers	Synthetic fiber fabrics
1950	296.4	22.1	74.1	—	—
55	721.3	23.7	82.6	—	
60	1,454.3	37.0	126.5	4.0	11.6
65	3,026.1	17.9	108.6	31.0	66.8
70	6,900.3	5.7	67.5	103.0	225.2
75	16,330.2	4.4	77.1	124.4	386.3
80	29,080.6	10.4	110.0	144.2	510.5
85	41,574.1	16.9	158.6	139.0	486.5

Source: General Affairs Office, *Nippon Choki Tokei Soran* (A Conspectus of Long-Term Statistics for Japan).

Table 7.2
Production indexes for the fiber and textile industry (1980 = 100)

1926	16.1	1965	64.0
1930	20.1	1970	97.1
1935	30.9	1973	109.3
1940	28.1	1975	92.2
1945	2.4	1980	100.0
1950	11.6	1985	98.3
1955	27.4	1990	91.4
1960	44.2		

Source: General Affairs Office, *Nippon Choki Tokei Soran* (A Conspectus of Long-Term Statistics for Japan).

The fiber industry's continued growth in the 1960s coincided with a period of unprecedentedly high growth of the Japanese economy. However, before the dramatic expansion of heavy chemical industries like electric machinery, transport equipment, petrochemicals, and metals, the fiber industry's relative proportion within the whole of the Japanese manufacturing industry or Japanese economy had begun a steady decline.

Fundamentally, while the Japanese fiber industry's technology underwent further improvements after the war, and productivity rose, its labor intensiveness which was the foundation for its international competitiveness declined. Starting in the 1970s exports of Japanese cotton goods were further affected by the yen's appreciation with the abolition of the gold exchange standard coupled with the development of the fiber industries in South Korea and China.

As the Japanese economy entered a period of slow growth after the oil crisis of 1973, the fiber industry's production plummeted. Since 1970 its exports have been curtailed such that the Japanese fiber industry now caters mostly to domestic demand.

Since the late 1970s imports of fiber products have started to rise. Exports from South Korea, China, and other Asian countries—particularly of cotton clothing—have taken over a large section of the domestic market.

Present State of the Fiber Industry

The period following the oil crisis of 1973 saw the Japanese fiber industry transformed from a huge export industry into an industry centered around domestic demand and its preference for luxury

Table 7.3
Number of employees (thousands)

Year	Manufacturing total	Fiber and textile industry	Garments and other finished products
1950	3,860	812	96
55	4,958	964	123
60	7,602	1,163	187
65	9,921	1,327	311
70	11,680	1,264	414
75	11,296	996	531
80	10,292	691	498
85	10,733	627	522

Source: General Affairs Office, *Nippon Choki Tokei Soran* (A Conspectus of Long-Term Statistics for Japan).

products. The number of employees in the industry dropped dramatically with the introduction of technology to raise labor productivity and with subsequent reductions in output (see table 7.3). As the shifts in the production structure advanced, low-productivity areas as well as low-quality and low-price products were foregone. Many companies in this way made directional changes from volume-centered to high value-added production.

Such changes were on the way to full completion when after 1985 the yen began its progressive rise. The export surplus of fiber products ended in 1986, and since 1987 the fiber trade has faced a rapidly expanding deficit. A fixed volume of exports has been maintained at present, but imports have swelled to twice the number of exports both in monetary and quantitative terms.

The many firms that strove in 1980 to improve labor productivity with measures like automation have since 1985 seen that process approach tentative completion. However, amid the present circumstances, the Japanese fiber industry has been seeking new directions for development. The industry is currently heading toward globalization and raising its technology. It has opened up part of the vast domestic fiber goods market to foreign products. For that reason it has also enlarged its production to fit the demand of world markets.

Problems

Especially in the apparel field the finished product involves many suppliers as it passes through a complex series of stages from processing of raw materials to the final stitching and pressing of the garment sold to the consumer. Thus a complicated structure exists for the allotment of added values to the industry. There are numerous related areas to consider as well, for example, fashion designers, wholesale and retail distributors and trading houses. Hence the final added values in the fiber industry reflect many more sections than in other manufacturing areas.

While, in general, production in the fiber industry has undergone reduction and the number of employees has been greatly cut back, the fibers and clothing areas have not become smaller. Add to that the increase in imports, and the weight of distribution becomes larger than manufacturing in the industrial chain involving fibers. This means that the weight of distribution has also become larger in the apportionment of added values.

In the case of fashion apparel, prices vary greatly depending on whether or not the item is in vogue. Sales are also very unpredictable, posing great risks to manufacturing and marketing. The question is who will bear those risks, or who can obtain considerable profits in return for taking risks. In reality the commercial margin is quite large for apparel, but so are the risks.

The entire fiber industry faces the great challenge of how to curtail these risks. Moreover the imbalance between manufacturing and distribution suggests the need to allot more added value to manufacturing. Thus the challenge is to find a way to transmit information about market trends quickly and accurately from the retail field to the raw thread production field in order to cut down on unreliability of the industry. This way the fiber industry can prevent waste due to surplus stock, excess production, and unsold goods, but also it then cannot continue to be so trendy in its desire for large profits.

In the apparel field foreign fashions are popular in Japan. Japan's designers still do not measure up to those of Italy and France, for example. Therefore Japanese designers face developing their creativity in fashion which belongs to the realm of soft technology.

A problem confronting the Japanese fiber industry more directly is the shortage of skilled labor power. With the spread of automation in the fiber industry, which had traditionally been labor intensive, the number of workers at the direct production sites has declined dramatically. But at the same time skilled workers have become the minority and are being replaced by inexperienced part-time workers. Experienced technicians who are well-versed in several areas or else technicians with artistic talent are becoming scarce. So that poses yet another challenge for the industry, whether it can secure the necessary qualified technicians.

The decline in the number of experienced workers in the stitching of garments is a particular problem because it is hard to replace this delicate operation with robots and computer-controlled processes. Although robotization and automation are advancing, we must not think that the skilled technician will ever become obsolete. Finding and training capable workers is a problem faced by the entire fiber industry.

7.2 Adjustments in the Japanese Fiber Industry—Five Directions

While contending with such problems as growing labor costs, a shortage of labor power, competition from the NIES countries and China, or else the stagnant domestic market, the Japanese fiber industry is presently working to open up new directions. In particular, there are improvements in five areas: in labor productivity, high-quality goods, value-added efforts, business risk-taking, and development of overseas locations.

Improvements in Labor Productivity

In response to market trends the Japanese fiber industry has been moving to raise the production of fine thread. In the Japanese spinning industry, for example, with 100 percent cotton yarn, a thread count of twenty is taken as standard, and 40-count thread calculates to 2.329 times that of 20-count thread while 60-count and 80-count threads, respectively, come to 4.226 and 6.34 times the standard count. In other words, as production of cotton yarn is being cut back, it is compensated by the rise in the thread count. Such is the case that among plants affiliated with major cotton spinning companies, the average thread count of products in 1988 was 38, and four years later the figure went up to 54, which means that the amount of unit production rose 1.7 times. Ever since the liberalization of the dollar-yen exchange rate in 1971, efforts have been made at these factories to move away from mass production. The refining of thread count has proceeded rapidly in recent years and has now been fully accomplished. Attempts at increasing labor productivity in the fiber industry are being made by greatly accelerating and connecting automated production processes (by shortening some and combining other processes).

In the case of synthetic fibers, the speed of the spinning yarn, which pulls out thread from a raw material polymer, was at first 1,000 meters per minute. Now with the development of direct spin draw technology, which integrates yarn-spinning with stretching processes, the speed has been raised dramatically to 3,000 to 3,500 meters per minute. A further improvement in productivity is the development of the new draw textured yarn technology which produces processed thread in one stroke by stretching it while adding the twine.

As a result of these technological improvements in super high-speed spinning, the industry has prospered since 1985. In some areas the speed of spinning yarn went up as much as 6,000 to 7,000 meters per minute.

In the case of spinning cotton yarn, greatly accelerated methods of cotton carding, rough spinning, and thread curling, as well as auto-mation of wrap-raising equipment for making cotton carding and continuous pipe thread, have been adopted. All have speeded up production from raw cotton to cotton thread. Recently new spinning methods, such as rotary-style open-end spinning and bundle spinning through jet spinners, have been developed; putting them into practical application is the next challenge. Compared to ring spinning, the physical productivity of open-end spinning and of jet spinner spinning is, respectively, six to seven times faster.

Even at the weaving stage improvements in speed have increased productivity. The fly shuttle, which makes the woof go back and forth, had been used in looms since the Industrial Revolution. But in 1964 the water jet loom, which drives the woof by a completely different principle, was developed, and it primarily improved productivity in filament weaving. Next the air jet loom, which uses air instead of water, was developed, and it has improved the productivity of span weaving. Further advancements in the fly shuttle raised the number of loom revolutions to 200 per minute and then 350 per minute for the original water jet loom and to 700 per minute for the later air model. Today the average number of revolutions for the air jet loom is 750 per minute, and it can go up to 1,000 per minute at maximum.

The most labor-intensive job traditionally carried out by human hands was the work of passing the warp to the composite satin. It has also come to be automated. As a result the preparations of the warp for one loom, which used to take two days, can now be done in 90 minutes.

As a result there have been substantial reductions in the labor power invested in the production site. If we look at the example of a certain weaving factory in the Hokuriku region (along the Japan Sea coast), in 1926 there was one worker for one loom, but now there is one worker for 100 looms. In addition, while the number of staff has dropped from 800 to 200 in the past 20 years, the volume produced has undergone more than a fourfold increase, and the amount produced by one worker has seen more than an eightfold rise.

The number of workers operating looms at both the spinning and the weaving factories has dropped to the bare minimum. Human hands are mostly needed for feeding the raw materials and carting the finished products and for installing conveyances. Since such simple work does not require skill, many part-timers are hired for it. But plans are underway to replace them with robots.

Just like the looms, knitting machines have rapidly been automated to operate at a very high speed. The pantyhose-knitting machine moves at the speed of 1,000 revolutions per minute. Actually, since threads are supplied from four spots per knitting needle, the machine moves at a total of 4,000 revolutions per minute. This knitting machine is kept running for 24 consecutive hours, 8 hours of which are manned, and the remaining 16 hours unmanned. During the manned operations one employee handles 200 machines.

Presently in the areas of color-dyeing and finishing are methods of both advanced dyeing, whereby the threads are first dyed and then woven into a finished product, and finished dyeing, whereby plain woven cloth is colored. Continuous automation for all advanced dyeing processes has been established, and the result has been helped considerably by rationalization. Furthermore, with liquid dye-flowing machines, efficiency has risen three- to fourfold in the finished dyeing processes. The cycle of injecting the cloth, dyes, and chemicals and then dyeing has increased from three batches per day to eleven or twelve batches daily.

In the apparel field, assembly-line methods have been brought into the production of men's suits. The patterns are put together via computer control and cut automatically, speeding up the whole process.

Many other ceaseless efforts by individual company have led to improvements in productivity. Although much of the new technology had originated in the United States and Europe, technicians primarily at the production site have adapted and even transformed it, oftentimes to the top level in the world.

Improvements in the capacities of microelectronic (ME) technology have had a particular significance in these reforms. Often machinery development and improvements in this industry are conducted jointly by the manufacturer and the company that utilizes the equipment. It is also not rare for equipment to be further reworked and rebuilt at the manufacturing site. In this way machinery specifically suited to the shop floor has been developed.

Through such attention to speed and automation, production workers with experience and skill are no longer a necessary component of the manufacturing process. Any remaining manual labor can now be sufficiently executed by people with little training, namely by part-timers.

Making High-Quality Textiles

To make something high quality not only means to improve the character of a product, it is also connected with value-added productivity. High-quality products cost more to produce. High quality of raw materials and intermediate products have enabled automated and high-speed processes at the later production stages.

The shag quality of synthetic fibers determines the quality of a woven product. Shag is formed by a simple thread cut. With polyester, Japanese makers have succeeded in keeping the shag down to five for 100 million meters, and their next goal is to get this to one per 100 million meters. It is said that the figure at present in European countries is 100 per 100 million meters. The fibers produced in Japan are way ahead of other nations in terms of quality, which is why they still have a steady export market despite the high yen.

Cotton thread, which is the main natural fiber, is first produced as card yarn through a process that arranges the direction of the fibers while removing impurities. The yarn spun after combing this further and removing poorly developed fibers is called "comber yarn." While this comber yarn has been steadily becoming the standard count, recently products with high thread counts are being added.

Knotless yarn, which fastens the bends of thread cuts without knots, is made by a spinning process. The operation to eradicate knots consists in an automatic, high speed untwining of both cut ends and then immediately retwining them.

Delicate color matching has come to be conducted swiftly and accurately in the dyeing stage by a computerized color system that does not rely on skilled workers. Cloth printing sometimes requires 12 separate printings using 12 different negative plates. The colors are analyzed from the print sample, and a print with the necessary number of colors is traced on film. After photosensitizing the film, the negative is assembled and repeatedly printed on the same fabric. Accuracy is required in all these stages. For example, a printed cloth of outstanding quality is made by utilizing a 180-mesh (about 0.1-millimeter openings) negative film. Recently CAD (computer-aided design), CG (computer graphics), and ink jets have been brought into the print field. Technology to shorten delivery periods and robotize the process is being explored now.

The development of synthetic fibers is a particularly good example of the quality control. So-called new synthetic fibers are being made that have unique, outstanding qualities different from natural fibers like silk. They are being created by delicate combinations of technologies that can transform polymers, slice different ultrathin shapes, and blend or twine fibers in complex strands. These new synthetics have been the fruits of joint efforts by each area of the fiber industry to study not only their raw thread states but also their thread processing, dyeing, and finishing qualities. The concept behind these synthetics is not just to make a certain product from a certain material but to create the very material with characteristics that are essential to a stronger product. This intensive effort to produce the new synthetic fibers has thereby been successful in creating added value in the fiber industry.

Creation of a New Price Structure

There are many other efforts being carried out in diverse areas of the fiber industry that have contributed to added value in terms of their new concepts or higher qualities that are not widely known up to now. Some examples follow.

Complex spun yarns that twine together natural and synthetic fibers at the thread stage are being produced now in the spinning stage. Produced in this way the yarns have different characteristics from those of mixed spun yarn, and they are finding wide use in men's garments, women's clothing, and knitted sportswear among many other examples.

Cloth can now be produced and dyed in the weaving stage, that has multiple characteristics of being water-permeable, water-proof, and antistatic, among other things.

Double-spun yarn whereby ultrathin nylon yarn has been wound once to the left and once to the right around polyurethane elastic fiber, which serves as a wick, has been developed for support pantyhose.

The automobile industry's style of assembly line has been brought into the apparel field, leading to the establishment of a ready-on-order system that produces order-made men's garments at the factory. This system can now produce suits, at approximately half the price of high-quality, custom-made suits, within at least 24 hours after receiving an order, with the style of suit, materials, and size matched to the order. Via computers and on-line communications, information about the client is relayed immediately to the factory. Then cutting is carried out automatically, and the garment is sewn together under an assembly-line system. Except for difficult jobs like fastening on sleeves, the finely divided work processes are left to part-time workers in an effort to reduce labor costs.

New uses for fibers are being pioneered as well in fields other than clothing. For example, the ceiling of the Tokyo Dome baseball stadium is made of woven glass fiber. Its raw materials were American products, but in cutting them, the Japanese manufacturer used an automatic laser cutter to raise quality and labor productivity.

Other synthetic fibers are being developed nowadays to be utilized as structural materials for civil engineering and general construction projects, enabling engineers to use sharp angles in raising ground levels, and levees to be built that have good drainage. The existence of synthetic structural materials also promises construction practices that do not harm the natural environment, particularly if attention is to be continued to be paid to preserving the wild life and landscape in public construction works. There is much hope for synthetics in the future of the construction industry. Table 7.4 shows the production of various fiber and textile products in Japan.

International Strategies

The overseas market for the Japanese fiber industry declined with the introduction of a fluctuating monetary exchange rate in 1971 and the oil crisis of 1973. Now, with the growth of fiber industries in Asian countries that have large low-wage labor forces, Japanese mass-produced products have lost their competitive edge.

To compensate for the loss of exports, Japanese companies have started to invest heavily in overseas and local production (see table 7.5). Since the rapid appreciation of the yen in 1986, numerous fiber goods produced at local plants abroad have been imported into Japan. Among the imports at present are clothing from the overseas branches of Japanese companies or from Japanese companies set up abroad. There are also many other cases in which designs and production standards have been transferred to other countries so that on-order production can be carried out.

Table 7.4
Production of fiber and textile products and its previous peak

	Peak	1950	1960	1970	1980	1985	1990	1991	Ratio to peak
Discontinuous fibers (kilo-tons)									
Viscose rayon	1973	379	67	285	353	274	242	175	170	0.45
Nylon	1985	24	—	7	16	18	24	15	14	0.58
Vinylon	1971	66	0	22	66	40	27	34	32	0.48
Acrylic	1987	404	—	22	261	350	380	359	363	0.90
Polyester	1985	323	—	18	182	320	323	311	301	0.93
Continuous fibers (kilo-tons)									
Viscose rayon	1957	93	43	88	60	58	49	41	37	0.40
Fortified rayon	1960	27	0	27	8	4	2	—	—	0.00
Cuprammonium rayon	1973	25	4	15	27	22	22	25	25	1.00
Acetate	1973	37	0	14	33	32	28	27	27	0.73
Nylon	1980	300	0	34	287	300	291	274	265	0.88
Polyester	1991	428	—	4	127	305	329	406	428	1.00
Spun yarn of discontinuous fibers (kilo-tons)									
Pure cotton	1960	536	235	536	495	473	393	390	340	0.63
Cotton blend	1987	49	1	8	12	31	45	36	34	0.69
Combined wool	1972	147	15	94	132	74	70	76	81	0.55
Carded wool	1984	54	17	39	50	46	53	29	26	0.48
Silk	1973	3	1	1	2	2	2	2	2	0.67
Hemp	1974	124	23	67	121	24	13	5	3	0.02
Pure rayon	1957	248	39	191	156	97	83	73	63	0.25
Rayon blend	1971	88	1	17	48	13	22	13	11	0.13
Nylon blend	1957	14	—	13	9	7	11	5	4	0.29
Acrylic blend	1985	266	—	34	151	233	266	184	182	0.67
Polyester blend	1980	269	—	27	204	269	243	175	176	0.65
Raw silk	1969	21	11	18	21	16	10	6	6	0.29
Woven fabrics (million square meters)									
Cotton	1961	3,383	1,289	3,222	2,616	2,202	2,061	1,765	1,603	0.47
Combed wool	1972	393	31	242	361	233	230	285	298	0.76
Carded wool	1980	95	34	74	65	61	95	50	47	0.49
Silk	1959	222	110	220	201	152	115	84	81	0.36
Linen	1970	178	52	102	178	27	26	16	13	0.07
Viscose rayon	1964	422	NA	NA	354	121	80	86	93	0.22
Cuprammonium rayon	1963	465	NA	NA	202	132	100	122	116	0.25

Table 7.4 (continued)

	Peak		1950	1960	1970	1980	1985	1990	1991	Ratio to peak
Acetate	1969	177	NA	NA	161	82	63	71	73	0.41
Spun rayon	1957	1,136	175	1,057	827	546	476	430	390	0.34
Nylon	1970	933	—	153	933	465	307	289	286	0.31
Vinylon	1968	226	—	84	224	83	71	68	59	0.26
Acrylic	1976	185	—	—	72	152	125	83	77	0.42
Polyester	1984	2,596	—	—	1,662	2,278	2,386	2,029	1,987	0.77
Knitted fabrics (kilo-tons)										
Fabrics	1971	215	10	57	198	170	173	168	170	0.79
Industrial materials and other products (kilo-tons · million square meters)										
Tire cords	1980	105	—	21	79	105	95	81	76	0.72
Towels	1980	65	—	—	51	65	62	62	62	0.95
Hose	1972	1.4	0.5	0.6	1.0	1.1	0.6	0.6	0.8	0.57
Rugs	1973	8.6	0.4	2.8	4.8	8.1	4.5	3.6	3.2	0.37
Tafted carpets	1990	98.7	—	—	20.2	80.1	83.9	98.7	95.0	0.96
Hook rugs	1972	2.3	—	3.0	1.3	1.3	1.5	1.4	1.3	0.57
Felt	1970	18.1	2.4	10.9	18.1	6.5	5.3	4.8	5.0	0.28
Unwoven cloth	1991	67.4	—	—	10.6	25.3	35.1	61.1	67.4	1.00
Needle unwoven cloth	1991	65.2	—	—	21.6	44.9	48.1	63.4	65.2	1.00
Thin-width cloth	1990	27.7	1.8	8.3	13.8	23.8	24.6	27.7	27.4	0.99
Braided rope	1973	7.5	1.4	4.4	7.5	5.2	5.7	5.5	5.5	0.73
Fishing net	1973	31.0	7.9	10.6	22.9	29.9	25.9	25.7	24.2	0.78
Hemp rope	1960	48.5	23.5	48.5	26.1	7.2	4.6	3.1	2.9	0.06
Synthetic fiber rope	1972	51.2	—	3.0	37.3	41.5	35.5	36.6	33.4	0.65
Dyed products (million square meters)										
Woven fabrics	1985	6,459	1,462	5,029	6,312	6,138	6,459	5,877	5,744	0.89
Knitted fabrics	1991	1,104	—	—	563	995	1,056	1,096	1,104	1.00
Apparel products (million items)										
Outer garments	1985	683	17	77	284	653	683	624	618	0.90
Underwear	1979	561	21	101	232	546	512	391	397	0.71
Sleepwear	1969	33	1	5	33	27	26	25	28	0.85
Socks/stockings	1989	1,550	6	24	120	1,325	1,444	1,530	1,434	0.93
Gloves	1982	62	3	10	35	53	58	51	52	0.84

Source: MITI, *Sen-i Tokei Nenpo* (Fiber Statistics Annual).

Table 7.5
Overseas investments by Japanese industries and the fiber and textile industry

	Number		Amount ($million)	
	All industries	Fiber and textile industry	All industries	Fiber and textile industry
1970	730	43	904	49
1971	904	43	858	65
1972	1,774	72	2,338	163
1973	3,097	181	3,494	326
1974	1,912	74	2,395	175
1975	1,591	28	3,280	98
1976	1,652	38	3,462	112
1977	1,761	43	2,806	158
1978	2,393	65	4,598	172
1979	2,694	52	4,995	89
1980	2,442	63	4,693	91
1981	2,563	71	8,932	91
1982	2,549	62	7,703	67
1983	2,754	54	8,145	174
1984	2,499	47	10,155	85
1985	2,613	40	12,217	28
1986	3,196	45	22,320	63
1987	4,584	94	33,364	206
1988	6,076	146	47,022	318
1989	6,589	174	67,540	533
1990	5,863	200	56,911	796

Source: Ministry of Finance Statistics.

Meanwhile, although the volume of Japanese luxury goods is not all that high, they have maintained their reasonable market share overseas. It demonstrates that the Japanese fiber industry has the technological edge in producing high-quality goods that more than compensate for the steep costs due to the high yen and high wages.

7.3 Future Outlook

Immediate Concerns

Like other fields of manufacturing, the Japanese fiber industry has been directly affected by the inflation due to the high yen and by the labor power shortage. Yet this industry has managed to rise above such trying ordeals as the 1973 oil crisis and the yen's dramatic appreciation since 1985 by transforming itself from a mass-production-oriented export industry that depended on cheap labor power to a high value-added industry that has utilized automation in order to lower productivity costs and stay competitive in world markets.

Will the fiber industry be able to continue in this practice in the future? On the surface, the present changes have been accompanied by quantitative reductions in production and equipment as well as by the liquidation of low-productivity firms and low-value-added product areas. Anticipations are that imports from abroad, including products made overseas by Japanese companies, will increase. However, on supplying merchandise that will satisfy the consumers of Japan, who can be extremely demanding with their high standards, we can say that the Japanese fiber industry has a range of technology and adaptability that cannot easily be matched by foreign producers. It has maintained a very stable domestic market and has found a stable market overseas as well. Moreover each Japanese fiber company is continually working on raising its added values.

Nevertheless, some important concerns remain about the future directions for the advancement of the fiber industry. Foremost is the issue of apportioning added values. Distribution and commercial relations are a problem. Besides raising the allotment to the manufacturing side, fluctuations in price and demand must be controlled. High-level information communications and computer technology now allow trends in demand to be transmitted quickly to areas close to raw materials. For that reason a larger share of production must be apportioned to on-order sections that respond to actual demand. Soft merchandise planning, which includes fashion design, is another potential area of market strength. Indeed cooperative efforts could raise added values in a wide range of industry operations. We can hope that in creating fashion, the fiber industry will henceforth take advantage of the sensibilities, traditional designs, and color sense of the Japanese people.

Then there is the notion of developing new demand. The discussion in this chapter has so far concerned mostly garments, but there are also uses for fibers in furniture, bedding, personal effects, and interior walls—not to mention industrial use. In fact the market here is quite extensive. The Japan Chemical Fiber Association has compiled data that show apparel, products for housing/household use, and industrial use each account for one-third of total production.

Housing and household uses are likely to grow in both the domestic market and trade in the future, along with the building of new homes and housing repairs. The various manufacturers of the fiber industry have more latitude here to develop fresh concepts and products.

In materials related to structural engineering and construction, there is much possibility for growth along entirely new directions in industrial use. For this reason more cooperation and joint effort with other industries should be made in developing merchandise, and that entails the creation of a completely new information network.

In industrial uses it will also be necessary to monitor the distribution of added values, particularly in cases where the customer may be a monopoly or an oligopoly so that the item's price is not forced down. Let us look, for example, at tire cords which are produced in very large quantities. Both supply and demand consist in about the same number of companies, but the power to determine prices is on the demand side. Thus, using market trends overseas as a reference, conditions ought to be created that allow appropriate prices to be set.

An international market for fiber products for industrial use has yet to be established. There appear to be more than a few markets capable of being opened up overseas. Therefore some research is necessary on popular trends and latent demand in other countries.

A final point is how to deal with the new labor structure due to the shortage of new members and the aging of the present labor force. The so-called Japanese-style management based on lifetime employment and wages according to seniority is rapidly coming apart. On the one hand, the fiber industry acquired fairly early its Western capitalistic character, so it has relied not all that much on Japanese-style management. On the other, its industrial structure is complicated by numerous small satellite firms that depend largely on cheap labor. This industrial structure is being reorganized because of the labor shortage and the rise in wage standards, but it will need a complete overhaul soon.

Currently, however, the Japanese fiber industry still depends on female workers as part-timers and other diligent, but inexperienced, low-wage workers. It has not yet made a full break from labor-intensive activities. What has been mechanized and automated is work relating to the supply of raw materials and the transport of goods.

The Japanese fiber industry now needs to restructure its labor force, including software engineers on the shop floor. The impending end of Japanese-style management is reason enough for a discussion of changes and new directions. Company managers and labor unions leaders must deal with the present changing circumstances and find new ways of thinking.

Japanese Fiber Industry's Future

The structure of the Japanese fiber industry cannot avoid change as it heads toward the twenty-first century.

Already, with competitive superiority in labor-intensive industries now transferred to the NIES countries, Japanese fiber companies have improved labor productivity via automation and made efforts to add high values by turning out high-quality and luxury products. They have also advanced into other industrial fields and worked on diversifying management. Their activities now extend to the manufacturer of food products, cosmetics, pharmaceuticals, and chemicals, for example, and they have entered the service industry too.

While in many cases the technological stock in the fiber industry has up to now been put to good use, the fiber industry has aged. That is precisely why its technology, which was accumulated over long years of experience, is highly sophisticated and can also be employed effectively in other areas as well. Indeed Japanese companies—even the smaller ones—have made technological improvements not only in their fiber products but also in the industry's machinery, ME, and chemistry, and that strong technological foundation should enable them to expand their areas.

There are signs that the fiber industry will take up greater challenges. One is that several companies have aggressively invested in basic chemical research relating to biotechnology. With the continual breakthroughs in this field, the fiber industry can be expected to contribute significantly and possibly extend its expertise to other fields as well.

Then there is the potential that closer attention to consumer demand for clothing and personal effects may aid the development of an integrated life-style industry that responds to all material needs arising in work and leisure designed as one package of garments, personal effects, sports goods, furniture, and interior articles. These are in fact only a few of the endless applications to consider. To achieve this goal, the fiber industry is required to diversify its business activities.

III Common Problems

8 Paradigm Shift

Haruo Shimada, Hiroyuki Itami, and Kei Takeuchi

For performance to be maintained in manufacturing, the various support systems must be kept healthy. However, Japanese society and economy have been experiencing recently a conspicuous system fatigue. Signs of system fatigue were already underway when Japanese manufacturing industries were doing well. But because of their impressive outward success, the fatigue that had creeped into their structure was overlooked.

Limitations in the traditional social system supporting manufacturing industries are becoming visible today, and Japan's whole economic order is being challenged to proceed with a paradigmatic shift in industrial objects from a focus on upward economic growth to preparing a new socioeconomic system for the twenty-first century. This chapter will discuss the different modes of corporate activity known as Japanese management and Japanese capitalism. It will also deal with environmental changes in the market and competition.

Japanese manufacturing industries have both expanded and protected their market share. These dual tendencies have served to limit the creativity necessary for further development of the industries. In the future it will be necessary to shift the competition paradigm to a more genteel rivalry with its basis in innovation.

Japanese employment practices such as lifetime employment, the seniority system, intercompany labor unions have traditionally contributed to economic well-being and enhanced the manufacturing industry's productivity. Now these practices are being viewed as depleting corporate profits and impeding needed changes in the industrial structure. Promotions based on merit and staff rotations are unavoidable choices to be taken. Both management and labor must change their attitudes and seek out creative ways to add value to their productivity.

Top management is facing a serious crisis in the manufacturing industry today. In particular, the demands on the top management of internationalized corporations have increased. Yet companies in Japan have only recently begun training programs for top management. Up to now the merit system of the Japanese corporate organization consisted in offering equal opportunities for success to many people and maintaining order in the workplace through the seniority system, and that has caused a shortage in the supply of top management recruits. The changing of the generational guard makes this now an urgent matter.

A distinguishing feature of Japanese competition in the marketplace is the presence of a large number of small firms. This domination of competition by small firms has led to improvements in productivity and lower costs. Yet it has also brought about a decline in profitability due to competition for shares, overinvestments, and the like. Furthermore buyers often have the advantage in Japanese markets, for aggressive competition among the firms concerned has led to both cost reduction and higher-quality products. On the other hand, it is also a fact that both profitable and unprofitable industries appear in the market. As the scale of a market is being expanded, such rules of competition contribute in their own way. Nevertheless, the need to alter these rules is likely to arise as the Japanese economy approaches maturity.

8.1 Economic Changes Affecting Manufacturing Industries

At present, despite the yen's rapid appreciation, there is increasing demand from foreign countries that Japan open its markets and relax regulations because of its trade surplus which is starting to become institutionalized. Meanwhile, to counteract the high yen, manufacturing industries have tried to raise productivity further and strengthen their rationalization effort. Out-of-date operations are becoming apparent in the distribution system represented by wholesalers, and with the high yen raising rather than lowering prices, the disparity between purchasing power parity and the nominal market rate continues to grow.

Although the Japanese should now be wealthy in view of their nation's productivity, these present circumstances have not contributed to their well-being. Rather, along with a long recession has come a serious rise in unemployment. Moreover joining the ranks of the unemployed are white-collar workers, a condition unknown of up to now, and thus the problem is getting much attention by the press.

The unemployment problem has also brought to the surface the issue of personnel training systems, including in R&D, which is the foundation of Japan's economic development. But, despite Japanese economic development, the fact is that the country remains backward in fundamental research. In particular, the universities, which should carry the standard of basic research and be a training ground for scientific and technical human resources, were neglected in the period of economic growth. As a result their facilities have fallen to ruin.

These oversights during the high economic growth period into the bubble economy of the 1980s have only made apparent the urgent need for structural changes in every area of the social system that has supported manufacturing. From their very beginning manufacturing industries have not existed by themselves; their development has been possible only through the various interrelated factors that comprise the Japanese social system. These industries have worked closely with a variety of institutions such as the education system for training and supplying qualified workers, universities for professional specialties, and the government for rules of competition. Also included may be foreign companies that sometimes have worked toward the same goal and at other times became rivals, industries supplying the raw materials, and industries that purchase products.

The relationships between these diverse elements and the manufacturing industries depend on steady support. Like the glacier in the ocean whose great mass of ice remains mostly below the surface, once the invisible support starts to melt, the visible mass will steadily diminish as well. Eventually the glacier will break up into many pieces and melt away.

Recent changes in our nation's social economy have revealed the growing seriousness of the fatigue in manufacturing industries, which has progressed from the very institutions that have supported manufacturing. This system fatigue had started back when Japanese industries were experiencing favorable growth. But, because the glacier above the water was then so solid, the system disintegration below the surface went unnoticed. Or else it was noticed by some people but ignored.

From this standpoint we will, in part III, scrutinize the diverse systems that have enabled manufacturing industries to function smoothly both internally and externally and also the part they have played in setting principles and constraints. We will also look at more recent problems that have arisen due to environmental issues. Particularly in this chapter we will discuss traditional corporate Japanese-style management and Japanese-style capitalism. We will consider the basis for a paradigmatic shift and how that affects competition.

8.2 Limits to the Paradigm of Conformist Competition

Policies to Curb the High Yen and the Vicious Circle of Trade Friction

The Japanese economy has experienced a number of recessions brought on by the high yen. The manufacturing industry, which shoulders most of the exports, has been strongly affected by the high yen. Every time there is a recession, the Japanese manufacturing industry has recovered its international competitiveness through cost-cutting efforts. While some strategic cost reduction has been attempted by transferring production lines overseas, the main effort has been to raise productivity of domestic plants. Both management and labor have generally become united in striving without rest toward this purpose. The vast amounts of export-oriented consumer goods like electric and electronic equipment and automobiles produced as a result have not only been of outstanding quality but have also shown extreme price competitiveness.

However, in raising productivity, an industry has to have a market above a certain scale in order to recover investments. Since the scale of the domestic market is limited, Japanese products will unavoidably be directed toward export. This has resulted in the Japanese manufacturing industries sending out exports like intense torrential downpours. Each time trade friction gets stirred up again, and the yen appreciates further. Meanwhile the Japanese manufacturing industries are cutting costs and raising productivity literally by blood, sweat, and tears.

Nevertheless, it is by this means that improvements were made in Japanese manufacturing, resulting in their strong international competitiveness. Cheaper goods are also now supplied to the domestic market. So the vicious circle of trade fiction has benefited the Japanese economy.

While the effort gathered to reduce production costs has not been negative, cost cuts are not a panacea. In the high yen recession result-

ing from the Plaza Accords of the mid-1980s, the feasibility of transferring production bases overseas was considered in order to cut
domestic production costs, but manufacturing industries have proceeded here in a donut fashion.

The high yen recession of the mid-1980s was checked by the domestic market's expansion during the bubble economy and by improvements in corporate earnings. Japan was able to recover without having
to establish basic strategies for handling the high yen. But it next met
with the current ongoing long-term recession, and this time Japan must
make strategic shift in order to recover.

Will Japanese companies be able to deal with the recession just by
reducing costs again? Even if that were possible for individual firms'
survival strategies, they all cannot repeat the adjustment process of
dumping exports and incurring trade friction; that would only lead to
another upward spiral of yen and then more effort to cut costs, and so
on. Naturally there are limits to cost-cutting measures, and other ways
must be explored for overcoming the present problems than the competition paradigm that has been familiar up to now.

Toward Courteous Creative Competition

Problems exist with the traditional competitive strategies. The increase
in demand during the rapid swelling of the bubble thrust Japanese
companies into fierce competition, they could not let their market share
slip away to other companies in the business. As they competed with
each other, they expanded their capital investments despite the long-
held opinion of some stakeholders that the market scale in Japan and
in the world had become excessive. However, such thoughts had no
effect because, under Japanese-style conformist competition, being late
to join the rivalry in their product area was viewed as heading toward
defeat.

Indeed the vigorous competition among similar companies had been
an important source of the energy that had bolstered the growth of
Japanese industry. That functioned effectively when the Japanese economy was catching up with Europe and the United States. Then as Japan
became industrially advanced, both in terms of earnings and technology, such excessive competitiveness rather started to hamper further
development. In the struggle to win in the competition among companies in the same business, each firm has inevitably wound up with
dizzyingly trifling differentiations and excessive details, not to mention superfluous capacities.

Such rivalry suggests overlapping resource investments. The dissipation of precious human resources is a problem, in particular. Long working hours is one aspect, but valuable human resources are already becoming scarce. In addition, as is typical in fields of advanced technology, like the electronic industry and the software industry, companies have turned to subcontracting because they cannot continue with profitless production while paying high prices to the United States for intellectual property rights.

The contradictory effect of conformist competition suggested by the Japanese corporate system could not be helped when the economy moved to maturation. The greatest challenge will be how to curb that urge to compete and expand production which has characterized corporate behavior. Another important issue is how to redesign the corporate mind-set with an aim toward creative value-added production.

Rather than invite world criticism by being the sole winner in a desperate competition, Japanese companies should seek a direction that enriches economic vitality and the well-being of corporate workers. There is also pressure on corporations to make strides toward bringing into company life the notion of leisure time. The competition paradigm must be made to accommodate a controlled courteous rivalry that allows for leisure in life, international harmony, and separate niches for companies.

8.3 Limits of Japanese-Style Employment Practices

Changes in the Employment Environment and Japanese-Style Employment

The lifetime employment and seniority systems traditionally worked to raise the effectiveness of corporate training and improve the quality of Japanese labor. The presence of outstanding workers in Japan has contributed improvements in productivity and reforms in quality, and that has been a source of economic growth. However, the current recession has caused such Japanese-style employment to crumble. The financial strain of maintaining that kind of employment is becoming evident.

During the bubble economy, many firms—particularly those in the electric/electronics field—rushed to hire vast numbers of recent graduates. As the recession became more serious, employment adjustments had to be made by each company. However, because of lifetime employment, employment adjustments meant only waiting patiently for current employees to reach the mandatory retirement age or to retire voluntarily. That structure has oppressed corporate earnings.

Japanese employment practices took root at the beginning of a period of high economic growth in order to fit the system within a high-growth-oriented economy. There is no sign that this system will be appropriate for the future economic society. It can be easily imagined that unemployment and disparities in wages among firms will occur because of company bankruptcies, a decline in corporate earnings, the demise of certain industrial fields, and so on, during a period of low growth. Will it be possible to maintain lifetime employment in such circumstances? Lifetime employment may very well become an unrealistic ideal for both companies and workers. Unlike the earlier era of catching up, Japanese companies now must take up risky challenges on their own. Should there really be a framework that determines wage standards just on the basis of the number of years on the job? Should lifetime employment and a seniority system be retained in a maturing society facing a decline in the population of young people?

In these changing circumstances we should recognize that our unavoidable alternative is a meritocratic approach, whereby outstanding personnel are selected for promotions, with flexible use of other human resources. While lifetime employment and wages according to seniority will probably not disappear entirely, the conditions for accepting other employment practices should be set up as soon as possible.

Intracompany Labor Union and Employment Problems

The intracompany labor union system has created a cooperative relationship between labor and management and contributed to stable corporate development. To workers, it is a safety valve that has protected them from worry about unemployment.

However, now that the industrial structure is undergoing change, the guaranteed employment system supported by intracompany labor unions which acts as a brake on structural shifts may end up increasing unemployment. That is to say, the company unit's employment guarantees have worked to delay a reform of the industrial structure. As a result the opportunity to create more employment in new industries and markets that could arise from structural reforms is lost. Therein lies the dilemma. Localized employment guarantees made possible through intracompany unions can lead to wide-ranging and grave unemployment problems.

Intracompany unions must therefore try to contribute toward creating employment opportunities by working with new industries not bound by the corporate framework. More precisely, they must grapple with matters like setting up educational and job-training systems that can help workers change jobs.

Toward an Age of Creative Labor

It is only natural for a company to restructure in recovering from the collapse of the bubble economy. However, the real question is how exactly does a company restructure? Does reforming the corporate structure mean just cutting out unprofitable divisions and lowering personnel costs? That simply amounts to a quantitative reduction.

For example, work hours have been shortened with the reduction of overtime during the recession, but has labor been thus made more efficient? If cost-effective measures are not in place when the economy turns a favorable corner, a company will simply return to its old ways of quantitative expansion of production.

How to raise creativity and put together a corporate structure capable of improving creativity and not just profits is a challenge for both management and labor. At the national level that means creating markets and employment through new industries.

8.4 Crisis in Top Management

Among the issues debated by the industrial sector, there should be included attention to the problem of acquiring top managers. Mainly there seems to be a shortage of leaders due to the leadership structure of Japanese companies. The demand for qualified leadership is high, but the supply is lacking, since programs to develop leaders are weaker than ever before.

Excess Demand for Top Managers with Leadership Skills

Two mechanisms may explain why demand for top leaders exceeds supply. One may be that the country has experienced a time lag in catching up internationally. The other may be due to the dramatic changes in the 1980s as Japan's industries rapidly overdeveloped. The time lag between demand and supply of leaders has led to greater demand, since from an early stage supply could not keep up with demand. This experience is not limited to Japan, for several other countries that have developed rapidly have had a similar history. Rapid domestic development has caused human resources having the potential for leadership in international affairs to be directed to domestic management. As a nation develops, the demand for international leadership increases such that it always is in excess of demand.

The historic changes in the 1980s that pushed Japan's industries into the front lines of international technology also created a demand for top leaders in Japanese companies to be knowledgeable in international affairs. Until then Japan had been in the run by tagging onto the coattails of the United States and Europe, so corporate decision-making was relatively easy. The top executives followed the models used in the West. As the trade environment began to change, Japanese executives had to come up with a plan and concepts relating to their growth. Many changes became necessary, but the Japanese companies were not sufficiently prepared to make them. Thus began the painful realization that they were a front-runner without a plan.

Shortage in the Supply of Top Managers with Leadership Skills

The shortage of top leaders can be related to two crises that arose simultaneously. One had to do with the inexperience of a generation of people who were the top management. The other was more systematic having to do with the Japanese corporate management structure which does not allow for a means to cultivate new leaders and is thus starting to wear away.

Let us first consider the inexperience of the current top management which is mostly formed of people who joined the company in the mid-1950s to late 1960s. These are men who have spent their youth in the confusion of the postwar period, and they represent a generation that has looked up to the United States as a superpower, since they were the actual midlevel fighting forces in the period of high economic growth. Most have had the experience of following the leadership of the United States and the Japanese who were leaders generations before them.

The second factor of the Japanese management system itself has the merit of giving many people an equal chance at leadership, and it is careful about creating order in the workplace through a seniority system. However, the effect is a subdivision of work that makes each individual's responsibility not very big. The emphasis on seniority also means that a person has to spend many years on the job before being given a comparatively important task.

These two distinguishing features indicate there are few chances for bright young people to be put in a position of high responsibility. In other words, the younger work force has comparatively fewer opportunities to practice and take charge of a large initiative, bringing it to its resolution through the propitious blood, sweat, and tears.

Avoiding a "Naked Emperor" Syndrome

With at the root of the problem being the times and the system, our main resolve should be to speed up the wheels of history in the generational change of the guard. Revising the system means forsaking time-honored customs, if only temporarily, in order to bring new human resources to top management. It will entail reorganizing the personnel framework to give the younger workers an opportunity for major responsibilities. While the postwar Japanese companies had not failed in providing leaders of the next generation, the most outstanding aspects to postwar management has made it at the same time difficult to cultivate younger leaders.

It is hard to produce leaders where there is poor egalitarianism. Japan might easily blunder in that way if it fails to raise such societal leaders, for it will enfeeble its next generation of youth who ought to challenge positions of leadership. As a result there has been prolonged a reign of the old which at times has tended to be dictatorial or enervated by age. The crisis in top management at some Japanese companies has been compounded by such lack of restraint that an old company dictator can easily end up a "naked emperor" before anyone notices it. Some firms may have fallen unaware into such an unthinkable dictatorship.

Essentially the crisis in top management lies in the problem of leaders accustomed to a society full of consensus. This is the "naked emperor" syndrome, for any apparatus that might restrain top management has become powerless. Such a critical issue needs to be addressed by these very leaders.

8.5 Characteristics of the Market and Reforms in the Rules of Competition

So far we have outlined the necessary paradigm shift and structural changes in companies with Japanese-style management. However, we need to look at how the market, which is the venue of corporate action, and its rules of competition which stipulate corporate action, have contributed to the Japanese economy's development. And we need to consider the problems they now face.

"Oligopolistic Competition" as the Motivating Force behind the Japanese Economy

The Japanese market is said not to be sufficiently open. On the other hand, there are also claims that for manufactured products Japan has the lowest tariffs and that import barriers do not exist at all. Theoretically the Japanese market is completely free. However, the prices consumers pay in Japan are strikingly high compared with other countries when they are calculated in the current exchange rate. Foreign products are sold at extremely high prices too, or else inexpensive foreign goods are not imported into Japan. These characteristics of the Japanese market suggest that at least for manufactured goods, the market in Japan is not entirely free. Nevertheless, on that basis one ought not to conclude immediately that nontariff barriers and producers' monopolies exist in Japan.

As far as major manufactured goods go, a totally free competitive market, as described in economic textbooks, cannot in fact be found in any nation. In every country the vast majority of the supply is dominated by a relatively small number of producers, whose goods pass through a complex distribution structure to reach consumers or the final source of demand. That mechanism is completely different from the perfect competition model whereby "a great number of suppliers and users react together to a suggested price; then the price becomes determined where the amounts of supply and demand match, and finally direct transactions are carried out."

In reality the functioning of the markets for many goods varies by country, period, and product. It is not easy to decide which is closest to being a complete market and which is the farthest from it. A characteristic of the markets for manufactured goods in Japan in most cases is the presence of a complex number of suppliers. However, it is customary for a handful, or perhaps 15 or 16, of the comparatively large companies among them to control a big portion of the supply. Moreover, not only does a complex number of large companies exist in the same field, but also in many cases those companies produce exactly the same product.

In this respect an almost monopolistic state has come into being. Or else even when a complex number of large companies is present within the same industrial field, the situation in Japan is quite different from that of the United States and the European countries, where specialization into product niches is far from rare. In that sense the vast majority of Japanese manufacturers can be said to be characteristically oligopolistic.

Basically these Japanese oligopolies vie fiercely with each other rather than mutually cooperate in any monopoly. In effect what has materialized is a "competitive oligopoly."

However, there are several cases in which fixed rules exist for such oligopolistic competition. Those fixed rules of competition are tacitly understood in order to avoid falling into a situation akin to the prisoner's dilemma of game theory. Even among oligopolistic Japanese companies, rules of competition appear to exist to prevent them from collapsing together while also vying with each other. That cannot necessarily be called monopolistic action, such as would sacrifice the consumers or the sources of demand.

Japanese oligopolistic companies seldom carry out price warfare. Instead, it is quite common for them to follow a powerful "price leader" company and compete for their share in the overflow of demand. Moreover each firm works to lower costs by raising productivity. But rather than suddenly rushing to reduce prices ahead of other companies, they turn to increase profits by expanding the difference between price and cost. Conversely, in order to maintain a market share, it is not unusual for a Japanese company to continue production even when the price drops below the cost. Competition for market share is often conducted over fine differences in quality, design, and capacities, and that is one reason why there are very many types and models of manufactured goods in Japan.

Buyers' Market and Distribution Problems

A distinguishing feature of the Japanese merchandise market is generally its enormous and complicated distribution structure, among which are included complex mechanisms for wholesaling and retailing. As a result many workers are employed, and the net profits are high as well. Distribution is not an issue for the time being. However, in the manufacturing industry the net profits to producers have become relatively low, while consumer prices have become comparatively high with in terms of production costs. These are facts worth noting here.

Some distributors have almost monopolistic distribution powers. They can limit both the amounts purchased and marketed, lower the prices of purchases from producers as well as the market prices for consumers, and also obtain monopoly profits. Since distribution monopolies are barely given attention compared to production monopolies, these circumstances are not very clear. However, it is common for distributors to wield great power in consumer goods made by several different producers.

The source of demand for capital goods is often the large corporation. As a result there has materialized a situation approaching a demand monopoly, whereby the supply prices are lowered and monopolistic profits accrue to the demand side. The companies involved in these demand monopolies are often large preeminent companies rather than the great many subcontractor firms. Nevertheless, this situation exists in accordance with market logic and does not necessarily comprise "domination" through logic external to the market.

There has traditionally been a tendency in the Japanese market for the purchaser to have the advantage over the seller. In the case where both the supplier and the source of demand are oligopolistic, often competition arises on the supply side while the demand side maintains a monopolistic superior position. In particular, a single company's demand has been known to create a situation akin to a monopoly by differentiating its demands with those of other companies.

Within the Japanese manufacturing industry, there are capital goods suppliers in advantageous positions vis-à-vis the market as well as those at a disadvantage. The capital goods producers that are comparatively large in number of companies are the most disadvantaged. This is because not only are these companies placed in a bad position in terms of price when faced with circumstances akin to a demand monopoly, but also they are often faced with requirements from the source of demand that set the amount and conditions of the supply. On the other hand, the producers that purchase these capital goods and produce the finished consumer goods stand in an advantageous position in both respects. A consumer goods company has an advantage when it can directly control distribution and marketing. The automobile industry is in a particularly favorable position in this regard marketwise. Much of its success in management can be attributed to the aforementioned factors or else because it has used its position effectively.

Oligopolistic Competition That Encouraged Technological Innovation

The influence of technological innovations depends on the market's structure. As long as technological innovations lower the producer costs, there will be a consumer surplus. How the consumer surplus is distributed between the producers (supply) and the consumers (demand) depends on the supply curve, the slope of the supply curve, and the existence of a monopoly or a mix of monopoly and oligopoly. If the supply curve is nearly horizontal in a situation close to perfect competition, the reduction in production costs will mostly benefit the consumer because of the lower market prices. On the other hand, if the demand functions are nearly horizontal, the prices will not drop, and reductions in production costs will mostly benefit the producer. When a monopoly exists in supply, demand, or distribution, large profits will naturally accrue to the monopoly-holder.

Reductions in production costs are not linked directly to lower prices under oligopolistic competition, probably because profits coming from monopolistic earnings are considered to be unfair. However, we should take note of the fact that they also have the effect of encouraging technological innovation by lowering the risk of a price drop.

Besides promoting technological innovation, Japanese manufacturing's style of oligopolistic monopoly has enabled improvements to be made in labor productivity in terms of a rationalization that has maintained the employment levels. The fact that the sources of demand always benefit from technological innovations—especially when these demand sources are large companies—indicates that contributing to the suppliers' technological innovations has been mutually advantageous. In Japan stable long-term relationships are maintained with subcontractor companies, sometimes involving joint technological development. That exchange of technological innovation benefits both companies and makes good market sense. These developments make it impossible to oppose the economic logic behind the collaborations.

There has been some reservation expressed about the effect of monopoly on technological innovation. But it should be noted that by being somewhat free from the risks of competition, Japan's oligopolistic companies have been guaranteed the benefit of technological innovation and thus can keep on encouraging technological development.

Limits to Oligopolistic Competition

Until the present time Japanese manufacturing industries were able to prosper and develop under oligopolistic competition as the market kept on expanding. In principle, then, when a market comes to a halt or has diminished, the oligopolistic companies that "share" competition face the danger of falling into a state of surplus equipment and excess supply. When additionally the economies of the scale are large with a production curve descending to the right, oligopolistic competition can very well force market prices to drop below production costs. The logical move then is for the companies to export in order to maintain production even at low prices—and that has also been for Japan a factor leading to trade friction.

Now, however, the Japanese economy has entered a stage of maturation; it has come to the point where it must revise the rules of oligopolistic competition premised in an endless expansion of market size. That may mean that both the distribution structure and the rules for doing business in Japan may need to be relaxed in order to ease entry by foreign firms such as has been stressed by these other countries.

We still cannot say anything about the long-term effects. On the surface the rationalization of the distribution mechanism seems to have made the share of profits more reasonable and has contributed to the development of Japanese industries. On the other hand, concepts like just-in-time which have been characteristic of Japanese-style management have favored the position of the purchaser, and that may be impossible to maintain in the future. Once more, these are issues for corporate management policy of Japanese manufacturing industries and issues that need to undergo deliberation.

9   Manufacturing Technologies

Yasunori Baba

In the 1980s Japan's manufacturing technologies concluded their process of catching up with the United States and Europe. At present, about 60 percent of the world's industrial robots can be found in Japan. As is plainly indicated by this figure, Japan has become a pivotal country in promoting manufacturing's microelectronic (ME) technologies such as computer control, robotics, and advanced processes stimulated by the induction of informatics.

In this chapter I will touch upon the factors that have led Japan's manufacturing technologies to its current position and will also suggest the sources of its competitiveness. Attention ought to be paid to the fact that in a single, almost forty-year period in the second half of the twentieth century, Japanese firms have regarded the dramatic changes in their economic environment as challenges and boosted their competitiveness by overcoming them. Let us then not be satisfied with partial optimization of the existing system and define as "dynamic capabilities"[1] the ability to give rise to positive new ways of doing things by using environmental changes as a lever. The dynamic capabilities shown by Japanese firms in some forty years after World War II have definitely had a worldwide impact.

Looking at manufacturing technologies from this perspective, we must stress that Japanese companies have taken to advantage their factories as experimental laboratories. In factories used as laboratories, innovations in process technologies have been continually accumulated through the participation of a wide range of employees. New manufacturing knowledge created here was put into application and made considerable contributions to the industry's competitiveness.

The vitality of Japanese manufacturing industries and their technology has been strongly colored more as a product of history that appeared in a specific period than as something Japan is uniquely endowed with.

Japan's manufacturing technologies are currently faced with three inherent problems. They are namely (1) the tendency to become rigid through the standardization of work/operations because of the simple introduction of information technologies, (2) an inclination toward the eliminating versatile, skilled workers, and (3) a system fatigue in a corporate society that used to pride itself on a culture of diligence. Once these tendencies begin to accelerate, the corporate vitality of Japanese manufacturing industries will become substantially enervated and, no doubt, will stimulate a decline in international competitiveness.

At present, what Japanese manufacturing industries must ask themselves is not limited just to how to keep on improving productivity. They must also turn their attention to the fact that the industrial principles forming a new type of international competitiveness have been appearing from outside of Japan. Since the production system pursues productivity seemingly to the point of excessiveness, will it really be possible to come up with radical innovations that can open up prospects for the industrial society of the twenty-first century?

9.1 Characteristics of Japanese Manufacturing Technologies

What Are Manufacturing Technologies?

Manufacturing technologies can be broadly divided into production technology and production administration technology. Production technology links goods with the manufacturing site and clarifies what can be done by doing things a particular way. Production administration technology's direct objective lies in the factory network system, arranging and running the information system and also seeing that manufacturing is carried out rationally. Production administration technology is generally concerned with production administration systems comprising the production system, information-processing system, and the control system in the administration of direct manufacturing processes.

Indispensable elements behind a manufactured good's existence are the product technologies that are specialized in the materialization of the item. Scale-up technology is necessary to enable production of a substantial volume when going beyond the realm of one product to have marketable goods constantly. In order to compete successfully in the market, the technology for reducing costs and raising productivity are required. Manufacturing technology embracing a broad range of interconnected technologies will be necessary for maintaining products at a certain standard and price for a long time.

Orders fulfilling military needs in the United States have rather tended to be for single items. They require high product quality but allow steep costs. By comparison, in Japan, where mass production and lower costs have been the consistent corporate goal, the civilian-oriented demands most certainly made great contributions to the formation of the present Japanese system of manufacturing technologies. In order to realize a system of such technologies with abundant competitiveness, the existence of human power will clearly be needed as an aggregate in one country to make that possible. Moreover, appropriate social and cultural bases will be necessary, too, as given conditions.

Development Process of Japanese Manufacturing Technologies

The present Japanese manufacturing technologies have emerged as a result of the dynamic mutual operations of the following three factors: (1) the accumulation of traditional production technology and skills in Japan, (2) the introduction of production technology from Europe and the United States, and (3) the market and competitive conditions as external environment. In other words, the production and production administration technology from the West was transplanted into Japan's environment of manufacturing—culture that stipulates the basic conditions of development. Then a series of reforms as well as changes in technology occurred under specific environmental conditions, and manufacturing technologies developed into their current state.

We will take up three points.

First, we will briefly discuss traditional Japanese production technology and the special characteristics of the proficiency accumulated therein by using the example of the Japanese sword. Attention ought to be drawn here to the high level of production technology traditionally attained by the Japanese, as evinced even by the observation of historians on the finishing of the Japanese sword, which suggests a technology carried out by experts specializing in metallurgy.[2] Since the properties of metals can be grasped visually, the sword-maker had to develop an eye for correctly evaluating their malleability during the forging process. The presence of such workers in large numbers cannot be ignored in the history of fabricating technologies since the Meiji period.

Unlike Europe, Japanese production technology never followed a path of general systematization. It did not manage to go beyond the practice of craftsmen's work even with respect to the acquisition and chain of expertise. This makes for also a strong contrast with the administration of technology centered around mass production, the use of conveyor equipment and of gauges and jigs for interchangeability of parts, that was born in the small hand-driven American manufacturers of the nineteenth century. Even after the Meiji period, the traditional craftsman's art maintained its integrity and continued to flourish primarily in small- and medium-sized companies. That Japanese spirit for making things suggested here still lives in the emphasis on manufacturing knowledge gained from experience on the shop floor.

Second, we will illustrate how Japanese companies transplanted production and production administration technology from the West into their own manufacturing climate by reaffirming an institutional framework present in Japan that supports manufacturing to this day. As in the case of the fabrication of the sword, the Japanese had already, by tradition, a high sensibility toward the culture of manufacturing. Indeed, since the Meiji period the emphasis on manufacturing met the policies of a wealthy nation with a strong military and high economic growth. The conclusion that Japanese universities were not like those in Europe and the United States has glossed over the advancement of technological expertise compared to the theoretical sciences. Japanese universities had rather put their emphasis on that realm of science relating to engineering practice. From their very start in the early Meiji period, the scientific aspects of manufacturing were explored at Japanese universities in the teaching of engineering courses, which had accompanied the machinery imported from the United States and Europe. At the beginning of the Showa period (1926–1989) courses in the study of manufacturing were set up in Japanese universities ahead of their Western counterparts. As a result a great number of outstanding workers entered the Japanese manufacturing industry after studying in college engineering departments.

In taking such a direction, the Japanese tradition of manufacturing became fortified with knowledge on advanced technologies imported from the West passed via universities. This institutional framework worked to make the technology introduced into the manufacturing site consistent with the Japanese production practices.

To take a further example,[3] when troubles arose in blast furnace operations at the establishment of the government-run Yawata Steel Mill at the beginning of the twentieth century, Japanese engineers cited as one reason for the failure the formalistic blast furnace design by the foreign engineers who had ignored the special attributes of Japanese raw materials. Then these Japanese engineers instituted changes in the original foreign blast furnace design. The technological imports that have succeeded as a result were not wholesale introductions but rather have generally been modified to uniquely Japanese conditions.

Compared to the introduction of production technology, the production administration technology came late. The statistical process control (SPC) textbook method that arose in the United States in the 1940s was brought into Japan after World War II. TQC (total quality control), which is currently in vogue around the world, was added to this SPC by a Japanese group in order to reinforce the group's objective in the activities of the group unit.

Third, we will turn to external environmental factors. These include the nature of the domestic market, which had constantly expanded in the high economic growth period following World War II, the markets in the United States and Europe, which in principle advocate free trade, and the fierce competition in the Japanese market. However, Japan's compressed technological growth period cannot be ignored[4] in its effect on the flexibility of Japanese companies, such as was suggested in our hypothesis of the people's dynamic capabilities to adapt. This means we must pay attention to the fact that despite historical constraints, production was able to undergo rapid expansion while capital and technological resources were in relatively short supply.

In the automobile industry, for instance, American manufacturers have constructed a rigid technological system from highly specialized factors through their long history of mass production and mass marketing. By contrast, Japanese manufacturers did not have enough leeway timewise and financially to renew their own technological system completely in line with the rapidly expanding volume of production. Thus it seems that by combining existing technological factors flexibly, they made the system efficient step by step. Faced by the historical constraints of compressed technological growth, the postwar Japanese manufacturing industries had to manage its production by putting the existing technological factors into maximum application.

Positive Introductions of ME Technology onto the Shop Floor

The impetus for the introduction onto the shop floor of ME technology—an idea that had surfaced in the 1970s—was the need for Japanese production technology to catch up with that of the West. In the 1970s programming control of equipment was brought about by mechatronization, and this flexibility enabled manufacturing to produce variable amounts of different products. In the 1980s industrial robots were introduced to cut down on the number of human workers without changing the production volume. Since then industrial robots have been used by the automobile industry and by the electric industry. The number of industrial robots active in Japanese firms in 1990 came to 274,000, which is 60 percent of the world share. In the equipment industry, process computers were set up in the 1980s in production processes, and efforts were made to raise the level of the automation in production.

In searching for the reasons why ME technology was successfully integrated in Japanese industry, we cannot ignore the fact that industrial robots were made possible due to extensive education and training programs. Through education and training blue-collar workers were brought into the fold of factories used as laboratories, which encouraged workers to develop technological familiarity with the robotic equipment. In Japan factories that have introduced robots have thoroughly reeducated and retrained their employees in small group sessions. Important in this regard is the emphasis on a comprehensive system that includes workers of the upstream and downstream processes in the production system. In that way a working environment is set up where human beings can interface with computers in managing the processes—that was a very difficult procedure with earlier robots. It is an environment where not much intelligence is required of robots.[5]

Concerning social and economic factors, the intracompany labor unions in Japan have acted in an entirely different manner than the unions in the United States and Europe which have rather worked to block the introduction of robots. For Japanese unions the shift to robots and repositioning of employees was easily accepted, since there was little chance of unemployment occurring within the firm. In effect the Japanese unions took a wait-and-see stance in endorsing an active use of robots: "Let's see if robots can strengthen the company's competitiveness" was the general opinion. Another reason why labor-saving investments did not suggest dire consequences on the employment front was due to the fact that Japan had maintained steady economic growth in the 1980s.

Let me next give a brief explanation of the introduction of ME in the equipment industry by using the example of the development of expert systems (ES) to control blast furnace operations in the steel industry. The development of ES was advanced by selecting the most capable veteran workers and interviewing them for their job knowledge; their experiences were then used in making operational decisions and incorporated into a computer program. The success of this mission to acquire manufacturing knowledge can be summarized by the following three factors:

1. The operating staff had among its workers expert technicians who had developed their skills by using the factory as a laboratory via team work activities.

2. Those expert technicians also excelled in statistical and analytical approaches to the operational activities because of company policies concerning the career development of personnel on the shop floor such as selecting some to attend steel technology junior colleges—a course that usually leads to promotion for the middle-level technicians.

3. The engineers who interviewed these technicians were well-versed in blast furnace operations and thus were sufficiently equipped to draw out the technicians' knowledge.

In other words, the complex career paths of both the veteran technician and the AI engineer were an important factor here. In particular, steel industry workers take charge of blast furnace operations only after spending nine years from their entrance into the company at physical labor. Then after further experience, some are trained as foremen and work in the staff department; they return to operating the blast furnace and spend at least another ten years at that. From work in the staff department, they gain experience that allows them to develop analytical skills related to operation of the blast furnace. Having within the company this sort of career path for extensively enriching manufacturing knowledge and skill have been the key to success in the development of ES.

Propagation of Manufacturing Knowledge on the Shop Floor

Taiichi Ohno, the father of the Toyota production system, has said: "If Henry Ford were alive today, I think he would be doing the same things we are doing with our Toyota production system."[6] These words evoke the entire postwar period of high economic growth when Japanese firms using an American-style mass production system evolved into a uniquely Japanese system. But, just like the student who ends up surpassing his/her teacher while the latter is simply looking on with arms folded, the Japanese system, as represented by Toyota's production system, brought preeminent competitive power to the nation's manufacturing industries through a series of organizational innovations.

The objectives of Japanese mass-production manufacturers have been standardization and mechanization of operations. After Taylorism and the Ford system were introduced to Japan, the old-fashioned craftsman system involving a master and his students nearly disappeared from the mass-production plants. But the craftsmanlike skills that were standardized and manualized by management have been revitalized and reintroduced at Toyota, and some other companies, in manualized manufacturing operations on the shop floor.

Under the Ford system only the IE specialists had data about work standards and process administration. There were no strategies for reforms of shop floor operations by effective application of such data at the production site. By contrast, Toyota, in making operational improvements for the workers on the shop floor, reformed its policies so that employees could have access to production information in order to make their own improvements. From this process was born the *Kanban* (front line), which is the key to the Toyota production system. The *Kanban* is applied as production information in terminals on the shop floor. Then the flow of things from the prior processes to the later processes is synchronized with the flow of information from back to front so that delivered is only the necessary amount of parts for a work post on the production line at a certain point in time.

This production system makes it possible for high-level information to be handled on the shop floor and to be assimilated in further manufacturing. That has made workers versatile. Unlike the specialization and division of labor that had proceeded under the American system, the Japanese-style production system does not close off workers into fractionalized processes. At Toyota each worker handles several tasks. In this way a worker acquires a wide range of production skills, and the evolution of the Japanese system greatly relies on the worker's active participation in setting improvements on the shop floor. Let me use an example of revisions in standardized operations to touch briefly on how manufacturing knowledge is propagated on the shop floor.

One distinctive feature of standard operations in the Toyota system is that the shop floor foreman freely uses his own experience and knowledge to frame the operations. At other companies the preparation of standard operations is often the responsibility of IE engineers based on their professional assessments of the work. By contrast, in the Toyota system, the technologies and skills to be attained by the workers are provided in a manual of standard practices. That information is also computerized. Standard operations are discussed by the foreman when he shows the workers how to do a job at the appropriate speed, and eventually the worker develops that skill.

However, the standard operations are always undergoing revision. Both the administrators who oversee standard operations and the workers who maintain them in succession are constantly on the lookout for improvements. Any improvements appearing on the shop floor become incorporated into the manual, so the standard operations get revised continually.

9.2 New Challenges

Japanese manufacturing technologies at present have to contend with problems of avoiding rigidity, phase-outs, and system fatigue.

Danger of Rigid Production Systems

At first the Ford system utilized mechanically versatile foremen and workers, treating factories as laboratories as well. Soon rigidity started to appear in the production system because economies of scale became emphasized. The system then was rapidly on its way to becoming estranged from its purpose of making things. In contrast, the *Kanban* system is reputed to be flexible and capable of promptly handling market needs. But, if manufacturers are not careful, the system could become rigid and lose its vitality. The meaning of the words "History repeats itself" should not be taken lightly.

In this regard attention ought to be given to the introduction of information technologies, such as CAD and CAM, on to the shop floor. Factories have steadily raised their levels of automation and seem to be moving in the direction of unmanned operations. The production efficiency attained by automation is generally high. However, the truth is that no matter how well production technology is programmed and even if the computer system is fully utilized, factories have to contend with a new series of problems once they meet with success.

As soon as a system emerges that has worked in specific production applications, the problem of maintaining that system in its present form arises. At this time the following concerns have generally been pointed out: (1) A system starts to become obsolete from the time it is built, and if further it is made an unmanned system, the shop floor will become fixed from that moment on; (2) the larger the scale of the system becomes, the harder it is to update it; and (3) if lopsided increases in production are not anticipated, it is difficult to recoup investments made for necessary maintenance of the system in adjusting processes. The dismantling of a system is unavoidable from the standpoint of profit management.

Further the manner of locking knowledge into the production system of Japan can be problematic. In other words, production system knowledge has become rigid in the United States because of the established automation and dependence on manuals. The manuals have yet to be definitive in their descriptions. The implementation of automation in Japan in the 1970s and 1980s, however, did not change the uniquely Japanese practice of accumulating knowledge by interpositioning people on the shop floor, without depending only on manuals. It has heeded the notion that "nothing remains if automatization takes place."[7] At present, automation has been proceeding in Japan, but there is the danger that creativity in manufacturing may be lost as a result.

Danger of Job Phase-outs

In quantitative terms job phase-outs mean the extinction of technologies and skills. This phenomenon accompanies the retirement of technicians and skilled workers who had been the backbone of high economic growth. Middle-level technicians, who have the brains of a college graduate in production technology and the skilled hands of a craftsman, are starting to leave the workplace in succession. Also the skills of all-round mechanics, who had managed to survive mainly in small- and medium-sized companies, will likely disappear because of a lack of successors.

As important is the phase-out of personnel from the organizational and institutional perspective. As described earlier, dynamic learning in the workplace has shaped Japan's versatile work force. However, there is no guarantee that the shop floor will continue functioning as a place for learning. The introduction of information technologies (e.g., AI expert systems) has begun to standardize the shop floor and reduce the number of workers. Traditionally the shop floor was where skills were formed based on the sharing of experiences through teamwork, but a decline in such learning effects has come with labor-saving moves.

In reducing maintenance personnel in the equipment industry, can one ignore the observation that "in order to make highly reliable products, people who may seem to be playing are necessary on the shop floor?" Moreover, how has the shop floor managed to survive as a place of learning in assembly industries, which have been shifting production overseas to be cost competitive in the wake of the high yen from 1985 on? Hidden fabricating activities like trial samples and the fabrication of dies and molds occur at strategic points of product development. Such fabricating capabilities are indispensable when developing new products. The extinction of fabricating skills is directly connected to declining product development capacities.

Manifestations of "System Fatigue"

Behind the danger of phase-out lies systemic fatigue, which has been appearing within the Japanese corporate structures that have been making changes in manufacturing technologies. There are changes occurring that are separating the manufacturing industries and their shop floors from the science departments of universities.[8] I will rely on a recent survey made by the National Institute of Science and Technology Policy (NISTEP)[9] and outline the outlook for the human resources estranged from the shop floor in Japan. This survey compared the career paths of Japanese and American graduates of engineering departments at the University of Tokyo, Tokyo Institute of Technology, and Massachusetts Institute of Technology.

First, the percentage of the University of Tokyo and Tokyo Institute of Technology graduates who aspire to work connected with the shop floor (formed of the shop floor and production management) underwent a dramatic decline from 12.2 percent in 1960 to 3 percent in 1985—a figure lower than the 3.9 percent for MIT graduates in the same year. Although the sample was very limited, it suggested that the idea that the Japanese aspire more than Americans to the shop floor is a myth.

Next 60 percent (well over half) of the MIT graduates gave the answer that they have the work "they had very much hoped for" to the question, "to what degree did your individual wishes play a part when deciding on the type of job?" But, by contrast, a mere 17 percent of the University of Tokyo and Tokyo Institute of Technology graduates gave the same favorable answer. Even when the subject of the survey was limited just to work "connected with the shop floor," more MIT graduates than those from the University of Tokyo and Tokyo Institute of Technology indicated that their individual wishes were respected when the job type was determined. This means that the percentage of Japanese university graduates who aspire to work related to the shop floor is much lower than the proportion who are actually given such jobs. That gap appears to get buried through the Japanese spirit of loyalty to the company, in which an employee obeys the organization's directions even when the job given was not the preferred one.

Seen from this standpoint, we cannot be optimistic about the Japanese shop floor's prospects for securing competent engineers and technicians as it traditionally did, once employees begin to voice their grievances about the work selected by the company and press for their personal job choices. Now that the traditional respect for diligence is on the decline, as indicated by demand for shorter working hours and the lack of full-time, versatile mechanics, the emphasis is on people-friendly production technology in order to keep human resources moored to the shop floor.

Complexities in the Issues and Policy Tasks

The three problems just discussed are structurally complex and present new challenges to Japanese manufacturing technologies. If these tendencies are allowed to intensify, the dynamic capabilities to adapt manufacturing technologies will become enervated and lead to a decline in international competitiveness. To protect manufacturing technologies from these dangers, investments must be made in maintaining the Japanese-style system's vitality. All manufacturing knowledge needs to be collected and analyzed. Let me put together the managerial/organizational way and the engineering way of dealing with these points.

At the managerial/organizational level the measures conceived are based on the notion that the burden is particularly high for the worker on the traditional shop floor. The objective then is to create resonance between human beings and machinery so that some of the burden can be lifted. From this standpoint, the trend toward the people-friendly conveyor system of Toyota would intersect with the current competitive, breakaway from the conveyor system at Volvo, and that could well be a good compromise in this post-Ford manufacturing era. Attempts are being made to construct an open knowledge-sharing system in manufacturing by utilizing information technologies. A knowledge-sharing system will enable the knowledge and know-how possessed by technicians and skilled workers to be used flexibly on the shop floor, starting from the product development stage.

Taking a Quantum Leap in Manufacturing Technologies

The era for manufacturing is coming to an end in which competitiveness is determined by the superiority of the shop floor technologies. The principles forming a new type of competitiveness have appeared from outside Japan. Let me introduce as an example the pattern of development and commercialization of the RISC processor.[10] This processor is building a new industrial order for computers in the United States.

The RISC theory was originally conceived as part of business research in the mid-1970s at the IBM Watson Research Center. That theory's effectiveness was proved by using prototypes. But IBM had to wait ten years to commercialize RISC machines because the introduction of the technology caused the company's existing product lines and their supplementary software to become completely obsolete.

In contrast to IBM, which was inclined to retain the status quo, research at the University of California at Berkeley and Stanford University served to lead the basic research and development toward the commercialization stage. In bringing the commercialization of RISC to fruition, crucial positions were fulfilled as well by Sun Micro Systems and MIPS, venture companies which were intimately involved with university researchers. Noteworthy here is the fact that at the time both firms specialized in the development and design of RISC processors and commissioned their manufacture externally.

In what way should Japanese manufacturing industries prepare for this new course? Now that trade friction has become a constant issue, the Japanese manufacturing industry should be aggressive about creating distinctive new products. Perhaps the creativity of all the people who operate computer terminals with activities related to products—

such as development, design, manufacturing, maintenance, and recycling—should be pooled to become a source of competitiveness and added value. A collaboration like this could provide the same leverage as "making things" has done on the shop floor. Rearranging the institutional framework through reforms in university studies is another consideration that can take advantage of the latent creativity in Japanese society. This will be a big challenge for the future of the Japanese manufacturing industry.

In closing, let me touch briefly on the manufacturing technologies' possibilities for meeting global environmental challenges over the long term. In the context of global warming, there is the example of curtailing CO_2 emissions. We cannot imagine that a solution will be found in the incremental innovations of existing technologies. A quantum leap in manufacturing technologies is needed to bring about a change that improves on this incremental technological evolution which has shown only limited results because of profit imperatives. The question is how to effect such a quantum leap. Relying on the Yoshikawa's model[11] on technology's evolution, let me suggest a way to make such a leap in progress possible.

First of all, we know that the basic research carried out in laboratories and gradually put to practical application and commercialized has become the precompetitive stage where real competition exists in the rivalry among different companies' products. Then, after technology matures and the founder's profits disappear, the rivalry moves to a postcompetitive stage when the accumulated manufacturing knowledge can be codified into textbook knowledge. In this way a product's engineering will become standardized. Its generic nature becomes the seed of technological innovation of the next generation. Science and technology develop in this spiral as knowledge is systemized in a product's postcompetitive stage. By carrying out further basic research, science and technology continue to evolve from generation to generation, each qualitatively higher than its predecessor.

How can the evolution of Japanese manufacturing technologies be glimpsed from this model? For one thing Japanese science and technology appear to be quite concentrated in the competitive stage which has been the wellspring of Japanese manufacturing technologies' present strength. Further this concentration of R&D in manufacturing has caused university research facilities to be phased out, despite their important mission in the postcompetitive stage. It is clearly the investments in universities that are necessary for a quantum leap to new technology to take precedence over the evolutionary spiral paradigm. On a global scale that would make manufacturing technologies stronger everywhere, and this should be an important policy objective.

Notes

1. Teece, D., Pisano, G., and Shuen, A., *Firm Capabilities, Resources, and the Concept of Strategy*, Center for Research in Management, University of California at Berkeley, 1990 Mimeo.

2. Smith, C. S., *A History of Metallography*, University of Chicago Press, Chicago, 1990.

3. Iida, K., *Nippon Tekko Gijutsushi* (A History of Japanese Steelmaking Technology), Toyo Keizai Shimposha, Tokyo, 1979, pp. 168–69.

4. Fujimoto, T., Technology System ni Kansuru Note: Nichibei Jidosha Sangyo no Hikaku o Chushin toshite (Notes concerning Technology Systems: Centered around a Comparison of the Automobile Industries in the United States and Japan), in Tsuchiya, M., ed., *Gijutsu Kakushin to Keiei Seisaku: Hi-Tech Jidai no Kigyo Kodo o Saguru* (Technological Innovations and Management Strategies: Grouping for Corporate Activities in the Hi-Tech Age), Nihon Keizai Shinbunsha, Tokyo, 1986.

5. Aida, S., *Eco-technology; Kyosei Gijutsu ga Maneku Shinjidai* (A New Age Initiated by Eco-technology; Symbiotic Technology), *Shukan Asahi*, September 11, 1992.

6. Abernathy, W. J., and Clark, K. B., Nippon no Jidosha Kojo Kenbun-Roku: Seisansei, Hinshitukanri, Romukanri o Chushin toshite (Visiting Records of Japanese Automobile Factories: From Productivity, Quality Control and Personnel Management's Viewpoints), *Will*, November 1982.

7. From private correspondence dated October 8, 1992, from Tetsuo Tomiyama (Associate Professor of Engineering Department, University of Tokyo) to Yasunori Baba.

8. The first policy research group of the National Institute of Science and Technology Policy (NISTEP), *Rikokei Gakusei no Shushoku Doko ni tsuite* (Employment Trends among Students in the Sciences and Engineering), NISTEP Report No. 1, 1989; *Daigaku Shingaku Kibosha no Shinro Kettei ni tsuite* (Career Decisions by Youths Intending to Enter University), NISTEP Report No. 12, 1990.

9. The first policy research group of NISTEP, *Kogakubu Sotsugyosei no Shinro to Shokugyo Ishiki ni Kansuru Nichibei Hikaku* (A Comparison of Japan and the United States Concerning the Career and Employment Consciousness of Engineering Department Graduates), NISTEP Report No. 28, 1993.

10. Khazan, J., and Mowery, D., The Commercialization of RISC: Strategies for the Creation of Dominant Design, *Research Policy* (forthcoming).

11. Yoshikawa, H., Technoglobalism (in Japanese), *Japan Society for Mechanical Engineering Bulletin* 94, no. 868.

10 Management of Research and Development

Konomu Matsui

Characteristics that notably differ from the manufacturing industries in Europe and the United States can be recognized in the technological management of research and development activities in Japan. Essentially Japanese research and development are based on technological imports. A way for Japan to raise its own technological concepts has not yet taken sufficient form.

Nevertheless, tremendous effort over many years has worked to overcome Japan's weaknesses in research and development. Recently, as a result, the number of fields in which Japanese industries are among the top level in the world in terms of technological standards and product quality has started to rise. It is now recognized that in some fields Japan does not need to catch up any more. However, from the point of view of the numerous problems in the education system, such as Japanese industries' lateness in developing software in contrast to the progress made in the hardware aspects of technology, we cannot afford to be overconfident. Japan still has not broken away from the catching-up process.

On the one hand, Japan successfully grappled with improvements in the potential for technology of utilizing natural energy, and with the reconstruction of technological systems that consume low units of energy, Japan was able to overcome the oil crises of the 1970s. On the other, when in the 1980s Japan began to reexamine its scientific-technological policies and its management of research and development in order to address the problem of trade and high-tech friction, it found that many of its industries did not make the grade internationally. In striving for balanced exchange, the government, industry, and universities then reviewed Japan's singularity, and they worked to reconstruct R&D management and scientific-technological policies to meet worldwide standards, while bolstering their strengths and compensating for their weakness internationally.

Those efforts are now steadily coming to bear fruit, although there remain several Japanese historic and cultural barriers, such as the nation's late industrialization, its group-oriented culture, the university climate which has not traditionally cooperated with industries, the hierarchy of lifetime employment, the effete military sector, and a lateness in setting up a social foundation for R&D. Additionally Japan's economic recession and global environment problems, among other macro issues, have worked to restrain growth and will likely continue to do so in the near future.

Japanese breakthrough toward international standards, and the recent framework for R&D that has started to produce results, are largely the work of the Japanese Exploratory Research for Advanced Technology (ERATO) program.

Although there is yet no nationwide system in Japan for the support of individual creativity in technology, the recent establishment of Tsukuba Research City and the Kansai Cultural Scholarship and Research Town has engaged the attention of several local governments. It has also started an interest in reforming educational institutions.

Up to now money laid out for corporate growth was conceived of as the prerequisite investment in equipment and not in research and development. However, this practice has been superseded in the processing industries by R&D investments which now surpass the outlays for new equipment. The guiding principle of future Japanese research and development must shift from notions of rivalry consisting in winners and losers within and among companies to a symbiosis that also encompasses other countries so that there is shared prosperity for all.

10.1 Problems in the Catching-up Process

Research Personnel and Barriers in Industrial Ownership

During World War II Japan lost about 67 percent of its GNP, and 33 trillion yen's worth of assets corresponding to around 14 percent of its national wealth (according to auditing by the Nomura Research Institute). Japan had no choice during its reconstruction but to strengthen its technological base and establish an open market system in order to overcome such troubles. However, many young educated Japanese men who had research talent were killed during the war or else left research institutions because of the difficulty of making a living in postwar Japan. Thus there were delays in arranging a research system, on which work could only proceed at a snail's pace.

A fatal blow was struck when, under a policy of the Allied Forces occupying Japan, the victorious countries' rights of ownership to industrial property rights were extended unconditionally for a ten-year period. To hasten the fortification of technological power, Japan was forced to utilize industrial property rights then owned by foreign countries (the victorious nations).

Up against such walls, Japan's R&D workers abandoned their practical application style (or discovery-driven style) that relied on internally developed discoveries and inventions and adopted an import- driven technological style instead. In other words, Japan selectively introduced foreign technology that could be adapted to its pressing market needs. Thus was born the Japanese market-driven style of productivity.

This practice has also been the reason why the companies carrying out research and development directly linked to market needs shoulder over 80 percent of R&D expenditures in Japan, while universities and national research laboratories bear less than 20 percent of the remaining costs, contributing more or less to the prerequisite R&D. This ratio is dramatically different from that in other advanced industrialized nations.

Discovery-Driven Style versus Market-Driven Style: "Japanity"

Since unlike discovery-driven productivity, market-driven productivity depends on technological innovations developed externally, it is a free-rider style of operation where science is concerned. In 1976 the National Science Foundation (NSF) of the United States pointed out (NSF-SU-76-1) that "While the United States has made 65 percent of contributions to precedent-setting breakthroughs, Japanese contributions amount to only 2 percent. Japan's display of innovation has been extremely low in comparisons of revolutionary technology that has given rise to innovations in every country." Considering the essentially market-driven course of Japan, that is a natural conclusion.

The results of that survey stimulated discussion in Japan on the market-driven style compared with the discovery-driven style. In the next decade, during the second Japan-Britain High-Tech Forum held in 1987, discussions were held on the effectiveness of Japan's market-driven style of research and development, dubbed "Japanity," which had proved to have strengthened Japanese companies' international competitiveness. From about that time the Japanese position of inferiority in discovery-driven activity was gradually being replaced by the confidence of its industries in their market-driven approach.

According to Tsuneo Nakahara, vice chairman of Sumitomo Electric Industries, who was one of the Japanese attending the conference, the debate grew lively after a researcher with a British civilian company pointed out that, "Serendipity, freedom, and Japanity will be necessary to connect research with success in business enterprises." Japanity was the term coined by the speaker to evaluate Japanese abilities and characteristics. It means that "if all the needed materials are available, the Japanese have a high capacity for assembling them into something." In other words, the British have originality but are weak in coming up with industrial applications, while the Japanese are the exact opposite of that. Therefore the gist of the discussion was that things might work out quite well if Japan and Britain joined forces.

People involved in research and development in Japan used to have a strong inferiority complex. But partly because of such debates, interest in comparative analyses of the discovery-driven style of the West and the Japanese market-driven style bonded.

Efficiency of the Catching-up Process

The Japanese style of research and development, which tends to be somewhat too much affected by market considerations, came unavoidably from postwar circumstances such as the shortage of personnel and restrictions on industrial property rights. Yet it has ended up being a strikingly positive development.

To understand the full economic effect of such research and development, we ought to measure the degree to which technological progress (improvements in productivity) has contributed to Japan's gross national product. Therefore let us look at how Japanese R&D efficiency has fluctuated according to data calculated by the Japan Development Bank.

Technology is a factor equivalent in importance to labor and capital in a highly developed industrial society. Research and development, involving considerable investments of human and material resources, are the means for creating new technology. Japanese technology had actively relied on technological imports from overseas during its pe-

Table 10.1
Fluctuations in the rate of technological progress (%)

	Manufacturing industries	Materials type	Processing assembly type
Era of high economic growth (1966–70)	7.5	8.7	7.9
Era of adjustment (1971–75)	2.3	3.6	4.5
Recent times (1978–82)	4.5	3.6	7.1

Source: Japan Development Bank, *R&D no Keizaigaku* (The Economics of R&D), 1985.
Note: Because of the influence of other industries, the measurements in the manufacturing sector is not always distributed between the materials type and the processing assembly type.

riod of high economic growth (1961–1971). The rate of technological progress in Japan around this time was 7.5 percent (see table 10.1), and it signifies the productivity of all factors, which should come to more than the total amount invested in production elements like labor and capital.

Since research and development during that period was basically mass production of technological imports, it was easy for the Japanese to manifest the Japanity in which they excelled. In addition nobody had any doubts about that management style back then. During that period the rate of technological progress was 8.7 percent for the materials type of industries and 7.9 percent for the assembly-processing type of industries. So an almost balanced level of technological progress was maintained among all industries.

Afterward, advancements were made in catching up with the United States and Europe. Then partly because of the oil crisis, Japan entered an era of economic adjustment from 1971 to 1975. In other words, there was a temporary pause in developing mass-production technology by such means as superenlarging and automating production equipment promoted earlier during the period of high economic growth. Moreover, partly in reaction to criticism that Japan's market-driven style was taking a free ride on technology, the foci of research themes also moved to matters not directly serving a quantitative expansion of production such as the environment, security, and conserving resources and energy. As a result the rate of technological progress during the adjustment period dropped to 2.3 percent for the entire manufacturing industry. Furthermore a gap was clearly formed between the rate of

3.6 percent for the materials type of industries and the 4.5 percent for the assembly-processing type of industries.

While, as mentioned earlier, this was a time for self-reflection over the management style of Japanese R&D, it was simultaneously the era when catching-up (relying on technological imports) was coming to an end.

In late 1970s the Japanese economy, seeking a new growth process, began a positive effort to transform basic research and develop some fundamental technology. From 1978 to 1982 such changes could be seen in the technological progress of assembly-processing type of industries, since they could easily deal with new business ideas in their overseas markets and the like; its rate of technological progress rose to 7.1 percent, which was respectably close to the 7.9 percent it had during the period of high economic growth.

By contrast, the rate for the materials type of industry stayed at 3.6 percent, which was a substantial decline over the 8.6 percent known during the period of high economic growth. That was because efforts to give high added value to the new materials and products that the R&D departments of materials-type industries were energetically grappling with did not work in such a way that their effects could be gauged as a rise in the rate of technological progress.

10.2 Rediscovery of the Market-Driven Style of Management

Problems Underlying "Japanity"

Aware that Japanese research and development's catching up process had ended, various surveys came to be carried out from the first half of the 1980s. At the start of the 1980s, the Institute of Industrial Technology of the Ministry of International Trade and Industry (MITI) began an investigation on the actual level of Japanese industrial technology. Then research commissioned by the Institute of Industrial Technology, the Japan Techno-Economics Society (JATES) carried out a detailed international comparison of the technological standards of Japan. The JATES report pointed out that the Japanese level had caught up in a majority of forty-three technological fields. This international comparison triggered other research surveys.

One analysis receiving much attention was conducted by the Institute for Future Technology, and it brought in the concept of the age (youth) of technology. The Institute claimed that "The true state of research and development in this country probably cannot be grasped just by comparing the technological level of Japan, which has depended on imported technology, with the technological standards of the discovery-driven West, where a vast stockpile of prerequisite technological knowledge exists." It provided a provocative conceit for the stages of technological development, that technological standards could be viewed in terms of youth and old age involving birth, growth, maturation, and decay (see figures 10.1 and 10.2).

As figure 10.1 indicates, much of high technology utilizes older equipment that is close to the maturation level. Also embodied in young technology can be a number of low-standard items. The comparison of technological development standards shown in figure 10.2 confirms this tendency. These facts suggest blind spots in Japan's technological potential and consequently the necessity for strengthening promising new technological fields.

This analysis should make us see that while the Japanity cited at the Japan–Britain Forum focuses on the strength of industrial technology, it also brings out weaknesses that we simply cannot feel easy about. Research and development engineers generally prefer to keep weaknesses from being exposed and rather strive to improve the development of young fields of technology.

Rediscovery Opportunities

The fact that close management of market-driven research and development can fortify a company's international competitiveness cannot be ignored. The impetus for rediscovering that fact was the considerable interest shown by various other countries in Japanese-style management of research and development.

One such case was the survey conducted by John Irvine and his colleagues—a report evaluating research at national research centers in Japan affiliated with either MITI or the Science and Technology Agency. Irvine and his group carried out surveys for five weeks in 1987 and published their findings in 1988 in a report entitled *Evaluating Applied Research—Lessons from Japan.*

This survey was made at the request from the British Department of Commerce and Industry. Its conclusion was that "applied research in Japan has had a good reputation in the downstream of the R&D process, and there have been some outstanding results. However, many problems exist in the methods of evaluating the upstream, and

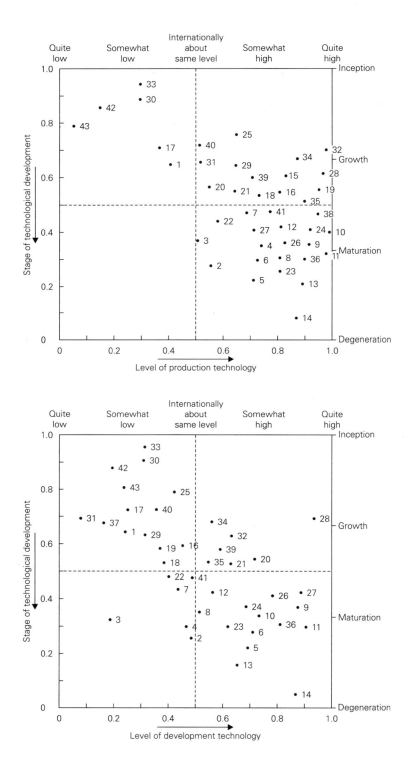

1. Apparel
2. Urea fertilizers
3. Synthetics dyes for use in polyester fibers
4. Polychlorobiphenyl (PCB)
5. Long polyester fibers
6. Surface active agents for use in the fiber industry
7. Antibiotics, cancer-inhibiting drugs
8. Colored paper
9. Cement
10. Ceramics for use as electronic industry parts
11. Ordinary steel
12. Special steel
13. Ordinary aluminum metal
14. 9.5 mm. co-axial cables
15. Optic fibers (graded form)
16. Powdered forged metal
17. Gas turbines for generating electricity
18. Construction machinery
19. Machining centers
20. POY yarn-spinning machinery for use with polyester fibers
21. Air jet looms
22. Injection plactic-molding machinery for heated multi-use plastics
23. Wet-style desulfurization from exhaust equipment
24. PPC copiers
25. Assembled robots for industrial use
26. 275–500 kv ultra-high voltage transformer
27. 200–300 liter electric refrigerators/freezers
28. 1/2 inch VTRs for household use
29. Multi-use super computers
30. Digital radiography
31. Spectrum analyzers (scanner-type)
32. IC memory
33. Fuel cells
34. Semiconducter lasers
35. 1800–2500cc. automobiles costing $7,000 to $8,000
36. General vessels
37. Civilian aircraft
38. LSI probers
39. Theodolite
40. Liquid chromatography
41. Light water reactor
42. Communications satellites
43. 30 Kilo-step class package software

Figure 10.1
Stages of growth and decline of production technology. Note that the stage of technological degeneration is indexed at 0 and that the stage of its introduction at 1. Source: "Konomu Matsui, Nihon no Gijutsu Kaihatsu Sokushin Joken no Bunseki" (An Analysis of the Conditions for the Promotion of Japan's Technological Development), *Kogyo Gijutsu* (Industrial Technology), October 1983.

Figure 10.2
Comparison of the stages of growth and decline of production technology with standard technological development. Note that the stage of technological degeneration is indexed at 0 and that the stage of its introduction at 1. Source: "Konomu Matsui, Nihon no Gijutsu Kaihatsu Sokushin Joken no Bunseki" (An Analysis of the Conditions for the Promotion of Japan's Technological Development), *Kogyo Gijutsu* (Industrial Technology), October 1983.

the judgment know-how is low, too. Reforms in the evaluation methods have just begun, as well."

Various rediscoveries were started in succession from the fields of policy science and science of management at national research centers in Japan as if to respond to the matters pointed out in this report. First of all, the Scientific and Technical Commission (chaired by the prime minister) established the Research Evaluation Policy Formulation Commission (headed by Jiro Kondo, chairman of the Japan Academic Council) and presented guidelines for desirable research evaluations.

Another incentive came when the American National Science Foundation (NSF) published in 1988 *The Japanese Exploratory Research for Advanced Technology* (ERATO) *Program*—a report on the present state of exploratory research in Japan's advanced technology. This report surveyed the efforts to advance innovation by ERATO, an open national program of an international nature promoted by the Japanese government. The NSF survey evaluated Japanese technology and introduced ERATO in the following way: "Begun in 1988, ERATO not only promotes high-tech creation and aims to bring academic scientific research to a high level for the future, but it can also be expected to seek out a better system for basic research."

The NSF report further pointed out that, "This ERATO program is of a nature that can definitely be called a social experiment in Japan, and it fulfills an important role in strengthening basic research for the sake of scientific discovery. . . . ERATO is useful for filling the gap between the basic research carried out at Japanese universities and the applied research conducted by industry." The NSF report additionally praised the ERATO as a program for its appealing characteristics to both the university and industry. The NSF report also observed that, "Under the ERATO Program, the annual budgets and a number of projects have continued steady growth (see figure 10.3). But despite the fact that they are open to foreign researchers, too, there are still few non-Japanese participants. Therefore, we hope that consideration will be given toward seeing that more non-Japanese can participate." (See table 10.2.)

Such interest by other countries in Japan's research and development caused the Japanese to realize the power of its market-driven innovations, which clearly was posing a threat to the nations where R&D had been conducted in a discovery-driven style. This rediscovery of its strength raised the desire of the Japanese to take up the challenge of making their own technological discoveries.

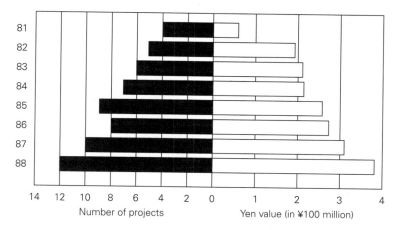

Figure 10.3
ERATO's Growth: Fluctuations in the annual budget and the number of projects. Source: Data from U.S. government's JTECH (Japanese Technology Evaluation Program) and from the Japanese discussion group's report, *The Japanese Exploratory Research for Advanced Technology (ERATO) Program,* 1988.

Table 10.2
Researchers in the ERATO program (as of March 31, 1988)

Project	From industry	Neutral	Foreign	Other	Total	(Technicians)
Hayaishi	3	12	1	2	18	(6)
Horikoshi	10	10	2	0	22	(6)
Yoshida	10	2	1	0	13	(1)
Kuroda	13	2	3	1	19	(1)
Goto	7	4	1	0	12	(1)
Hotani	4	6	2	0	12	(1)
Inaba	5	5	1	0	11	(3)
Nishizawa	2	0	0	3	5	(3)
Furusawa	2	1	1	0	4	(1)
Kunitake	9	1	1	0	11	(0)
Total	65	43	13	6	127	(23)

Source: Compiled from the U.S. government's JTECH (Japanese Technology Evaluation Program) and from the Japanese discussion group's report, the *Japanese Exploratory Research for Advanced Technology (ERATO) Program,* 1988.
Note: 51.2% from industry; 18.1% technicians.

10.3 Challenge to a Discovery-Driven Leadership

Dealing with Lack of Experience and Know-how

The challenge to discovery-driven productivity, where Japanese R&D management lacks experience and know-how, is just beginning to be taken up primarily at national research centers and universities.

Even in Japan there was once a period when the management of market-driven R&D was still experimental and overseen by the R&D activities office of the Institute of Physical and Chemical Research, the largest national research center prior to World War II; considerable results were produced then too. Among the noteworthy achievements were the discovery of vitamins (by Umetaro Suzuki), the discovery of monosodium glutamate (by Kikunae Ikeda), the invention of KS steel (by Kotaro Honda), the origination of the meson theory (by Hideki Yukawa), and the origination of the renormalization of the atomic nucleus theory (by Shin-ichiro Tomonaga); see table 10.3. However, its management expertise, which created such an outstanding research record, was barely transmitted outside the Institute's walls, and within the Institute itself there may have been knowledge not adequately shared.

Since 1992 the Institute of Physical and Chemical Research has been carrying out thorough reviews of its research evaluation system. Thus, in addition to its lengthy research reviews and special research hearings, there have newly been enacted Institute reviews too. Since aspects of the Institute's mission and vision, such as operation policies, the establishment of research fields, and the allotment of resources, are the most important to the management of discovery-driven style research, the idea behind the Institute reviews is that all of its review activities are to be checked by fifteen reviewers (half of them foreigners) every two years (see figure 10.4).

These reforms at the Institute of Physical and Chemical Research did not end at just one national research center; they became the model for structuring research and development at companies and universities in order to ease in a discovery-driven management style. For example, at the end of the 1980s, the University of Tokyo established the Research Center for Advanced Sciences and Technology (RCAST) to function as a center for research in advanced basic technology in order to bring the Center of Excellence (COE)[1] to fruition. Each successive director of RCAST is elected based ability to conduct COE. When we interviewed people at the RCAST, they all said that they were selected to work there because their standards of evaluation differed from those of the director. The strong sense of mission that "the reform of the University of Tokyo will begin from RCAST" seems to have moved things in that direction.

In the meantime major reforms have begun at national research centers under MITI's umbrella. In the 1990s the nine existing research centers were reorganized into eight. Traditionally intersecting or combined spheres of study were separated and made into the independent areas at the Affiliated Industrial Technology Spheres Research Center (see figure 10.5). The first director of this Center was the University of Tokyo Professor Emeritus Takahiro Okoshi, who had earlier served as the first director of RCAST. It would seem that strict evaluations about who is most suitable for bringing the new mission into fruition went into operation here too.

At the Institute of Industrial Technology an atom technology research group was organized in order to provide a partnership with the atom technology research group at the newly established Affiliated Industrial Technology Spheres Research Center and the research center (Angstrom Technological Research Institute) of a technological study group organized by private corporations. Scientists from both within and outside universities as well as from other research centers in Japan and abroad participate in the activities of the Institute of Industrial Technology. In addition new strategic cooperation is taking place among industry, the government, and academe (see figure 10.6).

Adjustments in Private Industry

Measures for dealing with discovery-driven productivity in private industry were adopted at an earlier time than at universities and national research centers. Yet their external influence was hardly great. Another effort in establishing research centers occurred among private companies in the 1980s (see figure 10.7). The first effort saw the new construction of mostly central research centers at corporations. But the second effort has maintained a succession of new construction of basic research centers. Hitachi and NEC have provided leadership in this respect.

Hitachi took 1 percent of total R&D expenses of the entire company as the standard amount to be allotted for studies at its basic research and applied principles center, which is open to the general public for reviewing the results of research. Hitachi was the first private company in Japan to set up rules for steadily providing research expenses to a

Table 10.3
Achievements of the Institute of Physical and Chemical Research (RIKEN)

Year	Achievements in research	Order of cultural merit	Japan academy prize
1920	Vitamins (Suzuki) Monosodium glutamate (Ikeda) KS steel (Honda) Synthetic sake (Suzuki) Alumito (Miyata)		Torahiko Terada, Toshiyuki Natsushima Shoji Nishikawa, Toshio Takase Umetaro Suzuki, Katsumi Takahashi Bunsuke Suzuki
1930	Metal whittling theory (Okoshi) Neutron electronic effect (Kikuchi) Estimation of meson weight (Nishina) Revolving metamers of chemical combinations (Mizushima)		Jiro Tsuji Sankichi Takei Miichiro Mizushima, Teruhiro Ogata
1940	Theory of mesons (Yukawa) Low-pressure enzyme manufacturing method (Oyama) Renormalization of the atom theory (Tomonaga)	Hantaro Nagaoka Kotaro Honda Umetaro Suzuki	Teijiro Yabuda, Isamu Nishida Muyuji Kotake, Rian Iimori Kentaro Kimura Shoichi Mashima Ranzaburo Taguchi Shin-ichiro Tomonaga Jun Okoshi Shinji Fukui
1950	Ferrite magnet (Takei)	Yoshio Nishina Toshiyuki Natsushima Shoji Nishikawa Masashi Kikuchi Shin-ichiro Tomonaga	
1960	Gibberellin (Yabuda) Polyoxygen (S. Suzuki) Turbo molecular pump (Sawada)	Miichiro Mizushima Teijiro Yabuda Isamu Nishida	Kazuo Nakahara, Fumiko Fukuoka Hiroshi Kubota Juzo Udaka Shingo Mitsui Saburo Suzuki Ryukichi Hashiguchi

Row grouping labels (left margin):
- Institute of Physical and Chemical Research (first) — 1920–1940
- Science Research Institute — 1950–1960

Institute of Physical and Chemical Research (current)			
1970	Thin board, deep extraction theory (Fukui)	Kin-ichiro Sakaguchi Shoji Seto	Saburo Tamura Saburo Nagakura
1980	Electron beam exposure equipment (Goto) Favorable alkaline microorganisms (Horikoshi)		Koichi Shimoda Masanao matsui
1990	X-ray laser (Aoyagi, Hara)	Saburo Nagakura	Tomoashi Mitsuoka

Source: Toshio Sakuda (current vice chairman of the Institute of Physical and Chemical Research), Riken no Hyoka Seido Ni Tsuite (About the Institute's Evaluation System). Data adapted from a speech presented before the Evaluation Work Group at the meeting of the Planning Research and Technology Society, 1992.

(1) Research lab review
- Every 7 years after the chief researchers arrive at their posts
- Reviewers: 4 (in most cases, including a company researcher)
- Time:

Morning:	1 hr, 30 min	Presentation by a chief researcher
	40 min	Questions (open)
Afternoon:	1 hr	Debates (closed)
	2 hr	Visits to research labs

- Reports from reviewers (within 1 month)—study objective drawn up
  Director in charge of research relates study objective to the appropriate chief researcher
  Study objective is reported at a board of directors meeting

(2) Special research hearings
- Project plans are drawn up and presented every year regardless of whether they are for new or continuing work
- Meeting of chief researchers   Hearings by the budget committee for the task at hand (attended also by members of the board of directors)
  Presentations: 20 min   Questions: 10 min
- Votes by ballot after discussion by the budget committee on the task at hand
- The board of directors considers the results as well as managerial policies for the Institute, which will be reflected in the budget application

(3) Institute Review (since 1933)
- Purpose: To hear the reviewers' opinions on operational policies for the research center, the fields concerned, the allotment of research funds, etc.
- Reviewers: A total of 15 people, with three each from the fields of physics, chemistry, biology, life science, and engineering. Foreigners comprise about half of the reviewers. Everyone's term as a reviewer is six years.
- Materials: Materials on the objective of the research center, its budget decision process, its selection of personnel, operational policies, etc., are formulated and sent out in advance.
- Review: Conducted for 3 to 4 days (in April) every 2 years and completely in English.

1st day:	Morning—report by the chairman of the board.
2nd day:	Afternoon—study tour (including the latter half of the afternoon of 1st day). Reports on the study objective by the chief researchers according to the field of specialization. Questions and observational tours of research labs. Night—discussions among the reviewers only
3rd day:	Morning—discussions among the reviewers only. Afternoon—reviewers release the results.

- Report: Reports are accepted from each reviewer and the chairman.
  The board of directors holds discussions reflecting all ex post facto operational policies.

Figure 10.4
Research evaluation system by the Institute of Physical and Chemical Research. Source: Toshio Sakuda (current vice chairman of the Institute of Physical and Chemical Research), *Riken no Hyoka Seido ni Tsuite* (About the Institute's Evaluation System) (Adapted version of data given by the Evaluation Work Group at the meeting of Planning Research and Technology Society), 1992.

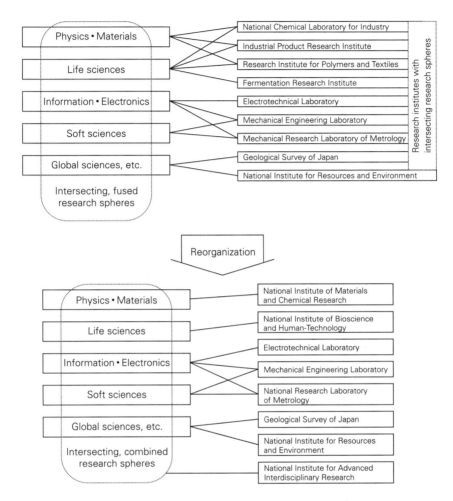

Figure 10.5
Scheme for the reorganization of research centers affiliated with the Institute of Industrial Technology. Source: Eiichi Maruyama (director of the Atom Technology Research Center), Proc. Symposium Commemorating the Tenth Anniversary of the Japan Interdisciplinary Conference's Founding, *Nijuseiki no Kagaku Gijutsu no Kozai to Nijuisseiki e no Tenbo—San-kan-gaku no Atarashii Paradigm o Motomete* (The Merits and Demerits of Twentieth-Century Science and Technology and the Outlook for the Twenty-first Century—Seeking a New Paradigm for Industry, the Government, and Academe), 1993.

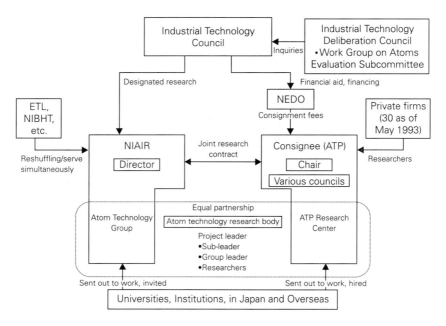

Figure 10.6
Interactions among universities and institutions in Japan and overseas. ATP: Angstrom Technology Partnership; NIAIR: National Institute for Advanced Interdisciplinary Research; NEDO: New Energy and Industrial Technology Development Organization; ETL: Electrotechnical Laboratory; NIBHT: National Institute of Bioscience and Human-Technology. Source: Maruyama, Eiichi (director of the Atom Technology Research Center), Proc. Symposium Commemorating the Tenth Anniversary of the Japan Interdisciplinary Conference's Founding, *Nijuseiki no Kagaku Gijutsu no Kozai to Nijuisseiki e no Tenbo— San-kan-gaku no Atarashii Paradigm o Motomete* (The Merits and Demerits of Twentieth-Century Science and Technology and the Outlook for the Twenty-first Century— Seeking a New Paradigm for Industry, the Government, and Academe), 1993.

basic research center and also to establish a completely open system for the results of its research. Moreover Hitachi's rule of allotting 1 percent of the total R&D expenses to basic research in the corporation became the guiding principle for other companies' attempts to grapple with basic research.

In the meantime, almost at the same time as Hitachi, NEC began operating a similar basic research center in the United States. Attention was also given to the fact that the German company Siemens had already established its basic research center near NEC's center some years earlier.

Sharp experimented with the challenge of discovery-driven management by taking an approach different from Hitachi's and NEC's. Sharp's move was aimed at changing the generations in R&D manage-

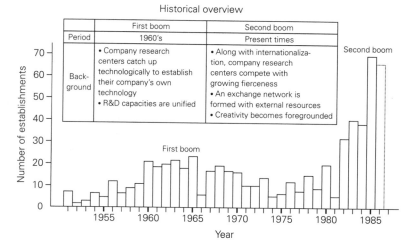

Figure 10.7
Historical pattern of growth of company research centers. Source: Survey by the Industrial Technology Council (March 1987).

ment (see figure 10.8). Namely the company reconsidered its R&D activities by means of a rice crop metaphor. It saw the first generation of management as "planting rice seed" (merchandization) and the second generation as "tending the seedbeds" (goal-oriented basic research), and then the third generation as "producing new types of seeds" (fundamental research). From around the mid-1980s the shift in emphasis to the second generation began, and in the early 1990s prerequisite experimentation with the third generation's management has started.

While private firms in Japan are just beginning to take up the challenge of the discovery-driven style, none has gone beyond the realm of experimentation. It would be desirable for these companies to present their plans of the logic, methods, and system of management that they anticipate will reduce the weaknesses of the discovery-driven style and maintain the strengths of the market-driven style. Establishing a balance between the two is a formidable managerial task that could boost Japan's international competitiveness.

10.4 New Directions in Research and Development Management

In what direction might problems be solved by companies that have conflicting values and management styles? Let us consider this

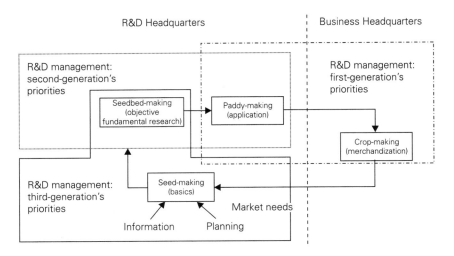

Figure 10.8
Generational changes in priorities managing R&D at Sharp. Source: Konomu Matsui,
Sharp no Kenkyu Kaihatsu Senryaku (Sharp's Research and Development Strategy),
Diamondo Harvard Business, 8, no. 2 (March 1983).

question by viewing, as in figure 10.9, the flow of research and development as upstream and distribution and marketing as downstream
tasks. The management of the market-driven style, in which Japan is
strong, emphasizes the downstream, whereas the management of the
discovery-driven style, such as that of the United States and Europe,
emphasizes the upstream.

At present in Japan there is a strong preference for the upstream
discovery-driven type over the market-driven style. By contrast, the
tendency is toward the downstream in the West. This means that both
sides can take advantage of each other's strengths and offset their
weaknesses. However, while it is comparatively simple to enhance
one's strengths, it is extremely difficult to compensate for defects. In
other words, it is not easy for either Japan or the West to meet with
much success. So what can be done?

Let us begin by comparing the guiding principles of the two. The
guiding principle in the United States and Europe can be expressed by
the key words "not invented here" (NIH). The NIH view values
technology only if its origin is its own and does not want to copy
something originating from elsewhere.

By contrast, the guiding Japanese principle can be indicated with the
key words "reform oriented." This view engenders strong interna-

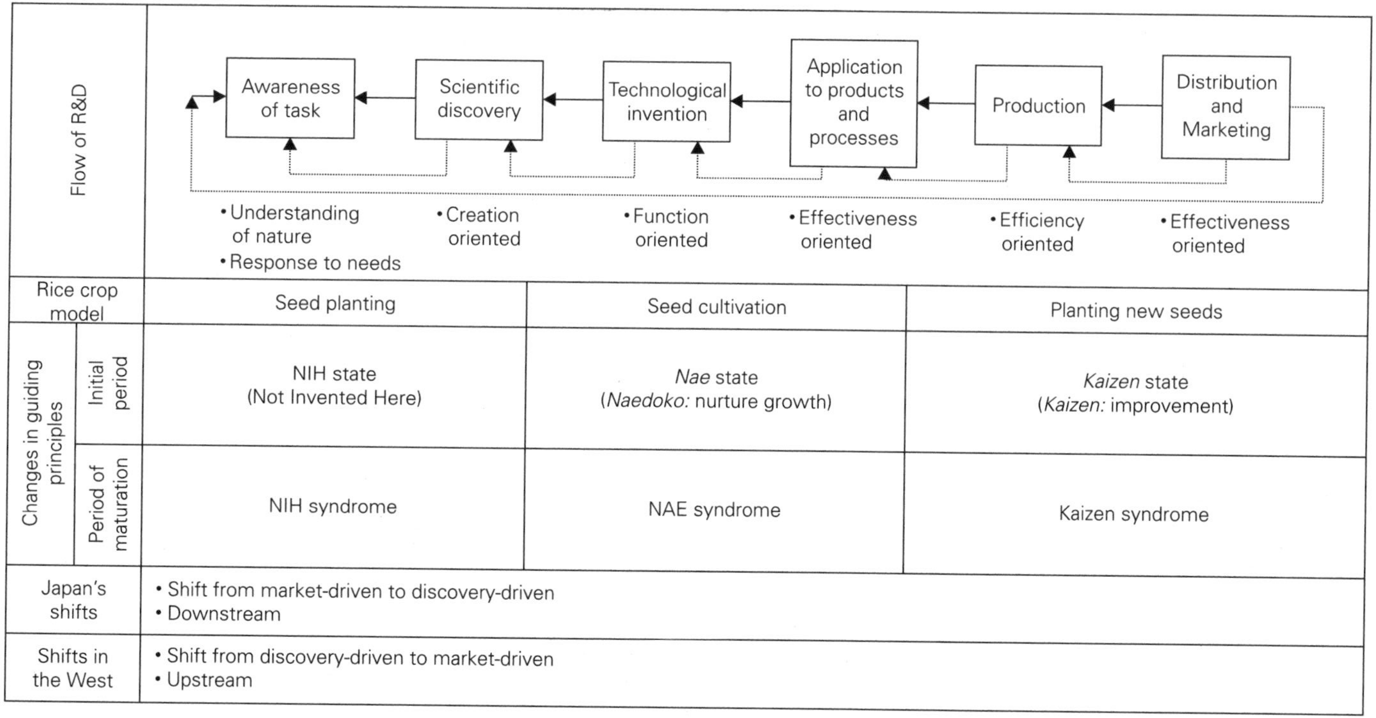

Figure 10.9
Schematic of integrated R&D Management. Source: Konomu Matsui, Kenkyusha no Kokusaika to Jinji Seido (The Internationalization of Researchers and Personnel Systems), Research and Development Management Forum '90 (Kenkyu Kaihatsu Management Forum '90), Text, Nihon Keizai Shimbun, Inc., November 20, 1990.

	Stage 1 Localization overseas of marketing capacities • expand exports to stimulate the market
Globalization within Japan	**Stage 2** Localization overseas of production capacities • set up a production system integral with the market
	Stage 3 Localization overseas of R&D capacities • strengthen technological support for overseas production, product development integral with the market, technological development, the research system, etc.
Globalization outside Japan	**Stage 4** Reconstruction of a management style based on local standards • establish corporate roots locally with natives included in management
	Stage 5 Management innovations for making the company in Japan suitable for globalization • practice true internationalization

Figure 10.10
Projected development stages in managing globalization. Source: Konomu Matsui, *Kenkyusha no Kokusaika to Jinji Seido* (The Internationalization of Researchers and Personnel Systems), Research and Development Management Forum '90 (Kenkyu Kaihatsu Management Forum '90) text, Nihon Keizai Shimbun, Inc., November 20, 1990.

tional competitiveness in that it means taking technology whose origin lies elsewhere and continually transforming it. The NIH and the reform views are separated considerably conceptually and likewise by managerial style. It is not easy for either to shift to the other direction. Moreover the NIH view has become obsessive, and its arrogance has been manifest in refusals to show an interest in other technological proposals. It has taken the form of an NIH syndrome.

However, obsession with reform can also corrupt, and this is only one of the symptoms. Finding a cure for both syndromes and reconfiguring them to a balanced state is necessary for shifts in management styles to occur.

Let us recall the case of Sharp where attention is given to the next generation of management. This is management that cultivates ideas. Let us tentatively call that concern for guiding growth the *nae* (nurturing) principle. To shift the guiding principle from the NIH to the nurturing kind is far easier than switching to the reform view. The nurturing view is concerned with developing the seeds of new technology and making connected discoveries. It is much easier for the reform view to switch to nurturing than for it to shift to NIH. Japanese firms and Western firms could come to a mutual understanding of one another's guiding principles and management styles in cooperative or joint research in related areas.

Efforts in Japan to strengthen R&D capacities by a management shift could include international exchange, cooperation, and joint work in overseas localities. There is much promise also in participating in open research programs based on principles such as those of the Japanese ERATO. (See figure 10.10.)

10.5 Strategic Cooperation among Industry, Academe, and Government

Partnerships Overseas

Under the present state of Japanese globalization, the activity of research and development has not been generally shifted abroad, nor has there been effort to promote international exchanges, cooperation, and joint work. Alternatively we can turn to discovery-driven universities and promote their cooperation with market-driven companies.

Professor Takeru Masumoto of Tohoku University (and director of the Metallic Materials Research Center), who has served as group leader of the Science and Technology Agency's ERATO program, drew on his experience in running international joint research teams from universities and corporations to build a new system of cooperation among industry, academe, and the government. He has thus set up a system with great merits for both the university and industry. This system, as shown in figure 10.11, has a research structure that gives practical application to patents held by the university for amorphous lightweight alloys. Professor Masumoto's method has promoted joint research by a complex number of corporate study teams with different purposes that use the university research labs as a base of operations.

From the standpoint of the university, this arrangement provides a practical focus for every major study area. Universities also benefit from new research themes arising out of the bottlenecks encountered by companies.

Since joint research teams are organized according to purpose, different corporations can work side by side and forget their competitiveness, and companies and the university can moreover carry out joint research with objectives much closer to their own. Since, as is often the case in research, there can be a shortage of suitable personnel at a

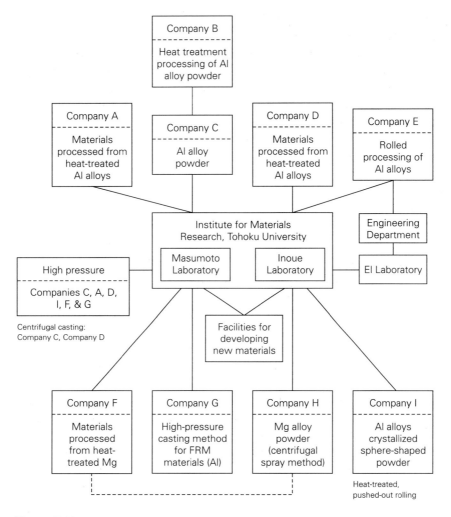

Figure 10.11
Organization of research on amorphous lightweight alloys. Source: Compiled in 1992 from lecture notes by Prof. Ken-ichi Masumoto (director of the Institute of Materials Research, Tohoku University) for the Japan Productivity Center's Technological Management Forum.

company, university faculty and graduate students can provide research assistance, and thus make it simple to secure the necessary
research data.

Conditions for the Success of Strategic Cooperation among Industry, Academe, and the Government

At Tohoku University and other universities several points in common
have been observed in the new strategic cooperation among industry,
academe, and the government. The following three conditions for
success are based on interview surveys taken at these institutions.

The first condition for success is that the stakeholders share the
concept of strategic cooperation. That strategic cooperation is generally
accomplished by several companies cooperating, without losing their
uniqueness, on short-term high-risk projects that they could not undertake alone. The contributions of the partner may not be uniform,
yet it is important for all partners to recognize the essential purpose
of their collaboration.

The second condition is that a virtual corporation be formed. The
term "virtual" is used as in the virtual reality of film technology, in the
sense of an imaginary credible reality. The partners in a relationship
of strategic cooperation create an imaginary company and likewise a
management team that resembles that of a corporation.

The third condition calls for the united effort to be nonbinding.
Although the participation of partners may be based on limited goals,
and mutual links among them make for a united body, everyone, in
principle, is free to leave.

For example, under condition two, several firms could choose to
form a temporary network by which they can accommodate certain
technology and merchandise licensing, and develop a new market for
new products.

Under condition three, several companies with shared goals could
undertake a relationship of mutual learning by which they could pick
up in areas where they lack expertise while mutually supporting
managerial resources. Withdrawal from such a relationship is free but
joining it is restricted. There are many cases of success in Japan of
virtual corporations. Evidence of success among corporations of nonbinding ties can be seen in the Tohoku University example mentioned

earlier in which the initiative for collaboration came from the university.

According to a survey by the Chogin Research Center, there have been a number of instances of strategic cooperation among industry, academe, and the government in the semiconductor field that have met with failure. In general, these seem to be cases where companies made a mistake in selecting a partner of a different corporate climate, cases where the partner company carried out a major strategic switchover, cases where the partners were at cross-purposes with each other, and cases where the partners began vying in the same market.

10.6 Conclusion

Japan's prudent transformation from a management style formed while it was catching up in research and development has been widely respected. There has yet to be explored a way of broadening cooperation among industry, academe, and government to exchanges and sharing among the R&D organizations worldwide that hold different values and guiding principles, such as with similar institutions in the United States. Japan's experiments suggest mutually beneficial growth in each country's research and development. Furthermore the Japan Productivity Center and the Japan Techno-Economics Society have continually held international forums with the Industrial Research Institute (IRI) of the United States on these points and have exchanged management expertise with U.S. businesses.

At the fourth R&D Executive Forum held between the Japan Productivity Headquarters and IRI in September 1993, debates and exchanges of information were carried out on improving R&D management productivity, such as would unite Japanese and American research and development in order to face the challenge of a society going beyond zero-sum growth. A fundamental agreement was obtained on maintaining frequent exchanges of research on this theme in the future. Thus steps leading to a new direction known as symbiotic competition in each nation's research and development are steadily being made.

Note

1. The COE (Center of Excellence) was set up on the ideal of a research center open to all researchers.

References

Imai, K., and Kasai, Y., ed., *Nijuisseiki o Mezasu Kenkyu Kaihatsu-gata Kigyo* (Research and Development-Style Companies Aiming for the Twenty-first Century), Toyo Keizai Shinpo-sha, Tokyo, 1984.

Irvine, J., *Evaluating Applied Research—Lessons from Japan,* Pinter, London, 1988.

Japan Development Bank, *R&D no Keizai gaku* (An Economic Study of R&D), Tokyo, 1985.

Ministry of International Trade and Industry, ed., *Sangyo Gijutsu no Rekishi no Keisho to Mirai e no Sozo* (The Successive History of Industrial Technology and Outlook for the Future), Tsusho Sangyo Chosakai, 1992.

MIT Commission of Industrial Productivity, *Made in America,* MIT Press, Cambridge, 1989 (trans. into Japanese by Yoda Naoya, published by Soshi-sha, 1989).

Nihon Gakusai Kaigi, *Shin-Sangakukan Kyoryoku ni Kansuru Kenkyu: New Paradigm no Kakuritsu o Mezashite* (Research on New Cooperation among Industry, Academe, and the Government: Aiming for the Establishment of a New Paradigm), Tokyo, 1993.

Peace Education Academy, *Knowledge,* March 1988.

U.S. National Science Foundation (NSF), *The Gehrman Report* (NSF-SU-76-1), Washington, DC, 1976.

11

Structural Distinctions within Japanese Manufacturing

Yukio Watanabe

This chapter will consider the distinguishing features of the social structure of labor in Japanese manufacturing industries and what they signify for the industry's international competitiveness. It will additionally discuss changes to that structure already underway.

Along that line some preliminary structural distinctions must be recognized: that manufacturing industries have continued long-term expansion under the leadership of the fabricated metal products and machinery industry; that the number of employees per plant including in the machinery industry has declined; that the proportion of medium-sized, small, and very small plants has rapidly increased in the machinery industry; that the level of dependence on imports of manufactured goods is low while domestic fulfillment is high; and that a considerable number of small-scale factories are gathered in a narrow region compared to the situation in other industrialized nations.

This chapter will largely consider the fabricated metal products and machinery industry whose structure of labor is sociologically unique. It depends on clusters of specialized small- and medium-sized plants segregated by scale or according to region. This setup makes for complex interrelationships, with these plants vying rigorously among themselves for a share of the manufacturing business.

As a result related industries as well as small- and medium-sized businesses have advanced simultaneously, and many serve as subcontractors. That additionally has engendered the efficiency and flexibility needed for coping with technological changes in the manufacturing industries.

However, this industry structure began changing both internally and externally in the 1990s. The small- and medium-sized enterprise strata have not reproduced themselves, and the likelihood exists that these businesses may cease to function. With bases of production moved to

East and Southeast Asia, the structure of Japanese manufacturing industries has begun to range throughout these regions. The future of manufacturing will be largely influenced by whether or not the Japanese corporations abroad can introduce an efficient structure of labor division in these areas.

11.1 Characteristics of Japanese Manufacturing

Structural Characteristics of Manufacturing

Except for the recession following the first oil crisis, Japanese manufacturing industries have almost continuously expanded production. Their progress has been swift compared to their counterparts in the United States and other Western nations, and the fabricated metal products and machinery industry[1] has been the driving force behind this rapid long-term expansion. Simultaneous with the growth in manufacturing has been the increase in the number of factories. The number of plants, which had continued to grow until the beginning of the 1980s, has now surpassed the increased number of persons engaged at them, which in fact reflects the decline seen in the number of workers per factory. Amid that change has come a big shift in the composition of the fabricated metal products and machinery industry. In this industry, with the increase in the number of total workers in factories have come larger increases in the number of medium-sized, small, and very small plants engaged in manufacturing, resulting in the decline in the number of workers per factory. There has further been low reliance on imports for manufactured goods because of the high level of completeness within domestic manufacturing. These characteristics and the remaining disparities of scale are important structural aspects of manufacturing in Japan. But particularly the locating of manufacturing activity in a vast number of medium-sized, small, and very small plants and the low number of workers per factory are features that cannot be found in other countries.

Consistent Expansion of Manufacturing

Ever since the mid-1950s when its high growth began, Japanese manufacturing industries have been expanding production almost continuously, except for the 15 percent reduction in industrial production at the time of the first oil crisis. The only other decline was the 0.2 percent drop from 1985 to 1986 after the Plaza Accords. Let us consider some of the changes during this long expansion period.

From about the mid-1950s until the recession brought by the first oil crisis, the production of all goods—particularly durable consumer goods and capital goods—expanded dramatically. From the mid-1970s until the mid-1980s, durable consumer goods experienced astounding growth. Then in the late 1980s the growth of durable consumer goods dropped below average for Japanese manufacturing while the growth of capital goods rose conspicuously. Production related to the machinery industry expanded during both periods.

Production indexes for the American manufacturing industry showed a 99 percent increase from 1960 until 1973—the part of the post–World War II period when its industry expanded most favorably. By contrast, the production indexes for the Japanese manufacturing industry showed a 362 percent increase during the same period. Within that figure, the increase in the machinery industry was, at 612 percent, way above the average for the entire manufacturing industry. In addition, while the U.S. manufacturing production index showed an increase of 61 percent in the period spanning from its peak in 1973 (just before the first oil crisis) to 1990, the index for Japanese manufacturing within the same timeframe has revealed a 77 percent increase. But the rate of increase seen in the Japanese machinery industry was even higher at 183 percent.[2] Then after the first oil crisis the rate of expansion of Japanese manufacturing's production changed considerably. Nevertheless, compared with other countries, Japanese manufacturing industries, and especially the machinery industry, have maintained a high rate of growth.

Rising Number of Plants and Declining Number of Workers per Plant

Now let us look at the changes in the number of plants and the number of persons engaged in Japanese manufacturing industries from 1963 to 1990.[3] As can be seen in table 11.1a, the number of plants, which totaled over 560,000 in 1963, grew to over 700,000. This means an increase of some 140,000 plants, or 25 percent, during the nine-year period from 1963 to 1972, which is just one year prior to the first oil crisis. After 1972 the number of factories kept on increasing at a slower pace reaching 780,000 in 1983, for an increase of 11 percent in eleven years. Thereafter this number statistically fluctuated at around 740,000; in 1993 there were 730,000 plants, indicating a slight decline.[4]

Table 11.1
Changes in number of establishments and number of persons engaged in them, 1963–1990

a. Changes in establishments

Size (persons engaged)	1963	%	1972	%	1978	%	1983	%	1990	%	Increase rate % 1963–90
1–9	415,544	73.77	522,864	74.42	569,866	76.56	595,686	76.34	536,860	73.66	29.19
10–19	65,032	11.54	92,717	13.20	83,689	11.24	87,088	11.16	86,533	11.87	33.06
20–99	70,069	12.44	71,313	10.15	77,058	10.35	83,028	10.64	89,213	12.24	27.32
100–299	9,263	1.64	11,508	1.64	10,231	1.37	10,919	1.40	12,407	1.70	33.94
300–999	2,720	0.48	3,365	0.48	2,820	0.38	2,909	0.37	3,137	0.43	15.33
1,000–	699	0.12	819	0.12	673	0.09	650	0.08	703	0.10	0.57
Total	563,327	100.0	702,586	100.0	744,337	100.0	780,280	100.0	728,853	100.0	29.38

b. Persons engaged in the establishments (thousands)

Size (persons engaged)	1963	%	1972	%	1978	%	1983	%	1990	%	Increase rate % 1963–90
1–9	1,634	16.80	2,056	17.45	2,178	20.00	2,248	19.81	2,071	17.57	26.74
10–19	911	9.36	1,315	11.16	1,152	10.58	1,196	10.54	1,193	10.12	30.95
20–99	2,706	27.82	2,945	24.99	2,987	27.42	3,184	28.06	3,450	29.27	27.49
100–299	1,501	15.43	1,872	15.89	1,651	15.16	1,762	15.53	1,995	16.92	32.91
300–999	1,374	14.12	1,712	14.53	1,412	12.96	1,463	12.89	1,577	13.38	14.77
1000–	1,602	16.47	1,883	15.98	1,512	13.88	1,495	13.17	1,502	12.74	-6.24
Total	9,728	100.00	11,783	100.00	10,892	100.00	11,348	100.00	11,788	100.00	21.18

Source: MITI, *Kogyo Tokei-hyo* (Census of Manufactures).

On the other hand, the number of persons engaged in industries, as can be seen in table 11.1b, went up from 9,720,000 in 1963 to 11,960,000 in 1973, indicating an increase of 2,690,000 workers, or 29 percent, in ten years. That number once experienced a slight decline to 10,890,000 in 1978 but began to rise again thereafter; in 1990 it came to 11,790,000, indicating a recovery to almost its 1973 level.[5]

If we look at the number of workers per plant, the figure in 1963 came to an average of 17.3 people at each factory. But it next underwent a rapid decline to 16.8, 14.6, and 14.5, respectively, in 1972, 1978, and 1983. Thereafter it increased again and reached an average of 16.2 workers per plant in 1990. From the time of the first oil crisis until 1983 the rate of increase in the number of factories surpassed that in the number of employees, indicating a decline in the number of workers per plant to less than 15. The average number per plant began increasing once more in 1983, but it has remained at 16.2 workers per factory since 1990.

The expansion of production occurred simultaneously with a decrease in the number of workers per plant. This, coupled with the fact that the number of persons engaged in each plant averaged about 15, is a distinguishing feature of Japanese manufacturing industries. By contrast, the number of factories in the United States in 1982 was less than 350,000, while the number of employees totaled 17,820,000, averaging 51.4 workers per factory.[6] However, family-run companies without outside employees are included in Japanese industries statistics and not in the U.S. manufacturing's statistics. Such small company plants are estimated to total about 170,000 in the United States.[7] If that were taken into consideration, the number of workers per plant in the United States would come to just over 33.

As a further comparison, in the former West Germany the number of manufacturing plants in 1976 was 90,000, and the number of workers came to 7,400,000, that is, 82 people per factory. However, in 1977, for example, just under 230,000 manufacturing-related workshops existed, and if they are included, such as in the Japanese classification of the manufacturing industry, the number of workers per plant will come to 28.[8]

Rapid Shift toward the Fabricated Metal Products and Machinery Industry

Since the mid-1950s the composition of Japanese manufacturing industries has moved rapidly from heavy industry and chemical materials to fabricated metal products and machinery. In 1956 the proportion accounted for by the fabricated metal products and machinery industry in the number of workers in Japanese manufacturing was 25 percent— a figure only slightly higher than the total of 21 percent for the textile and apparel industries, both of which were also the leading industries at the time. In 1971 the fabricated metal products and machinery industry accounted for 38 percent of the total number of persons engaged in manufacturing, and in 1990 this figure came to 45 percent.[9]

While the proportion of chemical materials and heavy industry in the composition of the added value was high in the mid-1950s, accounting for 28 percent of all manufacturing, this percentage declined during the high economic growth period of the 1960s. It had dropped to 20 percent by 1971, and by 1990 it was down to 17 percent. By contrast, the fabricated metal products and machinery industry's percentage was 24 percent in 1956, rising to 41 percent by 1971 and then to 47 percent in 1990.[10]

Within the composition of Japanese manufacturing, the fabricated metal products and machinery industry now alone accounts for nearly 50 percent. In the United States this machinery industry accounted for 42 percent of the composition of workers in manufacturing and of the structure of added value in 1977.[11] Clearly the Japanese fabricated metal products and machinery industry's dramatic rise in percentages has brought it to about the same level as its counterpart in the United States and even surpassed it just a little.

Function of Medium-Sized, Small, and Very Small Enterprises

In 1990 medium-sized, small, and very small facilities with less than 300 workers accounted for 99.5 percent of all the plants in Japanese manufacturing. Within that number, very small facilities with less than ten workers accounted for 74 percent of the total as well as 18 percent of all persons engaged in manufacturing in Japan. This means that an overwhelming majority of the people working in the industry are based at smaller facilities (see table 11.1).

From 1963 to 1978 there was a dramatic rise in percentages of both medium-sized, small, and very small plants and of their workers. Manufacturing activities rapidly expanded along with the rise in the number of plants and workers, showing increases of 32 and 11 percent, respectively, while the proportion of very small plants out of the total number grew from 74 to 77 percent. Medium-sized, small, and very small factories altogether also increased in number during these years, from 69 to 73 percent, as did the percentage of people working at very small factories, rising from 17 to 20 percent (see table 11.1).

The statistics for the United States show that in 1982 plants employing over 500 workers accounted for 38 percent of all workers. Unincorporated enterprises, with no employees besides the owners, account for less than two-thirds of American manufacturing industries.[12] That makes for a great difference with Japanese manufacturing, where nearly three-quarters is composed of medium-sized, small, and very small plants. In the former West Germany, a vast number of very small handicraft workshops exist, but 42 percent of the total workers in manufacturing in 1976 were at factories with over 500 people.[13] The high proportion of medium-sized, small, and very small facilities within the very large number of plants overall is an important distinguishing feature of Japanese manufacturing.

Let us take a closer look at the fabricated metal products and machinery industries that have been the driving force behind the Japanese manufacturing expansion. In 1966 medium-sized, small, and very small machinery metal factories accounted for 22 percent of the total number of such factories and 28 percent of all persons engaged in Japanese manufacturing industries. These percentages rose substantially to 33 percent of the total number of plants and 37 percent of all workers in manufacturing in Japan by 1990. The percentage of medium-sized, small, and very small factories in the fabricated metal products and machinery industry also went up from 98.9 percent in 1966 to 99.1 percent in 1990 in number of factories, and from 59 percent to 63 percent in number of workers during the same period. The average number of workers per plant dropped from 26.7 in 1966 to 19.5 in 1978. While this figure picked up slightly to go up to 21.9 people per plant in 1990, it is still considerably lower than the average for 24 years earlier.[14]

Thus, in the case of the leading sector, the fabricated metal products and machinery industry, the increase in the number of medium-sized, small, and very small plants above the manufacturing average has been accompanied by a downsizing of plants.

Low Dependence on Imported Manufactured Goods

In examining the state of dependence on imported manufactured goods in Japan, we found that imports other than food products accounted for 5.2 percent of all processed goods in 1990. The highest percentages have been in the fiber and apparel industries, amounting to 9.1 percent.[15] In contrast to the 4 percent import rate in the Japanese machinery industry, this figure came to 31 percent in 1986 in the United Kingdom. The import rate for all British manufacturing, including food products, is 27 percent.[16] Compared to their British counterparts, all Japanese manufacturing industries are pretty much supplied by domestic production. Moreover, even though Japan almost completely relies on imports for raw materials, the proportion of imports in its GNP in 1990 came to 7.9 percent, which is less than the U.S. 9.5 percent.[17] This is because Japan has such a strikingly high rate of domestically supplied manufactured goods.

Existence of a Relatively Large Difference in Scale

Now let us look at the differences in wages per worker according to the scale of wages. Here the indexes for factories in Japanese manufacturing industries with over 1,000 workers will be taken as 100. Accordingly the indexes for plants with 100 to 299 workers were 61 in 1955, and this difference was 71 by 1972. Thereafter the discrepancy narrowed to 66 in 1990.[18] The disparities in scale still remain and do not appear to be declining in any way.

The indexes in the United States for plants with 100 to 249 workers were 88 in 1947 and 67 in 1977.[19] Although the discrepancy in the United States shortly after World War II was small, now it does not differ much from its Japanese counterpart.

Meaning of Structural Distinctions

Manufacturing industries in Japan are characterized by the fact that over 700,000 plants, including a vast number of medium-sized, small, and very small ones, exist within the country's narrow territory enabling these industries to be almost completely established domestically. The presence of enormous numbers of plants and companies produces an atmosphere of fierce rivalry that has led to a unique structurization of labor. These circumstances have contributed to Japanese manufacturing's advantage internationally. In the following sections we will consider these points more deeply by taking up the example of the fabricated metal products and machinery industry.

11.2 Characteristics of the Japanese Fabricated Metal Products and Machinery Industry

As was mentioned earlier, the fabricated metal products and machinery industry leads Japanese manufacturing and is at the main force of its international competitiveness. A distinguishing feature in its structure of labor is a division into clusters of small and large factories that specialize in producing certain parts or provide certain services. Its labor force has also been segregated into tiers according to size of the operation and/or according to region. As a result the labor interrelationships are intricate and complex. For this reason we need to look at the structure of labor from three angles: the way a plant has specialized, its tiers of labor, and regional divisions of labor.

Broader Spheres of Activity and Industry Conglomerates

Although we are focusing on Japan, we should recognize that facilities in East and Southeast Asia are importing and exporting parts to different regions and that diverse companies are involved in these overseas transactions. However, East and Southeast Asia are not uniform in a social-minded distribution of labor. The industries aggregate according to their specializations and unique capacities. The clusters of companies exist interdependently with the core industries within their surroundings.

Let us take a look again at Japan, at the Keihin (Tokyo to Yokohama) region which is the area with the greatest number of machinery companies. In this area the connections among companies are so close that an order request made at night can be filled the next morning. This area commutes with a broader region beyond that ranges throughout East Asia. Within Japan this area spreads from Tohoku (northern Japan), the Kanto-Koshin-Etsu (greater Tokyo area along with Yamanashi, Nagano, and Niigata Prefectures) to the Hokuriku (prefectures along the coast of the Japan Sea), Tokai (Shizuoka and Nagoya areas), and Kansai (Kyoto-Osaka-Kobe) regions and is linked by a network of highways.

There are 245,000 fabricated metal products and machinery industry plants nationwide. Of them, 26,000 can be found in the 23 wards of Tokyo. When the rest of the Keihin region, including Kawasaki and Yokohama, is added to the aforementioned figure, it comes to 35,000 plants. In the four prefectures comprising the greater Tokyo area, there are 70,000 plants and just under 88,000 in the entire Kanto region, to account for 36 percent of the nationwide total. The Keihin region has just under 170,000 plants that each morning fill order requests made the night before—about two-thirds of the nation's total.[20] By contrast, in the United States, for example, in the 410,000-square-kilometer state of California where the machinery industry is concentrated, there are 16,000 of such factories.[21] So compared to the United States, a tremendous number of plants with interdependent activities are concentrated in a very narrow region of Japan.

High Development through Specialization

Since a great many plants are located within a relatively small region, competition is fierce. Yet at the same time very close mutual dependence exists. In order to survive these tough circumstances, the factories are forced to specialize to a high degree. Specialization has also been fostered because of the great proximities among the plants.

There are two directions a company's specialization in the fabricated metal products and machinery industry can take. One is by manufacturing unique products that are mainly finished goods and parts. The other is by providing unique production and assembly services. The huge plants around which the factories cluster specialize in manufacturing products for which company groups supply finished machinery and parts for mass production. However, a large number of these middle-level factories are medium-sized, small, and very small enterprises that have created niches for themselves in small finished machinery goods and parts. Market niches are important to survival in industrial equipment fields.

Among the operations of factories that specialize in processes are lathe turnery, milling, heat treatment electroplating, and gilding. These plants do not limit themselves to a particular product field but accept orders across fields. Their specialization diverges on points like the size of production, namely whether it is mass or small batch production, and the quality or the size of the materials to be processed. The levels of specialization can get even more sophisticated.

Dedicated subcontractors are to be found in the plant clusters that specialize in assembly sources. In the other direction lie a number of companies specializing in very narrow areas on diversification, increasing production numbers and customers.

The ability to adapt to changes has been a strength of plants specializing in processes and assembly, so there are few risks involved in complete specialization. An exclusive company accepting orders for assembly work can count on receiving similar orders from firms in different fields. In particular, the firms that have specialized in very sophisticated processes are in a good position to receive orders in a wide variety of areas. This way risks are reduced. Furthermore a firm's high level of specialization signifies the existence of company groups that have specialized together. Risks are also lowered when such firms are used as subcontractors.

The small workshops in the Jonan area of Tokyo are a good example of a plant cluster that has devoted itself to exclusive processing techniques. This cluster is composed of nearly 10,000 small subcontractor plants that rely on orders for jobs from a wide range of areas. Among the very small enterprises specializing in lathe turnery, differences exist in the aspect of the work in which they excel. Therefore they form complementary relationships in a mutual exchange of work.[22] Thus not only is each company highly specialized, but the relationships of mutual dependence, including the strata of very small enterprises, have become complex. The management of specialized firms rendered stable by such relationships has enabled their proliferation.

Competition within the Strata

A reason for the fierce rivalry among plants is that only a small amount of capital is necessary to enter a field depending on the size of the operation, and as a result a considerable number of diverse enterprises are constantly being formed. The expenses are not at all near what gigantic corporations need to enter a field. For example, setting up a standard automobile factory with the capacity for an annual production of 200,000 would entail expenses amounting to ¥100 billion.

There are in fact many fields that can be entered by very small enterprises or plants. Say the field is machine processing, which processes a small amount of parts for one-off products. Skilled workers can enter it just by relying on family members for labor. If circumstances allow the purchase of rather sophisticated machinery by installment payments and the use of a leased plant, it is quite easy for a skilled worker who so aspires to start an independent business. In general, as the level of specialization gets higher in the fabricated metal products and machinery industry, more division of labor becomes necessary and

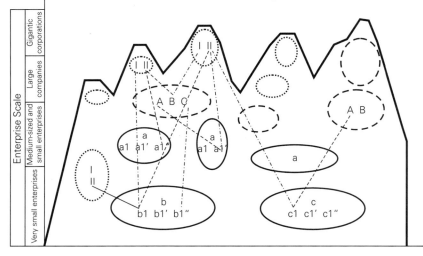

Subcontracting transaction relationships   Spheres of (quasi-)direct competition in
                                             Japanese industries
    ⋯⋯ Equal
    – – Dependent   ⋰⋰ Finished product manufacturers' sector
    —— Independent   ◠ Finished components manufacturer's sector
                                                 ◯ Small, medium-sized subcontractors' sector

Medium-Sized, Small Subcontractor
a, b, c, b1, c1, b1', b1" etc.

    a : Enterprises specialized in components   b1 :   Autonomous enterprises specialized in
    b : Enterprises specialized in processing   processing for major customers
    c : Enterprises specialized in assembling   b1' : Enterprises specialized in processing
                                                          with little capability of leaving main customers
                                                   b1" : Subsidiary enterprises specialized in processing
                                                          for major customers

Figure 11.1
The wide-ranging division of labor by scale of enterprise.

the fields of these small and very small enterprises start to spread out. Many businesses have grown in this way in the fabricated metal products and machinery industry, so many are encouraged to join this strata activity which rose to success in Japan's period of high economic growth.

Labor Specialization and Strata Formation

The high number of specialized companies in the fabricated metal products and machinery industry with their various divisions of labor can be seen in figure 11.1. Their interactions are divided by final products so that, even at the finished component level, the market is formed by the finished components. These supplier companies are further divided by their finished components. Among the medium and small firms that specialize in processing, the clusters of rival companies exist as companies according to their specialized processes.

The division of labor in the fabricated metal products and machinery industry does not have a singular industrial type or company at its peak. The structure of labor over the entire fabricated metal products and machinery industry, which includes many industrial subdivisions, however, can be expressed as a series of pyramidal forms. The gigantic firms producing large finished machines are positioned at the high peaks. In contrast, the large number of medium-sized, small, and very small enterprises that form small market niches for finished components cluster at lower peaks. In the valleys are the clusters of medium-sized, small, and very small subcontractors that specialize in processes common to many fields of finished machinery goods. These companies are not constrained by company or by the finished product. They exist according to the need for their particular skills.

Subcontracting relationships can be subordinate or autonomous. Their transactions with corporations are expressed in aggregate terms.

The subcontracting structure of labor from the perspective of a gigantic corporation making finished goods could be shown as a pyramid. The medium-sized, small, and very small enterprises would form strata according to their levels of specialization. Premised in this stratified way gigantic corporations can be seen to use subcontractor companies to their advantage. Included would be several diverse division of labor relations, including those among medium-sized, small, and very small enterprises that manufacture their own products, among them various forms of transactions by medium-sized and small companies that produce their own goods, small and medium-sized firms that have specialized in particular processes, and subcontracting relations with large corporations that make parts.

Formation of a Spatial Division of Labor Based around the Industrial Agglomeration

Medium-sized, small, and very small enterprises cannot function away from the industrial agglomerations in which they are located. These firms are regulated by the character of their industrial group, and they fulfill their functions accordingly. But these functions can vary by region, even within agglomerations of the same fabricated metal products and machinery industry. One extreme is the industrial group in the Keihin region of Tokyo. This is the oldest industrial concentration in Japan; it is also the largest base of machinery operations in the

Regions	Core metropolitan area		Periphery rural area		Overseas (NIES ASEAN)
Changes in content of products / production	severe ⇨	⇨	⇨	⇨	stable
Quantitative fluctuation in each product	large ⇨	⇨	⇨	⇨	small
Batch sizes	small ⇨	⇨	⇨	⇨	large
Value-added productivity	high ⇨	⇨	⇨	⇨	low
Regional division of labor / transaction relationships	complex ⇨	⇨	⇨	⇨	simple
Large corporations Division of labor between regions within the corporation	R & D • Prototype production • One-off product		Mass production Maturation of production technology ⇨ ⇨		
Middle-level, medium-sized and small enterprises Division of labor between regions within the enterprise	Development • Prototype production • One-off product • Small batches • Fluctuation • Changes (small production of diverse types)		Steady production ⇨ ⇨		
Agglomeration of medium-sized and small enterprises Specialized functions	Small production of diverse types • Fluctuation • Changes Vast amount / diversification of transactions within agglomerations		Mature product, steady production Maturation of production technology for small / simple transactions within agglomerations ⇨ ⇨		
Types of very small enterprises	Industrial agglomerations in metropolitan area	Industrial agglomerations in rural areas			Cottage industries

Figure 11.2
Division of labor among machinery industries by Japanese region.

country. Many industrial groups parcel out work to the companies gathered in the Tokyo area. The structure of these relationships is explicated in figure 11.2.

The different interactions among regional industrial groups can be explained in the following manner: In the older industrial areas there is a core of many highly specialized medium-sized, small, and very small enterprises. The level of production there is sophisticated and diverse, and characterized by small batch sizes and continual techno-logical changes, both gradual and radical. By contrast, in the surrounding vicinities, massive quantities of stable products are turned out. Distribution of labor in industrial groups is based on such differences in production.

Uniqueness of the Labor Structure in the Fabricated Metal Products and Machinery Industry

The large number of factories gathered within a relatively narrow area in Japan are of two types: those that specialize by product and those that specialize by a certain process or assembly method. By their specialization they have managed to survive fierce competition. Moreover, depending on the completeness of their specialization, the minimum capital they require varies. Likewise their subjection to vigorous competition depends on their scale of operations. At the same time each factory is regulated by the geographical conditions of its location and by the character of the industrial group that encompasses it and toward which its specialization is directed.

11.3 Subcontractor Relationships within Manufacturing Industries

In this section we will discuss the distinguishing features of the subcontractor transaction relationships with large manufacturing companies and their composition of labor. The future changes in their structure will be considered as well.

Significance of the High Development of Related Industries

Japan took off as an industrialized but backward nation after World War II. Manufacturing industries were led by the heated competition among huge companies, which pursued wholeheartedly the country's goal to catch up with the industrialized countries. These companies managed to bring about rapid growth and simultaneously to build up the industry and the domestic economy. That accomplishment also advanced the development of medium-sized, small, and very small enterprises—a stratum of industry lying at the base of the industrial structure and isolated since the beginning of World War II. Premised in the rivalry among oligopolistic companies, these latecomers of small and medium-sized operations faced the problem of catching up amid rapid growth. They survived because the gigantic corporations intervened establishing subcontracting relationships with them.

As a result of the vertically integrated subcontracting relationships, high technological development became possible for small and medium-sized enterprises, and as a result of the vigorous competition among the oligopolistic corporations, this development spread throughout the entire strata.

Improvements in On-Demand Style of Subcontractor Relationships

Based on technological imports, the process of rapidly catching up with advanced industries was backed by a fierce, stratified rivalry. It quickly became a competition of differentiation among products with complex product distinctions. That competition of differentiation unfolded in layers of improved product technology that closely adhered to users' needs and in reforms in production technology. The vertical integration of subcontracting enabled unlimited technological progress outside the core technologies of the giant corporations. Moreover, due to this verticality in the subcontracting relationships, the subcontractor firms could share in the technological reforms of the companies making the orders. To the companies making the orders, the reforms were crucially dependent on parts from the subcontractor firms. Overall fine reforms became possible through the joint efforts of both sides.

Flexible Production Structure

The enormous number of medium-sized, small, and very small subcontractor enterprises form a unique established source of supply for large manufacturers of machinery. In a short period of time at a relatively low cost they can obtain parts and meet their levels of production. These circumstances have come to be regarded as natural and dependable. Even in times of excessive demand, an odd number of parts can be guaranteed by a deadline as a matter of course. As a result the Japanese fabricated metal products and machinery industry has at the very base of its structure the advantage of flexibility which gives it strength in international competition.

Because of this important feature of having at their disposal a wide range of subcontractor firms, the large machinery manufacturers no longer feel that they can fall behind in modernizing their products. The fierce competition that encouraged specialization and the subsequent high development has advanced these medium-sized, small, and very small firms technologically.

Possibilities for Structural Changes in the 1990s

What changes the structure of Japanese manufacturing's future? With the ongoing slowdown in growth in the Japanese manufacturing, industries need to reexamine their survival strategies which are premised on growth and high specialization. Any difficulties that arise in sustaining the medium-sized, small, and very small enterprise strata will considerably affect the whole structure of the fabricated metal products and machinery industry. The advancing labor crunch and a decreasing number of new startups present a threat to this flexible production system in Japanese manufacturing industries. For the time being, any parts that are difficult to automate get sent as external orders to small and medium-sized subcontractor firms, and the industry has freely depended on the skilled workers there. But doubts exist about whether the skills of these workers can be preserved. It will then be up to the large corporations to reproduce these skills within their premises.

At the start of the 1990s both the increasing gravity of the recession on the fabricated metal products and machinery industry and the decline in the establishing of new enterprises in manufacturing have been viewed as problems, and they present major industry challenges. As such circumstances become long-lasting, the uniqueness of Japanese manufacturing industries in their distribution of labor and industrial structures is likely to undergo considerable change.

Added to that is the matter of giant corporations developing production bases in East Asia which duplicate the domestic structure of the machinery industry. Not only manufacturers of finished products but also parts makers and many mass-production firms, including small and medium-sized enterprises, have begun building and establishing bases of production in the East Asian region, including China.

Significantly the domestic completeness that had characterized Japanese manufacturing industries up to the 1980s is starting to disintegrate. Some call this the bottoming out of industry, but it is not at all similar to what has been happening in the United Kingdom. The structure of the division of labor among regions in Japan mentioned in this chapter might even be viewed as the reorganization of East Asia, including Japan, as an industrial sphere.

While retaining production capacities amid an expanding division of labor among regions, manufacturing industries within Japan are undergoing a transformation. Just as the industry cluster of the Keihin region was reorganized in the past by transferring mass-production plants to other parts of the nation, reorganization of the regional divisions of labor is now proceeding among other industrial clusters in Japan and areas of East Asia. If East Asia is to be included in this industrial sphere, the distribution of labor, with its Japanese style of completeness, will have to be maintained there. In effect Japan's manufacturing industries may not be facing a collapse of a structure but rather the wide possibilities arising from a broadening of their structure beyond national borders with a reorganization of Japanese domestic manufacturing as its center.

Notes

1. The term "fabricated metal products" refers to the fabricating industry within the heavy machinery and chemical industry. There are six industrial classifications here: manufacture of fabricated metal products, manufacture of general machinery, manufacture of electrical machinery, equipment and supplies, manufacture of transportation equipment, manufacture of precision instruments and machinery, and manufacture of ordnance.

2. Information about the rate of increase in the volume of production for manufacturing industries is from the Secretariat to the Minister of International Trade and Industry's Survey and Statistics Section, ed. *Showa 50-nen Kijun: Kokogyo Shisu Soran* (1975 Base Year: A Conspectus of Indices of Industrial Production for Mining and Manufacturing) and *Showa 60-nen Kijun: Kokogyo Shisu Soran* (1985 Base Year: A Conspectus of Indices of Industrial Production for Mining and Manufacturing). Information about the rate of increase in the United States is from OECD's Main Economic Indicators.

3. The rate of growth of very small establishments (plants) in the *Kogyo Tokei-hyo* (Census of Manufactures) has risen since the 1963 survey.

4. The aforementioned numbers come from the Secretariat to the Minister of International Trade and Industry's *Kogyo Tokei-hyo, Sangyo-hen* (Census of Manufactures, Report by Industries). Until 1980, surveys were carried out annually. After 1963 very small establishments have tended to increase every three years; 1963 was the year in which the *Jigyosho Tokei* (Establishment Census of Japan) was begun. The trends in the number of establishments were derived from comparisons made chronologically in multiples of three from 1963 to 1978. The statistics for the years following 1981 cover all establishments in which *Kogyo Tokei-hyo* surveys were made: 1983, 1985, 1988, and 1990. *Jigyosho Tokei* surveys were taken in 1981, 1986, and 1991. There are no years in this period in which both types of statistic surveys were taken, which is why it is extremely difficult to discuss trends in the number of very small establishments in the 1980s on the basis of statistics.

5. From *Kogyo Tokei-hyo, Sangyo-hen* (Census of Manufactures, Report by Industries).

6. From Department of Commerce, *1982 Census of Manufacturers*, vol. 1.

7. From estimates based on taxation statistics from A. D. Star, Estimates of the Number of Quasi and Small Businesses, *American Journal of Small Businesses*, no. 2 (October 1979).

8. From Statistiches Bundesamt, *Statistiches Jahrbuch 1978*. The statistics on the number of employees by plant size in West German plants have not been released for the

manufacturing industry. Only the places of business with more than twenty employees have been included in the surveys.

9. From *Kogyo Tokei-hyo, Sangyo-hen* (Census of Manufactures, Report by Industries).

10. From *Kogyo Tokei-hyo, Sangyo-hen* (Census of Manufactures, Report by Industries).

11. From Department of Commerce, *1977 Census of Manufacturers,* vol. 1.

12. From Department of Commerce, 1982 *Census of Manufacturers,* vol. 1.

13. From *Statistiches Jarhbuch 1978.*

14. From *Kogyo Tokei-hyo, Sangyo-hen* (Census of Manufactures, Report by Industries).

15. The rate of import permeation has been calculated on the basis of figures from MITI's *Heisei 3-nen Tsusho Hakusho, Kakuron-hen* (White Paper on International Trade, Japan's Trade Statistics in 1991) and *1990-nen Kogyo Tokei-hyo, Sangyo-hen* (Census of Manufactures, Report by Industries in 1990), and taken as the ratio of imports value to the sum of imports and domestic shipments' values.

16. Based on statistics printed in Department of Trade and Industry, *British Business,* 15 May 1987. Here the rate of imports has been calculated as the ratio of imports value to the sum of exports and domestic demands values.

17. From MITI's *Heisei 4-nen Tsusho Hakusho, Kakuron-hen* (White Paper on International Trade, Japan's Trade Statistics in 1992), p. 825.

18. From *Kogyo Tokei-hyo, Sangyo-hen* (Census of Manufactures, Report by Industries).

19. Takizawa, K., America Chusho Kogyo no Kozo Bunseki (An Analysis of the Structure of American Small and Medium-Sized Enterprises in Manufacturing), in Chusho Kigyo Jigyodan Chusho Kigyo Daigaku-ko Chusho Kigyo Kenkyusho, ed., *America no Chusho Kigyo ni Kansuru Kenkyu* (Research on Small- and Medium-Sized Enterprises in the United States), 1983, p. 62.

20. *Kogyo Tokei-hyo, Sangyo-hen* (Census of Manufactures, Report by Industries in 1990).

21. Refer to the Department of Commerce, *1977 County Business Patterns,* and to Watanabe, Y., Chusho Kogyo no Sonritsu Jitai to Mondaisei (The State of Existence of Small and Medium-Sized Enterprises in Manufacturing and Their Problems), in *America no Chusho Kigyo ni Kansuru Kenkyu* (Research on Small- and Medium-Sized Enterprises in the United States).

22. Concrete details concerning the state of existence of the small and very small plant cluster in the Jonan area of Tokyo can be found in Watanabe, Y., Daitoshi ni Okeru Kikai Kogyo Reisai Keiei no Kino to Sonritsu Kiban: Tokyo-to Jonan Chiiki no Baai (The Very Small Business Capacities and Foundation of Existence of the Machinery Industry in Large Cities: The Case of the Tokyo Jonan Area), in *Mita Gakkai Zasshi* 72, no. 2 (April 1979).

12

Educational System in Raising Human Capital

Shin-ichi Kobayashi

A driving force behind Japan's economic development, particularly of its manufacturing industries, has been its excellent educational system.

Compulsory education was established in Japan in 1900, and in a little over twenty years after its institution, more than 99 percent of school-age children were enrolled in primary education. By 1940 almost 50 percent of the population had had a secondary education. After World War II junior high school education was made compulsory, and the curriculum of public education was standardized, raising the educational level of a large number of workers. Compared internationally, Japan's education in mathematics and the sciences was maintained at a very high level. In general, the labor forces' high scholastic ability in mathematics and the sciences has helped make improvements in productivity and technological innovations possible. This fundamental condition has also contributed to economic growth.

In the postwar period, particularly starting in the 1960s, institutions of higher education rapidly expanded. As the labor force quickly attained a higher level of education, in the sciences and technology, the number of researchers and engineers increased enormously. Together with the foreign technologies introduced in the 1960s, this led to Japan's preeminence in research and development in the 1980s. During this time, within companies, educational and training activities premised on the permanent employment system promoted competent shop floor technicians and contributed to the development of an industrial philosophy.

However, although both public and private education in Japan have supported economic development and industry's success, and the economy has largely continued to develop, the educational system that has served as its backbone is, at this point, starting to show signs of fatigue. Overheated competition in entrance examinations in Japan has created a dependence on cram courses, which can hinder the development of creativity and leadership among the potentially bright youth who will some day be entrusted with the nation's future.

A drift away from the sciences and technology is another phenomenon seen among young Japanese, and this has caused discussion about whether there will be enough engineers and researchers available in the future. There have been delays in setting up graduate schools and a deterioration in the research environment. Although universities have contributed to economic development in response to social demand up to now, this combination has rendered them incapable of fulfilling their responsibility to the nation's industries in the training of a creative work force.

Japan's industry is now being faced with a situation in which it can lose the educational resource it has known so far. An urgent task for the Japanese manufacturing industry is to encourage scientific education among children and young people as well as to support society's expectations about schooling.

12.1 Contributions to the Economic Development of Education

Elementary and Secondary Education and Fundamental Abilities

The basic framework of public education in Japan was put together in 1872 during the Meiji period, and it underwent great changes in both the Taisho period (1912–1926) and after World War II. The postwar changes remain to this day. With the establishment of compulsory primary education in 1900, both boys and girls of the appropriate age entered elementary schools. Secondary education was launched in the 1890s, and by 1940 more than 50 percent of boys and 40 percent of girls went on to such higher education.[1]

An entirely new educational system was instituted after World War II. Compulsory education was raised to junior high school, and high schools came into existence. Japan's subsequent economic growth was blessed by the fact that compulsory junior high school education provided a tremendous number of middle-level workers with an education. By 1950, 42.5 percent of the population had a high school education and this rate increased rapidly during the postwar period of high economic growth. In recent years 95 percent of young Japanese have been going on to high school.[2] In this way primary and secondary education was set up early in Japan so that nowadays almost all Japanese have had some secondary schooling.

School curriculums have become uniform throughout the country through various education ordinances and supervision by the government. The Japanese educational system has endowed Japan's industry with homogeneous and high-quality work force.

The excellent level of the scientific and mathematic teaching in Japanese elementary schools was pointed out quite some time ago. Japanese elementary and junior high school children placed first in all fields of mathematics in an international survey[3] comparing elementary, junior high, and high school youngsters' scholastic abilities in mathematics and science, and Japanese high school students ranked second to those of Hong Kong in all mathematical fields. In the sciences, Japanese grammar school children tied for first place with those of South Korea, and Japanese junior high school students placed second after those of Hungary. As for high school science, Japanese students ranked third for general science in the liberal arts group. In the sciences they placed fifth for physics, seventh for biology and general science, and eleventh for chemistry. Thus, except for high school students, the scholastic abilities of Japanese youngsters in mathematics and science are at a rather impressive level internationally.

Definite other signs of the high scholastic level of elementary and secondary school education in Japan can be seen in the rate of advancement of pupils to higher education. The fundamental conditions of education that have ensured that Japanese workers have high scholastic abilities, particularly in mathematics and science, have further made it possible for workers to cope flexibly with technological innovations in efforts to raise productivity on the industrial shop floor.

Nevertheless, the excellence in elementary and secondary education has had a negative effect on the Japanese people as well. Although compulsory schooling has brought uniform affordable education to Japanese youth, it has failed to nurture original thinking. The emphasis is rather on study techniques in amassing huge amounts of knowledge in preparation for the highly competitive entrance examinations, resulting in "cram" learning that nips the buds of creativity and individuality. For this reason alone the system needs an overhaul, but there is also the matter of the Ministry of Education, Science, and Culture's iron control over elementary and secondary school education.

Higher Education and Higher Training Levels of the Labor Force

Advancement of Higher Education

Higher education in Japan was inaugurated with the establishment of the Tokyo Imperial University in 1877 (renamed the University of Tokyo in 1947). It underwent expansion as many other colleges and universities were created in the Taisho period. By 1945 the number of people enrolled in institutions of higher learning came to just under 400,000. It was at this time, after World War II, when the present system of higher education came into being with the establishments of a new university system in 1949 (some of it already instituted in 1948), a new graduate school system in 1953 (partially begun in 1950), a new junior college system in 1950, and then some years later the technical college system in 1962.

The number of people entering institutions of higher learning rose from the 1960s to the first half of the 1970s. In 1960, 10 percent of young Japanese proceeded on to institutions of higher education; in 1976 this proportion had reached 39.2 percent. Thereafter the percentage fluctuated in the upper 30 percentiles, and recently it has gone over the 40 percent mark. Moreover, after the vocational school system was established in 1976, the proportion of Japanese entering postsecondary educational institutions, including vocational schools, has fluctuated at around 50 percent.

From an international perspective the percentage of the people advancing to higher education in Japan is on the high side. The figures for the number of people attending institutions of higher education from the total population and the number attending from the appropriate age group show that Japan had already surpassed the European levels by about 1960. For example, the enrollments in 1958 came to 69 for every 10,000 people. By contrast, the figures at the same time for the United Kingdom (in 1957), France, and West Germany were, respectively 42, 50, and 33 per 10,000 people. The figure for the United States was 185 out of 10,000 people.[4] This increase in the rate of enrollment in higher education progressed rapidly among the Japanese labor force as well.

However, in contrast to the Japanese elementary and secondary schools which have placed high internationally, the nation's higher education system has not fared as well. An American instructor who had taught at a Japanese university has pointed out problems like low attendance rate among Japanese students, frequent cancellation of classes, and easy grading. His article on this subject has been widely discussed in both the United States and Japan.[5] Unfortunately, his criticisms accurately reflect one aspect of Japanese universities. After all the fervor over college entrance examinations, the schooling received in universities tends to be inadequate and the curriculum lacking in organization. There are even company people in Japan who say, "It's enough for youths to cram to get into a (prestigious) university. After they get in, they should be free to enjoy their four years of campus life."

Science and Technology in the Curriculum and the Education of Engineers
Science and technology, and particularly engineering curricula have traditionally been an important feature of Japanese higher education. Even today about 20 percent of college students are enrolled in engineering departments—a rate that is quite high by international standards. Within the Imperial University, in the late nineteenth century, an Engineering College was set up as a separate school. To place an engineering college within a university was a pioneering experiment not yet attempted in the advanced nations of North America and Europe at the time.

Important in connection with the economy was the policy to expand higher education in science and technology because of the so-called boom in certain fields just prior to Japan's period of high economic growth. The government's economic policies included a plan to educate scientists and engineers, so the quota of university students in science and technology was more than doubled in just seven years. Another great expansion of higher education began in the mid-1960s to meet the needs of the baby-boom generation; the number of students in science and technology continued to increase until about 1975. As the introduction of foreign technologies bustled in the 1960s, these science or engineering graduates, now engineers, were critical in making that possible.

Among these engineers were the people who developed technological ideas in the 1970s, and then took strides to turn them into products that came into great demand in the 1980s. Consequently the introduction of science and technology into higher education did not simply produce large numbers of engineers. It also supplied the leaders in the research and development who built the foundation for economic growth in the 1980s. Both the economic and technological success of

domestic manufacturing industries can be attributed to the importance
of college education in Japan.

Education in Industry

On-the-Job Training

Industrial education in Japan primarily consists in on-the-job training
(OJT). Premised in lifetime employment, OJT contributes to effective
collaboration among workers. It has been pointed out to be especially effective in the process-assembly industries where skills have
to be frequently adapted to technological innovations. Although
public schooling is relied on for the most part in cultivating job
skills, OJT enables a worker to cope speedily with changes in
circumstances.

Japanese firms pay huge amounts for education and training. Because OJT is the principal form of training, it is not easy to calculate
the costs. However, the total amount spent on in-house training in
Japan, including the costs of OJT opportunities, adds up to the equivalent of 3.3 percent of the GNP.[6] This corresponds to about 60 percent
of the total educational expenses from elementary school to college
and is three times the cost of higher education.

Even at the corporate level, it is not rare for ¥10 billion to be spent
yearly just on the direct costs of education and training, which do not
include the costs of opportunities for off-the-job training (Off-JT). It is
common for the number of employees receiving Off-JT in a corporate
group, which includes its regional marketing companies, to go up to
hundreds of thousands yen. Therefore, for such a vast number of
employees, the direct expenses for Off-JT alone, of which the company
headquarters takes charge, can come to an enormous sum of money.

Cultivation of Skilled Technicians

Historically industrial circles in Japan have been extremely responsive
to education and training needs. Accordingly companies occupy an
important position as institutions of education and training.

Before secondary and higher education was developed in Japan,
companies had systems that supplemented public education. Preliminary and ongoing professional training existed in Japan for skilled
technicians. In 1993 these systems underwent change. Specialized vocational training schools, advanced vocational training schools, and
vocational training colleges were set up to take the place of company

facilities. Nevertheless, orientation and training are still provided within companies. Together these programs comprise an approved corporate training system.

The position of approved in-house job training has changed along with the times. During the period of rapid economic growth, the hired machine technicians, electricians, and construction workers were mainly from among junior high school graduates. The number of companies participating in such a system and the number of people trained kept on increasing until around 1970. Education was a matter of both academic study and practical experience. Approximately two-thirds of the curriculum consisted of courses normally taught at high schools. Meanwhile the work experience provided hands-on practice. The trainees generally worked in training facilities set up either within the company or else jointly by some firms.

It also was not rare for businesses to establish part-time high schools for workers who had a junior high school education. From around 1970, when going to high school became the norm in Japan, the training system expanded to include courses geared toward high school graduates and for existing employees. The number of businesses with approved training within the firm increased as well.

In this way, during the period of high economic growth, companies possessed training and practice facilities internally and developed skilled technicians. Great contributions have been made by such in-house training to industrial activities in Japan.

Nevertheless, there has been worry in recent years about the shortage of skilled technicians and the decline in technical skill. A major factor behind this is that Japanese have tended to stay in school for more years, with schooling becoming single tracked. The educational route for providing outstanding technicians has essentially disappeared. Capable youths, who would have in earlier times become skilled technicians after attending industrial high school, tend to proceed onto higher education; in fact all competent youths now enter the general course program in high schools with the aim of going to college. Thus the academic level of those attending vocational high schools has dropped astoundingly. However, the route for becoming a skilled technician after college graduation has yet to be established. Moreover, since companies have been enthusiastic about automating production processes, they have tended to become lax about cultivating skilled technicians within the firm. This has added all the more to the shortage of skilled technicians.

The lack of outstanding skilled technicians is a sign that the accumulation of technological knowledge on the shop floor has disappeared. While, as automation proceeds, "on-the-job knowledge has been lost, in some cases even productivity has been adversely affected. This situation has been transported to the level of engineers, and this has aroused a general concern about a possible breach in the transmission of past technological knowledge.[7]

Companies as Institutions of Higher Learning for Engineers
The increase in high school graduates has both caused an increase in the number of college graduates and has changed the style and meaning of in-house training in a way that has caused transformations in the approved educational programs within businesses. First of all, the main recipients of in-house training have come to be college graduates. According to several surveys, there are more opportunities for the college-educated workers who undergo in-house training, and the greater the expenses involved, the more the opportunities increase. The second factor is that there are more people who have doctorates just on the basis of submitting qualifying dissertations.[8] In particular, out of the total number of doctorates conferred in engineering, the percentage of those who attained their degrees on the basis of dissertations alone rose sharply in the 1980s. A great many of these Ph.D. recipients seem to have been engineers and researchers working for companies.

This trend is a clear indication that in Japan company research and training in technology has an educational function equivalent that of graduate school. Universities themselves seem to have accepted this doctorate-by-dissertation-only system. Indeed Japanese companies, by maintaining and developing personnel training and supplementing public education, have been able to adapt well to the circumstances of each era.

12.2 Loss of Motivation toward Education

Collapse of the Myth of Human Capital

As mentioned earlier, education in Japan has contributed enormously to industrial development. However, recently occasional tears in its seams have become visible. The myth that education has worked to benefit economic development in Japan is now at the point of breaking. Entrance examination competition has worked its way down to the elementary school and even kindergarten level. Much to blame is the national government's lack of interest and low investment in education, as is reflected in its neglect of problems in the high schools where it is hard to both teach and learn, the delays in setting up graduate schools, the degeneration of the research environment at universities, the shortage of teaching staff at universities, and so on. In addition there are the problems of the younger generation's drift away from the sciences and technology, the growing disinterest in the manufacturing industry among students majoring in fields of science or technology, and so on. There is really not enough space in this chapter to enumerate all the signs of trouble. The government's loss of interest in education which is at the root of the problems we are facing in cultivating human resources may very well be exaccerbating these troubles.

In the past education was aimed at character building and improving human nature. The aim of education was considered to advance not only the knowledge of the individual but also society and the entire human race. Education was viewed to have the capacity to bestow childhood with curiosity, imagination, and initiative that could improve the welfare of society overall.

Today's education has not succeeded in imparting the proper curiosity and initiative to children. Notions of character building, stamina, and diligence have become obsolete. The stiff entrance examination competition is deceptive; it suggests that the Japanese people have considerable interest in education, whereas reality reveals otherwise. Success at entrance examinations might suggest stable employment in a large corporation, and thus a guarantee of easy life by their educational background. However, these hopes are not connected with education's original purpose of bestowing on citizenry responsible conduct.

Younger Generation's Drift Away from Science and Technology

In the first half of the 1980s, a big change occurred in the Japanese employment structure. The need for engineers doubled in the first five years of the 1980s. This increase exceeded that of the 1960s, which was a boom time for science and technology. Moreover a considerable portion of the increase was covered by shifts in job types among existing workers. This rapid rise was especially striking among electronic and information engineers, both areas that expanded 2.5 times in those five years.[9]

At first the rise in R&D personnel appeared to have halted with the recession brought about by the high yen rate. However, because of the expanded need for personnel after the economy's recovery, the labor crunch became all the worse in the manufacturing industry. Particularly during the so-called software crisis, there arose awareness of the shortage of people in the information fields. Then government bureaus and the affected industries worked out, in succession, measures to deal with the lack of information engineers.

This situation came to a head with the rapid decrease in the number of graduates of science and engineering departments seeking employment in the manufacturing industry. The phenomenon became striking at leading universities. The fact that a great many students from these universities went into the financial market, instead of engineering became a social issue. The slogan "Revitalize manufacturing" was popularized, which lessened some of the alienation from manufacturing.[10]

While the disregard for the manufacturing industry among students in science and technology was often discussed, signs that youngsters taking college entrance examinations were avoiding science and engineering departments became an issue as well. Then there was noticed a general shift away from science and technology among prospective college students.[11] A public opinion survey taken by the prime minister's office struck another blow, for it revealed that in a sharp decline from the 1980s, Japanese men in their twenties had little interest in science and technology; nearly half of the young respondents said that science or technology did not interest them.[12] These phenomena coming in the wake of the turning away from manufacturing by students in science and engineering then came to be known as the problem of reorienting the "younger generation's drift away from science and technology." As was obvious, the Japanese youths' alienation from science and technology would result in a shortage of researchers and engineers would affect the quality of research and development in the future.

As debate was proceeding on the prospect of science and technology shunned by college students, the decline in the number of students who completed high school courses in physics came to be discussed as well. A revision of the high school curriculum in 1982 had made physics, chemistry, biology, and geology elective subjects. Although before those changes, nearly 85 percent of high school pupils completed courses in physics, this number was more than halved to 35 percent after the curriculum revision.[13] The revision was the direct impetus for the pupils avoiding these subjects. There was also discussion of another commonly held view that the way science is taught in elementary and junior high school causes youngsters to end up hating science. Whichever the cause of this disinterest in science subjects, it is symbolic of the weakening in educational fields in which Japan has traditionally been said to be strong.

Both the decrease in high school pupils studying physics and the increase in the number of university graduates in science and technology seeking employment at banks reflect a problem of the present times. The real problem is that today young people are self-absorbed and are thus losing sight of time-honored values. The motivation behind getting an education has become askewed.

Manifestation of Problems

Overall, education in Japan has succeeded in raising the people's level of literacy. Yet it has failed to produce leaders with a vision and to cultivate human ingenuity. In pre–World War II Japan the educational system offered a greater variety of educational routes in the form of the imperial universities that supplied high-level bureaucrats, the private universities that supplied the professional fields, the trade schools that supplied the specialized workers, the practical business schools that supplied office workers, the teachers' schools that trained instructors, the military-related schools, and so on. Each occupied a unique position within the educational system, which was designed to meet the educational needs of the rising middle class.

With the post–World War II reforms in education the schooling was unified into a system of progression going from elementary school to junior high school and then to high school. The increase in youngsters entering high school among the baby boom generation leveled off the educational background of the Japanese. In addition higher education, which prior to World War II was only within the reach of the elite, rapidly became available as private universities expanded.

Along with the rise in the number of youngsters going to college, higher education declined in quality. There thus emerged a higher education completely different from the elite schooling seen at prewar universities. Moreover the idea of egalitarian elementary education spread to secondary schooling and even to university education. It all led to a strong inclination to deny even functional differentiations within higher education[14] and brought about a higher educational system that emphasizes homogeneity where differences can only be measured by entrance examinations.

Although, as a result, the work force on the whole proceeded to get more schooling than ever before, the educational system came to neglect its responsibility for cultivating creativity and leadership.

The company methods of training employees become more generalized as well, and leaders have often been chosen from among these employees. Demand for creative individuals has been strong on the corporate side. Yet when it comes to hiring such individuals and promoting them, the companies have been unable to adjust their existing personnel structures, which are based on the seniority system. Consequently it is no exaggeration to say that nowhere in Japan today is there an institution taking the responsibility to cultivate creative workers and leaders.

Indeed, Japanese society has yet to agree on where to foster creativity and leadership and how to involve education in this goal. While such a circumstance may have been acceptable in the postwar period when Japan took western education as its model, Japan ought to start to think and act on its own. The role of education in cultivating creative people and leaders is crucial, and must be viewed as an important task.

12.3 Impoverishment of the University System

It is not only children and their parents who are estranged from education. The government has lost faith in it as well. Further, although the industrial sector has recently, finally, come to show interest in research activities and teaching at universities, its expectations about universities do not appear to be particularly high.

Underdeveloped Graduate Schools

The graduate school system makes for one bottleneck in Japanese higher education. The graduate school system began in Japan with the establishment of the Imperial University. However, the university act of that time did not stipulate the objectives of graduate schools clearly, so they did not function adequately under the prewar system. The number of graduate students in Japan in 1925 came to 1,037 and increased to about 2,600 in 1935. Afterward the enrollment began decreasing, and it fell to under 2,000 in 1940.[15]

An accreditation program for standardizing graduate schools was instituted in 1974, and it pertained to the curriculum in the master's degree programs. The foundation was thus laid for expanding the master's curriculum, especially in engineering fields. Graduate schools could establish majors departments and programs with exclusive faculties. Thus it at last became possible to found autonomous graduate schools not dependent on college departments.

Since the 1980s the number of students in master's degree programs at graduate schools, especially in science and engineering, has increased. In recent years over 20 percent of college graduates have advanced to graduate school in engineering fields, which has produced a continual excess of engineers. Facing the leading universities have been over 50 percent of college graduates who have proceeded to master's degree programs. Further the number of foreign students attending graduate school particularly at national universities in Japan has grown. The number has increased with such frequency that at certain universities even more foreign students can be seen in Ph.D. programs than their Japanese colleagues.

Such an increase in the number of graduate students highlights the discrepancies in the graduate school system. That is to say, at some universities and in some faculties (research programs) graduate education gets overemphasized, and undergraduate activities get short shrift, with graduate programs all the while remaining financially dependent on the undergraduate faculties and facilities. This setup has hindered the development of university educational and research resources.

However, as master's programs have expanded, fewer students have advanced to the Ph.D. programs, which are supposed to train successors to the current teaching staff. There are worries about a future shortage of teachers in the social sciences and engineering. If Japan is to remain in a leadership in research and development, it must promote creative thinkers. Particularly in Ph.D. programs, which call for high-level research methods, the number of Japanese students finishing is low by international standards.

Crisis in the University Research Environment

The research environment at Japanese universities has degenerated substantially since 1982 because of zero ceiling/negative ceiling fiscal budget policies of the government. At a time when it is necessary to renovate and conserve the facilities constructed when higher education expanded, these facilities are going to waste because monetary investments for that purpose have decreased. Research expenses have essentially been in a period of decline, and the discrepancy in the research conditions between the universities and the industrial sector has rapidly expanded, calling for increased government investment in higher education.

Of course, the constraints of the national budget have only roused to the surface the deteriorating research conditions. The root of the problem is very deep. While universities may be responsible for assuming the dual function of education and research essentially from the time the new national university system was launched, they had to give priority to expanding the educational side because of financial constraints; they could not take sufficient measures to promote research. Thus, from the very outset, there have been worries about the relative weakening and dispersion of university research capacities.

Even in the 1960s, when higher education underwent expansion, similar problems were evident. Proposals to intensify the research capacities were made both in the 1971 report by the Central Council on Education and the 1973 report by the Science Council of the Ministry of Education, Science, and Culture. However, after the University of Tsukuba was established, hardly any moves were taken to change and strengthen the research functions at existing universities. The problem was rather tackled with measures like establishing interuniversity research institutions outside of the universities, but the question of improving research capacity within universities was left alone.

For this reason the decline of Japanese university research has to be attributed to a university system centered around undergraduate education. It has positioned the education and research capacities of graduate schools as supplementary functions to undergraduate departments. Reform of the research environment is an urgent task. More students must be encouraged to go on to high-level research and raise the human resources needed to shoulder the future of Japan.

In the 1990s the sense of crisis has at last been growing strong. Demand for prompt reform of the research base has come from both the industrial sector and the government.[16] Reports in 1992 by the Science and Technology Council and by the Science Council have taken in the debates and recommended reforms in the university research environment. The general opinion expressed is that the government budget for science and technology must be doubled. However, there has been little progress in bringing this to fruition. Debates over money have waged on, and the effort of finding a solution has been delayed further by the lack of a fundamental vision for reforming higher education and the research systems.

Engineering Education and the Industrial World's Obligations

The deterioration of the university research environment is especially serious in fields of engineering. As was noted earlier, the engineering fields already have to contend with a shift of interest away from science and technology among the younger Japanese. That has surfaced as an important challenge for engineering education and research. The first problem is that engineering education is incapable of handling changes in industry and industrial technology flexibly. Reports, for example, "Engineering Education in the Period of Transition" (in Japanese by the Higher Education Bureau of the Ministry of Education, Science, and Culture, 1989), and "Cultivating Human Resources and Arranging a System to Support the Future" (in Japanese by the Engineering Education Committee of the Engineering Academy of Japan, 1990), have pointed out sore points like the imbalances in the supply and demand for human resources, the decline in quality of engineers, the lack of an educational system that will guarantee the quality of graduates, and the deficiency of internationalism in the cultivation of personnel. At the base of these discussions have been anxieties that the existing structure and educational content of engineering departments have become incapable of responding flexibly to the demands of the age.

Next is the problem that internal self-help efforts alone cannot raise engineering education in Japan from its impoverished state. There have been claims for some time that universities must revitalize education on their own and respond effectively to the demands of the age by taking charge. However, university engineering departments have been placed in circumstances where at present it is difficult for them even to make self-help efforts.

"Engineering Education to Pioneer the Future," a report put together in Japanese in 1991 from a roundtable discussion by the chairs of engineering departments at eight leading universities, describes the basic problem in the following way, "In response to societal needs after World War II, the engineering departments at universities contributed to Japan's high economic growth by cultivating human capital from a stock of knowledge built up since the Meiji period. But that stock is now diminished." Expressing misgivings about a structure that, if anything, has impoverished universities, while allowing Japanese industries to become rich, the report recommends that: "A portion of the wealth of private sector ought to be returned to rebuild the faculty and facilities at universities."

The lack of government investment in science and technology at universities has become an international issue as well. Further lack of financial resources has made it difficult for universities to support creative initiatives that can launch new industries. This situation is endangering the future of manufacturing. Has Japan, which now ranks as an economic giant, produced any new industries? Fields in which Japan has succeeded prominently like steel, automobiles, and semiconductors are all imported industries. It is probably no exaggeration to say that there are no industries (at least in manufacturing) that Japan has created on its own.

The university culture in the United States has produced the new field known as the information industry. It is a clear case of mutual support between universities and industry. The universities in Japan today do not have the strength sufficient for creating new industries. If things are left as they are, the outlook for Japanese manufacturing can only be bleak. Japanese industries must recognize that they are about to lose a vital force in the form of the universities if they continue with their enthusiasm for in-house education and scant attention to the educational facilities at Japanese universities. The very companies that have made enormous investments in their own R&D activities have ignored the impoverishment of their native university research environment.

It is only recently that the serious decline in university research activities and engineering education has been brought to the attention of Japanese industries though the industrial sector should have shown interest in university problems before now. A communications forum is needed whereby the relationship between the industrial sector and the universities can be worked out. A position on cooperative education (not limited to higher education) between industry and academe needs to be agreed on.

Japan needs creative leaders for its industrial future. The younger generation's turning away from science and technology has been casting a dark shadow across engineering education and manufacturing industries. It is in the interest of the industrial sector to find ways to improve the prospect of engineering education so that young people will be attracted to the field.

Notes

1. Ministry of Education, Science, and Culture, *Nihon no Seicho to Keizai* (Growth and the Economy in Japan), 1962.

2. Ministry of Education, Science, and Culture, *Waga Kuni no Bunkyo Shisaku:Showa 63-nendo* (Education and Culture Policies in Japan: 1988), 1988.

3. National Institute for Educational Research, *IEA Kokusai Sugaku oyobi Rika Kyoiku Chukan Hokoku* (IEA Interim Report on International Mathematics and Science Education), 1988. In Japan, this survey was for mathematics in 1980 and for the sciences in 1983.

4. Ministry of Education, Science, and Culture, *Nihon no Seicho to Keizai* (Growth and the Economy in Japan), 1962.

5. Zeugner, J. F., The Puzzle of Higher Education in Japan: What Can We Learn from the Japanese? *Change* 16, 1983.

6. Yano, M., Muta, H., and Kobayashi, S., *Kigyonai Kyoiku no Henka to sono Hiyo-Koka Bunseki ni kansuru Kenkyu* (Change in In-house Education and an Analysis of Its Cost-Effectiveness), Tokyo, 1990.

7. Concern about these circumstances has brought cries for the succession of technology, such as in proposals for "A Bank of Living Witnesses to Industrial Technology." See the Ministry of International Trade and Industry, *Sangyo Gijutsu no Rekishi no Keisho to Mirai e no Sozo* (The History of Industrial Technology and Plans for the Future), Tsusho Sangyo Chosakai, 1992.

8. Graduate schools in Japan have a system whereby a person, without undertaking courses in graduate school, can receive a Ph.D. by submitting a thesis for the approval of a committee.

9. Kobayashi, S., Gijutsusha no Ichijirushii Zoka to Ichijirushii Koreika (The Startling Increase in Aging Technicians), *Spectrum-Japan* 3, no. 11 (1990): 38–39.

10. Kobayashi, S., Rikokei Gakusei no Seizogyo-Banare: Jittai to Tenbo (The Move Away from Manufacturing by Students in the Sciences and Technology: Actual Cases and Prospects), in *Jinpon-Gata Kigyo e no Henkaku* (Becoming People-Oriented Companies), Kikai Shinko Kyokai Keizai Kenkyujo, Tokyo, 1991, pp. 26–82.

11. Sato, E., Kikuchi, H., and Hirano, C., *Daigaku Shingaku Kibosha no Shinro Sentaku ni tsuite* (The Choices Made by Prospective College Entrants), Kagaku Gijutsu Seisaku Kenkyujo, Tokyo, 1990.

12. Nagahama, H., Kuwabara, T., and Nishimoto, A., *Kagaku Gijutsu to Shakai to no Communication no Arikata no Kenkyu* (Research on the Effects of Scientific Technology on Society), Kagaku Gijutsu Seisaku Kenkyujo, Tokyo, 1991.

13. Karaki, H., Kiki ni Tatsu Koko Butsuri Kyoiku (High School Physics Education in Crisis), *Parity* 5, no. 6 (1990): 60–63.

14. In a report by the Central Education Council in 1971, there were discussions on functional stratification of universities. However, hardly anything in this way has been enacted up to now.

15. Ministry of Education, Science, and Culture, *Gakusei Hachijunen-shi* (An Eighty-Year History of the School System), 1954.

16. For example, the Federation of Economic Organizations (Keidanren) has pointed out in its 1991 report, *Nijuisseiki o Mezashita Kenkyu Kaihatsu Taisei no Kakuritsu o Nozomu: Daigaku Kokuritsu Shiken Kenkyu Kikan no Jujitsu to Kagaku Gijutsu Bunya no Kokusai Koken no Tame ni* (Aiming for the Establishment of a Research and Development System Directed at the Twenty-first Century: In Order to Perfect the Universities and National Testing and Research Institutions and to Bring about International Contributions in Fields of Science and Technology), that the deterioration of the research environment at universities is threatening to destroy Japan's development at its very base. It therefore called for improvements in basic research and in the education of researchers and engineers.

13 Changing Circumstances of Employment: From Homogeneous to Heterogeneous Work Force

Atsushi Seike

The present employment structure in Japan has evolved by adapting to the economic circumstances of Japanese companies which had to find a means of catching up with the companies of industrialized nations. Two characteristics of this economic environment have been that Japan's companies have a pyramid-shaped labor structure with many young people at the base and that companies compete by volume producing as much as they possibly can sell.

Currently this environment is undergoing a major change. Japan has become one of the most industrialized nations in the world and has reached a point where it now has to compete more by added value than by volume. The pyramid-shaped labor structure has also been rapidly changing. As the twenty-first century approaches, it is becoming clear that Japan will soon be a nation of few young people and many people in the mid to elderly years. In line with such societal changes, the Japanese employment structure will unavoidably shift from a labor force composed mainly of young to middle-aged men to a diverse work force that includes more women of all age groups and elderly men.

Along with these changes the employment system will also have to be rearranged to allow individuals with professional skills to make the best use of their abilities. The current vision is that the system in which employers have a large homogeneous labor force working long hours will be replaced by a.system in which a small heterogeneous labor force does high-level work.

13.1 Employment in the Period of Change

Japan's labor force is widely known to be the wellspring of Japanese competitiveness. Indeed, for Japan, which has few natural resources, the labor force is the one economic resource that it has had in plenty. Indeed other countries often regard with awe the diligence of Japanese workers and their company loyalty. Japan further offers a modern industrial labor force of high ability in terms of measurable qualities like literacy and educational level.

However, these qualities do not mean that the Japanese labor force was born to work long hours and be unquestioningly loyal to the organization. Certainly Moto-o Endo's research[1] investigating the life-styles of handicrafts workers of the Edo period (1603–1867) shows that Japanese workers have traditionally taken professional pride in their high skills. But the loyalty of those times had more to do with the vertical relationship between the master and his disciples which ensured his control. Actually the craftsmen's working day was quite leisurely, for it entailed a break in the morning, a break at noon, another break for a snack, and then ended at sunset. Now, as far as loyalty to the company goes, the factory owners in the mid-Meiji period must have had a lot of headaches, for there was a high rate of job-changing among migrant workers who wandered from plant to plant in groups centered around a master seeking the most favorable labor conditions.[2]

More than anything, the present strength of Japanese companies lies in the incentives that they have put together to motivate their employees to do their jobs well with full loyalty to their companies. Today these incentives include a system of seniority in wages and guarantees of long-term employment until mandatory retirement. According to Odaka, the system only originated in the Japanese heavy industries around 1920; it became widespread during the postwar industrial recovery effort.[3]

World War I had provided the stimulus for Japan to build heavy industries. Before then, up through the Meiji period Japanese manufacturing had been centered around light industries. Thereafter manufacturing firms focused on shipbuilding, electric equipment, and so on, and imported advanced technology from overseas.

However, such imported technologies were completely new to Japan; there were no skilled workers within or without the companies who knew how to handle them. The firms therefore chose to hire young, promising unskilled laborers who had just finished their compulsory education and to offer them a full-fledged education and training so that they could acquire the necessary skills. The program entailed not only simple hands-on training but also an education in fundamental academic subjects that served as the basis for learning advanced technology. That was the beginning of a sort of work-study program.[4]

Then labor structure in fact had a clear pyramid shape that reflected the population structure. The young working force was plentiful and could be obtained cheaply. The opportunity of education provided by a company attracted outstanding youths who could not otherwise proceed to a higher level of schooling because of the income limitations of their families.

For such a full-fledged education and training program to be carried out at considerable cost to a company, it had to be viewed as a human resource investment. The firm had naturally to feel that it could recoup its full investment, since there would be financial losses if the workers it had educated and trained were fired or quit on them. For that reason Japanese companies created a structure of wages based on seniority and lifetime employment that ensured that those who work hard while young would enjoy the benefits later. In this way workers became encouraged to stay employed at a company for a long time.

About the time when technology was imported into Japan in the 1950s and 1960s, the system of wages according to seniority and lifetime employment guarantees—which had been enjoyed by white-collar workers and only blue-collar workers at a small number of large corporations before the war—came to be extended to blue-collar workers at most companies. The pattern then took root whereby workers could decide to stay permanently with one company and enrich their lives along with the company's development. In this way companies acquired capable and dedicated employees.

The long postwar period of peace allowed Japan moreover to expand its world markets. Japanese workers were in a situation whereby they would be rewarded if they tried hard and served their companies well. This easily raised their morale, prompting more dedicated effort. Even though the income level of each worker was low, dissatisfaction hardly surfaced toward the company that gave the individual an employment opportunity at a time of a still abundant labor supply.

At each and every benchmark in the growth of the Japanese businesses, there have been moderate crises like the liberalization of capital, the oil crises, and the high yen. Through these troubles the workers have maintained their enthusiasm for their workplaces despite continual inflation of the economy which can easily dampen morale.

Essentially Japan's strength until now has been maintained by the advantages of being a latecomer with a young, low-cost labor force that could learn high-level technology already developed elsewhere, by company management being ready to develop during a period of postwar peace and high growth in the world's economy, and by high worker morale brought on by plentiful labor supply and occasional unemployment crises.

All these favorable conditions are starting to change. Today Japan, which stands among the top industrialized countries, no longer holds the advantages of a latecomer. Company populations are aging and not easily being replaced by younger workers. As the Japanese economy has neared 15 percent of the world's GNP, the rest of the world has intervened not to allow Japan to continue unlimited growth. Japan is on the brink of an age of scarce employment opportunities and diminishing workers' morale. Recent accounts from Japanese corporate circles suggest already the end of an age when people show unconditional loyalty to a company just for giving them the chance for employment.

Japanese companies must look toward creating distinctive technology and concentrate on high-quality products such as can be expected from a mature working population. These challenges will be major challenges to employment practices as well.

13.2 Changes in the Labor Force

Labor Supply

Let us consolidate the factors that will fundamentally transform Japanese employment. We will begin by looking at the trends that have occurred in the supply and demand for labor.

The supply of labor is determined by the number of people over the age of fifteen who can be legally employed and the percentage of that population who want to be employed. The proportion of the people employed to the people looking for work is what is called the *labor force participation rate*.

As can be seen from table 13.1, the population over fifteen years old has continued increasing, from about 60 million in the 1950s to 100 million in 1990. According to birth rate forecasts, the figure is expected to peak at about 108 million in 2000 and then to decline. However, a closer look at these data reveals that the population aged 15 to 19 has

Table 13.1
Changes in the population structure (ten thousands)

Year	Over age 15,	15–19	20–29	30–39	40–54	55–59	60–64	Over 65
1955	5,949	863	1,601	1,123	1,316	321	250	475
1960	6,536	931	1,653	1,356	1,404	364	293	535
1965	7,310	1,085	1,743	1,576	1,554	400	334	618
1970	7,889	906	1,975	1,658	1,802	442	373	733
1975	8,468	795	1,987	1,767	2,137	467	428	887
1980	8,947	827	1,688	1,997	2,362	561	447	1,065
1985	9,497	898	1,602	1,979	2,530	700	541	1,247
1990	10,114	1,002	1,711	1,682	2,783	773	673	1,490
1995	10,537	854	1,883	1,589	2,850	792	746	1,823
2000	10,805	747	1,849	1,690	2,714	872	765	2,170
2025	10,756	722	1,400	1,274	2,549	843	749	3,244

Source: Bureau of Statistics, Department of General Affairs, Prime Minister's Office, *Kokusei Chosa* (National Census) Population Research Center, Ministry of Health and Public Welfare, *Shorai Jinko Suikei* (Future Population Estimates), 1993.

already peaked in 1990 and that the population aged 20 to 29 will reach its peak around 1995. This means that the employable population (age 15 and over) will start to decrease over the next ten years.

How will this change affect the percentage of the population who wants to work? The change in the population of men in their prime years from their 20s to 50s who have an almost 100 percent need to work no matter what matches the transformation in the labor force population. The question is the younger generation of women, women in all age groups, and elderly men.

Unlike men in their prime, the work force participation rate among these groups is less than 100 percent and also happens to be fluctuating. Even under the same population structure, if the labor force participation rate goes down, this labor force population will drop. In the opposite situation, it will increase.

Figure 13.1 shows the statistics on the labor force participation rate for the younger generation (men and women aged 15 to 19), women in general, and older men (aged 60 to 64). Since the labor force participation rate among the younger generation is the exact opposite of the rate of advancement to higher-level schools, it has declined along with the rise in the percentages going onto high school and college. Then, as the rate of advancement to universities hit an all-time high

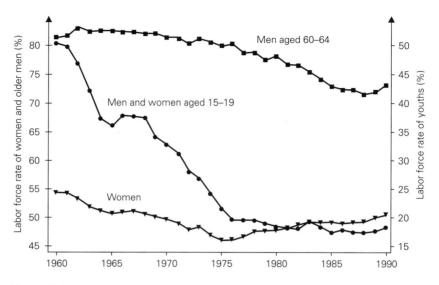

Figure 13.1
Labor force participation rate of older people, women, and youths. Source: Bureau of
Statistics, Department of General Affairs, Prime Minister's Office, *Rodoryoku Chosa Nenpo*
(Annual Report of Labor Force Surveys).

around 1980, the work force rate bottomed, remaining at a 17 to 18
percent level thereafter.

By contrast, the labor force participation rate among women has
dropped along with the decline in the proportion of the self-employed,
such as farming households where the husband and wife work together. However, in the late 1970s, after the drop in the proportion of
the self-employed bottomed and also after employment adjustments
ended right in the wake of the first oil crisis, labor force participation
started to rise. This can be attributed to an increase in the number of
housewives taking part-time employment coupled with a rise in continuous employment of women in their twenties. The decline in household income spanning from the late 1970s to the 1980s explains why
housewives sought employment. The rise in the number of women
who continued working into their late twenties can be attributed to
the rise in the average marriage age of women. This rise in the female
labor force participation rate contributed to a leveling out of the trough
between the two peaks that form the M-curve vis-à-vis women's employment.

Similarly the labor supply rate of older people which has been on a
decline since the 1960s is due mainly to a drop in the percentage of

the self-employed. However, the decline since the mid-1970s, when the proportion of the self-employed in this age range stopped decreasing, was because of adjustments in their circumstances. The most significant factor is that rapid improvements in the standard pension benefits following major revisions of the pension system in 1973 enabled salaried workers to retire.

Along with the improved conditions of retirement, the labor conditions offered by companies conducting outage management following the oil crises was unappealing to older people. An increasing number of older people opted for free time to do what they want to do while they still had their health, and this appears to have been another factor behind the drop in the labor force participation rate.

So what is the current outlook given these employment trends among the younger generation, women in general, and older men? First of all, it is hard to imagine that the labor force participation rate among the younger generation will reverse itself and rise. Since 1980 the decline of the labor force participation rate has halted among the younger generation, but this is attributable to a drop in the rate of advancement to college after it reached an all-time high. The rate of advancement to college has, in part, been affected by college admissions quotas which have not been increased despite increases in the college-aged population because in the future the youth population is expected to decline. In part, it has also been affected by the rising operation costs of universities and rising faculty salaries.[5] In fact it is hard to think of any circumstance that could reverse the labor force participation rate of the younger generation despite the decline in the rate of advancement to college.

In general, the labor force participation rate for women depends on the extent to which the trough of the M-curve rises. The working environment has accommodated women workers by the enactment of the Equal Employment Opportunity Law in 1985 and recent regulations on maternity leaves, but some problems remain. As fewer youths enter the work force in the future, the participation rate of women will likely rise further provided that companies continue to improve wages and working hours in ways that attract women to the workplace.

As regards the situation for older men, first of all, the minimum eligible age for pension benefits will inevitably be raised in the near future, with more stringent controls over conditions for receiving these benefits. For this reason the labor force participation rate will probably not drop if there is a surfeit in pension funds. As in the case of women, if a company facing a shortage of youthful laborers sets up the right environment and improves working conditions to utilize the skills of retirement-age people, some may be inclined to come back to the workplace. However, most older Japanese people seem to want the free time, so companies must work to attract them by arranging an environment that does not interfere with their hobbies and social activities. Along this line, it should be pointed out that in the early 1960s, when public pensions were not fully set up and the percentage of self-employed was still high, the labor force participation rate among those aged 60 to 64 was over 80 percent. This suggests that given attractive circumstances, many older workers may choose to delay retirement, although it seems unlikely that an 80 percent employment level of these workers will ever be reached again.

Nevertheless, the population numbers show that the labor force cannot help but decline from now on, since the population of younger people is decreasing. The labor force participation rate of women and older men must be raised to offset this decline, and companies must strive to attract these two groups to the workplace. This means that the labor force must be transformed to a more diverse composition in gender and age. As this occurs, the Japanese company hierarchy will be forced to reflect the change as well.

In general, we can expect such heterogeneity that includes skilled older women and men to raise the quality of the human capital component of Japanese companies. No doubt, the level of education of people who will be senior citizens in the near future will be markedly higher because of the increased rate of advancement to higher education. Likewise job skills, for example, of married women who reenter the labor force will be higher, since many would have had an earlier work record. Although some older workers today may have trouble learning how to use high-tech machines, the senior workers of the future will be people who used personal computers while young. The percentage of such older workers having high-level white-collar job experience will go up as well. The quality of labor force is already starting to rise as more young people advance to higher education.

Finally, there is the issue of the foreign labor supply. First of all, highly capable foreign professionals and researchers are definitely welcome in Japan. Such people, and of course women and men in Japan with new ways of thinking, can stimulate the Japanese corporate organization and help it to become more open and forthright. However, the idea of importing low-skilled, low-waged work force to deal with any labor shortages seems, if anything, to go against the tide of structural reforms in Japanese companies. Such a move would also leave Japan with industries and firms that are otherwise unable to maintain competitiveness by the nation's wage and labor standards.

Such industries and companies would be better off anyway moving to the countries that supply this low-waged work force and thus contributing to the economic development and expansion of employment there. To set Japanese industry on a high value-added track, it is important that it coordinate with other countries by means of an international distribution of labor. Japanese industry should turn away from any temptation to bring in low-waged foreign workers but rather should seek to motivate an exceptional labor force with high wages.

Nevertheless, Japan cannot afford to ignore people in developing countries. Transferring Japanese industrial technology there may improve the distribution of labor internationally, and promising youths from developing countries could be brought for training to Japanese firms. While companies themselves could pay for such training, there should be additional support from the government's ODA budget, among other considerations.

Demand for Labor

Let us now look at the changes in the demand for labor. Since the employment of government public servants is frequently decided outside of market forces, we will regard here as demand for labor the number of people employed in nonagricultural private companies as well as in publicly managed corporations (other than those serving the public).

Table 13.2 gives the employment trends of both private and publicly managed corporations. As the table shows, the number of employees was about 31 million in 1972 and rose to approximately 46 million in 1992, for an increase of about 15 million. The total work force, including self-employed individuals and working members of family businesses, went up during this period from approximately 51 million to about 64 million, for an increase of about 13 million. Overall the demand for labor increased 1.6 times during this twenty-year period.

However, the distribution of employment was not uniform. As can be seen, in manufacturing industries, which form the core of labor demand, the number of employees was between about 11 million and 13 million, which means that there was not much change.

Table 13.2
Changes in the number of employees by industry

	Private enterprises								National corporation	Local government corporation
Industries	Total (excluded agriculture, forestry and fishery)	Mining	Construction	Manufacturing	Electricity, gas, heat, water supply services; transport; communications	Wholesaling, retailing, food and/or beverage-dispensing	Finance, insurance, real estate	Service	National corporation	Local government corporation
Number of persons engaged (thousands)										
1972	38,794	187	3,981	13,298	2,230	11,691	1,793	5,615	1,419	1,901
1975	39,641	146	4,161	12,664	2,243	12,329	1,964	6,134	1,427	2,090
1978	42,295	133	4,616	12,509	2,372	13,556	2,151	6,958	1,443	2,195
1981	45,720	129	4,949	12,863	2,555	14,850	2,315	8,059	1,426	2,356
1986	48,995	103	4,789	13,342	2,980	15,673	2,498	9,611	919	2,429
1989	51,676	97	5,021	13,682	3,272	16,617	2,708	10,279	—	—
1992	54,792	78	5,282	14,087	3,488	16,875	2,987	11,995	694	2,497
Number of employees (thousands)										
1972	30,639	174	3,355	11,736	2,098	7,553	1,557	4,167	1,419	1,901
1975	30,929	133	3,446	11,051	2,093	7,968	1,686	4,551	1,427	2,090
1978	33,070	121	3,804	10,879	2,213	8,960	1,826	5,268	1,443	2,195
1981	35,473	115	3,971	11,102	2,361	9,862	1,925	6,137	1,427	2,356
1986	39,200	92	3,838	11,712	2,793	11,066	2,081	7,619	919	2,429
1992	45,519	68	4,319	12,650	3,290	12,751	2,520	10,042	694	2,497

Source: Bureau of Statistics, Department of General Affairs, Prime Minister's Office, *Jigyosho Tokei Chosa* (Statistical Survey on Business Enterprises).

Consequently the proportion of manufacturing employees has declined from a onetime high of nearly 50 percent to the present 30 percent level. By contrast, wholesaling, retailing, and the service industries increased their number of employees. Taken together, wholesaling and retailing nearly doubled in workers from about 7.5 million to approximately 13 million, thus exceeding manufacturing which nevertheless alone more than doubled from about 4 million to approximately 10 million.

Within the manufacturing industries a great change has been occurring in the number of job types. There has been a decline in the staffing of blue-collar production processes. Figure 13.2 compares the employment trends of workers in agriculture, forestries, and fisheries (first sector); workers in mining, transport, and communications, including engineers and operators of machinery (second sector); employees in sales, security, and service fields (third sector); and employees in professional occupations including managerial and clerical jobs (fourth sector).

As can be seen from the figure, while the number of blue-collar jobs in the first and second sectors decreased or stagnated, white-collar jobs in the third and fourth sectors increased. Particularly striking is the increase in the fourth sector, which reflects the rising demand for high-level professional work.

Clearly, as these labor trends indicate, major changes in job types and the composition of labor have occurred since the 1970s. They reflect the "white-collarization" of the industrial structure. We could say that a tertiary industrialization structure has raised labor demand to a higher level.

The figure also reflects improvements in productivity, especially in the manufacturing industry. From 1966 to 1990 the production indexes in mining and manufacturing industries increased approximately fourfold, while the number of employees in manufacturing stayed approximately the same during this period. Thus the growth in productivity per worker rose nearly fourfold. In fact, labor productivity index by the Japan Productivity Center showed a quadruple increase during this period as well.

This increase of productivity was brought about by the rise in capital investment in the manufacturing sector, which was accompanied by a greater number of workers hired with high-level professional skills. The rise in manufacturing's productivity, the slump in the total number of employees in manufacturing, and the improved composition of job types have entirely changed the employment structure in Japan.

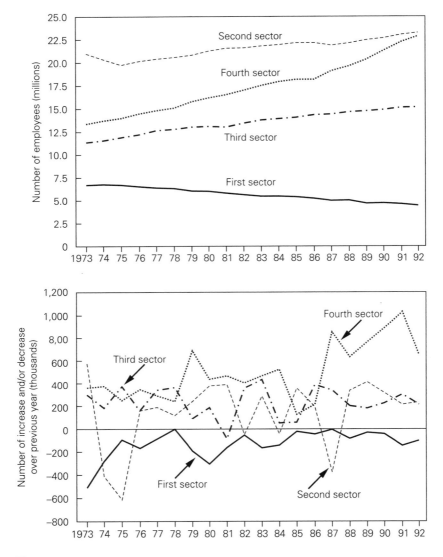

Figure 13.2
Changes in the number of employees according to jobs in four sectors. *First sector:*
Agricultural, forestry, and fishery workers. *Second sector:* Miners, workers in transport
or communications, technicians, production process workers, and laborers. *Third sector:*
Salespeople, security personnel, and service industry workers. *Fourth sector:* Workers in
specialized/technical fields or administrative positions. Source: Bureau of Statistics,
Department of General Affairs, Prime Minister's Office, *Rodoryoku Chosa Nenpo* (Annual
Report of Labor Force Surveys), 1992 ed.

Fundamentally, these trends are expected to continue in the near future with some further improvements in the industrial structure and a shift to added-value productivity. The demand for white-collar work is expected to go up still more, while that for simple blue-collar work will decline. By the year 2000, according to the Economic Planning Agency's "Development of Human Resources in a Period of Transition in the Employment Structure," there will be shortages of about 2.8 million professional workers and 500,000 office workers. Conversely there will be a surplus of about 3 million mechanics and factory workers.

The demand for labor eased after the Japanese bubble economy burst. As the children of baby-boomers, whose birth rate should be increasing until the mid-1990s, mature, the present state of economic retrogression will easily yield to widespread unemployment. We cannot ignore the fact that unemployment is already becoming an issue due to the excessive investments and overemployment that took place during the bubble economy. We have again circumstances that resemble the 1970s when Japan was hit with the oil crises during a period of high economic growth, affecting tremendous numbers of employed people.

13.3 Changes in the Ways of Working

Rationale in the Era of Abundant Labor

At the present time the configuration of Japan's supply of labor is changing and approaching an era when youthful workers will be scarce. The labor force will be composed of advanced workers and include many women and retirement-age men. Already, labor demand has shifted away from blue-collar in the manufacturing sector to white-collar workers oriented around tertiary industries. Changes in the composition of the population and in the development of the economy seem to be the factors behind this trend.

Up until now the Japanese economic strength has been inherent in the fact that its economic development and the population structure meshed with each other. It was primarily focused on the objective, understood by Japanese companies, of catching up with the Western market and new technology. In fact, until each Japanese household was fully equipped with the necessities of daily life such as televisions and refrigerators, what to sell was not an issue among electrical appliance manufacturers. It was clear back then that all they had to do was to make and sell more refrigerators and televisions to meet consumer demand.

Such major appliances had been disseminated for quite some time in the United States and other industrialized nations, and the technology to make these products had to be imported from overseas—especially from the United States. Some westerners like the American Dr. Deming even came to Japan to teach companies how to make high-quality appliances, though basically using imported technology.

Competition then meant expanding Japan's share by producing and marketing cheaply a large volume of good quality products that companies knew would sell. To make productivity more efficient and at the same time to improve quality so that the products were durable were the main objectives.

Indeed it was the efficiency in the manufacturing production processes, where cost control combined with the excellent workmanship of blue-collar workers, that formed the basis of the competitive edge. It was important for white-collar workers, particularly engineers, to fully understand and assimilate the production technology. Likewise at the marketing end, since they only had to promote many more of the same products, this also meant doing work that required little relearning. Even in tertiary industries, for instance, on days when bank interest rates completely restricted lending, each bank would issue the same rate to savers. Competition was carried out by leg work, by making the rounds to clients.

Work, in a manner of speaking, meant doing the same thing, sweating away for long hours, in order for a company to succeed in the marketplace. And, at that time, these companies were blessed with a labor supply structure that allowed an abundant young work force to be hired cheaply and easily. These vast numbers of young workers, who learned on the job, later would put their minds together to carry out all the company initiatives. Competition was conducted by quantitative expansion, which, along with a company's growth, was also easy to maintain given a pyramid-shaped organization. As the number of people hired was increased every year, the veteran staff gradually taught the newcomers the understood work and moved on to administrative positions.

Since the perceived wisdom was to proceed in as great a volume as possible and combine experience, it was especially convenient to have a homogeneous labor force that could quickly take hints from one another. Moreover, since fundamental work knowledge was involved, how to absorb it efficiently had to be considered in terms of a capacity to learn. In this corporate world individuality was not necessary and in fact got in the way of work.

So far Japanese companies have continued this practice and have succeeded in the marketplace by fundamentally carrying out the notion of common long-term learning and depending on an abundant and relatively low-cost homogeneous labor supply.

However, for the worker, the abundant labor supply meant that having a job opportunity was of primary importance. In that sense the aforementioned circumstances where employment chances were increased by a quantitative expansion of the economy were desirable. Inefficiencies were inevitable in the rush to expand job opportunities. There appeared a rationale for not only excess corporate activities like product services but also for excess societal services. For example, the work of automobile garages was increased because car inspections now had to be conducted every two years.

Employment became a buyers' market, so it was difficult to attain happiness by moving from company to company. Once a person obtained employment, it was best to work hard at that company and try to raise one's living standard as the firm grew. The underlying idea was that in order to have a good life in retirement, a person must work harder in the prime years and put up with low wages so that the company can grow. This was a logic an individual could identify with easily.

Rationale in the Era of Scarce Labor

The practice of Japanese companies to depend on an abundant homogeneous, and consequently low-cost, labor force has suited the worker quite well up to now. Today the socioeconomic conditions that were a mainstay of Japanese companies are undergoing tremendous change.

Companies have begun to face product markets and technological competition that are no longer as simple as they used to be. In a society filled with a wealth of daily essentials, consumer needs are not as easily understood as before. Companies must either guess what consumers want or stimulate their latent desires. Competing by making at lower cost the same sort of things as other companies no longer works.

Likewise the rationalization of production processes to manufacture high-end goods at low cost has come to pass. Long work hours and contrivances on the production line are no longer enough when the rivalry is waged through full-fledged technological innovation and product development. In other words, to compete successfully, companies need to venture into uncharted areas in order to raise the character of their product lines.

Competition is no longer the question of making and selling as much as possible of the same product. Value-added productivity and nuances of quality are the objectives instead. Companies, as a result, need to attend to changes in the work required of people who develop their products. The knowledge one brings to a company is more important than just working long hours. It is not just long-term experience that counts but what a veteran with such long experience can teach the junior members of the company.

For this reason companies now look to employ people with diverse education and interests. Indeed, the individuality inherent in a heterogeneous labor force is much preferred over a homogeneous group that performs the same way no matter what the task is.

Fortuitously, this tendency is reflected, overall, in the structure of Japan's work force, since it has been becoming more advanced and heterogeneous. We must admit then that the Japanese economy is fortunate enough to have sustained these changes while the corporate framework and ways of working have been undergoing readjustment. Nevertheless, the Japanese companies are faced with exploring new products, and they now have to do so with a scarce, consequently high-priced, well-educated heterogeneous labor force.

Of course, for worker, there will be many employment opportunities, so the necessity to stay with one company will be moot. Likely, as has appeared in recent criticisms of so-called corporate society, there will be a reaction against company control of all aspects of life, in particular, affecting wages which will necessarily rise because people who do high value-added work must be paid well (no doubt, for the common production-line worker, wages will remain low). In general, however, people cannot be expected to be willing to work hard for long hours at low wages while in their prime in order to be compensated with a comfortable life later on.

Use of Human Capital in an Era of Scarce Labor

A labor force that is scarce and of high value cannot be used wastefully. Of course in the past it was often cheaper to hire an abundant low-cost work force than to buy more machine equipment. In the future, however, as laborers become scarce and expensive, companies will find it extravagant to give work to people that a machine can do. Human "work" will be mostly jobs involving decision making and providing services to others. Most decisions cannot be made by machines, and the same is true for services such as sales work and administrative positions that involve direct contact with people.

Such a high-level labor force will not come cheaply. For this reason the company must make an effort to attract and keep these workers. The following four considerations should top the company's list of priorities: Make the company benefits attractive to workers so that they stay with the company; hire highly capable workers; set up their work in the most efficient way; keep job conditions pleasant.

The next extremely effective policy is to shorten the work hours. If working hours are not shortened, the aforementioned requisite conditions will fall short. Shorter hours are particularly important given the scarce number of workers who will need to be supplemented by women with young children at home and older people who cannot work long hours. Indeed, older people are often forced to retire because there are no suitable working hours for them. Companies will be incapable of filling their labor needs unless they attract those people with the will to work but not willing to do so under the hours currently required to be spent on the job.

The second effect on business if hours are not shortened concerns the worker's capacity to function and grow on the job. In the golden age, when a person knew what to make and how to make it, the worker learned skills and knowledge from his seniors on the job. So as long as he developed his abilities through diligent effort with his colleagues, his work would improve the longer he stayed at the company. However, as the market and technology continue to advance, in the future abilities like a market sense for predicting consumer trends, analytical ability, and creativity will become the decisive factors in corporate strategies. Since the market and technology will be changing constantly, there will be more areas that cannot be handled with the common sense and knowledge accumulated in the workplace. To take the time to upgrade one's abilities on one's own, aside from doing the work during company hours, is already becoming a condition for remaining a first-rate employee.

As can be seen in the left panel of figure 13.3, today an employee is so busy with the work right before him while he is in his prime years that he does not have the time for self-enrichment. Therefore by the

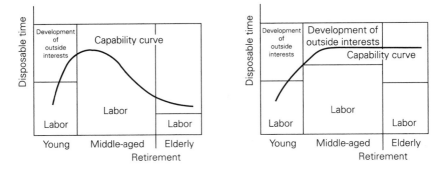

Figure 13.3
Hours worked related to the development of capabilities. Source: Atsushi Seike, White collar no rodo jikan tanshuku (The Shortening of White-Collar Workers' Hours), *Rodo Hogaku Kenkyukaiho* (Labor Law Research Review), no. 1854, December 1991.

time he attains seniority he cannot present his capabilities adequately because he is worn out physically and mentally. As is indicated in the right panel of figure 13.3, it is indispensable that one cultivate interests outside the work environment while one is still in his prime in order to have a long and fulfilling work life and to be able to function energetically even on reaching retirement age.

The third effect on business if hours are not shortened concerns efficiency. For instance, in order to reach the same living standard as the Germans, the Japanese people have to work longer hours, which amounts to two months longer per year. The longer work day is due to the little effort made to cut down on waste on the job or to encourage ingenuity in work performance. This is particularly evident among white-collar workers whose proportion of the work force has been on the rise in Japan. A reconsideration of the extensive time spent on the job is essential in order for improvements to be made in productivity.

The work ethic is the fourth business resource that will be lacking if hours are not shortened. As was mentioned earlier, in Japan advanced technical work is at the heart of the new competitive spirit. The environment that is everywhere emerging is one where every worker must compete with his or her analytic abilities; no longer will it suffice for productivity simply to increase as one works longer hours. The matter of diligence has shifted from number of hours worked to number of timely results. With diligence less rewarded, the work ethic is starting to decline in workplaces where the former evaluation structure coexists with one where a reputation for excellence is earned by the person who produces impressive results without doing overtime and also takes full vacations.

To summarize, labor power is indeed Japan's biggest economic resource. But this source of power is already becoming scarce. Since Japanese industries to survive in the world economy, they must alter their view of competition from quantitative to qualitative production, that means they must cultivate their scarce labor force to do increasingly sophisticated work.

In that regard there should be created incentives for workers to want to improve their level of productivity. The crucial factor is worker satisfaction. Rather than making this a company goal, a framework is needed whereby workers can take charge of their own careers and attend to their own on-the-job needs.

Up to now Japanese workers have been allotted jobs, undergone training, and uniformly worked long hours in accordance with company directions. This may to some extent promote diligence, but it does not allow for individual responsibility, since all an employee has to do is work long hours and display loyalty to the company. However, when in the future a scarce labor force begins to do advanced work, the notion of diligence will likely be redefined. Diligence might be viewed as self-responsibility, and a person demonstrates this by the personal choices and further educational investments he or she has made. Yet, even self-responsibility, in the attempt at personal growth, is a wonderful thing as long as there is a satisfaction in the work that goes along with this growth. Therefore we are very fortunate to be able to welcome an advanced industrial society where our growth will be connected to our improvements in productivity. With an eye at this objective, we must construct an employment framework befitting the new company person of tomorrow.

Notes

1. Endo, M., *Nihon Shokunin-shi no Kenkyu* (Studies in the History of Japanese Craftsmen), Yuzankaku, Tokyo, 1985.

2. Odaka, K., *Rodo Shijo Bunseki* (An Analysis of the Labor Market), Iwanami Shoten, Tokyo, 1984.

3. Odaka, K., Ibid.

4. Odaka, K., Ibid.

5. Higuchi, Y., Kyoiku o Tsujita Sedaikan Shotoku Iten (Transitions in Income among Generations through Education), *Nihon Keizai Kenkyu* No. 22, March 1992.

14

Fixed Investments and Finance Sources: From a National to a Global Perspective

Hisashi Yaginuma

It is no exaggeration to say that Japan's high economic growth was brought to fruition mainly by the fixed investments of private companies in heavy industries. Innovations occurred because new technology was introduced, the Japanese people consented to the idea of catching up with the industrialized nations, and so on.

Rapidly expanding demand for funds for fixed investment in the private sector could not be met with internal funds alone, so there was an increasingly strong tendency to rely on external funds—particularly indirect financing from banks. There were distortions in this setup such as overborrowing and excess loans brought on by a firm control of capital transactions; the deficiencies in the indirect financing system; and the policy-oriented, inflexible fixed interest rate system. But these conditions began to normalize at the beginning of the 1980s.

A main bank system set up by private financial institutions served to ease the limits on the private sector's internal funds by gathering and analyzing a company's information and also informally providing that to other financial institutions. Governmental financial institutions experienced a similar capital-driven effect as the main bank in long-term financing.

By the late 1980s all traces of the stagnation that had followed the oil crises of the early 1970s were fully effaced by a bubble economy brought on by the energetic investments of the private sector. These were investments funded by equity financing such as stocks newly issued at market prices, convertible bonds, and warranted bonds. With the progressive diversification of these financing investments came the collapse of indirect financing in Japan, and that instigated a re-examination of the main bank system and governmental financial institutions.

Amid tremendous changes in the economic environment in recent years, the unique Japanese financing system that had supported private fixed investment was ended. In the future Japan can make global contributions by sharing these experiences so that other countries and economies may learn from them.

An important challenge to major Japanese corporations today is how to proceed with globalization. Investments overseas in production, marketing, and development are being steadily advanced regarding particular localities. In the future it will be only natural that Japan take a global perspective in procuring funds for investment, including direct foreign investment, and in diversifying the sources of funds.

Although under the current recession private fixed investments have been shrinking, sufficient opportunities exist for domestic investments in areas such as global environment, urban infrastructure, community activities, and cultural institutions. There is a need for Japan to break away from the intense concentration on exports, competition for shares, and the like, and to take the initiative in constructing an internationally open society.

14.1 Private Fixed Investment and Its Finance

Fixed Investment That Led High Economic Growth

In the 1960s, in the period when the income-doubling plan was launched, until the oil crisis of 1973, fixed investments were the mainstay of Japan's economy. The ratio of private fixed investments to the GNP during that period stayed at 12 to 20 percent of GNP, an unprecedented high not seen in other advanced industrialized nations up to then. Private investments contributing to the increase in the GNP likewise rose, by 40 to 50 percent, and surpassed that of private consumption.[1] Whether referred to as "technological innovation" or as "investments engendering investments," it was indeed an age in which the entire economy was absorbed in Schumpeterian "innovation."

In 1973 as demand stagnated due to the oil crises, and during the subsequent years of adjustment, private fixed investment fell. There resulted a slump in the entire economy. The economy had to be sustained by public investment. Not until the expansion of the economy from 1986 to 1991 could fixed investments by the private sector reemerge and their proportion to GNP shot up over the 1960s peak to top the 20 percent mark in 1990. During those years fixed investments by private companies in Japan fundamentally transformed the whole economy leading to high growth.

Individual industries' contributions to the increase in the total amount of fixed investment from 1958 to 1961 were high in primary metals like steel, the manufacturing of precision machinery and children's toys, transportation machinery like automobiles and ships, and chemicals such as petrochemicals.[2] Understandably the allocation of investments among industries was directed at the time mainly to so-called heavy industries and related fields. From 1965 to 1969 contributions by each industry were largely in commerce like wholesaling, retailing, and manufacturing industries; primary metals; transport/communications including both marine and overland shipping; and the agricultural, forestry, and fishery industries. Likewise at this time the weight from heavy industries shifted to investments connected with the industrial infrastructure.

Heavy industry and related products have had remarkably high resilience to demand and are areas for which economic growth-driven market expansion can be forecasted with accuracy from the experiences of other industrialized nations. Moreover several of these industries embodied the innovations in the industrial technology that had appeared during World War II. They also happen to be fields with the greatest promise for lowering production costs and boosting international competitiveness.

Indeed this is the fundamental reason for the investment activity that was concentrated in these industries. The following points perhaps ought to be added as well: First of all, the outlook for the future was debated by deliberation councils and other advisory groups composed of members from the government and industry for each industrial field. Thus common perceptions were formed among them. Since the Japanese people concurred with the idea of catching up with the advanced industrialized nations, this country could deal positively with the introduction of new technology and improvements in productivity. Competition among corporate groups typified by the so-called one-set philosophy (or desire to have one set of every industry) strengthened all the more their will to invest. Furthermore protective policies and preferential measures were taken by the government toward industry.

Investment Funds Furnished with Domestic Savings

In 1955 the capital formation of the entire Japanese economy consisted of roughly ¥2 trillion. This rapidly swelled to over ¥29 trillion by 1970.

Just how amazing this growth was is indicated by the fact that the capital composition in 1955 accounted for 19 percent of the GNP, whereas by 1970 it came to 35 percent. Even today the capital formation continues to be maintained at more than 30 percent of the GNP.

Interestingly in Japan's case funds for this rapidly expanding capital formation were almost entirely covered by domestic savings, even during the high-growth period of the 1960s. This is an important point. While there are variances in the social and systemic background, it is a pattern completely different from the way the Asian NIES are currently accomplishing high growth through the rapid expansion of their capital formation (including equipment investments) by supplementing their insufficient domestic sources with foreign capital.

In fact, since private corporations hardly produced any savings because of their lack of internal reserves, the household sector, the source of domestic savings, and the government in general accounted for the vast majority of Japan's high growth in the initial stage. By 1970, however, while households savings continued to be the greatest source of funds, nonfinancial corporations became the number two supplier.

In this way, throughout the high-growth period, private corporations rapidly strengthened their internal reserves. Nevertheless, demand for funds exceeded those reserves and grew to amazingly enormous sums. Therefore, instead of being resolved, the deficiency of funds expanded. The ratio of this deficit to the GNP climbed from about 5 percent to between 7 and 10 percent in the 1960s. Thus was formed a structure in which the corporate sector had the greatest deficiency of funds and households and the government served as the suppliers of funds for that very reason. This pattern was consistently seen throughout Japan's period of high economic growth.

Overborrowing, Overlending, and the Financing of Funds

Overborrowing due to Expanding Demand for Funds

Japan's investment-driven high economic growth, coupled with an expansion of working capital, raised the demand for funds for fixed investments. This demand for funds, as was seen earlier, grew to surpass the funds accumulated internally (internal reserves and depreciations) by the corporate sector.

The composition of these sources continued to remain in a state where internal funds came to about 40 percent and external funds to

Table 14.1
The state of industry's supply of capital (¥100 million: %)

	1959FY	1962FY	1965FY	1967FY	1969FY
Total capital supply	36,895 (100.0)	67,717 (100.0)	89,880 (100.0)	136,335 (100.0)	215,300 (100.0)
Internal funds					
Internal reserves	5,683 (15.4)	5,509 (8.1)	6,493 (7.2)	19,895 (14.6)	37,600 (17.5)
Depreciated amortization	7,030 (19.1)	12,800 (18.9)	31,530 (35.1)	42,776 (31.4)	63,500 (29.5)
Total	12,713 (34.5)	18,309 (27.0)	38,023 (42.3)	62,671 (46.0)	101,100 (47.0)
External funds					
Public funds	1,943 (5.3)	3,625 (5.4)	5,132 (5.7)	6,747 (4.9)	9,800 (4.6)
Private funds	20,641 (55.9)	43,818 (64.7)	45,825 (51.0)	62,901 (46.1)	98,500 (45.8)
Stocks	3,407 (9.2)	7,388 (10.9)	2,459 (2.7)	3,398 (2.5)	8,500 (3.9)
Company debits	1,423 (3.9)	1,212 (1.8)	2,407 (2.7)	1,961 (1.4)	2,800 (1.3)
Loans	15,811 (42.9)	35,218 (52.0)	40,959 (45.6)	57,542 (42.2)	87,200 (40.5)
Total	22,584 (61.2)	47,443 (70.1)	50,957 (56.7)	69,648 (51.1)	108,300 (50.3)
Foreign capital, etc.	1,598 (4.3)	1,965 (2.9)	900 (1.0)	4,016 (2.9)	5,900 (2.7)

Sources: Based on surveys by the Economic Planning Agency and the 1965 and 1971 editions of the *Nomura Shoken Yoran* (Nomura Securities Handbook) Kamekichi Takahashi. Cited by K. Takahaski; see ref. 2.

around 60 percent (see table 14.1).[2] The financing of the capital needed by Japanese companies throughout the high-growth period was characterized by the generally low internal reserves. Financing through corporate bonds was much lower than in other industrialized countries, although, as has been pointed out, financing through borrowing was far higher than in other nations.[3,4,5]

The greatest distinguishing feature here is that loans, mainly from private financial institutions, have accounted for 40 to 50 percent of the total funds supplied. This phenomenon is called *overborrowing*. Not only is the dependence on loans (borrowing) in Japan higher than that in Europe and the United States, but it is distorted by deficiencies in both the stock and bond markets.

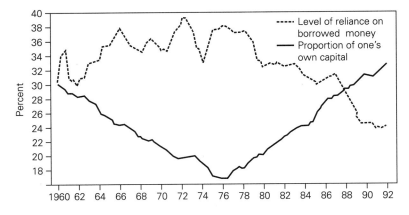

Figure 14.1
Financial structure of the manufacturing industry. Data based on the Ministry of Finance's *Hojin Kigyo Tokei Kiho* (Seasonal Report on Corporations' Statistics) for incorporated companies with at least ¥10 million in capital. Source: *Nissei Kiso Kenkyujo* (Nissei Basic Research Center).

The stock market in the 1960s consisted mostly of allocations to the stockholders issued at their face value, so publicly offered bond flotations could practically be ignored. Since the stock market was underdeveloped, dividends were treated disadvantageously taxwise compared to interest. (Specifically, although the interest paid was deductible as expenses, dividends were not.) The flotation of corporate bonds was severely controlled too. Over 80 percent of such bonds were possessed by financial institutions, so they essentially channeled their short-term funds into long-term capital.[2,6,7]

In addition, in those times, capital financing from other countries was closed off. Financing was regulated with priority given to indirect financing and restrictions on capital and exchange transactions.

In any case the percentage of major corporations' equity capital underwent a steady decline because of their dependence on loans for more than half of funding. The ratio of equity capital for entire manufacturing, which came to 30 percent in 1955, had dropped to 17 percent in 1972 (see figure 14.1).

Excess Loans due to the Financial System
The phenomenon of overlending occurs when private financial institutions (banks) are constantly in a state of excess credit over debt (a state in which loans and/or negotiable securities exceed deposits and/or capital), so they have to rely on money borrowed from the

Bank of Japan to cover the deficit.[8] The fixed investments by the private sector during the period of high growth which stimulated the demand for more loans were concentrated mostly in city banks. To those banks the increase in deposit accounts was the main way of securing funds. But to handle the shortage of funds as the demand for loans exceeded the amount of deposits, they could only rely on borrowing from other financial institutions (regional banks, mutual banks, credit unions, etc.), funds from abroad, loans from the Bank of Japan (credit from the Bank of Japan), and/or the credit-rationing to the nonfinancial corporations. In particular, the cost of borrowing from the Bank of Japan (the discount rate) was set at about 1 to 6 percent lower than the interbank rate (call rate).[5] Therefore, partly because of the constraints on collecting funds from overseas and partly because of the city banks' dependence on it, the Bank of Japan grew all the stronger.

Thus in some ways excess lending typical of city banks was encouraged by financial system itself, and these banks fulfilled an important role in supporting the rapidly increasing demand for funds. In fact, borrowing from the Bank of Japan existed among banks throughout the era of high growth. The amount borrowed went from ¥450 billion in 1960 to ¥2.2 trillion in 1970. The onset of a period of low growth during the oil crises and in the ensuing years caused a striking reduction in the demand for investment funds. Thus borrowing from the Bank of Japan by private financial institutions dropped to ¥1 trillion in 1981, almost bringing an end to excess lending. Whereas their proportion in the total of Bank of Japan credit deposits approached the 10 percent mark during the period of high economic growth, thereafter their proportion underwent a conspicuous decline following the oil crises; it has hovered at the 1 to 3 percent level in recent years.[9] From these figures we can understand the importance that Bank of Japan credit had in funding via city banks during the high-growth period.

Increasingly Higher Dependence on External Sources for Investment Funds
The proportion of industrial investment funds (loans, stocks, bonds, foreign debts) of the total industrial investment was 60 to 70 percent during the period of high growth starting in 1960. This pattern stands in sharp contrast to that of firms in the United States and Europe, which cover the majority of their investment expenditures with internal funds. Loans from financial institutions accounted for an overwhelming 75 to 90 percent of external funds in Japan.

This high dependence on external funds and loans cannot simply be explained as attributable to the lack of internal funds within an industry. To be sure, supplying funds to firms in such a situation is considered high risk. Kamekichi Takahashi[2] has pointed out the following benefits for the financial institution's side accompanying familiarity with the client's management: a reduction in risks, a cooperative system for dealing with unexpected circumstances, more complementary services among companies, and corporate development. Takahashi additionally touched on the fact that since throughout Japan the people concurred with its economic growth, the banks, with their systematic judgment powers, have effectively functioned in a leadership capacity allocating funds among industries.

In reality, in introducing new technology and vying with each other, banks that were positioned in the center of corporate groups seem at least not to have taken short-term profitability into account. Rather, incentives may have worked to supply funds as long as the risks accompanying the loan were on the low side, since during the period of high growth there were few portfolio assets beyond borrowing and the rate of return on assets was low as a matter of government policy.

Loans from government financial institutions accounted for more than 20 percent of the total amount of these extended by financial institutions during the first half of the high-growth period and over 15 percent even during the latter half. Therefore we can say that government loans were quite sizable (see table 14.2). Their impact on the allocation of funds for industrial investment cannot be ignored.

14.2 Private Fixed Investment and Private Financial Institutions

Modernized Industry Portfolio

Three industrial types appear in the top ranks of private financial institutions' investment funds supply portfolio in 1955. In order of loan size, these were electric power, metals, and overland transportation. In 1960 they were electric power, chemicals, and machinery; in 1965, chemicals, machinery, and overland transportation; and in 1967, chemicals, machinery, and steel. The portfolio gradually shifted from industries with infrastructure aspects to those with heightened autonomous power.[9] In addition the share itself held by the industries in the top three ranks experienced a striking decline, from over 40 percent at the outset to a percentage in the midtwenties. Thus the loan portfolio showed a structural change along with the industrial diversification that took place in the process of economic development.

Table 14.2
Government funds in equipment funding (%)

Industry	Average for 1954–60		Average for 1961–67	
Mining (including the coal industry)	25.7	(17.0)	39.9	(18.8)
Coal mining	37.2	(31.2)	65.9	(45.3)
Steel	4.6	(2.5)	3.6	(1.0)
Machinery	11.3	(2.6)	9.5	(3.1)
Chemicals	8.1	(3.4)	7.1	(3.8)
Fibers	14.2	(2.1)	14.7	(2.2)
Agriculture, forestry, fishery	52.9	(0.5)	47.9	(0.4)
Electric power	32.4	(13.1)	19.7	(8.3)
Marine transport	33.9	(29.5)	50.9	(39.0)
Land transport	10.4	(0.7)	21.9	(2.2)
All others	21.6	(6.8)	15.7	(4.3)

Sources: From the Bank of Japan, *Honpo Keizai Tokei* (Economic Statistics for Japan) and *Keizai Tokei Nenpo* (Economic Statistics Annual). Cited by A. Horiuchi and M. Otaki.[3]
Note: Land transport for 1954 to 1960 is the average for 1956 to 1960. In the parentheses is the proportion of Development Bank financing. After 1968 related statistics were not released to the public.

The portfolio of governmental financial institutions, as will be explained later, has clearly tilted toward the infrastructure-related and declining sectors. By contrast, private financial institutions have made modern growth sectors the focus of their financing activities.

Main Bank System, Its Merits and Decline

The role fulfilled by corporate groups in Japan's postwar industrial development has often been emphasized. In particular, the financial conglomerates (*keiretsu*) are groups composed of banks, related financial institutions, and their main clients. Based at the main bank, which has considerable say in matters, these groups have supplied funds for investment, given diverse financial support when a business was having trouble, and coordinated the industrial activities of each corporation in the same group.

Shiro Yabushita[10] has picked up on the following six stylized facts about main banks:

• They are the greatest lender (particularly of long-term funds) to the appropriate company.

- They are the main stockholder in the company concerned.
- They have long-term, uninterrupted trade relationships.
- They offer human relationships such as dispatching executives.
- They have integrated transaction relationships (deposits, exchange, transferring salaries into savings accounts, managing bond issues, etc.).
- They function to insure and stabilize the management when companies have fallen into a business crisis. (This includes publicizing activities to promote the companies concerned.)

Given the uncertainty of investment opportunities and the system of limited responsibility for stockholders, the suppliers of external funds tend to establish high interest rates because of the risk in the premiums they are facing (agency costs). Not just anybody has the ability to acquire, analyze, and stock the variety of information concerning the profitability of investment opportunities, the reliability of management, and so on. The main bank can acquire various information by screening a company and monitoring its daily transactions. If the information thus obtained is analyzed and presented to other suppliers of funds as public goods, other financial institutions will be able to utilize them. Since that will keep their costs lower than making autonomous judgments, they have naturally come to follow the decisions made by the main bank.

Consequently the main banks have eased the order of the existing sources as firms procured external funds. More precisely, they were able to mitigate restrictions on internal funds and bring the costs of borrowing from other financial institutions down as well. Such functions stemming from the main bank have been confirmed econometrically in cases where they were checked according to whether or not the financing costs of a firm belonging to the corporate group had declined.[11]

The main bank must bear the expenses of collecting and analyzing such financing information. However, the burden of these costs is beneficial to the main bank in that it makes the client company avoid action disadvantageous to the main bank and prevents moral hazard to the client. Moreover these costs can often be recouped through various, long-term transactions with the borrower company. This has already been pointed out by Takahashi.[2]

This main bank framework has allowed other financial institutions to utilize company information at low cost and served the corporate sector with its abundant demand for funds. The main bank led the fixed investment competition during the high-growth period based on a one-set philosophy within each corporate group that focused on heavy industries like petrochemicals, steel, and home electric appliances. In this sense these main banks have provided Japanese industries with more than the necessary funds. From such a perspective, Okazaki and Horiuchi[12] concluded that "the constraints of internal funds on investment activity have been mitigated through main bank functions in its share in the amount of investment expenditures. And main banks also worked to make borrowing from other financial institutions easy."

In recent years the role of the main banks seems to have been undergoing a gradual decline. It has been pointed out that significant differences in the rate of corporate growth between firms in the groups with a main bank and other nongroup firms have not been apparent since the oil crises.[11,13] The group firms have consisted of heavy, large-scale industries in general. The many firms outside these corporate groups belong to the assembly-processing industries and have constructed an efficient system known as the production *keiretsu*. Taking all this into the picture, it would seem that the historic role of the main bank system is now coming to an end.

Moreover uninterrupted trade relationships with particular companies serve as a premise for the main bank system to function adequately. But because of the enhanced ability of firms to finance the necessary funds and the accumulation of internal reserves within the firm itself, some 20 percent of major companies have changed the banks from which they borrowed the most within the past five years.[14] This hints of a relative improvement in the companies' position and of unsteadiness in the main bank system.

14.3 Private Fixed Investments and Government Financial Institutions

Portfolio in Infrastructures and Declining Sectors

Government Financial Institutions for Long-Term Capital
Government financial institutions that supplied investment funds existed well before World War II (the former Nihon Kangyo Bank and the former Nihon Kogyo Bank, both of which were privatized after the war). During the postwar reconstruction period, the Financing Corporation for Reconstruction was established (in 1946). A vast amount of funds was injected into coal, electricity, and marine transport for

financing the *keisha seisan* or priority production system, relief to private financial institutions, and the deficit that originated in the maintenance of official prices. In particular, it accounted for 75 percent of the investment funds supplied by all financial institutions. This corporation supplemented the shortage in funds from private financial institutions and served as virtually the only institution providing investment funds. [15]

In addition the People's Finance Corporation was established in 1949 in order to secure long-term industrial funds and to control inflation by expanding the supply capacity. Afterward the Japan Development Bank; the Agriculture, Forestry, and Fisheries Finance Corporation; the Japan Finance Corporation for Small Businesses; the Hokkaido-Tohoku Development Corporation; and the People's Medical Business Finance Corporation were set up in 1951, 1951, 1953, 1956, and 1960, respectively. Then in 1967 the Environmental Sanitation Business Finance Corporation was established to complete a full array of government financial institutions providing investment funds.

All of these financial institutions were established under special laws with 100 percent of their capital from the government. Their purpose was to finance investment expenditures by private companies in specific regions or industrial fields in line with policy objectives at low interest rates and for a long duration. The financial sources for these institutions have basically come from a special account collected from the financing operations conducted by the government.

At the outset the rate of domestic savings was low and per capita financial assets quite minuscule. Only deposit accounts in private financial institutions existed other than postal savings as financial assets for savings. The total amount of funds collected by the financial operations of government, postal savings, postal life insurance, post-office annuities, and welfare insurance reached roughly one-third of deposits from all banks during the period of high economic growth. Therefore it may have been a natural development for these governmental financial institutions to be set up and provide the needed industrial funds.

Financial Activities in Infrastructure-Related and Declining Sectors
Similar to the case of private financial institutions, the three main industrial recipients of funds from governmental financial institutions were, in 1956, electric power; agriculture, forestry, and fisheries; and marine transport; in 1960, again electric power; agriculture, forestry,

and fisheries; and marine transport; in 1965, marine transport; agriculture, forestry, and fisheries; and land transport; and in 1967, agriculture, forestry, and fisheries; marine transport; and land transport.[9] Moreover, although the amount of concentration in the three main industries dropped from its original 70 percent, it still came to nearly 40 percent in 1967. Thus from these figures we can tell that the portfolio of these governmental financial institutions was clearly concentrated in infrastructure-related and declining sectors.

In general, governmental financial institutions have a loan portfolio quite different from private institutions. However, their loan portfolio has been as diversified just as it was for private financial institutions.

Although there was concentration in infrastructure-related industries, the share of demand for investment funds in certain industries was hardly low. As can be seen in table 14.2, the share of government funds in the second phase (1950 to 1960) and the third phase (1960 to 1973) of high economic growth came to 21 and 16 percent, respectively. It was particularly high in coal; marine transport; agriculture, forestry, and fishery; electric power; and textiles, followed by machinery.

By comparing the share of government funds with the contributions to the increase in investment expenditures by industry, we can confirm a positive relationship between them only within the machinery industry in the second phase, and for the agriculture, forestry, and fishery and the transport/communications industries in the third phase. It is hard to say that government funds on the whole influenced the interindustry allocation and growth of private fixed investments to a large degree. In that respect it is justifiable to state that rather than having effects on the allocation of private investment, the role of governmental financial institutions has had a complementary character, functioning qualitatively and quantitatively in specific industries.

Let us look at the loan portfolio of the Japan Development Bank and the Japan Finance Corporation for Small Businesses as representative examples. In the case of the Japan Development Bank, financing centered around the transport, communication, and electric power industries continues to this day, and financing going to manufacturing industries has been experiencing a rapid decline in recent years. In the case of the Japan Finance Corporation for Small Businesses, the manufacturing industries still remain the main force and the proportions for trade and distribution have been rising.

The shares of both institutions have remained low in industries on the whole. Yet they have been substantial in a limited number of fields, and this is indicative of the direction being taken in the allocation of investment as a matter of policy. As seen in table 14.2, which shows the percentages of the Japan Development Bank's industrial equipment funding, during the third phase of high growth, considerable weight was given to the coal and marine transport industries, followed by electric power. The weight allotted to the manufacturing industry was generally low; even in the chemical field, which had the highest proportion, it was under 4 percent. Consequently, in terms of volume, the role played by policy intervention in private investment through loans by the Japan Development Bank never consisted of more than inducing funds to industry-related infrastructures and declining sectors as well as quantitative supplements within those areas.

Role and Reputation of Government Financing

Favorable Loan Conditions for Private Fixed Investments in Certain Industries

As already mentioned, the government financial portfolio that supported fixed investment in infrastructure-related industries and declining sectors was different from that it reserved for private financial institutions. Government funding was especially important during the period of high economic growth when not only corporations but also private financial institutions were faced with constraints on the supply of funds and could not easily allocate their funds to those industries. Therefore government financial institutions came to the aid of certain industries.

Second, intervention through the distribution of funds was combined normally with preferential economic conditions of low interest rates and long-term financing. The interest rate on standard loans from government financial institutions during the high-growth period was set at the same level as long-term loans from private financial institutions. However, there was a broader range of application of special interest. For example, a 6.5 percent interest rate was applied to about 80 percent of the total amount of loans from the Japan Development Bank in 1955—a figure considerably lower than the 10 percent on long-term loans from city banks. (The situation was generally the same for 1960.) Furthermore loans with a repayment period of over fifteen years accounted for more than half of the loans extended, and many of them were three to five times longer than those for loans from private financial institutions.[15] As a result it became possible for private nonfinancial corporations to lower their interest burden to pay, and they could accordingly increase internal funds to be used for fixed investment by the same degree.

Ogura and Yoshino[16] have estimated the incentive effect on private firms' fixed investments through preferential tax measures such as special depreciations and financing from governmental financial institutions through fiscal investments and loan programs. If this is calculated with the contribution of the Fiscal Investment and Loan Program removed, it will amount to approximately 10 percent in the marine transport, electric power, and transportation machinery industries. There have been few incentive effects in industries other than these specific fields; for instance, they come to less than 1 percent in the entire manufacturing industry. Here too the role of government financial institutions can be recognized as effective only in limited spheres.

Funding by Private Financial Institutions under Tight Money Conditions
As was noted earlier, excess lending by private financial institutions during the period of high economic growth occurred because these loans were extended so aggressively that they surpassed the amount of deposits. Consequently, as demand for fixed investment expanded rapidly in the third phase of the high-growth period, private financial institutions faced rather tight circumstances.

The policy objectives at the time seemed to aim for high growth and to strengthen industry's international competitiveness. Along this line governmental financial institutions can certainly be inferred to have fulfilled a role supplementing the private financial institutions. Especially at the outset, the internal funds (internal reserve and depreciation) of private nonfinancial corporations were insufficient, and the route for financing capital via the stock and bond markets had yet to be established. Under such circumstances the complementary role of government financial institutions to private financial institutions in quantitative terms definitely had its own significance within the limitations of a particular industrial area.

More precisely, government financial institutions extended loans in the form of "cooperative financing" with private financial institutions in order to supply funds for investment. According to Higano,[17] in the case of the Japan Development Bank, cooperative finance can generally be seen in almost all of its projects such as with private railways, marine transport, urban development, electric power, steel, and regional development. The actual proportion of cooperative financing during the latter half of the second phase amounted to 45 percent.[15]

Had no constraints existed on the sources of private financial institutions' funds, government and private financial agencies would have certainly fought one another over financing to these industries. In fact the government sector was once heavily criticized for oppressing the private sector. Whenever the lending conditions of government financial institutions become favorable, the likelihood of conflict grows stronger.

There are good reasons for private financial institutions to accept cooperative financing: (1) When money is tight, it can bring in government funds, while maintaining relationships with many clients as the main bank; (2) the risks are lower because of indirect guarantees by the government; (3) expenses for screening and monitoring clients are not necessary. For these reasons private financial institutions have actively made use of governmental financial institutions as well.

Effect of Limited Agency Costs
Consider the fact that companies may end up borrowing their needed funds, while stockholders bear responsibility only within the limits of their own contributions (limited responsibility system). This condition provides the incentive to invest in high-risk fields and thus brings on moral hazard. The lender who is aware of that outcome will demand high interest. That is one of the "agency costs" to firms related to financing through liabilities.[18] On the other hand, when a company is faced with an investment opportunity that produces low earnings and stocks are issued taking advantage of the information gap with investors, financing may be advantageous. The investor, taking this possibility into account, is unlikely to purchase the stock at a high price. The existence of such agency costs positions the internal fund as the lowest costing source of funds with respect to a firm's fund-raising structure and forms a hierarchy in the supply of funds.

From this description we may assume that government financial institutions, as producers of information, have a function in lowering agency costs. Indeed, it should be pointed out that hidden behind the government financial institutions' encouragement of lending by private financial institutions has been improved information-producing technology, which includes information collection and analysis capacities (screening capacities) vis-à-vis a repayment program as well as the release of information to the public (as the provision of public goods) in the form of a "government financial institution's decision to extend loans." The effect of lowering this agency cost is the so-called cow bell effect.[17]

These functions of government financial institutions resemble the main bank functions of private financial institutions. For this reason government financial institutions have sometimes conflicted with the main banks in releasing information. In general, main banks primarily utilize information on short-term loans, whereas government financial institutions are concerned with long-term loans. Private financial institutions undoubtedly must take into account such differences by combining these two sources of funds when they make loans to private companies.

14.4 Present State of Capital Finance

Knowledge Gained through the Diversification of Finance

The oil crises of the 1970s caused the demand for fixed investments to stagnate. In the final years of the adjustment period, 1985 and 1986, the proportion of the shortages of funds in the corporate sector to the GNP dropped to nearly 1 percent. The share of external funds in the total amount of funds supplied likewise went down to the 40 percent level.[19] Nevertheless, the proportion of external funds was still much higher than that in the Western nations. Therefore, in the eyes of foreign countries, Japanese companies remained in a state of overborrowing.

Thereafter from 1986 to 1990, while funds in the corporate sector were being depleted amid the expansion of the economy brought on by an upsurge in domestic demand, demand for investment funds rapidly declined, along with the collapse in the bubble economy.

To counter the decline in available external funds, corporations diversified their sources of external funds increasing their borrowing through such direct financing routes as corporate bonds and stocks. Thus in the case of major nonfinancial corporations, loans, which had served as the main source of external finance, plunged down to 40 percent in the late 1980s, while corporate bonds and newly issued stocks rose dramatically to nearly 30 percent.[19]

This shift in funding sources has been called a change from debt to equity financing. It is a phenomenon that is plainly apparent in the fact that convertible bonds, warranted bonds, and the flotation of stocks at market value underwent a startling expansion in the second half of the 1980s. In this period the financial market of Japan was liberalized, internationalized, and securitized, and increasingly straight and warranted bonds were floated in overseas markets. Thus financing came from both the domestic and foreign markets which became important sources of funds.

Under the current recession such instruments of finance as flotation at market value and warranted bonds, which are based on the presumption of rapidly growing corporate profits, have virtually disappeared from sight. Firms have acquired much know-how concerning the instruments of finance and are beginning to turn to financing activity that deals with steady demand for funds.

Shrinking Relative Advantages in the Cost of Capital

Shrinking Differences in the Cost of Capital with the United States
A firm determines its fixed investment by comparing any increased profits with the costs involved. The drop in the cost of capital signifies a decline in the cutoff rate. Consequently investment can be increased until the profits decline and reach the same level as the decreased costs.

As indicated in figure 14.2, after temporarily descending to a negative level of growth following the oil crises, the cost of capital in Japan has stayed within the 2 to 3 percent range. By contrast, it is in the 5 to 7 percent range in the United States—meaning that the cost of capital in Japan is constantly two to four points lower. This has been a strong investment incentive for Japanese companies.

The question is why the cost of capital in Japan is low. The primary reason for the disparity with the United States lies in the low level of the stock market costs. In other words, the returns to the stockholders in Japan are slight. The differences in the relationship with the stockholders in corporate management show up unexpectedly here. Japanese investors have unwillingly contented themselves up to now with low dividends with the expectation of large capital gains obtained from corporate growth. However, if corporate growth gets slower than it has in the recent past, the dividends for investors can be expected to rise, and the cost of capital for firms will likely rise over the long term as well. We are in fact approaching an era when not only Japanese but also foreign investors will be turned away by the low dividends from Japanese companies.

There has been some debate on the feasibility of active equity financing such as warranted bonds by which in the late 1980s Japanese companies greatly lowered the capital procurement costs. It is certainly

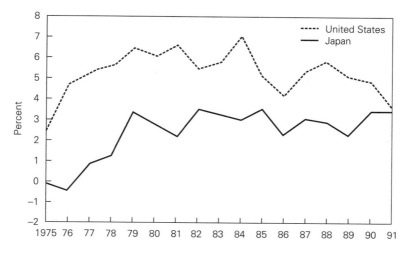

Figure 14.2
Funding costs in Japan and the United States compared. Sources: From the Economic Planning Agency[4] based on data from the Bank of Japan's *Keizai Tokei Geppo* (Economic Statistics Monthly) and *Kokusai Hikaku Tokei* (Internationally Compared Statistics), the Ministry of Finance's *Zaisei Kinyu Tokei Geppo* (Public Financing Statistics Monthly), and the Daiwa Research Center's *Analyst Guide* (in Japanese).

true that the capital costs at that time plummeted to barely more than the 2 percent level, with the effects of equity finance reflected to a corresponding degree. Yet that phenomenon was hardly different from the trends of the entire 1980s. Moreover companies that were pressed to finance enormous amounts of funds in order to repay warranted bonds are paying higher capital costs even now.

Recently, however, the cost of capital in Japan has been on the rise, placing Japan at almost the same level as the United States. This is partly a reflection of a brisk stock market and low interest rates in the United States and partly a result of the liberalization/internationalization of the Japanese financial market and the internationalization of its corporate activities. These circumstances have worked to raise the fluidity of capital among nations and to scale down differences in the costs of capital.

Effect of User's Cost on Research and Development
Today an important consideration for companies involved in dramatic technological innovations would appear to be to continue moving toward new technological frontiers. Investments in research and development are an integral part of that effort. Just as fixed investment,

R&D expenditures are determined by comparing the benefits to costs. If R&D costs are high, only programs guaranteeing high returns can be considered. From the late 1960s to 1980 R&D expenditures—personnel, depreciation, and other material costs—came close to doubling.[20] This increase was in fact rather small in comparison with the rise in fixed investments, and it means that R&D investments experienced a relative decline. To that same extent, it is advisable for companies to put their strength into technological development.

As we enter an age with heightened cost consciousness about R&D, we may very well in the future see cooperation among firms in R&D activities, research in Asia where there are abundant human resources and low wages, and research carried out within Japan by researchers from other countries, and R&D will take directions different from those known up to now.

Comprehensive data concerning the financing of R&D cannot be found. However, considering the secretiveness involved in R&D and the huge gaps in information among firms and outsiders (the existence of asymmetric information), it is only natural for agency costs to be high and for finance to be supplied mainly through internal funds.

14.5 Future Outlook

The economic boom of the late 1980s is already a thing of the past. The present seems to be a time for repaying debts and settling on future directions. But the decline of corporate activities in general raises cause for alarm. That decline suggests that Japanese industry got very much enveloped in a myth of its own competitiveness and technological power and did not sufficiently devise measures for attaining permanent strength. Given these present circumstances, such standard adjustments will require considerable time.

Regarding companies' need for funding, there is the view that since real investment will stay relatively stable, the rate of growth of corporate demand for funds will also remain at about the same level as in the early 1980s.[19] However, we should not be so pessimistic about the long-term trends if future investment activities are focused on the key areas of information processing, global environment, urban infrastructure, aging population, and cultural institutions. If the pace of fixed investment is somewhere between that of the period of high growth and the decline of the late 1980s, it will mean that domestic savings will continue to surpass the investment amount. Effort to build up human capital and to locate domestic investment opportunities can be expected. On the other hand, with the accumulation of national financial assets, the selected portfolio should become more diversified than ever before.

A decrease is already occurring in the amount of funds headed into indirect finance such as deposits in private financial institutions and postal savings, which serve as funds for government financial institutions. This suggests that the amount of funds headed into direct finance such as corporate bonds, stocks, and investment trusts is likely to expand.

Companies' internal funds will rise to much higher levels. Their diversification of external funds and their know-how for utilizing them will steadily improve. Funding will be pursued through various combinations of sources such as debt and equity finance, domestic and overseas finance, long-term and short-term funds, all involving global strategies. There will also be put into place policies for savings and for dealing with market uncertainties.

As has been seen in the cost of capital, the era of disparities between the financing conditions of Japanese and U.S. companies is about to come to a pass. We are entering an age in which the Japanese capital market will be synchronized with international markets and practices, and internationally compete on equal footing in financing capital. There is a need for such major transformations comparable to those in the domestic system.

In liberalizing the financial market, which involves the liberalization of interest, the barriers between financial *keiretsu* groups, between Japan and other countries, and between government and private financial institutions will come down. This new environment will bring about tremendous change in cooperative and complementary relationships among all parties as well.

The demise of the main bank system has already been discussed, and it should be pointed out that government financing has likewise declined. Private financial institutions are approaching an era in which they must select and commit themselves to only certain business areas. As commercial banking functions are upgraded to the main business of credit creation, private financial institutions will enter into business areas related to portfolio management such as financial brokers. To compensate for the disadvantageous shift into direct finance, they will necessarily deal in investment banking operations including underwriting corporate bonds and stocks, venture capital, and the like.

Then, the funding of venture capital as well as small- and medium-sized enterprises and consumer finance will inevitably be within the domain of indirect finance. In this environment private financial institutions will have more need to improve their screening and evaluation capabilities. Collateral finance has made it easy to manage financing operations without such capacities, but in the future it will be difficult to survive unless the banking business is operated on the basis of information technology. In this area the competition among financial institutions will become fiercer.

Finally, we need to consider how from now on the financing system used in Japan throughout the high-growth period can contribute to global needs.

The main bank system, to which traditionally private financial institutions had been committed for funding, may again be useful in supplying funds to the corporate sector in their setting up stock markets in developing countries. The cow bell function fulfilled by government financial institutions has been effective in supplying capital for industrial development. This experience in financial systems may be applied in developing countries—particularly in the Asian region but also in Russia and other eastern European nations that are in the process of becoming market economies.

In the future the Japanese industrial economy cannot avoid but to acquire characteristics compatible with other industrialized countries in financing capital, in corporate management, and in financial systems. But Japan's diverse and unique experience can be utilized by the rest of the world.

Notes

1. Economic Planning Agency, *Choki Sokyu Suikei: Kokumin Keizai Keisan Hokoku* (Long-Term Statistics Traced Back: Report on the System of National Accounts), Tokyo, May 1988.

2. Takahashi, K., *Sengo Nihon Keizai Yakushin no Konpon Yoin* (Essential Factors behind Postwar Japan's Rapid Economic Progress), Nihon Keizai Shinbun, Tokyo, April 1985.

3. Horiuchi, A., and Otaki, M., Kinyu: Seifu Kainyu to Ginko Kashidashi no Juyosei (Finance: Government Intervention and the Importance of Bank Loans), in Hamada, K., Kuroda, M., Horiuchi, A., *Nihon Keizai no Macro Bunseki* (A Macro Analysis of the Japanese Economy), University of Tokyo Press, Tokyo, June 1987.

4. Economic Planning Agency, *Keizai Hakusho: Heisei Yonnen-ban* (White Paper on the Economy), Tokyo, 1992.

5. Tomita, Y., *Sengo Nihon no Kinyu Keizai* (The Financial Economy of Postwar Japan), Taga Shuppan, Tokyo, 1993.

6. Sudo, M., and Takahashi, T., *Gendai no Kigyo Kinyu to Kinyu System* (The Present State of Corporate Finance and the Financial System), Yuhikaku Sensho, Tokyo, 1986.

7. Teranishi, S., *Kogyoka to Kinyu System* (Industrialization and the Financial System), Toyo Keizai Shinpo-sha, Tokyo, 1991.

8. Suzuki, Y., *Nihon Keizai to Kinyu: Sono Tenkan to Tekio* (The Japanese Economy and Financial System: Their Transformation and Adaptation), Toyo Kezai Shinpo-sha, Tokyo, 1981.

9. Bank of Japan, *Keizai Tokei Nenpo* (Annual of Economic Statistics), editions for each year.

10 Yabushita, S., Main Bank to Joho no Riron (Main Banks and a Theory of Information), in Horiuchi, A., and Yoshino, N., *Gendai Nihon no Kinyu Bunseki* (An Analysis of the Contemporary Japanese Financial System), University of Tokyo Press, Tokyo, 1992.

11. Okazaki, T., Shihon Jiyuka Iko no Kigyo Shudan (Corporate Groups Following the Liberalization of Capital Transactions), in *Hosei Daigaku Sangyo Joho Center* (Hosei University Center for Business and Industrial Research): Hashimoto, T., and Takeda, H., *Nihon Keizai Hatten to Kigyo Shudan* (The Development of the Japanese Economy and Corporate Groups), University of Tokyo Press, Tokyo, 1992.

12. Okazaki, T., and Horiuchi, A., Setsubi Toshi to Main Bank (Fixed Investment and Main Banks), in Horiuchi, A., and Yoshino, N., *Gendai Nihon no Kinyu Bunseki* (An Analysis of the Contemporary Japanese Financial System), University of Tokyo Press, Tokyo, 1992.

13. Odagiri, H., *Nihon no Kigyo Senryaku to Soshiki* (Corporate Strategies and Organization in Japan), Toyo Keizai Shinpo-sha, Tokyo, 1992.

14. Bank of Japan, Zaimu Data kara Mita Kigyo-Ginko kan no Torihiki Kankei no Henka (The Changes in Transaction Relationships between Companies and Banks as Seen in Financial Data), *Bank of Japan Monthly Report,* March 1992.

15. Japan Development Bank, *Nihon Kaihatsu Ginko Junen-shi* (A Ten-Year History of the Japan Development Bank), Tokyo, 1963.

16. Ogura, M., and Yoshino, N., Tokubetsu Shokyaku-Zaisei Toyushi to Nihon no Sangyo Kozo (Special Depreciation, Fiscal Investment and Loan Programs and the Japanese Industrial Structure), in Economic Research Center, Hitotsubashi University, Hitotsubashi Daigaku Keizai Kenkyujo-hen *Keizai Kenkyu* (Economic Research), April 1985.

17. Higano, K., Kyocho Yushi to Shinsa Noryoku (Cooperative Finance and Screening Capacities), in *University of Tokyo, Keizaigaku Ronshu* (Journal of Economic Theory), April 1984.

18. Ohniwa, T., and Horiuchi, A., Honpo Kigyo no Main Bank Kankei to Setsubi Toshi Kodo no Kankei ni Tsuite (About Main Bank Relationships with Japanese Companies in Relation with Their Fixed Investment Activities), in Nihon Ginko Kinyu Kenkyujo (Financial Research Center, Bank of Japan), *Kinyu Kenkyu* (Financial Research), Tokyo, 1990.

19. Nissei Kiso Kenkyujo (Nissei Basic Research Center), Ono, M., *Seminar: Kore kara no Kigyo Kinyu-Zaimu Senryaku* (Seminar: Corporate Finance and Financial Strategies from Now On), Toyo Keizai Shinpo-sha, Tokyo, 1992.

20. Research Institute of Capital Formation, Japan Development Bank, *Setsubi Toshi Kenkyu '81* (Research into Fixed Investments '81), July 1982.

15

International Development of Manufacturing

Hiroyuki Itami

Historically the international development of Japanese manufacturing industries took shape by exports expanding greatly first and then, in the 1980s, by an upsurge in direct investments overseas. Compared with the United States and Germany, the following characteristics emerge regarding Japan's exports and direct investments:

First, it should be noted that Japan's exports have been surprisingly low in number. The percentage of exports in Japan's GNP has been much lower than that in Germany's GNP. Japan's percentage of overseas production likewise has not approached by far that of Germany or the United States. This was still the reality at the start of the 1990s. It suggests that in the future Japanese overseas development can increase quite a bit, especially in direct investments.

Second, there is the high concentration of the machinery industry, and within that industry the production of automobiles and electric machinery are particularly high. Among regions of production, the United States has high standing. Moreover a small number of these companies have been involved in Japan's large overseas operations.

Third, both exports and direct investments have grown in an extraordinarily short period of time. Furthermore, advancements overseas have been carried out at a remarkable pace, as seen by the dramatic increase in exports following the oil crises and the rapid expansion of direct investments in the wake of the high yen.

Fourth, there is a tendency for Japanese companies to have high visibility abroad. As far as products go, there are many consumers' goods—especially automobiles and home electric appliances—that are prominent in overseas markets. Japanese products have moreover been concentrated in certain areas and have been rapidly gaining recognition for their quality. In addition many Japanese companies have branched out overseas almost as if to take the place of American companies.

This pattern of international development by Japanese companies has inadvertently led to the formation of a trade structure that easily arouses friction with other countries. The prominence of Japanese products tends to make Japanese firms more conspicuous than the firms from nations that quietly export machinery and materials for industrial use. In terms of industrial machinery, there have been many advancements overseas by the sort of industries in which high added values are found in Japan. Nevertheless, a relative decline has occurred in the position of American companies as Japanese firms have expanded. To prevent conflicts that could have easily arisen, Japanese companies made direct investments; the incentive was political rather than economical. In the future Japanese firms will need to make more effort to avoid various forms of conflict besides that concerning direct investments.

15.1 Growth of Exports

Worldwide Exports

The Japanese manufacturing industries' exports in 1991 came to $305.2 billion, and it accounted for 97 percent of Japan's total exports ($314.8 billion). The share of the world's total exports accounted for by those from Japan comes to 8.6 percent. Although that may seem like an enormous number, it is not the largest exports figure in the world, nor is Japan's dependence on exports exceptionally high.

Table 15.1 compares Japanese total exports, along with those of manufacturing, with exports from the United States and Germany (the former West Germany). Several distinguishing features of Japanese exports and, in particular, of the manufacturing industries' position can be found on this chart.

First of all, Japan's total exports place a distant number three in the world share, after those of the United States and Germany. Moreover, while the monetary value of its exports per capita is larger than that for the United States, it is much less than that for Germany. Likewise, while the relative weight of Japanese exports in the GNP (level of dependence on exports) is higher than that for the United States, it is much smaller than that of Germany. Germany is much more dependent on exports than Japan. Japanese exports, namely due to the inter-

Table 15.1
An international comparison of exports

	Total exports ($millions)	World share (%)	Exports per person ($)	Dependence on exports (%)	Proportion of manufacturing industry (%)
1965					
Japan	8,452	4.5	85	9.5	92.0
United States	27,521	14.6	142	4.0	64.0
Germany	17,892	9.5	303	16.3	88.9
1981					
Japan	151,495	8.1	1,288	13.0	96.6
United States	238,715	12.7	1,038	7.8	68.4
Germany	176,047	9.4	2,855	25.7	86.0
1991					**1990**
Japan	314,786	8.6	2,548	9.3	96.7
United States	422,158	11.8	1,689	7.4	76.0
Germany	391,884	12.3	6,198	24.8	91.0

Source: Bank of Japan, *Kokusai Hikaku Tokei* (Statistics for International Comparison).

nationalization of manufacturing industries, have really been surprisingly low.

Second, the growth of Japanese exports has been the largest among the three nations. Its exports in 1991 were 37 times the figure for 1965. From the fact that Germany's exports experienced a twenty-two-fold increase during the same period and those from the United States a fifteen-fold expansion, we can understand how startling Japan's growth has been. The speed of that growth has been number one among industrialized countries.

However, that is not because Japanese dependence on exports has become great. The level of dependence was roughly the same—just a little over 9 percent—in both 1965 and 1991. This figure once swelled to about 13 percent around 1980, but thereafter, in the 1980s, Japan lowered its dependence on exports. Nevertheless, since Japan enjoyed greater economic growth on the whole than Germany and the United States, its exports did increase their world share.

Third, in the sense that almost all Japanese exports have been from the manufacturing industries, their added values have been great. The manufacturing industries of other nations have all been increasing their weight in exports. Still the respective figures for Germany and

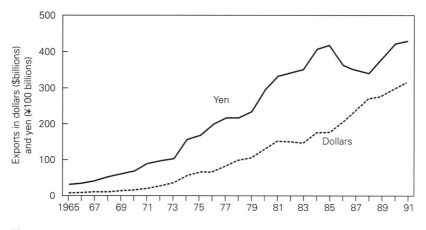

Figure 15.1
Development of Japanese exports. Source: Ministry of Finance Statistics.

the United States were 91 percent and 76 percent in 1991—meaning that the weight of their manufacturing industries was less than that of Japan's.

Leading Players in the Growth of Exports

Let us now look at the development of Japanese exports until they reached their 1991 size, as shown in figure 15.1. Both yen and dollar indicators are displayed on the graph.

As can be understood from this graph, while the dollar exports grew quite smoothly, those at a yen showed uneven growth. (The data begin in 1965, which is the first year Japanese trade turned a surplus; it was in that sense a benchmark year.) It is obvious here just what a big event the high yen of 1985 was. Exports then fell from their yen-base level of 1985, which was finally recovered in 1991. It was the first time in the history of Japan's postwar economic development that its yen-base exports had taken such a plunge. However, in dollar terms, exports continued to grow steadily after 1985.

Both the smooth development of exports and the effects of the high yen present differences that produce inevitable gaps in perception between the dollar world and the yen world. Although the tendency of Japanese exports in terms of yen has been to grow considerably, growth went in a zigzag pattern after the oil crises, and it plunged enormously with the high yen rate. Nevertheless, the view in the dollar

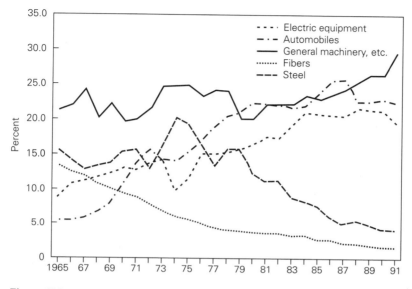

Figure 15.2
Composition of exports by industry. Source: Ministry of Finance, *Gaikoku Boeki Gaikyo* (Outline of Foreign Trade).

world is that Japanese exports have actually expanded steadily and continued growing despite the high yen. This is just how different things look in the yen world and the dollar world even under the same economic circumstances.

Japanese company people sense the yen indicator as reality, but the dollar-indicator figures are what foreign people see. The gaps in perception between these two worlds in fact present a lot of grief to the yen world, while in the dollar world it looks as if Japan has been enjoying a steady expansion that is virtually inexplicable. The sense that Japan had advanced abnormally was begot in other countries, and then a reaction to that view could not help developing, in turn, in Japan. These are gaps in perception that only fuel friction.

Over the twenty-five years that Japanese exports grew, the leading players have changed considerably. Figure 15.2 shows the changes in the composition of Japanese exports by industry for the top five industries. As is clear from the graph, from the latter half of the 1960s to the first half of the 1980s, the automobile industry's importance substantially increased, while exports of steel and textiles declined. However, especially after the high yen of 1985, the exports of the automobile and electric machinery industry began to drop, and exports

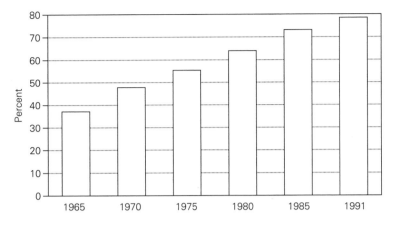

Figure 15.3
Export share of the machinery industry. Source: Ministry of Finance, *Gaikoku Boeki Gaikyo* (Outline of Foreign Trade).

of general industrial machinery began to rise. There are indications that the composition of Japanese exports will become centered around industrial machinery.

More generally, whether automobiles or industrial machinery, all these exports include the machinery industry. The share accounted for by the machinery industry in Japanese exports as a whole has steadily increased. That effect can be better seen in figure 15.3. Machinery industry's share, which was just under 40 percent in 1965, climbed to almost 80 percent by 1991; this indicates that the development of Japanese exports is largely because of the machinery industry.

Now let us look at the markets to which Japanese exports have been directed. Figure 15.4 shows the changes in the share of exports by region. With all of Asia regarded in the figure as one economic region, the exports there have been heavier overall than to the United States. This tendency became stronger with the high yen rate.

Although the United States has consistently been a major market for Japanese manufacturing industries as far as individual countries go, directly after the oil crisis of 1973, exports to Asia rose sharply, while those to the United States rapidly declined. But that was not because the absolute value of exports to the United States had decreased but rather because those to the oil-producing countries of western Asia began a rapid expansion. This is particularly true of the period following the oil crisis. The export share to the United States fell to almost

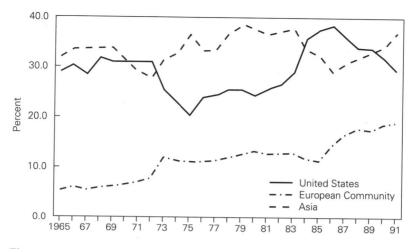

Figure 15.4
Composition of exports by region. Source: Ministry of Finance, *Gaikoku Boeki Gaikyo* (Outline of Foreign Trade).

20 percent in 1975, only to climb back to 38.5 percent in 1986. Especially in the first half of the 1980s, there was a striking rise in Japan's dependence on the American market. Even though that may have been brought about by Reaganomics which caused an expansion of demand, it was still an abnormally high degree of dependence.

Although Japanese exports to the United States fell significantly below 30 percent in 1991, overall the vast amount of Japanese exports, entailing a nearly 30 percent dependence on one country, has naturally led to imbalances of trade. Other nations importing Japanese products are, according to data for 1991, Germany with 6.6 percent, South Korea with 6.4 percent, and Taiwan with 5.8 percent. By comparison, the share of Germany's exports by country (according to 1989 data) is balanced, with France accounting for 13 percent, Italy for 9 percent, the United Kingdom for 9 percent, and the Netherlands for 8 percent.

As can be seen in figure 15.4 as well, after the yen rate peaked, there were substantial changes in the pattern of Japan's exports. More Japanese exports headed toward Asia and the EC. To some extent that was only natural since the high yen was a casualty of the devaluation of the dollar. Nevertheless, Japanese exports cannot shake the image of having deluged the EC and Asia after losing their great American outlet. The volume of Japanese exports did not decrease despite an enormous decline in the yen-base exports as the dollar-base exports gradually increased. Indeed it was that without increasing their dollar prices significantly, Japanese companies avoided a decline in their volume of exports, attributable to the high yen, by pioneering the EC and Asian markets.

15.2 Direct Investments and Overseas Production

Direct Investments

Direct investments overseas by Japanese manufacturing industries have also grown rapidly after the high yen rate of 1985. Clearly the high yen marked a turning point in the international development of Japanese companies.

As figure 15.5 shows, direct overseas investments were at the $2 billion level in the first part of the 1980s, but in 1985 they suddenly jumped nearly eightfold, to $16.3 billion. Japan's total direct investments overseas in the forty-year period from 1951 to 1991 came to $93.9 billion, and 70 percent of that figure was made during the four-year period between 1987 and 1991. From these figures one can understand just what a recent phenomenon the expansion of direct investments by Japanese manufacturing has been. In a sense direct investments by Japan's manufacturing industries have only begun, although, on reaching a high in 1989, they started to decline. The bubble economy of the second half of the 1980s had a strong effect on manufacturing's direct investments. Nevertheless, in the near future, these investments are unlikely to drop as far down as the level during the first half of the 1980s.

Despite the dramatic investments of recent times, the balance of Japan's direct investments is still not high by international standards. Table 15.2 shows data not just for manufacturing but for all industries. The percentage of direct investments for manufacturing in Japan has been fluctuating between 20 and 30 percent of the totals shown. Unlike exports, the direct investments for manufacturing do not account for the majority of investments. Direct investments in other countries made by companies in areas like real estate and finance have been tremendous. The balance of Japan's direct investments in 1990 was $201.4 billion—a figure only 28 percent of that for the United States. However, it is much higher than the German figure. Since Japan and Germany were at the same level in 1986, from this we can tell just how

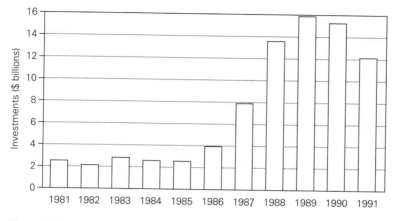

Figure 15.5
Direct investments by the manufacturing industry. Source: Ministry of Finance Statistics.

Table 15.2
International comparison of direct investment balances ($billions)

	1986	1990	1990 − 1986
Japan	58.1	201.4	3.47
United States	519.4	714.1	1.37
Germany	58.1	132.7	2.28

Source: Bank of Japan, *Kokusai Hikaku Tokei* (Statistics for International Comparison).

amazing Japan's direct investments became in the latter half of the 1980s.

As is seen in table 15.1, Germany had not quite 10 percent more exports than Japan in 1991. Yet Japan had a direct investment balance nearly 50 percent higher. This shows that Japan has been largely shifting its overseas operations from exports to direct investments. Nevertheless, Japanese investments are well below those of the United States.

I have already mentioned how exports from the Japanese manufacturing industries depend on the United States, where the direct investments tend often to be made as well. The regional allocation of the Japanese manufacturing's direct investments is shown in figure 15.6. Direct investments were centered in Asia before the 1980s, although since the end of the 1970s they had increased dramatically in North America. Direct investments in North America came to surpass 60

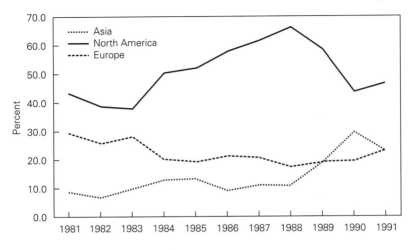

Figure 15.6
Composition of direct investments by region. Source: Ministry of Finance Statistics.

percent of the total partly because of the large acquisitions of companies, which peaked in 1988. Thereafter there was a shift to Europe
coupled with a revival of investments in Asia. Nevertheless, North
America remained in the lead at 48 percent in 1991. This majority of
direct investments headed for the United States indicates that Japanese
companies' dependence on the United States has been consistently
high.

Overseas Production

Direct overseas investments have led to production overseas on a large
scale by the Japanese manufacturing industries. According to the Ministry of International Trade and Industry's basic survey on overseas
business activities (data on 1,563 companies that are active abroad;
hereinafter, referred to as the "basic survey"), in 1989, there were 2,646
Japanese companies with locally incorporated manufacturing overseas
(incorporated companies carrying out manufacturing abroad, excluding those that conduct marketing activities only), and their sales came
to ¥22.267 trillion. The sales per firm were not large at ¥8.4 billion, but
this altogether accounted for 59 percent of Japan's total amount of
exports (¥37.8 trillion) for the same year. However, attention should be
paid to the fact that overseas sales and exports from Japan overlap in

Table 15.3
Overseas production activities, 1989

	Persons engaged (thousands)	Sales (¥billions)	Total assets (¥billions)	Profits after taxes (¥billions)
Overseas subsidiaries	922	22,267.0	23,043.4	227.9
Company headquarters	2,188	125,003.9	126,304.9	3,479.6
Ratio to headquarters (%)	42.1	17.8	18.2	6.5

Source: Ministry of International Trade and Industry, *Kaigai Jigyo Kihon Chosa* (Basic Survey on Overseas Business Activities).

the calculations where Japanese companies export half-finished products and have them assembled locally and where the incorporated manufacturers abroad put on the local market products imported from Japanese headquarters.

How far do overseas production activities go when compared with the production activities of company headquarters in Japan? As can be seen in table 15.3, 922 thousand people are employed overseas by Japanese companies—42 percent of their personnel. It should be noted that this figure is not 42 percent of employment for all the Japanese manufacturing industries but rather corresponds just to 42 percent of the employment in Japan of the 1,563 Japanese manufacturing companies that are active abroad. The locally incorporated producers overseas account for 17.8 percent of sales, and their percentage of total assets is roughly the same, while their profits figure at 6.5 percent. From all this, we can tell that the weight given abroad by Japanese firms is highest for employment and then descends from sales to profits.

Saying that the sales of locally incorporated producers overseas come to 17.8 percent of those of company headquarters will give the impression that production abroad accounts for close to 20 percent of Japanese manufacturing. But that is not so in reality, for there are many completely domestic firms that are not included in this basic survey. If we calculate the percentage of total Japanese manufacturing sales accounted for by the ¥22 trillion production abroad as the proportion of overseas production, it will be only about 5.7 percent.

Figure 15.7 compares Japanese and American production overseas since 1982. Overseas production by the American manufacturing industries has by far exceeded that of the Japanese. Moreover since the

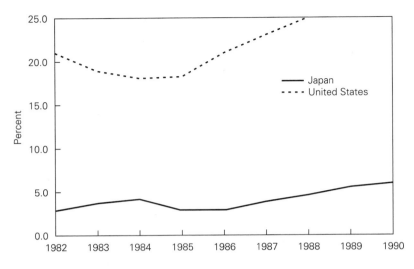

Figure 15.7
Comparison of overseas production. Source: Ministry of International Trade and Industry, *Kaigai Jigyo Katsudo Kihon Chosa* (Basic Survey on Business Activities Overseas).

mid-1980s the proportion of American production overseas has been increasing at a faster rate than Japan's. Overseas production by Japanese manufacturing industries is in fact rather low. The proportion of overseas production for Germany's manufacturing industry comes midway between those of Japan and the United States.

Other distinguishing features of Japanese overseas production activities are given, by region, in table 15.4. The Asian region accounts for almost half of employment and profits, but sales are highest in the United States. Total assets in Europe exceed the percentage of sales and employment by far, so it is the venue for priority investments, whereas in the United States Japanese subsidiaries have been losing money on the whole. Although the number of employees sent abroad from Japan is low at about 16,000, around 40 percent of them are dispatched to the United States, with nearly 40 percent of the total assets invested there too. Yet the local corporations in the United States still produce a deficit after taxes. From all this we can tell just how unprofitable they tend to be.

The main reasons for overseas production hardly seem to be attributable to the existence of many extraordinary deductions or because the advancements, being recent, are in the initial stage of investments.

Table 15.4

Regional composition of overseas production activities of Japanese companies, 1989 (%)

	Employment (thousand people)	Sales (¥ billions)	Total assets (¥ billions)	After-tax profits (¥ billions)	Number of persons engaged overseas
Asia	45.2	22.9	18.9	60.2	38.7
North America	30.6	55.2	37.6	−16.6	40.0
Europe	9.5	14.0	35.1	19.5	12.6
Other	14.6	7.9	8.4	36.9	8.6
Total	922	22,267	23,043.4	227.9	16,078

Source: Ministry of International Trade and Industry, *Kaigai Jigyo Katsudo Kihon Chosa* (Basic Survey on Overseas Business Activities).

Table 15.5

Overseas advancement and profitability (working income rate for 1989 sales)

Advancements	Prior to 1978	1978–80	1981–83	1984–86	1987–89	Average
Asia	4.1	5.3	6.0	3.4	−1.7	3.8
North America	1.2	0.8	2.4	−0.7	−2.3	0.2
Europe	2.9	3.0	2.8	1.0	1.0	2.3

Source: Ministry of International Trade and Industry, *Kaigai Jigyo Katsudo Kihon Chosa* (Basic Survey on Overseas Business Activities).

Table 15.5 shows the trends in the rate of ordinary profits to sales by region for Japanese companies' overseas subsidiaries in 1989 according to the period in which they made their advancement abroad. While profits certainly do tend to be low for recent advancements, North America is a region of low profitability for Japanese firms, even compared with Europe.

In other words, the Asian region is the most profitable for Japanese companies, followed by Europe, and then North America. This order of profitability was true not only in 1989; it has consistently been the pattern for some time.

The rate of ordinary profits to sales for Japanese companies in 1989 was 5.6 percent. The average rate of profits for their locally incorporated companies throughout the world was 1.8 percent, which should make us understand that advancements overseas have yet to become profitable business ventures. Nevertheless, as can be seen in table 15.5, the 1980 profits of the subsidiaries in Asia alone practically match up with those of the company headquarters in Japan today.

Impetus for and Expansion of Overseas Development

Why do Japanese companies in fact advance abroad? According to one basic survey, the main reason for turning to North America and Europe is to "maintain and expand the local market." About 80 percent of the companies responded this way. Undoubtedly, through local production companies can expand their local markets because they become more aware of local needs. But even more important is that companies can use local production to overcome political barriers (e.g., to circumvent trade friction). These companies apparently think that even low profits are preferable to losing a market share. This can also be surmised from the answers given to the question on reasons for advancement into the more profitable Asian region; the two most frequent responses were, "to take advantage of the local labor force" and "to maintain and expand the local market."

These motives are backed by the data on the locations of the sales markets for the locally incorporated companies shown in table 15.6. Subsidiaries of Japanese companies in North America and Europe seek, to an overwhelming degree, local sales markets (in the case of European subsidiaries not only in the particular country where the company is located but in the surrounding countries as well). In the case of Asian subsidiaries, a hefty 15.8 percent of sales are accounted for by exports to Japan. Nevertheless, 73.6 percent of sales are within the Asian region. The average proportion of exports for subsidiaries in all regions is 20.4 percent. And, perhaps just by chance, the proportion of exports for company headquarters in Japan—a figure included here for reference—is quite close.

In other words, direct investments overseas by Japanese manufacturing industries have focused on local markets. At least there has not been much tendency so far to produce in the most appropriate location globally and then offer from there goods to the world's markets or else to import them into Japan. In the case of American companies (according to data for 1988 from *U.S. Direct Investments Abroad: Preliminary 1988 Estimates*), 61.5 percent of the sales of overseas subsidiaries in the manufacturing industries was directed to their locality, 12.7 percent went to the United States, and 25.8 percent headed to a third country.

Table 15.6
Markets for the overseas production subsidiaries of Japanese companies, 1989 (%)

Regions	Domestic sales	Exports			
		Total	To Japan	Within region	Other
Asia	63.9	36.1	15.8	9.7	10.6
North America	93.1	6.9	4.5	1.6	0.8
Europe	66.5	33.5	1.7	29.6	2.2
Total overseas subsidiaries	76.9	20.4	7.9		
Japanese headquarters	80.7	19.3			

Source: Ministry of International Trade and Industry, *Kaigai Jigyo Katsudo Kihon Chosa* (Basic Survey on Overseas Business Activities).

Here we can see that U.S. management has been more global than that of Japanese firms.

However, the Asian subsidiaries of electric machinery companies are the sole exception to this general trend among Japanese firms; they operate more globally. The proportion of their sales in the local country is just 37.4 percent. They export throughout the world, with Japan accounting for 26.9 percent, North America for 13.3 percent, Asia for 16.7 percent, and Europe for 4.3 percent. Such global management has been a trend seen since the mid-1980s.

Even in this case we might observe that the large sales, at 54 percent, within the Asian region are proof of Japanese companies' strong inclination toward local markets. The figure is much lower for American companies. Only 12.5 percent of the sales of the Asian subsidiaries of American companies (in the electric machinery industry) go to the local region, 60.1 percent head to the United States, and 27.4 percent to a third country. Therefore this Japanese industry, which is the exception by being global, operates less globally than its American counterpart.

This inclination toward local markets among Japanese firms is connected with the recent shift in direct investments to the United States and Europe such that the basic pattern of the internationalization of Japanese companies has become

Exports → Economic friction → Local production

This pattern took shape in avoiding the strong trade friction with Europe and North America by launching local production. This way

Table 15.7
Share of overseas production investments by industry (%)

	Transport machinery	Electric machinery	Metals	Chemicals	General machinery	Machinery industry total
Overseas production, 1989	32.4	30.4	7.1	5.8	5.0	69.8
Total investments, 1980–91	14.5	25.7	10.9	12.3	10.1	50.3

Source: Ministry of International Trade and Industry, *Kaigai Jigyo Katsudo Kihon Chosa* (Basic Survey on Overseas Business Activities).

Japanese subsidiaries do not produce off the shores of Japan but locally in other countries for a market that has always been outside of Japan. Indeed one has only to look at the fact that the distribution of overseas production has been concentrated in industries that have experienced the greatest trade friction. Overseas production by the Japanese manufacturing industries came to ¥22 trillion in 1989.

Table 15.7 shows the share of production and the share of total investments overseas (from 1980 to 1991) by industrial field for the top five producers in 1989 (or expressed more accurately, the sales of locally incorporated overseas manufacturers). As far as production goes, automobiles and electronics account for more than 60 percent of that conducted by Japan overseas. If the data for general machinery and precision machinery are added to the production share for the machinery industry's total, this figure will come to 69.8 percent. Just as in the case of exports, Japanese production abroad has been driven by the machinery industry. In terms of total direct investments since 1980, the situation is somewhat different; the proportion of transport machinery in the total figure has declined. This may be due in part to some exports from Japan being included in the sales of the locally incorporated companies overseas of Japanese transport machinery manufacturers. But also in an industry like transport machinery, which involves many parts, a considerable portion of the overseas yield is covered by the export of parts from Japan in order to raise the amount of production while keeping investments in the locality relatively low.

This is more than a matter of simple arithmetic. Direct investments overseas may encourage industries in the export of parts and capital assets from Japan to the locally incorporated subsidiary such that would account for the major portion of the local yield. That hints of a great danger for Japan, of a vicious circle of trade friction occurring whereby the export of different assets will end up increasing as Japanese companies try to deal with the trouble caused by the export of products. Whatever happens, the fact that the Japanese manufacturing industry's development overseas is driven by the machinery industry will not change.

The pattern of the Japanese manufacturing industries' international development as described so far can be boiled down to an inclination toward local markets and machinery industry–driven growth. The response to the needs of local markets entails not using a region as a base of operations for other markets.

On the matter of Japanese imports, many of the goods produced offshore could be imported back into Japan. In a sense overseas production means opening the market of one's own country. The United States has done just that. However, Japan has hardly done so at all. The Japanese market has not been particularly open even to the overseas subsidiaries of Japanese companies. Recent changes in the electric machinery industry suggest that this is a viable course for Japanese manufacturing industries.

The machinery industry is centered around fields that must pass through several complicated stages of production. The machinery industry–driven international development has made it comparatively easy for Japanese competitiveness to last a long time. It has simultaneously become a structure that easily gives rise to trade friction. The basis for that friction will be explained in the next section. But there are other factors that distinguish the international development of Japanese manufacturing. Let us now take a look at the characteristics of this international development.

15.3 Four Characteristics That Distinguish Japanese Subsidiaries

The following four characteristics are representative of Japanese manufacturing's international development:

1. Small size
2. Concentration
3. Speed
4. Visibility

First, concerning small size, Japanese companies still conduct, relatively speaking, a surprisingly low level of activities abroad. For example, the proportion of its exports within its GNP is much lower than the equivalent figure for Germany, and the balance of its direct investments is not even one-third of that for the United States. In terms of employment, too, Japan's presence is still less than one-quarter of the American figure. The proportion of its overseas production is also much smaller than the equivalent figure for the United States, and the number of employees dispatched from Japan to subsidiaries abroad has been low as well, 16,000 in 1989. In fact the number of employees dispatched overseas is only 0.7 percent of the number employed at the headquarters of companies in Japan. At this level a shortage of international personnel has already been observed. Here we can tell at just what a tight spot the international management of Japanese firms has been.

Second, concentration refers to region as well as industry type. International activities have been carried out mostly in the United States. The United States is important both for exports and for direct investments. The United States accounts for nearly 40 percent of Japan's automobile and electronics exports, and the proportion of the machinery industry's exports is approaching 80 percent. Although direct investments significantly trail, they are largely driven, like overseas production, by the machinery industry. In terms of corporate concentration of certain dominant companies in industries like automobiles, electronics, and precision machinery, in 1988 the top twenty-five exporting Japanese firms accounted for approximately 50 percent of Japan's total exports. They also led in direct investments.

Third, speed has characterized these companies' rapid growth and rapid directional changes. Typical are the fast rising direct investments in the late 1980s. They followed earlier instances of prompt directional changes of exports in the aftermath of both the oil crises and the high yen. Japanese companies closely followed the American market after the oil crises. Shifts in direction to Europe could be seen in the wake of the high yen, and more recently there have been directional shifts to East Asia with extraordinary flexibility and speed.

Fourth, high visibility has been the inevitable result of the aforementioned three characteristics. A small number of companies in consumers' machinery goods (e.g., automobiles and VTRs) do enormous overseas production and exporting, and they also have concentrated markets. Since consumer goods are involved, they easily get a lot of attention. Because these companies get such popular treatment abroad, they become conspicuous in Japan as well. Our eyes easily spot what's hot in the marketplace too.

Such high visibility easily generates trade friction. If instead our overseas activities were divided among several companies centered around more subdued industrial products and spread among a greater distribution of countries, there would probably be a lot less friction for us to face, even if we maintain international development at the same level overall. German companies seem to have successfully used this stratagem.

15.4 A Structure That Easily Produces Friction

Inadvertently the machinery industry has submitted itself to a pattern of international development that easily rouses trade friction with other countries. This is a lesson for Japanese companies planning on internationalizing their operations; they should be aware of the consequences of high visibility and a strong international presence of their industry.

Japan's Future Growth

First of all, the generally low activity of Japanese companies abroad, and the concentration in the United States, suggests that there is room for Japanese companies to expand overseas. Currently production abroad for Japanese companies is less than half of that for the United States, so there is some leeway for Japanese firms to proceed with internationalization. Even in the machinery industry, among the large corporations only a small number have developed international subsidiaries. These and companies in other industries may find ample space for their international operations in Asian regions.

In exports it is of course difficult to predict competitive activity or whether products will experience a great decline in price, quality, and so on. Nevertheless, one should not overlook the potential for growth. Although we can hardly expect exports to the United States and the EC to increase boundlessly, there is no question about the effort of the Asian NIES to catch up with Japan. Given such markets outside of the United States and the EC, as well as the development of the international division of product lines with Asia, it is hard to imagine that the entirety of Japanese exports will ever stagnate.

As for the Asian countries, their most natural course would be for exports to Japan to increase as they advance into the world's export markets. Already since the high yen of 1985, exports from the Asian countries have been increasing, along with exports from Japan to the Asian NIES of the capital assets and intermediate equipment production (e.g., automobile and electronic parts). A type of division of product lines has begun to take place in Asia. Were by some chance the exports from the Asian NIES to countries beyond Asia to vie with Japanese exports, that would not erode significantly Japanese exports. Rather, Japanese exports would more likely be supplemented by the increase in capital assets and intermediate equipment sent to those countries.

In view of these circumstances we can expect the international presence of Japanese industry to grow larger over the long term. However, if that presence is concentrated and swiftly accomplished, as it has been up to now, then it will generate more friction. With this understanding of Japan's potential international contributions operating on the other side of friction, we must be cautious about overdoing the levels of concentration and speed.

Japan's High Added Values

The presence of Japanese industry abroad can be expected largely to continue to be centered around machinery. The distinguishing features of both exports and direct investments, which have been machinery industry–driven so far, were pointed out earlier in this chapter. They have enabled high added values to accrue to Japan, in addition to becoming a source of friction with the United States.

Fundamentally, this aggregation of added value is attributable to the fact that the machinery industry consists of end products—be they capital assets or consumers' goods—of long production processes that start with materials processing. In other words, several stages of production, involving materials, parts, and assembly, are built into these products.

Since multiple stages of production are involved, the country that exports machinery obtains higher added values, and its share of income is consequently larger. This is because added value emerges as income at each stage up to the end production, and when those end products are exported, all those earnings aggregate to Japan. High added values are very much attributable to long production processes.

Thus the income of the machinery industry is what countries scramble for, and it is in this industry that has piled up huge earnings in

Table 15.8
Export weight of the machinery industry, 1989 (%)

	Within total exports	Within manufacturing industry's exports
Japan	75.6	78.1
United States	46.9	66.0
Germany	51.7	57.0

Source: *Nihon Kokusei Zukai* (Explanatory Diagrams of the National Situation in Japan).

Japan. This is precisely why friction easily occurs over matters relating to employment. Since every country wants to have as much production as possible carried out within its own borders, machinery exports readily become a source of friction.

Furthermore, since the machinery industry involves multiple stages, impasses can easily occur over the issue of how many stages of production can be carried out locally. This can slow the shift to local production. A simple example is the procurement of parts. If parts are not procured, a machine cannot be assembled. The magnitude of the problem might better be grasped by calling to mind the vast number of parts required, for example, by 3,000 VTRs or 30,000 automobiles. To be sure, for final production to be conducted abroad, the assembly systems set up in these localities must include the parts industries. This is a hurdle that overseas production has to overcome, and for this reason changes in that direction have been proceeding at a slow pace. And that too has led to friction.

Still a company moving into overseas assembly while keeping the production of parts within Japan will show rising exports. There will be more added value to the production of parts, so added values will still aggregate to Japan. That is why assembling overseas while leaving the high value-added portion in Japan has been criticized as deceptive, and it has become yet another source of friction. The issue is one of constraints on overseas operations.

The fact that Japan's level of internationalization, driven by its multiple-stage machinery industry, has been higher than that in other countries exposes it to more friction. But it also is indicative of the diverse character of the local overseas operations.

The machinery industry has essentially formed the core of the manufacturing industry's international development in every other nation, large or small. Yet that has been taken to an extreme in the case of

Table 15.9
Number of top 500 manufacturing companies

	1980	1988
United States	217	176
Japan	66	102
United Kingdom	51	50
France	36	35
Germany	29	29
Others	101	108
Total	500	500

Source: *Fortune* 500.

Japan. The data on the machinery industry's weight in Japan's exports appears in table 15.8. The figure is significantly higher than that of its counterparts in the United States and Germany. Therefore Japan's composition of exports readily gives rise to friction.

An Unintended Zero-Sum Game

A final reason why the international development of the Japanese manufacturing industry has generated friction is that Japan's global presence has inadvertently expanded as that of American companies has declined. That is to say, these circumstances suggest that Japan grew at the expense of the United States. To put it more bluntly, the pluses and minuses between the two countries have contrasted so sharply that Japan could be said to have taken aim at the United States.

One aspect of this development has already been explained here as due to the concentration of exports and direct investments in the United States. As a result Japanese companies have appeared as if they have converged on American firms. Really, unconnected to any convergence, there have been many instances of pluses for Japan surfacing together with minuses for the United States. For example, the historic movements in the two countries' shares in the world's GNP clearly show pluses for Japan occurring together with minuses for the United States.

Table 15.9 shows the distribution of the *Fortune* 500 manufacturing companies in the world. Thirty-six Japanese companies newly appeared in these rankings in the 1980s, while 41 American firms disap-

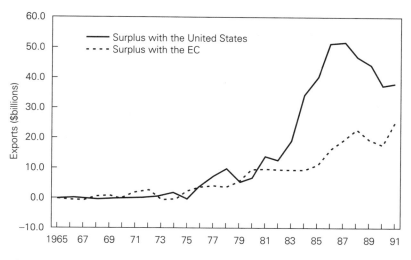

Figure 15.8
Japan's trade surplus with the United States and with the EC. Source: Ministry of Finance, *Gaikoku Boeki Gaikyo* (Outline of Foreign Trade).

peared from the list. The United States suffered a decline close to the share of Japan's increase, whereas other countries showed little change.

In contrast to the United States, Japan began experiencing a substantial trade surplus in the 1980s. Indeed, as shown in table 15.9, Japan's trade surplus underwent a rapid increase simultaneously with the changing of the companies in the rankings. This is depicted in figure 15.8. Until the mid-1970s Japan did not have such a big trade surplus with either the United States or the EC. In some cases Japan even ran a deficit. But things somehow changed from the second half of the 1970s. One difference was that the international competitiveness of the Japanese manufacturing industry became solidified. In addition, in the first half of the 1980s, it experienced an extraordinary rise in exports to the United States.

Regardless of what the cause of the demand for Japanese products was, the $52 billion trade surplus to the United States in 1987 became a sum of much political concern. Almost 50 percent of the U.S. trade deficit was with Japan. From the American perspective, if its trade deficit with Japan were solved, then half of its deficit would disappear. The sum is so large that we simply cannot say that it is illogical and incorrect to view the trade balance as just between two countries. That of course is not a zero-sum game that Japanese industry willfully built against the United States. However, even though it may have emerged unintentionally, it would be strange if the speed of the deficit's growth and its size did not arouse friction.

So far, as figure 15.8 shows, the trends indicate that the EC will become the next player in this so-called zero-sum game. While Japan's trade surplus to the United States dropped to $38.2 billion in 1991, its surplus to the EC rose to $27.4 billion. That is the same level as the surplus to the United States in the first half of the 1980s. Therefore it is not unreasonable for Japan to expect that affected Europeans will take political measures toward this deficit. Japanese industries must be careful about this one-way road to friction and make efforts to avoid it.

16   Role of Government (Industrial Policy)

Toshihiro Kodama

This chapter will consider the government's role in the development of Japanese industries after World War II. For that reason it will first give an overview of the changes in postwar industrial policies over time. Next, it will clarify the special features of Japan's industrial policy by investigating the appropriateness of popular characterizations of government involvement such as the "Japan, Inc." view and the target industries view. Last, it will touch on challenges to government's role in the twenty-first century. The following points summarize the thrust of this chapter:

• Postwar Japan's industrial policy from the end of World War II to the beginning of the 1970s underwent changes in basic structure concerning the government's involvement in the market economy, as shown in the return to and move from a controlled economy to a domestically free market economy and to an open economy. But considerable transformations have been occurring in the fundamental objectives since the 1970s as well. To be sure, the present industrial policy is different from the development-oriented policy of the past, and it has been increasingly oriented toward international cooperation.

• It is a wild exaggeration to regard Japanese industrial policy in terms of a "Japan, Inc." model. There is likewise a misconception in the interpretation of industrial policy as "encouraging resources to move into particular industries." The characteristics seen from the allotment of resources among sectors brought about by industrial policy, such as policy-based finance, show that the government has supplemented market functions of a cross section of industries rather than given preferential treatment to particular industries. This picture suggests that while being based in market principles, industrial policy has acted to supplement industry where the market mechanism functions only insufficiently.

• As can be seen in the experience of dealing with the GATT Uruguay Round concluded not so long ago and the currently increasing need for deregulation, political, administrative, and industrial systems have yet to be adjusted to conform with the times. Industrial policy must be formulated to serve the interests of the entire national economy, and not just the manufacturing industries. Supplementing market functions via the government at a complementary position must be a unified principle comprised of the market mechanism at the very foundation but with sufficient constraints to prevent its being violated by manufacturing industries.

16.1 Development of Postwar Industrial Policy

The industrial policy of postwar Japan underwent a transformation in the relationship between government intervention and basic market objectives of such policy.

From immediately after World War II to the beginning of the 1970s industrial policy-making can be divided into three stages according to the relationship between policy tools and the market economy. The first stage was the period directly after the war to 1952—an era when Japan was occupied by the victorious Allied Forces. Domestically Japan's economy was under transition and strict control, and external trade was extremely limited. The second stage lasted from the restoration of industrial autonomy in 1952 to 1960. While on the international front import control continued through a foreign exchange allocation system, on the domestic front an industrial policy was introduced indirectly through methods premised in a free market economy. The third stage was the period in which Japan proceeded into an open economy through the liberalization of foreign trade, followed next by the liberalization of capital movement (especially the liberalization of direct foreign investments into Japan).

Another important change in postwar industrial Japan was the transformation in the fundamental objectives of industries. From the Meiji period until before World War II and from the postwar reconstruction period to the beginning of the 1970s, the basic objective of industry policy was *shokusan-kogyo* (to increase production). This guided the promotion of heavy industries in the reconstruction of the economy and boosted international competitiveness carried out by the heavy and chemical industries. This objective, to put it more bluntly, consisted in "development" aimed at catching up with the United States and Europe.

Indeed, on entering the 1970s, Japan had already come to be referred to as a "GNP giant." The government authorities concerned themselves recognized that the process of catching up with the industrialized nations of the West had ended. As a result gradual shifts were introduced in industrial policy objectives. In other words, there seemed to be a strong consensus among government authorities that the traditional development-oriented industrial policy should shift focus to international cooperation and raising the well-being of Japanese citizens.

From the 1970s to the first half of the 1980s, a crucial task of industrial policy was to maintain smooth progress despite such exogenous shocks as the change to the floating exchange rate system and the two oil crises. The Japanese economy was forced to make painful adjustments and to set aside the objectives of directly working toward international cooperation and enriching the lives of the Japanese. Only by the late 1980s, when the Japanese economy broke away from the effects of the oil crises, could international cooperation in industrial policy once more be pursued. That tendency toward international cooperation became visible, for instance, in import expansion policy measures giving preferential treatment to foreign products. It could be found as well in industrial technology policy, making clear the idea that the fruits of research and development promoted by the national government are public property belonging to all the world and not just to Japan.

Industrial Policy Demarcated by Era

The following results have been obtained by consolidating the changes in industrial policy in accordance with the aforementioned demarcations in era.[1]

Reconstruction Period (1945 to about 1952)

The fundamental objectives of economic policy in general and industrial policy during the period directly after World War II to 1952 were reconstruction and stability—in other words, restoring production and allaying inflation. Industrial policy tools were based on such expedients as materials rationing, price controls, and subsidies for price maintenance. A system of production priorities was enacted from 1947 to March 1949; it took advantage of the structural expedients and of the Reconstruction Finance Corporation's funding. This funding was aimed at restoring the production levels of all industries which were prioritized by the recovery of bottleneck industries like coal, steel, electric power, and chemical fertilizers.

Simultaneously under the directions of the General Headquarters of the Allied Forces occupying Japan, the large family financial combines (*zaibatsu*) were dissolved, an antimonopoly law was enacted, and the gigantic corporations were broken up as part of a policy to democratize the economy. In this way was laid the foundation for a functionable market economy. As important production priorities, the mining and manufacturing industries were restored up to 60 percent of their prewar levels by 1948. In 1949 the "Dodge Line," which aimed to stabilize prices from the money supply perspective by forcefully tightening fiscal and monetary policy, was instituted. Prices thus became stabilized, and at the same time economic controls were gradually relaxed. These measures enabled the market economy to be accepted domestically. In addition, on the international front, although Japan was under a foreign exchange allocation system, trade with other countries was resumed.

Period of Achieving Economic Autonomy (1952 to about 1960)
In 1952 Japan's independence was restored as the San Francisco Peace Treaty went into effect. The temporary controls of materials supply and demand, which was fundamentally a law vis-à-vis control of the domestic economy, became null and void.

The fundamental objective of economic policy on the whole was to make the economy autonomous—meaning attaining a compatibility between economic growth and the balance of payments. However, the uniform fixed exchange rate of $1 = ¥360 established by the Dodge Line was too high for most manufacturing industries. Therefore industrial policy had to focus on (1) maintaining import restrictions to protect the balance of payments and (2) strengthening international competitiveness through rationalization of the domestic industry in order to raise production for export. While on the international front import restrictions were continued through the foreign exchange allocation system, domestically the market economy was restored and industrial policy based on indirect incentives unfolded.

As was noted above, industrial policy at this time was concerned with industrial rationalization and export promotion policy with the establishment of JETRO (Japan External Trade Organization). The industrial rationalization policy was horizontally implemented among industries and promoted by the Enterprises Rationalization Promotion Law, the Steel Industry Rationalization Plan, the Petrochemical Industry Promotion Program, the Synthetic Fiber Industry Promotion Program, the Temporary Measures Law for Promotion of the Machinery Industry (the Machinery Industry Promotion Law), and the Temporary Measures Law for Promotion of the Electronics Industry (the Electronics Industry Promotion Law).

These policy measures were accompanied by assistance tools such as tax concessions, accelerated depreciation on rationalized equipment investments, and policy-based financing through the Fiscal Investment and Loan Program (FILP). The Machinery Industry Promotion Law and the Electronics Industry Promotion Law helped formulate rationalization targets for certain industries as corporate goals, set up the criteria for assistance cases, and authorized the exemption of rationalization cartels from the Antimonopoly Laws. Other attempts were to improve productivity initiated by the Japan Productivity Center, the enactment of Industrial Standardization Law, and the development of infrastructures such as industrial water supply and electric power sources were important aspects of industrial rationalization policy.

Period of Shifting to an Open Economy System (1960 to about 1970)

Japan's economy became open by the enactment of the Trade and Foreign Exchange Liberalization Program in 1960. This was also a time of high economic growth, as is evident by the Income Doubling Plan, which was also formulated in 1960. The main objective of the economic policy in 1960 was to maintain high economic growth while completing the shift to an open economy.

This shift to an open economy went through a number phases, which included the liberalization of trade (the import liberalization ratio went from 41 percent in April 1960 to 93 percent in 1964 after the foreign exchange budget system was abolished), the lowering of tariffs (the average tariff burden rate dropped from 7.1 percent in 1968 to 2.7 percent in 1974), and the liberalization of the flow of capital (from the first liberalization measure of direct foreign investments into Japan in

1967 to the fifth liberalization measure of 1973). On the domestic front it advanced heavy machinery and chemical industrialization (which strengthened the international competitiveness of the heavy and chemical industries), since within the industrial structure both had the most promise for bringing rapid economic growth under intense international competition.

The scheduling of this phased move to an open economy was the most important aspect of this period's industrial policy, which began with the liberalization of trade. The strengthening of international competitiveness was seen as enabling a merits-of-scale economy, such as was published in the *Vision of the Industrial Structure in the 1960s*, which advocated carrying out heavy and chemical industrialization domestically. Government and business cooperation (see section 16.2) was conceived in the form of administrative guidance but not ever compelled. Rather, this concept allowing the government to intervene was primarily limited to coordinating equipment investments among industries.

Decisions to reorganize the manufacturing industry through mergers and business alliances were welcomed by the government except when they rankled the antimonopoly authority as progress toward international competitiveness. Moreover, since modernizing the small- and medium-sized enterprises (SMEs) was regarded as means of fortifying Japanese industry's international competitiveness, diverse policy measures were formulated to promote SMEs such as the *kodoka* ("upgrading") scheme of preferential loans combined with consulting services to support the upgrading activities of SMEs (sharing business expertise, plants, etc.), diagnostic advice, job training, and so on.

Adjustment Period (1970 to Early 1980s)

The 1970s was a period of grand-scale transformations in the international economy wrought by the changes in the international currency system. The so-called Nixon shocks (i.e., his announcement of plans to devaluate the dollar and to visit China), the shift to the floating exchange rate system, and the two oil crises threatened Japan's still fragile industrial foundation.

Japan had to adapt its fundamental objectives of industrial policy, which logically shifted from being development oriented with its sights on boosting international competitiveness and advancing the industrial structure, to emphasizing international harmony, qualitative improvements in the lives of the people, and generally public welfare. In addition industrial policy had to consider such markedly diverse new circumstances as how to overcome Japan's dependence on foreign energy, which was made painfully clear with the outbreak of the oil crises. Other problems concerned pollution and overcrowding in urban areas due to the depopulation of rural areas, but these were issues that had already started to become apparent in the 1960s.

Taking in the perspectives of environmental protection and the conservation of resources and energy, the *International Trade and Industry Policy Vision for the 1970s* advocated building a "knowledge-intensive" industrial structure. In the next decade, in consideration of the fact that Japan was advancing as a front-runner in technological development, the *International Trade and Industry Policy Vision for the 1980s* emphasized the need for building a "creative knowledge-intensive" industrial structure.

Research and development was promoted in government contracts, subsidies, and at national research institutions in order to build a "knowledge-intensive" and "creative knowledge-intensive" industrial structure. Specifically, the Large-Scale Industrial Technology Research and Development Program was expanded, and the R&D Program on the Basic Technology for Future Industries was established. In addition there were conceived major technological development projects for the semiconductor and computer industry typified by the research and development of VLSIs.

In the case of structurally depressed industries that persistently had excess production capacities, the government provided assistance for their industrial readjustment (reduction of production capacity). Antipollution policies had been set up and developed, starting in the late 1960s and continuing through the early 1970s. But after the oil crises energy policies focused on energy conservation, the development of alternative energy sources, and securing a stable supply of petroleum. At this time there was also discussion of industrial location policies for an industrial relocation program, in the 1970s, and then a technopolis program, in the 1980s.

International Cooperation Period (Since the Late 1980s)

Since 1985 the weight of international cooperation in Japanese economic policy has increased by leaps and bounds. Coexistence and co-prosperity within the world economy have become the most important

Table 16.1
Tariff rates and the number of items with residual import restrictions

	Imports	Japan	United States	European Community
Average tariff rate (effective 1990 rate, %)	All products	About 5	About 4	About 7
	Agricultural, marine products	About 9	About 3	About 12
	Mining industry products	2.1	4.3	4.6
Tariff burden rate (1989, %)	Total Average	2.9	3.5	3.5
Number of items with residual import restrictions (1992)	All products	12	17	99
	Agricultural, marine products	12	15	78
	Mining industry products	0	2	21

Source: GATT data, Ministry of International Trade and Industry data and the Ministry of Finance's *Zaisei Kinyu Tokei Geppo* (Public Financing Statistics Monthly).
Notes: Included in the data are (1) import surcharges on the average EC tariff rate and rate of tariff burden, and (2) EC items with residual import restrictions and items subject to variable tariffs.

issues, especially since they relate to securing a long-term base for industrial development. For this reason there has been an extraordinary increase in the number and variety of industrial policy measures aimed at international cooperation and international contributions.

By the mid-1970s Japan's trade system had already become open to a degree that compared well with those of the United States and Western Europe (see table 16-1)[2] in terms of the average level of tariff rates and the number of residual import restrictions on mining and manufacturing products. In the late 1980s some further policy measures expanded imports and improved the market access. Among these were reforms in the systems of standards and certifications which had been seen as institutional nontariff barriers. These reforms were begun in July 1985 and carried out over three years under the Action Program to Improve Market Access.[3] In 1990, under the Comprehensive Import Expansion Measures, tariffs were abolished on 1,004 manufacturing and mining products. These import measures, which were unprecedented worldwide, were devised to give preferential treatment to imported manufactured products by setting up a tax concession scheme to encourage imports of manufactured goods, establishing a program to unearth potential import products, and enacting low-interest financing to encourage imports of manufactured goods. In 1992 the Temporary Measures Law for Promoting Imports and Facilitating Foreign Investments in Japan came into being. This law stipulated government support through preferential treatment in policy-based financing and tax concessions for setting up import-related infrastructures in ports, airports, and their surrounding regions.

After 1985 various policies for international joint R&D research were established or expanded. In some cases, such as the Human Frontier Science Program, Japan was the initiator of a global research and development project. Moreover within Japan R&D projects in industrial technology are now being carried out under conditions that allow the participation of foreign companies. Promoting research and development as international public goods has become the position of Japanese government. Crucial other areas of international policy concern global environment problems, support for the industrialization of developing countries by making use of diverse economic cooperation and technological cooperation schemes, and promotion of economic cooperation in the Asia-Pacific region.

16.2 Characteristics of Japanese Industrial Policy

The following two points have by tradition been emphasized as characteristic of Japanese industrial policy: One is close cooperative relations between the government and private companies based on a government-guided economic constitution such as would correspond to both the "Japan, Inc." view and the revisionist view, which in fact developed from the former. The other concerns the promotion of certain industries through resource allocations—a view taken by many economists. These two claims have both complementary and conflicting connections. They have considerably influenced political debate on Japanese domestic industrial policy in other countries and informed their image of Japan and policies for dealing with Japan.

Popular Interpretations of Japanese Industrial Policy

Connection between the "Japan, Inc." and Revisionist Views
The popular interpretation of Japanese industrial policy as "Japan, Inc." began in the late 1960s in the West; in the 1980s this view underwent some revision in the United States which had regarded Japanese industry as responding exclusively to government goals. Although the "Japan, Inc." theory is repudiated by many economists

nowadays, Japan is still often discussed on the basis of this image abroad.

"Japan, Inc." was basically a conception of Japan as one enormous joint-stock corporation with the government—particularly the Ministry of International Trade and Industry (MITI)—as the company headquarters and large companies as its business departments. Such an image suggests a nation without a market economy whose government and businesses are locked into an intimate cooperative relationship and whose businesses are controlled by the government with the economy run according to its directions and plans.

This very simple image of Japan was partially revised in the *United States Department of Commerce Report*[4] of 1972. On the relationship between the Japanese government and business, the report took the position that "Japan, Inc." is not a simple system in which the government gives directions that are blindly followed by the business world.

The report's view was that Japan functions as one enormous body of government and business through a complex mechanism. By this mechanism, once a consensus is formed over the order of priorities and the targets of the economy as a result of interactions between the government and business, then the government will make good use of administrative guidance and inductive policy tools to bring the priorities and targets thus established to fruition. In the end, although the report says that the economy "does not run under the government's unilateral directions," it nevertheless asserts that "Japan is on the whole a managed economy, and it is a gigantic joint-stock company that presses on toward a unified goal."

The "Japan, Inc." view was passed on in new dressing as the revisionist view, which came to full flourish in the latter half of the 1980s. Chalmers Johnson's 1982 book, *MITI and the Japanese Miracle,* typified this view of Japanese industrial policy. Taking his political analysis from a comparative systems approach of the Japanese economy, MITI, and its predecessor—the Ministry of Commerce and Industry—from 1925 to 1975, in Johnson's eyes: "Japan is not a communist centrally planned economy, but within capitalism, it is different from the Western market economies. Japan consists of a state-guided market system, in which the government provides the economy with goal orientations based on a consensus, and the government and private business cooperate to aim to accomplish the goals." He dubbed the Japanese economy and state system a capitalist "developmental state."

Karel van Wolferen, James Fallows, and Clyde Prestowitz, in the latter half of the 1980s in works[5] representative of the revisionist view state opinions on the Japanese economy and industrial policy that are strongly influenced by Johnson, whose book is prominently quoted from. In other words, they all take the position that the Japanese economy is different from the free competitive economy of the West and claim that intimate cooperative relations between the government and private business as well as aggressive market intervention by the government exist in various fields of the economy for the sake of industrial development. According to these authors, this goes hand in hand with the private business practices, including those in bank *keiretsu* ("bank-centered corporate groups"), which account for Japan's economic success and cause economic friction with other countries. These writers see preferential treatment for particular industries as a distinguishing feature of Japanese industrial policy.

Such Japanese industrial policy and ways of the economy are viewed favorably in the aforementioned Johnson book as something the United States should learn from, whereas the later three writers find these points of criticism. That is to say, they censure Japanese industry for being protected in a market economy where private companies should compete on equal terms. They claim protection by the government through a variety of means, including nontariff barriers such as restrictions on foreign exchange, which hark back to controls from before and during World War II, and the exclusionism of distribution system seen after the liberalization of foreign trade. The three authors further assert that resources are invested to strengthen an industry's international competitiveness even at the expense of consumption, and that for that reason, American and European companies have been forced into a game with different rules.

This image of a government-guided economy as planned and apportioned by the state appears primarily to have become the basis for discussions in the United States claiming that, "Since the Japanese economy is different, it is all right when dealing with trade with Japan to apply rules that are different from those for the West"—such as spoken in 1993 on the institution of quantitative import targets by the American side in establishing the U.S.–Japan Framework Talks. Then, again, on the issue of the Eastern European countries making the transition into market economies, there has become evident the mistaken conception in some parts that Japanese industrial policy is due

to some semiplanned economy base. And this seems to be responsible
for arousing the reaction that industrial policy is inappropriate for the
Eastern European countries seeking to advance to market economies.

Industrial Targeting View
Industrial policy is often defined in economic terms as "a government
attempt to allocate resources to certain industries that it views as
important to economic growth."[6] In particular, Japanese industrial
policies have been characterized as having focused on certain important industries and making arrangements with them for preferential
policy treatment.[7] The following two types of arguments have often
arisen based on such an interpretation of industrial policy.

The first argument doubts the effectiveness of industrial policy and
its applicability to other countries. Its viewpoint is that the government's criterion for selecting certain industries for intervention is based
on mitigating market failure due to external economies and the existence of incomplete competition, whereas, in fact it is difficult for the
government to judge market failure and its extent. The selection of
industries inevitably ends up being arbitrary. Preferential treatment of
certain industries in the allocation of resources would mean sacrificing
other industries. It is consequently more appropriate to entrust the
development of industries to market mechanisms.[8]

The second argument, on the contrary, recognizes government intervention to be effective in promoting certain industries, but claims that
"it is unfair for the government to support certain industries in order
to develop their export competitiveness and invade the markets of
rival countries. Therefore competing trade countries are justified in
their use of countermeasures." Such criticism of Japanese industrial
policy characterized the U.S. government's view at the start of the
1980s. In the past Japanese industrial policy based on such an interpretation partially formed the ground for the demand by the Clinton
administration for managed trade such that quantitative import targets
be established for Japan.[9]

Characteristics of Japanese Industrial Policy

Is the "Japan, Inc." View Appropriate?
A major problem with any argument purporting the uniqueness of the
relationship between government and industry in Japan is that it
continues to pass on the view of "Japan, Inc." which appeared some

twenty years ago. The problem with Johnson's 1982 book which formed the basis of the revisionist view and became influential during the late 1980s is that it centered its analysis on the period from 1925 to 1975. These were the times of government control before, during, and right after World War II, and finally a postwar age in which direct intervention by the government existed in the form of foreign exchange allocation, foreign investment regulations, and the like. Indeed until the 1970s the Japanese had no authority to ration foreign exchange nor to regulate foreign investments. Consequently such positions emphasizing the government's or the state's power of control and planned economy methods are quite dated with relation to the current situation in Japan.

Even with regard to the Japanese economy up to the 1960s, the general view is that its growth was accomplished through dependence on market mechanisms.[10] However, numerous examples can be found that challenge the interpretation of the Japanese economy as a cooperative system between the government and private sector, or as government guided.

For one thing, there is the case in 1963 and 1964 when MITI advanced a bill with temporary measures for the promotion of specific industries (the Specific Industries Promotion Bill) and presented it to the Diet. This bill was to legalize the *kanmin-kyocho hoshiki* ("government-business cooperation formula") which would promote the specific industries needed for boosting international competitiveness. The intention was for the government, industry, and the financial sector to put together, through their deliberations, guidelines for each designated industry in order to establish a rationalized production system by mergers, joint ventures, specialization in production, and the like, and to prepare the financial backing. This bill, however, did not manage to obtain the support of industries nor of the financial sector, which was apprehensive about such bureaucratic control. Ultimately the bill was shelved.

It has often been pointed out that even after the rejection of the Specific Industries Promotion Bill, the "government-business cooperation formula" was instead brought to fruition through the enactment of "government-business cooperation discussion groups" in several industries. However, unlike the "cooperation formula" for various strategic industries, as was hoped for under the bill, these "discussion groups" undertook investment coordination for just three industries. They did not handle mergers and business tie-ups at all. Except for petrochemicals, the industries they dealt with, such as synthetic fibers, paper, and pulp, were on the brink of structural ruin.

In terms of funding too, the "structural finance scheme" was established within the Japan Development Bank for rationalizing firms' production systems premised in mergers and tie-ups. Yet this scheme was not accompanies by cooperative finance from private financial institutions, as envisioned by the aforementioned Specific Industries Promotion Bill. Moreover the amount of money borrowed was extremely small, so the cooperation system between the government and private sector postulated by the bill did not come to fruition.[11]

The details behind the abandonment of the Specific Industries Promotion Bill suggest that in Japan government industrial policy cannot be formed without the support of the private sector. It also shows that such a mechanism had already been set up in Japan back in the early 1960s.[12]

There are several other problems with the appropriateness of the "Japan, Inc." view. But the point we need to stress is the unique relationship between the Japanese government and industry that has encouraged mutual understanding and intimate exchanges of information between both sides. To be specific, a number of vertical sections corresponding to individual industries exist within the ministries such as MITI which deal with the industrial sector. Their normal daily activities include overseeing the current circumstances of individual industries. All policy proposals are conducted with such an awareness of each industry's present circumstances.

Their information is supplemented by exchanges of opinion and information gathering from a broader perspective through deliberation councils,[13] in which representatives from the concerned industries participate along with people from several related industrial fields, the academic world, journalism, consumers' groups, and so on. Such a system of policy formation contains absolutely nothing like the central government-directed restraints put on the decision-making of private companies assumed by the "Japan, Inc." view. The system has rather functioned to heighten objectivity in forming policy.

Is the Industrial Targeting View Appropriate?
Next we will investigate the appropriateness of the industrial targeting view, which is characterized by claims that Japanese industrial policy has encouraged resources to move into specific important industries and has aimed to promote them thereby. Here we will examine actually

Table 16.2
State of the new supply of capital from government financing for industrial equipment according to industrial type (%)

Industry type	1952–54	1955–59	1960–64	1965–67
Manufacturing industry		22.8	31.7	27.7
Food product industry		3.3	3.1	2.8
Fibers industry	2.5	2.8	3.9	3.6
Chemical industry	2.5	3.4	4.8	3.7
Machinery industry	2.8	4.1	7.2	6.2
Metal industry	4.3	3.6	5.0	3.9
Steel industry	3.3	1.8	1.9	1.3
Other metal industries	1.0	1.8	3.1	2.6
Ceramic industry	0.7	1.3	2.1	1.7
Other manufacturing industries		4.2	5.6	5.8
Mining industry	3.8	4.0	4.8	4.8
Metal mining industry		0.6	1.0	1.1
Coal mining industry	3.0	2.5	3.1	3.0
Other mining industries	0.8	1.0	0.7	0.7
Agriculture, forestry, and fishery	18.5	15.3	13.8	15.0
Agricultural and forestry industries	15.6	12.6	11.7	13.0
Fishery industry	2.9	2.7	2.1	2.0
Electric power, gas, and water supply	41.1	33.0	15.9	5.9
Electric power industry	40.6	32.5	15.5	5.5
Gas industry	0.5	0.5	0.4	0.3
Water supply industry			0	0.1
Transport and communications	17.5	14.4	20.0	27.7
Overland transport industry	1.6	2.1	7.8	12.2
Marine transport industry	15.3	10.0	8.6	13.9
Communications industry			0	
Other transport industries	0.6	2.3	3.6	
Other industries	6.1	10.4	13.7	18.8
Total for all industries	100.0	100.0	100.0	100.0

Source: Japan Development Bank, *Chosa Geppo* (Monthly Survey).
Notes: (1) Since the food product industry was not listed separately within the "manufacturing industry" prior to 1954, the data before then are unknown. (2) The water supply industry was not included in data for the "electric power, gas, and water supply industry" prior to 1956. (3) The data for the "transport/communications industry" prior to 1956 are for the transport industry only. (4) The data for "other transport industries" in 1967 are unknown. (5) The data for other "mining industries" prior to 1954 include metal mining.

Table 16.3
Concentration levels according to broad industrial classifications of the new supply of government-funded capital for industrial equipment

Industry type	1952–54	1955–59	1960–64	1965–67
Agriculture, forestry, and fishery	74.6	72.0	92.9	111.6
Mining	120.3	172.8	339.5	468.6
Manufacturing	30.7	78.3	94.4	85.1
Other industries		28.4	35.1	44.3
Electric power, gas, and water supply; transport and communications	590.3	445.6	327.4	323.9
Total	100.0	100.0	100.0	100.0

Source: Japan Development Bank, *Chosa Geppo* (Monthly Survey); Economic Planning Agency, *Kokumin Shotoku Tokei Nenpo* (Annual Statistics on Population Income).
Notes: (1) The numbers were calculated as follows: The structural proportion each industry accounts for in the source of new supplies of industrial equipment funds through government financing (government financial institutions and special funding budgets) divided by the structural proportion accounted for by each industry in purely domestic production (excluding financing, insurance, and public service) in essential expense indications × 100. Because of limitations on the materials, the real estate industry is included in the numerator but not in the denominator. (2) "Other industries" means the total of the construction, retailing, real estate, and service industries. (3) Because of limitations of the materials, distinctions cannot be made between the "manufacturing industry" and "other industries" from 1952 to 1954.

to what degree the allocation of resources was concentrated in specific sectors through policy-based finance (government financing activity mainly from government financial institutions), tax concession measures, tariffs, and other government tools that reduce resource allocation.

First, let us look at the level of concentration of resource allocation among industries under policy-based finance. Table 16.2 represents the proportion of government-supplied funds by the recipient industry out of the new supply of industrial equipment investment funds. The "government funds" represent the total of funding from (1) government financial institutions consisting of the Japan Development Bank, the Hokkaido-Tohoku Development Corporation, the Small Business Finance Corporation, the People's Finance Corporation, and the Agriculture, Forestry, and Fishery Finance Corporation, and (2) government financing other than that which passes through government financial institutions such as a special account for industrial investment. Because of data limitations, only the years from 1952 to 1967 are presented here.

Table 16.4
Concentration levels by industry type within the manufacturing sector of new government funding of industrial equipment

Industry type	1952–54	1955–59	1960–64	1965–67
Manufacturing industry		100.0	100.0	100.0
Food products industry		139.1	108.3	106.4
Fiber industry	95.0	103.0	125.2	145.8
Ceramic industry	72.7	115.9	137.6	124.3
Chemical industry	88.3	100.3	111.6	95.9
Metal industry	163.5	98.3	102.0	91.2
Steel industry	238.8	92.3	81.7	65.9
Other metal industries	79.2	105.2	119.6	112.4
Machinery industry	74.9	71.0	71.6	73.5
Other manufacturing industries		116.1	114.0	124.6

Sources: Japan Development Bank, Chosa Geppo (Monthly Survey); Industrial Statistics Association, ed., *Sengo no Kogyo Tokei-hyo <Sangyo-hen>* (Postwar Industrial Statistic Charts. Industrial Edition).
Notes: (1) The numbers were calculated as follows: The structural proportion each industry accounts for in the source of new supplies of industrial equipment funds through government financing (government financial institutions and special funding budgets) divided by the structural proportion accounted for by each industry in the manufacturing industry's value-added output × 100. Because of limitations on the materials, the structural proportion of the industrial types of new supplying industrial equipment through government funding gives the computation for the budget year, and the structural proportion of the industrial types in value-added output gives the calculation for the calendar year. (2) The 1952–54 figure is the relative comparison accounted for in the total for the fiber, ceramics, chemical, metal, and machinery industries. (3) The "chemical industry" here includes oil refining, rubber products, and leather in addition to chemicals. (4) "Other manufacturing industries" are formed of the lumber/lumber products, paper pulp, publishing/printing, and other manufacturing industries.

If the weight given a certain industry in the economy is high, that industry's demands for funds will correspondingly be high as will its share in the allocation of government funds. Therefore, in order to assess the level of concentration in the allocation of government funds, we need to study the relative size of the proportion by industry in the supply of government funds compared to each industry's proportion in terms of measures such as output.

From this standpoint, table 16.3 presents the indexing of the proportion of the value of the newly supplied government funds for industrial equipment investments by industry, divided by the proportion of the value of net domestic production in the National Income Statistics by industry according to a broad industrial classification. Similarly table 16.4 presents the indexing of the proportion of government funds by industry divided by the proportion of value-added production in the Census of Manufacturers by industry within the manufacturing industry.

Let us examine the level of concentration of government funds among industries according to tables 16.3 and 16.4. In terms of a broad industrial classification, they indicate primarily that the level of concentration was conspicuously high in the electricity, gas, water supply, and the transport and communication industries from the 1950s to the 1960s (which was particularly true of electric power and marine transport in the 1950s, and land and marine transport in the 1960s). This fact suggests that infrastructure was given priority. Second is the concentration in mining that rose rapidly toward the latter half of the 1960s. However, this may more accurately reflect the political and social demand for help in the coal-mining industry, which was losing its economic advantage, than it does any economic rationality.

Concerning the concentration by branch industry within manufacturing, excluding that of the newly supplied government funds to the iron and steel industry from FY 1952 to 1954 (strictly speaking, in 1952 and 1953 only), on the whole the degree of concentration has been high in light industries comprised mostly of small- and medium-sized enterprises; among these are food products, textiles, ceramics, other metal industries, and other manufacturing industries. The chart shows, however, that the concentration was relatively low in the industries that might be regarded as important such as chemicals, iron and steel, and machinery.

In terms of government funds, the concentration of loans from the Japan Development Bank and the Hokkaido-Tohoku Development Corporation in the chemical and iron and steel industries was comparatively high. However, government funding overall was allocated mostly to small- and medium-sized enterprises via the Small Business Finance Corporation and the People's Finance Corporation, and the concentration of funding was higher in light industries such as textiles and food products.

It has often been said that policy-based financing has traditionally mostly been allocated to so-called strategic industries that greatly contribute to economic growth and thus the expansion of exports. Of course, considering their relative importance to the economy, it is common sense that policy-based financing would be larger to electricity and marine transport. However, it is significant that, as table 16.3

Table 16.5
Concentration levels by industry in amortizations used in the manufacturing sector

Industry	1960–64	1965–69	1970–74
Manufacturing	100.0	100.0	100.0
Food products	35.6	45.3	65.2
Fiber	76.9	106.7	137.2
Pulp, paper, paper-processed	172.2	42.3	95.1
Chemical	64.1	95.4	89.6
Ceramics, earthenware/rockware	49.8	59.2	78.2
Steel	235.3	342.8	219.9
Nonferrous metals	121.5	69.4	61.6
Metallic goods	49.8	78.5	90.7
Machinery	91.7	70.1	71.6
Electric machinery equipment	64.0	71.0	67.5
Transport machinery equipment	217.8	182.1	203.5
Shipbuilding	89.1	247.8	127.7
Other manufacturing	104.7	51.8	74.6

Sources: Ministry of Finance, *Hojin Kigyo Tokei* (Statistics for Incorporated Companies); Industrial Statistics Association, ed., *Sengo no Kogyo Tokei-hyo <Sangyo-hen>* (Postwar Industrial Statistic Charts: Industrial Edition).
Notes: (1) The numbers were calculated as follows: The structural proportion accounted for by each industry in the actual worth of the special amortizations utilized divided by the structural proportion accounted for by each industry in the manufacturing industry's value-added output × 100. Because of limitations to the materials, the structural proportion occupying the actual worth of the special amortizations utilized is the computation for the budget year, while the structural proportion for each industrial field in the value-added output is the calculation for the calendar year. (2) "Other manufacturing industries" are formed of the clothing and other fiber product industries; lumber and lumber product industries; furniture and furnishing industries; publishing, printing, and related industries; oil product/coal product manufacturing; rubber product manufacturing; tanned skins, chamois product, and fur manufacturing; precision machinery/apparatuses manufacturing; weapons manufacturing; and other manufacturing industries.

indicates, among the manufacturing industries the concentration of financing has been higher in the light industries which are composed of small- and medium-sized enterprises, such as textiles and food products which developed rapidly after World War II.

As for the actual record on the various tax concession measures such as accelerated depreciations, income deductions, and reserves, only accelerated depreciations are available in a time series from the Statistical Survey on Incorporated Enterprises. Accelerated depreciations have been the most general form of tax concession measures for promoting equipment investments.

Table 16.6
Rate of effective protection in Japan

Industry	Nominal protection rate (%)		Effective protection rate (%)	
	1963	1968	1963	1968
Mining (excluding coal)	2.1	3.4	3.7	−1.7
Processed food products	31.5	29.7	74.5	57.9
Beverages	35.0	45.2	47.9	54.9
Spinning	18.9	17.0	51.6	26.7
Woven products, fiber products	19.0	18.9	56.7	32.1
Personal effects	24.1	25.5	67.2	51.7
Furniture	20.2	23.8	39.9	33.1
Pulp, paper	11.6	9.1	38.3	5.7
Leather, leather goods	21.4	22.8	71.2	28.3
Rubber products	13.0	15.4	21.0	12.1
Basic chemotherapeutants	16.2	15.1	27.0	17.9
Coal/oil products	9.7	10.0	23.4	13.8
Ceramics, earthenware/rockware	13.5	13.5	24.1	14.9
Pig iron, unrefined iron	10.8	12.6	37.3	20.7
Steel primary products	16.0	15.8	27.6	14.5
Nonferrous metal primary	16.6	17.7	54.3	18.1
Metal products for use in construction	15.5	18.7	19.7	18.5
General machinery	16.1	15.8	22.6	25.0
Electric machinery	19.3	17.6	30.7	22.9
Transport machinery	20.3	17.4	35.2	17.9
Other manufacturing	23.1	22.4	36.2	23.6
Simple average	17.8	18.4	38.6	24.2

Source: Norihiko Muto, *Kanzei Suijun no Kokusai Hikaku* (An International Comparison of Tariff Levels); *Kanzei Chosa Geppo* (Monthly Tariff Survey), vol. 24, 1971.

Using these data for accelerated depreciations, table 16.5 shows the levels of concentration by manufacturing industry compared with value-added production. A high concentration of accelerated depreciations can predictably be seen in major industries such as iron and steel, transport equipment, and shipbuilding from the 1960s to the first half of the 1970s. However, the accelerated depreciation formula given in the table notes can be used by any industry. So altogether, as the record indicates, accelerated depreciation was less utilized than policy-based financing and favorable tariff rates.

Let us turn next to the effect of tariffs on the allocation of resources among industries. After the Trade and Foreign Exchange Liberalization

Program was established in 1960, the quantitative import restrictions based on the foreign exchange allocation system were gradually abolished. In 1961 the tariff rates and tariff system were completely revised; in trade policy, tariffs came to replace quantitative import restrictions. After the Kennedy Round in 1968, tariffs began to be lowered. By 1974 they were close to average, compared to those in the United States and Western Europe. During this time tariffs largely influenced the allocation of resources among industries.

Using an existing study, table 16.6 compares the nominal rate of protection and the effective rate of protection by industry in 1963 and 1968. As is clear from the table, iron and steel, electrical machinery, transport equipment, and the like, did not receive any remarkable protection by tariffs; they were very close to average. Rather, light industries like food processing, beverages, spinning, fabrics and textile products, clothing accessories, furniture, and leather and leather goods were given such protection.[14]

As was mentioned earlier, the data on policy-based financing, tax concession measures, and favorable tariffs, which were the primary tools of assistance in industrial policy from 1950 to the first half of the 1970s, show that even the funding of capital equipment via policy-based financing and tariffs was not concentrated in the industries that later expanded their export competitiveness. Consequently, if we look at the actual results of resource allocation brought about by policy tools, it is difficult to characterize Japanese industrial policy simply as having selected certain industries for growth by preferential allocation of resources.

In the case of assistance measures in research and development, an area that has been becoming increasingly important since the 1970s, the tendency has been to concentrate on research-intensive industries. While we cannot overlook the government support in the electronic industry's R&D projects, we must note that overall the percentage of the Japanese government's outlay for research and development in industry has been markedly lower than that seen in the West.[15]

The many laws and policy measures that promoted industries existed in the 1950s and 1960s as was noted in section 16.1. Government promotional policies were industry specific because they needed to respond according to each industry's circumstances; it was not a matter of just choosing to allocate resources in certain industries.

Overall, we can say that the crucial fields where industrial policy allocated resources encouraged a cross section of industries to firmly establish themselves, promoted small- and medium-sized enterprises, and the advanced research and development, but no particular industries were favored. Policy also served to protect or save faltering industries when the problems relating to infrastructure, namely consisting of small- and medium-sized enterprises, and research and development were difficult to surmount by the market mechanism alone. Industries undertook improvements to their infrastructure and to research and development (especially basic research) in the face of uncertainty. Small- and medium-sized companies had to compete in the labor market and in the incomplete capital market.[16] Industrial policy thus functioned to supplement market forces in allocating resources to these areas.

The allocation of resources to weakened industries enabled smooth transitions to so-called positive areas of production, raised the morale of the labor force, and provided protection and relief but without preserving inefficient industries. The industrial policy in these cases were very different in nature from any policy that promotes strategic industries for economic growth.

16.3 Future Tasks

It is no exaggeration to say that the development of the manufacturing industries has been the driving force behind Japan's economic growth. In its history there was a period in which the government stepped up to intervene in the market, but it later moved to lessen its involvement. It can be said that industrial policy encouraged the growth of manufacturing industries in order to strengthen market principles. The resource allocation brought about through policy tools like policy-based financing, as described in section 16.2, is one such form of intervention in order to correct a market imperfection.

The discussion in section 16.1 showed that since the mid-1960s industrial policy has responded promptly to the diverse issues that have arisen successively in our times. Among the policy changes are various commitments to international cooperation to environmental issues of industrial pollution and energy waste, to abating the extreme concentrations of industries, to the advancement of basic research and development, and to the promotion of imports and international cooperation in research.

For example, the industrial policy of the 1990s is committed to seeking ways for dealing with global environmental problems such that a protected environment will coexist with economic growth. Industry is being challenged to help construct economic growth that is harmonious with the environment. This perspective also includes the thoughts on maximizing global productivity suggested in the prologue and in part I of this book. Along this line the Environment Basic Law of 1993 launched energy conservation measures for energy conservation, recycling, modernizing machinery, and the like. These policies have attracted much public attention, so from now on the activities of firms will be under greater public scrutiny.

While policies have generally coped flexibly with the challenges of each era, and in particular, have been kind to the manufacturing industries, the issues of the future will likely see coordination among the interests of the political and administrative systems. That is to say, on the one hand, wide-ranging economic policies such as contributions to international economy and the welfare of the third world, besides those concerned with the well-being of Japanese citizens, will become the province of industry, manufacturing as well as agriculture, construction, communications, and finance among the areas concerned.

On the other hand, with changes in economic circumstances in Japan and overseas and with the advancements in technology, reform will be demanded in conformity with the structure and system of the era concerned. This idea is easy to understand if we think about the ways in which international economic decisions by GATT/WTO and positions on deregulation are formulated.

Dealings with International Economic Systems Like GATT

No one can deny that the Japanese manufacturing industry benefited from the free trade system centered around GATT. Needless to say, given the enormous scale of growth of the Japanese economy, Japan must now take positive steps to maintain and boost the free trade system. Such involvement is indispensable for securing an environment that allows for the manufacturing industry's growth. In particular, it is even Japan's duty to contribute to international trade policy organizations like GATT in order to serve global society.

At the end of 1993, the Uruguay Round negotiations finally reached a settlement. For more than seven years, Japan has responded to this Round with positive moves in several fields. For instance, it further reduced its tariffs on mining and manufacturing products, even though they were already on the average lower than those in Western

Europe and the United States. However, on the tariffs restricting rice imports—which has received the most international attention—Japan has just managed finally to decide to open the market partially, succumbing to foreign pressure. This is why the country could not lead the agricultural negotiations, which held the key to the outcome of the Round. And for that reason, the international evaluations of Japan's contributions to it have been fairly low in comparison with the vast energy its government had actually expended toward the Uruguay Round overall.[17]

Concerning influence over international trade, the fact is that subsidies to agricultural exports in the United States and Western Europe are a much larger issue. Nevertheless, because of the obdurate attitudes of those involved in agricultural politics, for instance, the Diet's resolutions for the nation to be self-sufficient in rice, Japan was unable to make effective negotiations and strategies on cuts in subsidies to farm exports by other countries. By contrast, the United States demanded the abolition of or cuts in subsidies to agricultural exports as well as the tariffication of nontariff measures on all items including farm products for which import restrictions were allowed for its own country through a waiver measure, which meant exemption from GATT obligations. In this way the United States assumed a negotiation posture that tried to realize profits for its own agricultural industry as a result.

Maintenance and fortification of the free trade system, which should have been brought about by the success of the Uruguay Round, would have secured an environment for the Japanese manufacturing industries' growth. Besides that, Japan's conservative position on agricultural matters can be described only as having enormously diminished its force at the Round. During the Round negotiations, there were hardly any attempts within Japan to consolidate the stakes of the manufacturing industries, which supported the advance into a free trade system, with those of agriculture which demanded the continuation of the present form of agricultural protection. Also, unfortunately, there were hardly any clear political indications to the Japanese people that the so-called national interest in preventing tariffication without exception and blocking partial openings of the rice market is a structure in conflict with another national interest of Japan—that as a processing trade country it has to rely on international trade. To Japanese farmers, as well, that the government and the Diet even went against objective circumstances to take a public stance of rejecting tariffication and partial market openings to the very end served, instead, to delay the construction of a system for more efficient rice production.

This case affecting the manufacturing industries suggests that agricultural policy in the future will not be so isolated from other areas of production. During the liberalization of trade in the 1960s, through agreements between the government and industrial circles on growth targets, the manufacturing industries could move rationalization ahead by making use of a time schedule for liberalization set up product by product in advance. For rice, too, it will be important to take full advantage of the six-year period of grace for enacting tariffs and to use that time for finding ways to boost its international competitiveness. This initiative requires building a system and environment with incentives for efficiency. Of course agriculture is distinguished by having a much stronger reciprocal connection to the natural environment than the manufacturing industries. However, having in place both a system and a congenial environment can stimulate productivity and growth. If farmers do not respond to this, we can imagine that Japan will end up distressed once more in future international economic negotiations, once more by the contentious national interests of promoting both free trade and agricultural protection.

Deregulation and the Growth of Nonmanufacturing Industries

In recent years the necessity for deregulation has been an issue for various reasons. I will list some of the main arguments. First, inefficient systems and structures, as seen in the differences between domestic prices and those overseas, hamper any attempts by consumers to acquire and satisfy the feeling of actual wealth. By relaxing regulations, the nation's living standards will be finally raised.

Second, regulations ostensibly restrict corporate activities, and thus a more dynamic spirit of entrepreneurship. Deregulation may be a way to liberate the economy from the stagnation that has accompanied its maturation and allow businesses to expand and be stimulated by private investments. A similar argument can be made for the expansion of private investments as a way to correct the surplus in the current account balances due to savings substantially exceeding investments.

Third, from the standpoint of international economic cooperation, domestic systems and practices must be harmonious and fine-tuned. Several regulations are behind the times due both to changes in technology and in economic circumstances in Japan and abroad. In fact the problem with regulation is that the restrictions are mostly on business practices involving entry into nonmanufacturing industries like construction, public utilities, transport, communications, broadcasting, distribution, finance, and services rather than the activities of manufacturing industries. While industry-specific business regulations in manufacturing do exist in such areas as oil refining (licenses), shipbuilding (notifications), and cigarette manufacturing (a legal monopoly), in general, industry-specific business regulation laws prohibit entry in the nonmanufacturing industries.[18]

It is further frequently pointed out that labor productivity is lower in nonmanufacturing industries than in the manufacturing industry. That can be attributed to the wide-ranging regulations coupled with the fact that except for the agriculture, forestry, and fishery industries and mining, the nonmanufacturing industries are nontradeable goods industries that do not compete internationally.[19]

This is not to say that manufacturing industries will not be affected by deregulation. Deregulation and improvements in productivity in the nonmanufacturing industries will contribute to the business environment in manufacturing as well. As indicated in the introduction to part I and in chapter 8, increases in production costs have become a big concern in the manufacturing industry. Further, as noted in the introduction to part I, it has become a situation where a number of Japanese manufacturing industries are losing their advantage internationally because of production costs. Factors behind the high production costs are the continued rise of the high yen and the differences in prices between Japan and overseas. And they make clear the importance of a strong yen.

Deregulation may be seen as a way to rectify the disparities between prices in Japan and overseas, and likely also the surplus in the current account balance. While such is expected to indemnify the constitution of excessive saving, deregulation may be seen further as a means of shifting in the allocation of resources to the nontradable goods industries from manufacturing, which is oriented toward tradable goods, by opening up investment in nonmanufacturing industries.[20] We cannot deny the continuing surplus or the accumulation of the current account balance as the reason for the high yen trend. A reduction in the surplus in the current account balance, or expressed another way, an attempt to use the excessive savings within Japan by expanding investment opportunities in the nontradable goods industries, may curb the high yen (e.g., purchasing power parity that includes nontradable goods).

The regulations that exist emerged out of a need for safety, disaster-prevention, health and hygiene, consumer protection, environmental protection, and the like, besides the need to restrain natural monopolies. Therefore we cannot easily go along with arguments to abolish them. Nevertheless, the fact is that there have been technological advances and changes in economic circumstances in Japan and abroad since the regulations were launched. The economic effects of relaxing individual regulations need to be studied more fully. Although the effects of expanding domestic demand and curtailing the surplus in the current account balance are not always immediate, deregulation ought to be viewed as a way of expanding investment opportunities in the nonmanufacturing industries and thereby improving their industrial development.

Fixed Principles and Self-discipline

The established policies and systems of the industrial sector have proved to be insufficient for Japan in fulfilling its responsibility to the world's economy. They have also proved to be inadequate in raising the standard of living for the Japanese and securing a foundation for long- and medium-term domestic growth. Thus the familiar structures and systems of Japan's industrial sector must be revised in response to changing times.

Clearly there need to be fixed principles for Japan's economic activity. Basically companies ought to take responsibility for their economic development while adhering to market principles, and not depend on government to supplement their market function. Needless to say, there is further a strong call for Japanese industry taking an international perspective in redesigning its policies, since domestic economic problems are continually being linked with global economic issues.

Sections 16.1 and 16.2 described the policies in agriculture and other nonmanufacturing industries from the standpoint of manufacturing, whose markets are international. However, in maintaining their international operations, manufacturing industries and industrial policymakers must not forget the need for self-restraint. In other words, when a certain industry falls on rough times due to structural changes in the marketplace and a decline in demand, it should be left to expend its own effort in adapting to market forces. It should learn to recover, perhaps by rationalization and higher value-added production, or to make cutbacks and changes in its business practice. It is easy to insist that protective measures that work to preserve the status quo be put into motion. But it is up to policy-makers with the authority to protect our industries to make a consciousness effort to help it break away from such temptation.

Notes

1. Ministry of International Trade and Industry and the Editorial Committee for the History of International Trade and Industry Policy, *Tsusho Sangyo Seisaku-shi* (A History of International Trade and Industry Policies) Tokyo, was used for reference concerning distinctions in era.

2. Information in the Japan Tariff Association's *Boeki Nenkan* (Trade Annual), 1977 edition about the levels of tariffs for Japan, the United States, and Europe in the rate of the overall average in 1975 shows that the figure for Japan was 2.9 percent, in contrast to the 3.6 percent for the United States and 5.0 percent for the EC (tariffs for outside the region). The number of items with residual import restrictions in January 1976 came to 7 in the United States (6 of which were mining and manufacturing products), 25 in the United Kingdom (6 were mining and manufacturing products), 74 in France (35 were mining and manufacturing products), 39 in the former West Germany (20 were mining and manufacturing products), and 27 in Japan (5 were mining and manufacturing products).

   The most recent figures for the tariff rates and the number of items with residual import restrictions in Japan, the United States, and the EC are as shown in table 16.1. The import barriers in the Japanese trade system in respect to mining and manufacturing products have been at the lowest level among major industrialized nations.

3. The Action Program to Improve Market Access brought in for reconsideration a mix of six kinds of tariffs; import restrictions; standards, certifications, and import processes; government procurements; the finance and capital market; services and promotion of imports. In particular, in the case of standards, certifications, and import processes, the examination was generally from the standpoint of the free market principle with limited restrictions, which was compared with similar systems in other countries. Measures to reform 89 items, which entailed 42 laws, were devised during the three years of this program, with the idea that in the openness of its market, the Japanese system compares with those of other countries.

4. U.S. Department of Commerce, *Japan: The Government-Business Relationship*, 1972.

5. van Wolferen, K. G., *The Enigma of Japanese Power*, Macmillan, London, 1988.; Fallows, J., Containing Japan, *Atlantic Monthly*, May 1989; Prestowitz, C. V., Jr., *Trading Places*, Basic Books, San Diego, 1988.

6. Krugman, P. R., and Obstfeld, M., *International Economics: Theory and Policy*, 2d ed., Scott, Foresman, Glenview, IL, 1991, p. 263.

7. See Patrick, H., Japanese High Technology-Industrial Policy in Comparative Context, in *Japan's High Technology Industries*, ed. by Patrick, H., University of Washington Press and University of Tokyo Press, 1986; Krugman and Obstfeld, ibid. The representative view can be found in Peter J. Katzenstein's *Between Power and Plenty* (Introduction, University of Wisconsin Press, 1978), which characterizes Japanese economic policy-making as "a formidable set of policy instruments which impinge on particular sectors of the economy and individual firms."

8. See Patrick, H., ibid.

9. See Tyson, L. D., Managed Trade: Making the Best of Second Best, in *An American Trade Strategy: Options for the 1990s*, ed. by Laurence, R. Z., and Schultz, C. L., Brookings Institution, Washington, DC, 1990.

10. See, for example, Kosai, Y., Epilogue (in Japanese) in *Kodo Seicho no Jidai* (The Age of High Growth), Nihon Hyoron-sha, Tokyo, 1981, and H. Patrick, ibid.

11. See Ministry of International Trade and Industry and the Editorial Committee for the History of International Trade and Industry Policies, *Tsusho Sangyo Seisaku-shi 10-kan: Kodo Seichoki (3)* (History of International Trade and Industrial Policies Vol. 10: The Period of High Growth [3]), Tsusho Sangyo Chosa-kai, Tokyo, 1990, ch. 5, sec. 2.3.

12. Another good example concerns MITI's proposals for paring down the automobile industry, the People's Car Concept in 1955, and the Three Production Groups Concept in 1961, all of which were not brought to fruition because of opposition from the industry. See Ota, F., Tanigawa, H., Nagai, H., and Otani, D., *Sengo Fukkoki no Sangyo Seisaku: Keisha Seisanhoshiki—Sangyo Gorika—Jidosha Sangyo Seisaku no Saihyoka* (Industrial Policy in the Postwar Reconstruction Period: Reevaluating the Priority Production Method—Industrial Rationalization—and the Automobile Industry Promotion Policy), *Tsusho Sangyo Kenkyujo Kenkyu Series no. 16*, 1993; see, in particular, section 7–2, chapter 5, by the Ministry of International Trade and Industry and the Editorial Committee for the History of International Trade and Industrial Policies, 1990.

Administrative guidance in production coordination, equipment investment coordination, and the like, which occurred frequently in the 1950s and 1960s, set up the conditions for effective foreign exchange policies and the authority to approve technological imports that went along with the regulations of foreign capital. Corroborative research up to now indicated that clear administrative authority based on some kind of law lay behind their effectiveness. The research also shows that private companies did not always follow the government's guidance unconditionally. See Tsuruta, T., The Rapid Growth Era (ch. 3), and Miwa, Y., Coordination within Industry: Output, Price, and Investment (ch. 18), in *Industrial Policy of Japan*, ed. by Komiya, R., Okuno, M., and Suzumura, K., Academic Press, San Diego, 1988.

13. The Industrial Structure Council (set up in 1964), its precursor, the Industrial Rationalization Council (1949–64), and the Industrial Structure Research Committee (1961–64) can be mentioned as typical examples of deliberation councils. Refer to R. Komiya's Introduction in *Industrial Policy of Japan*, ed. by Komiya, R., Okuno, M., and Suzumura, K., Academic Press, San Diego, 1988.

14. From Muto, Y., Kanzei Suijun no Kokusai Hikaku (An International Comparison to Tariff Levels), in *Kanzei Chosa Geppo* (Tariff Survey Monthly) 24, 1971.

15. According to the 1984 edition of *Kagaku Gijutsu Yoran* (An Outline of Scientific Technology), in the percentage of government converge of research and development expenditures in the industrial sector, Japan's come to 1.7 percent (in 1983), those of the United States to 32.4 percent (in 1983), those of West Germany to 17.7 percent (in 1983), those of France to 24.5 percent (in 1981), and those of the United Kingdom to 29.2 percent (in 1978).

16. The infrastructure sectors referred to here are the electricity, gas and water supply, and transport and communications industries. Although most of these were under public utility regulations, they were not strictly public goods. However, the electricity industry, which is representative of the state of affairs in this field, had to maintain low rates even at the sacrifice of business stability in the 1950s, while working to solve quickly grave electric power shortages. This experience greatly affected the external economies of all industries especially manufacturing. The capital accumulation in private sector was still inadequate. Equipment in the electricity industry required large sums of money and considerable time to recoup capital, so substantial government funding was necessary for expanding its equipment.

This has been pointed out, also, in the following passage concerning the postwar industrial promotion policy: "National funds were much more directed into equipment in the external economy than directly injected into industrial activities." In Tsuruta, T., *Sengo Nihon no Sangyo Seisaku* (Postwar Japan's Industrial Policy), Nihon Keizai Shimbun-sha, Tokyo, 1982, pp. 67–74.

17. See, for example, the comment by Jagdish Bhagwati in the Post Shin-Round: Sekai Keizai no Yukue (Post New Round: The Future Direction of the World Economy) *Nihon Keizai Shimbun,* no. 4, December 22, 1993.

18. See table 3-6-4 on p. 320 of the Economic Planning Agency, *Keizai Hakusho* (White Paper on the Economy), Tokyo, 1992.

19. For instance, the disparities in productivity between the tradable goods and non-tradable goods industries are cited in MITI, *Tsusho Hakusho* (White Paper on International Trade), Tokyo, 1993, pp. 341–50, as causes for the differences in prices between Japan and other countries.

20. As of this writing in 1993, various debates have been waged by economists both in Japan and overseas on the cause and significance of the surplus in the current account balance. For example, writing for the *Shukan Toyo Keizai,* both economists T. Akabane and R. Koo have promoted the need to correct the surplus in the current account balance, the former in his article "The Inverted Arguments between the Surplus and Excessive Saving," August 28, 1993, and the latter in his "An Objection to Komiya's Position of Accepting the Current Situation," August 7, 1993. They maintain the necessity for policy measures such as deregulation.

In opposition are economist R. Komiya's essays, such as "Keijo Kuroji-berashi wa Hitsuyo ka?" (Is a Reduction of the Current Account Surplus Necessary?) in the July 10, 1993, edition of *Shukan Toyo Keizai,* and his interview "'Maekawa Report' wa Ayamari datta" (The "Maekawa Report" Was Mistaken), in the Nihon Keizai Shimbun-sha publication, *Isetsu Nihon Keizai: Tsusetsu no Gobyu o Utsu* (Divergent Opinions on the Japanese Economy: Striking at the Fallacies of Popular Views), 1992. He claims that since the surplus in the current account balance is the result of the high Japanese savings rate and the application of the excessive savings overseas, there is fundamentally no problem with it. He also asserts that from the standpoint of reducing the current account surplus, the effects of policy measures like expanding imports and deregulation will be only temporary and limited.

Economist H. Yoshikawa introduces in contraposition the Keynesian model and the neoclassic model, which form the theoretical background of both the negative and positive arguments about policy actions dealing with the surplus in the current account balance. I will not go further into this issue here. See Yoshikawa, H., Keijo Shushi to Kawase Rate (The Current Account Balance and the Exchange Rate), in *Nihon Keizai to Macro Keizaigaku (The Japanese Economy and the Macro Economics)*, Toyo Keizai Shimposha, Tokyo, 1992, ch. 6.

Afterword

Koji Kobayashi

Let me explain in brief the particulars behind how this book came to be put together by our Japan Techno-Economics Society (JATES).

The year 1989 was when Japan had reached the peak of its bubble economy, and at the international level, economic friction had begun to escalate. Discussions among various conscientious company managers in Japan led to the idea that they should thoroughly survey and analyze what can be done to allow Japan to continue growth and not be isolated from the world. They were particularly concerned about what direction to take with the manufacturing industries, and they decided along this line that they should also redefine management policies, in general, with an eye toward the twenty-first century.

At about the same time, *Made in America* was published in the United States by The MIT Press. Authored by an MIT Commission on Industrial Productivity, the book took up the issue of the present state of American industries and the problem of productivity they were facing. The book was promptly published in Japan, translated into Japanese by Naoya Yoda (then managing director of Toray Corporate Business Research, Inc.), and it caused quite a stir in the Japanese industrial world.

The Japan Techno-Economics Society's attention was drawn to the book as well. It began to undertake a similar analysis of Japanese manufacturing industries and held a special symposium to report on its progress in December 1989.

Thereupon emerged the idea that we ought to put together a book about Japanese manufacturing industries. Thus, with strong encouragement by the members of this society, who are the leaders of the Japanese industrial world, we came to produce this book *Made in Japan.*

A formal decision was made to undertake this book as a special project of our management research work at the 78th Board of Directors meeting on July 13, 1990. The Japan Commission on Industrial Performance (JCIP) was launched as a result. Its chairmanship was assumed by Shoichi Saba, a member of JATES's board of directors and advisor to the board of Toshiba Corporation, who was also one of the people who proposed this project.

Most readers will recall that the period of research for this project corresponded to a period of historic transitions befitting the turn of the century. For example, on the international front there was the end of the cold war between East and West in the wake of the Soviet Union's collapse, and domestically a great recession accompanied the collapse of a bubble economy. This confluence of events made it quite difficult for us to determine the perspective to take with this book, and we were forced to extend its publication way beyond the originally scheduled date. Nevertheless, we feel that it was to our benefit that the book was not written during the bubble economy period and that its writers, instead, got to observe closely the state of Japanese manufacturing industries during a recession, which enabled them to revise their concepts for the twenty-first century.

We are especially pleased that a book befitting our original objectives could be put together through the close cooperation between the academic and industrial worlds. I want to express my heartfelt gratitude for the hard labor put into this work by the writers belonging to the various study groups and to the cooperation extended by people from the thirty-four participating companies.

In addition, appreciation must be conveyed to Yoshio Ishikawa, executive director of the Japan Techno-Economics Society, and Bunya Tadano, managing director of the same, for the tremendous effort they expended in the overall organization and operation of this project. Our very deep appreciation has to be expressed also to Kazuaki Marumo, director of the Research Department and the JCIP Secretariat, and to all the JCIP staff for the diligent effort they put into the studies and research for this project.

We will be very happy if this book proves to be of some use to business managers in manufacturing in both Japan and abroad, and also to those who have interest in the present state of Japanese manufacturing industries and how these industries are expected to develop in the near future.

A list of the sixteen companies that helped with the launching of JCIP as well as of the members of the various JCIP organizational and working committees appears at the end of this book.

Appendix: Members of the Japan Commission on Industrial Performance

Representative Promoters for the Project

Koji Kobayashi, Chairman Emeritus, NEC Corporation; President, Japan Techno-Economics Society

Shoichi Saba, Adviser to the Board, Toshiba Corporation; Director, Japan Techno-Economics Society

Supporters for the Project (16 Companies, and the titles are as of November 1990)

Yoshio Maruta, Chairman, KAO Corporation

Hiroshi Saito, Representative Director, Chairman of the Board of Directors, Nippon Steel Corporation

Norio Ohga, President and Representative Director, CEO, Sony Corporation

Joichi Aoi, President and Chief Executive Officer, Toshiba Corporation

Yoshikazu Ito, Chairman of the Board, Toray Industries, Inc.

Shoichiro Toyoda, President, Toyota Motor Corporation

Yutaka Kume, President, Nissan Motor Co., Ltd.

Tadahiro Sekimoto, President, NEC Corporation

Haruo Yamaguchi, Chairman, Nippon Telegraph and Telephone Corporation

Isamu Yamashita, Chairman, East Japan Railway Company

Hirokichi Yoshiyama, Chairman Emeritus, Hitachi, Ltd.

Minoru Ohnishi, President, Fuji Photo Film Co., Ltd.

Takuma Yamamoto, Chairman of the Board, Fujitsu Limited

Akio Tanii, President, Matsushita Electric Industrial Co., Ltd.

Yotaro Iida, Chairman, Mitsubishi Heavy Industries, Ltd.

Masaki Yoshida, CEO and President, Mitsubishi Petrochemical Co., Ltd.

Commission Members

Chair

Shoichi Saba, Adviser to the Board, Toshiba Corporation

Vice Chair

Michiyuki Uenohara, Executive Advisor, NEC Corporation

Executive Director

Hiroyuki Yoshikawa, President, University of Tokyo

Members (34 Companies, and the titles are as of January 1994)

Kosaku Inaba, President and CEO, Ishikawajima-Harima Heavy Industries Co., Ltd.

Mutsumi Hongoh, President, Idemitsu Petrochemical Co., Ltd.

Nobuo Tateishi, Vice Chairman and Representative Director, Omron Corporation

Yoshio Maruta, Chairman, KAO Corporation

Hiroshi Takahashi, Chairman, Kureha Chemical Industry Co., Ltd.

Tetsuya Katada, President, Komatsu Ltd.

Masahiro Arashi, Chairman, Komatsu Seiren Co., Ltd.

Haruo Tsuji, President, Sharp Corporation

Hiroshi Saito, Representative Director, Chairman of the Board of Directors, Nippon Steel Corporation

Hideo Mori, Chairman, Sumitomo Chemical Co., Ltd.

Tsuneo Nakahara, Vice Chairman and Deputy CEO, Sumitomo Electric Ind., Ltd.

Norio Ohga, President and Representative Director, CEO, Sony Corporation

Hiromasa Nohmura, Vice Chairman of the Board, Taiyo Kogyo Corporation

Hiroshi Itagaki, President and CEO, Teijin Limited

Joichi Aoi, Chairman of the Board, Toshiba Corporation

Yoshikazu Ito, Chairman of the Board, Toray Industries, Inc.

Saburo Takizawa, Chairman, Board of Directors, Toyobo Co., Ltd.

Iwao Isomura, Executive Vice President, Member of the Board, Toyota Motor Corporation

Toyo Kato, President, Toyoda Machine Works, Ltd.

Yutaka Kume, Chairman, Nissan Motor Co., Ltd.

Tadahiro Sekimoto, President, NEC Corporation

Haruo Yamaguchi, Chairman, Nippon Telegraph and Telephone Corporation

Isamu Yamashita, Principal Executive Adviser, East Japan Railway Company

Hirokichi Yoshiyama, Chairman Emeritus, Hitachi, Ltd.

Seiuemon Inaba, President and CEO, Fanuc Ltd.

Minoru Ohnishi, President, Fuji Photo Film Co., Ltd.

Takuma Yamamoto, Chairman of the Board, Fujitsu Limited

Akio Tanii, Corporate Counselor, Matsushita Electric Industrial Co., Ltd.

Shogo Takebayashi, Chairman of the Board, Mitsui Petrochemical Industries, Ltd.

Yotaro Iida, Chairman, Mitsubishi Heavy Industries, Ltd.

Moriya Shiki, Chairman, Mitsubishi Electric Corporation

Takeshi Nagano, Chairman, Mitsubishi Materials Corporation

Akira Miura, CEO and President, Mitsubishi Petrochemical Co., Ltd.

Koh Kikuchi, President, CEO, Yasukawa Electric Corporation

Research Committee (consists of scholastic members and industrial members from the aforementioned 34 companies, as of January 1994)

Executive Director

Hiroyuki Yoshikawa, President, University of Tokyo

Members from Academe

Professor Hiroyuki Itami, Faculty of Commerce, Hitotsubashi University

Assistant Professor Sumihiko Ohira, School of Management and Informatics, University of Shizuoka

Associate Professor Toshihiro Kodama, Innovation Policy, Graduate School of Policy, Saitama University

Professor Fumio Kodama, Department of Industrial and Systems Engineering, Tokyo Institute of Technology

Associate Professor Shin-ichi Kobayashi, Graduate School of Information Systems, University of Electro-Communications

Professor Haruo Shimada, Faculty of Economics, Keio University

Professor Atsushi Seike, Faculty of Business and Commerce, Keio University

Professor Kei Takeuchi, Faculty of Economics, University of Tokyo

Ex-Associate Professor Hiroshi Doihara, Research Center for Advanced Science and Technology, University of Tokyo

Associate Professor Yasunori Baba, Research into Artifacts Center for Engineering, University of Tokyo

Assistant Professor Takahiro Fujimoto, Faculty of Economics, University of Tokyo

Professor Konomu Matsui, Department of Sociology, Rikkyo University

Professor Hisashi Yaginuma, Faculty of Business Administration, Hosei University

Professor Yukio Watanabe, Faculty of Economics, Keio University

Members from Industry

Kazumichi Motozuna, Managing Director and Administrative General Manager of Technical Development, Ishikawajima-Harima Heavy Industries Co., Ltd.

Kazutaka Yamaji, Director, General Manager of Business Unit 2, Idemitsu Materials Co., Ltd.

Takashi Kinoshita, Associate Director (Corporate) and Plant Manager (Kawasaki), KAO Corporation

Takaaki Aiba, Deputy General Manager, Polymer Processing Technical Center, Kureha Chemical Industry Co., Ltd.

Eisuke Nakanishi, Executive Managing Director, General Manager of Electronics Division, Komatsu Ltd.

Shigeo Kanazawa, Executive Director, Komatsu Seiren Co., Ltd.

Kozo Hayashi, Consultant, Sharp Corporation

Masayuki Hattori, Director, Technical Planning and Marketing Division, Nippon Steel Corporation

Ryuichi Sonoda, Director, General Manager of Chiba Works, Sumitomo Chemical Co., Ltd.

Nobuo Yumoto, Managing Director, Sumitomo Electric Ind., Ltd.

Seiichi Watanabe, Director, Sony Corporation

Yasuo Kume, Senior Vice President, Taiyo Kogyo Corporation

Masao Nishida, Senior Managing Director, Teijin Limited

Akira Kuwahara, Vice President, General Manager of Multimedia Division, Toshiba Corporation

Kohei Sakamoto, Chairman, Toray Corporate Business Research, Inc.

Junzo Masai, Director, Senior General Manager of Marketing Coordination Division, Toyobo Co., Ltd.

Iwao Isomura, Executive Vice President, Member of the Board, Toyota Motor Corporation

Yoshihiro Hirano, Managing Director, Toyoda Machine Works, Ltd.

Yoshiyuki Miyakawa, Managing Director, Nissan Motor Co., Ltd.

Koji Maeda, Counselor, NEC Corporation

Jun-ichiro Miyazu, Senior Executive Vice President, Nippon Telegraph and Telephone Corporation

Nobuyuki Sasaki, Managing Director, East Japan Railway Company

Yuichi Moriya, Executive Managing Director, Hitachi Research Institute

Kohei Ito, Executive Vice President, Fanuc Ltd.

Mitsutaka Sofue, Director of Patent Department, Technology Development and Information Department and Export Control Office, Fuji Photo Film Co., Ltd.

Shigeru Sato, Managing Director, Fujitsu Laboratories Ltd.

Reiji Sano, President, Matsushita Research Institute Tokyo, Inc.

Yoshio Abe, Managing Director, Mitsui Petrochemical Industries, Ltd.

Shoji Ueda, Corporate Adviser, Mitsubishi Heavy Industries, Ltd.

Eiichi Ohno, Managing Director and General Manager of Corporate R&D, Mitsubishi Electric Corporation

Masayuki Nagasawa, Senior Managing Director, Mitsubishi Materials Corporation

Naotoki Sawada, Managing Director, President of Industrial Chemicals Division, Mitsubishi Petrochemical Co., Ltd.

Hirotaka Miura, Director and General Manager, Tsukuba Research Laboratory, Yasukawa Electric Corporation

Steering Committee

H. Yoshikawa, Executive Director of JCIP, heads the committee. Two academic members, H. Shimada and K. Takeuchi, and two industrial members, S. Ueda and K. Maeda, provide support in managing research activities.

Scenario Committee

H. Yoshikawa, Executive Director of JCIP, heads the committee, which is composed mainly of 17 academic members, who direct research and evaluate and report on the results, etc.

Members

Professor Hiroyuki Itami, Faculty of Commerce, Hitotsubashi University

Assistant Professor Sumihiko Ohira, School of Management and Informatics, University of Shizuoka

Associate Professor Toshihiro Kodama, Innovation Policy, Graduate School of Policy, Saitama University

Professor Fumio Kodama, Department of Industrial and Systems Engineering, Tokyo Institute of Technology

Associate Professor Shin-ichi Kobayashi, Graduate School of Information Systems, University of Electro-Communications

Professor Haruo Shimada, Faculty of Economics, Keio University

Professor Atsushi Seike, Faculty of Business and Commerce, Keio University

Associate Professor Shinji Takai, Faculty of Business Administration, Kobe University

Senior Researcher Akira Takeishi, Business Strategy Department, Mitsubishi Research Institute, Inc.

Professor Kei Takeuchi, Faculty of Economics, University of Tokyo

Ex-Associate Professor Hiroshi Doihara, Research Center for Advanced Science and Technology, University of Tokyo

Associate Professor Yasunori Baba, Research into Artifacts Center for Engineering, University of Tokyo

Assistant Professor Takahiro Fujimoto, Faculty of Economics, University of Tokyo

Professor Konomu Matsui, Department of Sociology, Rikkyo University

Professor Hisashi Yaginuma, Faculty of Business Administration, Hosei University

Naoya Yoda, Executive Advisor to the Board, Toray Corporate Business Research, Inc.

Professor Yukio Watanabe, Faculty of Economics, Keio University

Working Groups for Industry Research

Working Group on the "Semiconductor, Computer Hardware, Software, and Communications Equipment Industries"

Chair
Professor Haruo Shimada, Keio University

Members
Akira Kuwahara, Vice President, General Manager of Multimedia Division, Toshiba Corporation

Koji Maeda, Counselor, NEC Corporation

Jun-ichiro Miyazu, Senior Executive Vice President, Nippon Telegraph and Telephone Corporation

Yuichi Moriya, Executive Managing Director, Hitachi Research Institute

Shigeru Sato, Managing Director, Fujitsu Laboratories Ltd.

Semiconductor Subgroup

Takeshi Nakagawa, General Manager, Semiconductor Marketing and Sales Division, Toshiba Corporation

Kyozo Shimizu, Chief Engineer, Semiconductor Group, NEC Corporation

Nobuaki Ieda, General Manager, LSI Design Division, NTT Electronics Technology Corporation

Hideki Fukuda, Senior Chief Engineer, Semiconductor and Integrated Circuits Division, Hitachi, Ltd.

Yoshio Tominaga, Ex-Chief Engineer, Semiconductor Design and Development Center, Hitachi, Ltd.

Taro Okabe, Associate General Manager, Administrations and Business Operations for Electronic Devices Group, Fujitsu Limited

Computer Hardware Subgroup

Akira Miyoshi, Senior Manager, Computer Administration Office, Computer Division, Toshiba Corporation

Takehisa Tokunaga, Chief Engineer, 1st Computers Operations Unit, NEC Corporation

Yasuhiko Takei, Senior Manager, Information Processing Technology Department, Information Systems Headquarters, Nippon Telegraph and Telephone Corporation

Toshiakira Ikeda, General Manager, Product Planning Operation, General Purpose Computer Division, Hitachi, Ltd.

Koji Yamaguchi, General Manager, Network Division, Open Systems Group, Fujitsu Limited

Computer Software Subgroup

Seiichi Nishijima, Director, Systems and Software Engineering Laboratory, Toshiba Corporation

Eiichi Yoshikawa, Associate Senior Vice President, NEC Corporation

Haruo Katsuyama, Executive Manager, Customer Information Systems Department, 1st System Development Division, Information Systems Headquarters, Nippon Telegraph and Telephone Corporation

Akihiro Kondoh, Chief Engineer, Product Planning Division, Computer Group, Hitachi, Ltd.

Hiroshi Kubo, Associate General Manager, Information System Factory Systems Engineering Group, Fujitsu Ltd.

Communications Equipment Subgroup
Toshihide Kawashima, Assistant to General Manager, Integrated Communication Systems Division, Toshiba Corporation

Shigetoki Sugimoto, Vice President, NEC Corporation

Hisao Iizuka, Executive Manager, Technology Research Department, Nippon Telegraph and Telephone Corporation

Michitoshi Koshiyama, Manager, Marketing Industry and Government Relations of Telecommunications Division, Hitachi, Ltd.

Shunroku Sasaki, General Manager, R&D Administration Division, Fujitsu Ltd.

Working Group on the Home Electric Appliance Industry

Chair
Professor Kei Takeuchi, University of Tokyo

Assistant Professor Sumihiko Ohira, University of Tokyo

Ex-Associate Professor Hiroshi-Doihara, University of Tokyo

Members
Masayuki Yamashita, General Manager, Liaison Department, Tokyo Branch, Sharp Corporation

Hachiro Irie, Manager, Liaison Department, Tokyo Branch, Sharp Corporation

Ryusuke Moriya, General Manager, R&D External Affairs, Corporate Planning Group, Sony Corporation

Akihiro Nakamura, Assistant Manager, Government and External Relations Division, Sony Corporation

Naoki Yamada, Manager, Engineering and Planning Department, Video and Electronics Media Group, Toshiba Corporation

Tadatoshi Banse, Chief Specialist, Engineering and Planning Department, Air-conditioners and Appliances Group, Toshiba Corporation

Koji Iwasa, Manager, Marketing and Product Planning Department, Household Appliances Division, Hitachi, Ltd.

Yoshio Suzuki, Manager, Marketing and Product Planning Department, Personal Media System Operation Division, Hitachi, Ltd.

Yoku Kudo, Manager, Research Relations Department, Corporate Research Division, Matsushita Electric Industrial Co., Ltd.

Yuuji Ito, General Manager, Products Planning Department, Personal Communication Division, Matsushita Communication Industrial Co., Ltd.

Working Group on the Metallic Materials Industry

Chair

Associate Professor Yasunori Baba, University of Tokyo

Associate Professor Shinji Takai, Kobe University

Researcher Akiya Nagata, National Institute of Technology Policy, Science and Technology Agency

Researcher Tokio Suzuki, International Christian University

Members

Hironobu Okubo, Planning and Administrative Department, Sumitomo Electric Ind., Ltd.

Toru Aramaki, General Manager, Technical Planning and Marketing Division, Nippon Steel Corporation

Toshiko Nishikawa, Assistant General Manager, Corporate Communications Department, Mitsubishi Materials Corporation

Working Group on the Automobile Industry

Chair

Associate Professor Takahiro Fujimoto, University of Tokyo

Senior Researcher Akira Takeishi, Mitsubishi Research Institute, Inc.

Members

Kazuaki Nakao, Assistant Manager, Corporate Planning Division, Toyota Motor Corporation

Naoki Miyazaki, Assistant Manager, Industrial Affairs Division, Toyota Motor Corporation

Toshio Kondo, Ex-General Manager, Production Planning Division, Toyota Motor Corporation

Takahiro Tsuchiya, Ex-Deputy General Manager, Production Planning Division, Toyota Motor Corporation

Masaharu Kasama, Ex-Manager, Corporate Planning Division, Toyota Motor Corporation

Takeo Ishikawa, General Manager, External and Government Affairs Department, Nissan Motor Co., Ltd.

Yuji Aoki, General Manager, Market Strategy and Product Planning Office, R&CV Product Planning and Development, Nissan Motor Co., Ltd.

Hiroshi Ono, Senior Manager, External and Government Affairs Department, Nissan Motor Co., Ltd.

Kaoru Tanaka, Assistant Manager, Corporate Planning Department, Nissan Motor Co., Ltd.

Working Group on the Chemical Industry

Chair

Professor Konomu Matsui, Rikkyo University

Associate Professor Shin-ichi Kobayashi, University of Electro-Communications

Members

Kazutaka Yamaji, Director, General Manager, Business Unit 2, Idemitsu Materials Co., Ltd.

Takashi Kinoshita, Associate Director (Corporate) and Plant Manager (Kawasaki), KAO Corporation

Kahei Sakaguchi, Ex-Director, Research and Development Division, KAO Corporation

Takaaki Aiba, Deputy General Manager, Polymer Processing Technical Center, Kureha Chemical Industry Co., Ltd.

Michio Nagao, Manager, Corporate Planning Office, Sumitomo Chemical Co., Ltd.

Masaaki Takimoto, Senior Associate, Technology Development and Information Department, Fuji Photo Film Co., Ltd.

Yoshihiko Kataoka, Director, Corporate Planning, Mitsui Petrochemical Industries, Ltd.

Kiichiro Tanabe, Director, General Manager of Management Planning Department, Mitsubishi Petrochemical Co., Ltd.

Working Group on the Fiber, Textile, and Apparel Industries

Chair

Professor Kei Takeuchi, University of Tokyo

Professor Atsushi Seike, Keio University

Members

Shigeo Kanazawa, Executive Director, Komatsu Seiren Co., Ltd.

Hayato Minagawa, Assistant Manager, Corporate Planning Department, TSP Taiyo Inc.

Kuniaki Matsumoto, General Manager, Public Relations and Advertising Department, Teijin Limited

Fumishige Imamura, Deputy General Manager, Corporate Planning Office, Toyobo Co., Ltd.

Fumio Taniguchi, Research Fellow, Toray Corporate Business Research, Inc.

Working Group on the FA Equipment and Industrial Machinery Industry

Chair

Professor Hiroyuki Itami, Hitotsubashi University

Professor Yukio Watanabe, Keio University

Associate Professor Hisanaga Amikura, Chiba University

Members

Toshiki Sato, Manager, Technical Planning Group, Technical Planning Department, Technical Development Division, Ishikawajima-Harima Heavy Industries Co., Ltd.

Shuzo Hasegawa, Corporate Business Planning Department, Omron Data General Corporation

Fujio Tokita, Tokyo Regional Sales Department Manager, Omron Corporation

Ken Furukawa, General Manager, Planning and Coordination Department, Business Development Division, Komatsu Ltd.

Tetsuro Aikawa, Manager, Transport Safety Department, East Japan Railway Company

Toru Hara, Assistant to the President, Fanuc Ltd.

Kenji Nomura, General Manager, Corporate Planning Department, Toyoda Machine Works, Ltd.

Chikayoshi Higuchi, Deputy General Manager, Patent and License Department, Technical Headquarters, Mitsubishi Heavy Industries, Ltd.

Yukio Satake, General Manager, Nagoya Works, Mitsubishi Electric Corporation

Michiaki Kohno, Manager, PLC Marketing Mechatronics Division, Yaskawa Electric Corporation

Secretariat

In order to execute this project, a secretariat has been placed in the Japan Techno-Economics Society. The members of the secretariat are as follows:
Chief Executive Kazuaki Marumo
Associate Chief Executive Moriji Matsumoto

Staff

Kunio Nishimura

Tatsuya Endo

Kazuyo Kaneko

Translation

Lora Sharnoff

Index

Action Program to Improve Market Access, 366
Added value, 130, 291, 337, 354–55. *See also* Value-added production
  in chemical industry, 148
  in electric appliance industry, 55, 62, 63, 66
  in fiber industry, 178, 183, 188
Affiliated Industrial Technolgy Spheres Research Center, 237
Agriculture, forestry, and fishery industries, 322, 373–74, 384
ALIS (artificial and logical intelligence system), 105–107
Angstrom Technological Research Institute, 237
Antimonopoly laws, 363
Antipollution policies, 365. *See also* Pollution
Apparel industry, 177–78, 181, 183, 186, 188, 260. *See also* Fiber industry
Asia, 165, 340, 341, 353–54. *See also* East Asia
  direct investment in, 83, 343–44, 346
Assembly-processing industry, 155, 158–59, 230
AT&T, 22, 29, 33, 34, 36
Audiovisual equipment industry, 51, 58, 68–69, 69–70. *See also* Home electric appliance industry
Automation, 4, 33, 129, 217–18. *See also* Robots
  in automobile industry, 82, 86, 94
  in electric appliance industry, 63, 67
  in fiber industry, 177, 178–84
  and labor supply, 138
  skilled technicians and, 178–79, 279

Automobile industry, xi, 158, 165, 288, 350
  automation in, 82, 86, 94, 214
  distribution in, 83, 84–85, 88–91, 94, 206
  exports of, 77, 78, 93, 335, 339–40, 352
  global management in, 91–92, 93
  labor force in, 74, 77, 78, 81–83, 86
  multilevel global networks in, 79–81
  production system in, 71–73, 79, 93–95, 213
  product strategies of, 9, 87–88
  reforming, 92–95
  sales in, 73, 84–85, 88, 89–91, 206
  and steel industry, 110, 111, 112–13
Automobile manufacturers, international rankings of, 75
Automobile parts industry, 59, 74, 76–78, 83–85, 87, 88–91

Bank system, 316–17, 319–21, 327, 331. *See also* Japan Development Bank
Blast furnace manufacturers, 100, 111, 114–15, 213, 215
  and ALIS, 105–107
  crude steel production of, 98
Bubble economy, ix, 7, 14, 137, 146, 154, 195, 198, 311
  and corporate restructuring, 200
  investment funds during, 303, 342

CAD (computer-aided design), 183, 217
Capital, 313–15, 316, 330
  financing of, 327–28, 331–32
  liberalization of, 293
Capital investment, and employment structure, 301
Capitalism, Japanese-style, 193, 196, 331

Center of Excellence (COE), 236–37
Chemical companies, major world, 150
Chemical industry, xi, 150, 155
  branches of, 142, 148–49, 151, 152, 157–
    60
  competitiveness of, 142–43, 144, 151–52,
    364
  diversity of, 147–49
  economic importance of, 141–43, 147
  environmental problems and, 143, 145–
    46, 156–57
  globalization of, 164–68, 350
  government financing for, 373–77
  R&D in, 141, 147, 160–64, 165
Chogin Research Center, 250
CIM (computer integrated manufactur-
    ing), 101, 103, 111
Commerce and Industry, British Dept.
    of, 231
Communications equipment industry,
    19, 20, 26, 33–34, 40–42. See also Indus-
    trial electronics industry, Japanese
  competitiveness of, 27, 28, 29, 36–37
Communications industry, government
    financing for, 373–76
Companies. See also Corporations
  family-run, 257
  pyramid-shaped population structure
    of, 291, 304
Competition, 5, 7, 124, 194, 250, 304, 306
  attitudes toward, 11–12, 15
  automobile industry and, 71–85, 92–95
  in chemical industry, 151–56, 158
  conformist, 196–98
  in electric appliance industry, 51–52, 56–
    57, 62, 64
  and FA industry, 124–26, 134, 138, 139–
    40
  in machinery industry, 261, 263–64, 266–
    67, 268
  oligopolistic, 202–204, 206–207
  in R&D, 126–29
  specialization and, 266–67
  in steel industry, 100, 104
Competitiveness, x, xvii–xviii, 326, 364
  of automobile industry, 71, 73–79
  of chemical industry, 142–43, 152, 154,
    168, 364
  and electric appliance industry, 57, 66
  of electronics industry, 19, 21–22, 24–25,
    27, 28–29, 31, 35–37, 43
  of FA industry, 123, 124–26

of fiber industry, 176, 184, 187
  and industrial policy, 360–61
Computer hardware industry, 19, 20, 23,
    30, 38–39. See also Communications
    equipment industry
  competitiveness of, 24–25, 29, 31, 35–36
Computers, 365
  in fiber industry, 172, 183–84
  in steel industry, 100–103
Computer software industry, 19, 20, 25–
    26, 38, 40–42, 129, 198. See also Com-
    puter hardware industry
  competitiveness of, 36, 129
  corporate characteristics of, 12, 13, 32–33
  outlook for, 39, 69–70
Conflict management, in automobile in-
    dustry, 71, 79, 81, 94
Consumer electronics industry. See
    Home electric appliance industry
Consumer goods, finished, 159–60, 165,
    166, 205–206
Consumers, 72, 79
  and automobile industry, 76, 77, 78, 89–
    90
  chemical industry and, 161, 165
  high standards of Japanese, 188
  income of, 4, 5, 296
Cooperation, 11–12, 167
  in automobile industry, 71, 79, 81, 83–
    84, 94
  and electric appliance industry, 52, 67,
    69
  in electronics industry, 19, 23, 39, 42, 45–
    47
  and industrial policy, 247–50, 359, 361,
    365–67, 384
  in steel industry, 104, 108–13, 119
Corporations, 5, 11–12, 211, 307. See also
    Companies
  adaptability of, 13–15, 97–98, 213–14
  and creativity, 44–45, 307
  management style of, 13, 189–90, 193,
    196, 198, 201–202
Cosmetics, 142, 148, 158, 159
Costs, 196, 197, 206, 211, 278, 304
  in chemical industry, 145, 146, 149–50,
    154–56, 157, 158, 161
  excessive service, 5, 155
  in FA industry, 126, 132, 133
  in fiber industry, 171, 184, 187
  and international competitiveness, 125,
    171, 384

of Japanese automobiles, 73, 74
  in steel industry, 103–104, 114
Cotton industry, 172, 173, 174, 180, 182.
  See also Fiber industry
Creativity, xviii, 221–22
  in chemical industry, 163, 164
  and education, 44, 274, 275, 284, 285
  in electronics industry, 35, 36, 37, 38, 44
  Japanese corporations and, 44–45, 307
  and technology, 12–13
  vs. profits, 200

Demand, xiv, xviii, 4, 8, 124, 197, 206
  automobile industry and, 94
  chemical industry and, 158, 163
  civilian-oriented, 211
  and FA industry, 132–34, 139, 140
  and fiber industry, 188–90
  and overborrowing, 314–16
  and perfect competition model, 203–204
Deming, W. Edwards, 304
Deregulation, 383–85. *See also* Regulations
Developing countries, 8–9, 298–99, 367
Diligence, notion of, 220, 308, 309
Distribution, 5, 204–205, 207
  in automobile industry, 83, 84–85, 88–
    91, 94, 206
  in electric appliance industry, 61–62
Diversification, industrial, 97, 98, 116–19,
    190, 291, 298
Dumping, 125, 197
Dyeing process, 142–43, 157, 166, 181,
    182–83

East Asia, 261, 269. *See also* Southeast
    Asia
EC (European Community), 8, 110
  chemical industry output of, 142–43,
    144
  Japanese exports to, 341–42
  Japan's trade surplus with, 357–58
Economic systems, 360, 362, 363–64, 381–
    83
Edo period, 172, 173, 292
Education, xviii. *See also* Training systems
  and creativity, 44, 274, 275, 284, 285
  decline in quality of, 273–74, 280–84
  engineering, 277, 285, 287–89
  and fundamental abilities, 274–76
  and industry, 44, 195, 247, 278–80, 288
  and labor force, 200, 292–93, 298
  science and technology in, 276, 277–78

Electric machinery industry, 51, 53–57,
    58, 339, 377, 378. *See also* Information-
    processing equipment industry
Electric power, government financing
    for, 373–77
Electronics industry. *See* Industrial elec-
    tronics industry
Electronics Industry Promotion Law, 363
Employees, 72, 76–78, 214, 309. *See also*
    Labor force
  numbers of, 299–301, 302
  overseas, 345–46, 352
Employment, xviii, 7, 305, 355
  and labor, 15, 291–94, 294–303, 347
  lifetime, ix, 4, 5, 198, 199, 273, 278
Endo, M., 292
Energy conservation, 67, 143, 365
Engineers, 83, 273, 274, 281–82
  education and, 277, 285, 287–89
  in FA industry, 128–29
  shop floor and, 219–20, 280
  in steel industry, 106–107, 215
Enterprises Rationalization Promotion
    Law, 363
Environment, 172
  and automobile industry, 92, 111
  chemical industry and, 142–43, 144–47,
    156–57
Environment, global, xix, xv, 97, 222, 330
  and industrial policy, 367, 380–81
  Japanese contribution to protection of,
    7, 10–11, 157
Equal Employment Opportunity Law
    (1985), 297
ES (expert systems), development of, 215
Ethylene center companies, 152–53, 154,
    155
Europe, xiv, 5–6, 83, 131, 174, 214, 317
  automobile industry in, 81, 84
  chemical industry in, 142–43, 149–51,
    154–55, 156, 160, 163, 164, 168
  electronics industry in, 29, 30
  environmental measures in, 143, 157
  overseas production in, 346
  product development in, 128, 204
Exchange rate
  floating, 361, 364–65
  and productivity measurements, 130–31
Exports, xv, 6, 8, 14, 97
  and added values, 337, 355
  of automobile industry, 77, 78, 93, 335,
    339–40, 352

Exports (cont.)
  of chemical industry, 142, 151, 152, 165,
    166
  of electric appliance industry, 52, 54, 56,
    65, 339
  of electronics industry, 20, 24–25, 27, 352
  of fiber industry, 171, 173–76, 177, 184,
    339
  growth of, 335, 338–42, 353
  international comparison of, 336–38
  of machinery industry, 339–40, 355–56
  productivity and, 196, 197
  of steel industry, 98, 110, 113, 339
  technological, xviii, 110–11, 128, 165–66

Factories, xix, 86, 209, 214, 215
Factory automation (FA) equipment in-
    dustry, xi
  automation in, 129, 138
  competition in, 134, 139–40
  and demand, 132–34, 139, 140
  and international competitiveness, 124–
    26
  labor in, 134–36
  productivity in, 123–24, 129–32
  R&D in, 126–29
  technological systems in, 137–38
Fallows, James, 369
Fiber industry, xi, 190, 260. See also Tex-
    tile industry
  added value in, 177, 183, 188
  changes in, 171–74, 177
  in global market, 175–77, 184, 187, 339,
    378
  government financing for, 373–77
  price structure in, 183–84
  production in, 176, 177, 178, 180–81,
    185–86, 188
  productivity in, 177, 179–83
Financial institutions, government, 327
  industrial recipients of funds from, 322–
    24, 325, 373–77
  and international competitiveness, 326
  and long-term capital, 321–22
  portfolio of, 318–19, 323
Financial institutions, private
  future of, 331–32
  investment funds supply portfolio of,
    318
  and tight money conditions, 325–26
Financial market, Japanese, 328, 329, 331
Financing, 327–28, 329, 330, 332

  government, 324–27, 331, 372–80
  and private fixed investment, 311–13
Financing Corporation for Reconstruc-
    tion, 321–22
Fiscal Investment and Loan Program
    (FLIP), 325, 363
Foreign Capital Act (1950), 164
France, 34, 276, 341
Fuji Photo Film Co., 161
Fujitsu Ltd., 23, 24, 25, 28, 29, 34
Furukawa Electric Industries, 144
Future Engineering Research Center, 230–
    31

GATT (General Agreement on Tariffs
    and Trade), 154, 360, 379, 381–83
Germany, 83, 102, 335, 336–38, 341, 343,
    346. See also West Germany
  labor productivity in, 55
Globalization, 247, 349–50
  of automobile industry, 91–92, 93
  of chemical industry, 164–68
  development stages in managing, 246
  and direct foreign investment, 312
  and electric appliance industry, 64–65,
    67
  electronics industry and, 45–47
  and trade friction, 355–58
GNP, Japanese, 294, 312, 314, 361
  chemical industry share of, 141, 147
  percentage of exports in, 335, 336, 351–
    52
Government, xv–xvi, 3, 7. See also Finan-
    cial institutions, government; Indus-
    trial policy
  and automobile industry, 79, 81
  and chemical industry, 145, 153
  and computer industry, 25
  and education, 275, 277, 281, 284, 285–87
  and industrial development, 195, 250,
    313–14
  and steel industry, 108, 109
Graduate schools, 274, 276, 284–85

Heavy industry, 313, 321
Heijunka (leveling the volume of produc-
    tion), 89
Higano, K., 326
Hitachi, Ltd., 22, 23, 24, 28, 51, 58
  research center at, 237, 242
Hokkaido-Tohoku Development Corpora-
    tion, 322, 374, 376

Home electric appliance industry, xi, 43,
158, 303–304. *See also* Electric machinery industry
competition in, 51–52, 56–57, 62, 64
distribution in, 61–62
electronics industry in, 51, 53–55, 57–59
exports of, 52, 54, 56, 65, 339
and globalization, 64–65, 67, 335
imports of, 52, 54, 57
industrial structure of, 57–59
long-term trends in, 67–70
postwar development of, 52–56
productivity in, 52–56, 60
structural reforms in, 65–67
technology in, 60–61, 63–64, 65
Honda, Kotaro, 236
Horiuchi, A., 321
Human Frontier Science Program, 367
Human resources, 198, 201, 330. *See also*
Employees; Personnel
and education, 44, 273–88
and scarce labor, 306–309

IBM Corp., 25, 32, 41, 221
and Japanese computer hardware
manufacturers, 22, 23, 24, 29, 35, 36
Ikeda, Kikunae, 236
Imports, 98, 351
of chemical industry, 151, 152, 154–56
of electric appliance industry, 52, 54, 57
of electronics industry, 20, 24–25, 28
of fiber industry, 171, 176, 177, 184, 260
low dependence on, 254, 259–60
restrictions on, 110, 366, 379–80
tariffs on rice, 382, 383
Income Doubling Plan, 363
Industrial electronics industry, xi, 9, 40,
198. *See also* Semiconductor industry
competitiveness of, 19, 21–22, 24–25, 27,
28, 29, 31, 34–38
cooperation in, 19, 23, 39, 42, 43, 45–47
and creativity, 35, 36, 37, 38, 44
internationalization and, 45–47
multimedia in, 19, 42–43, 69
overseas production of, 350
productivity of, 19, 20–21, 35–36
R&D in, 43, 44
technology in, 19, 21, 24, 25, 26–27, 30,
32–33, 34, 38
and trade friction, 22, 25, 27, 28, 37
Industrial policy, 2, 386
adjustment period of, 364–65

and deregulation, 383–85
and economic autonomy, 362–63
and electric appliance industry, 25, 64
industrial targeting view of, 370, 372–80
international cooperation period of, 365–
67
open economy system and, 363–64
popular interpretations of, 367–71
postwar, 359–60
reconstruction period of, 361–62
of 1990s, 380–83
Industrial Research Institute (IRI), 250
Industrial Standardization Law, 363
Information-processing equipment industry, 51, 52, 56, 57, 58, 69–70. *See also*
Audiovisual equipment industry
Information technologies, 172, 209–10,
219, 288
and banking business, 332
funding of, 327, 330
and production systems, 217
Infrastructure, 330, 363
Institute of Industrial Technology, 237,
241
Institute of Physical and Chemical Research (RIKEN), 236, 238–40
Intellectual property rights, 8, 25–26, 37,
198
International development
direct investments and, 342–44
and export growth, 336–42
Japanese subsidiaries and, 351–53
overseas production and, 344–51
and trade friction, 335–36, 354–58
Internationalization. *See* Globalization
International Motor Vehicle Program
(IMVP), MIT, 73, 85, 89
Investment, fixed
funds for, 311–314, 318–28
and high economic growth, 312–13
and overlending, 316–18
Investment funds, external, 72, 315–21,
328
Investments, direct
of automobile industry, 83, 165
of chemical industry, 165
compared with U.S., 351–52
of electric appliance industry, 64–65
of electronics industry, 46
of manufacturing industries, 342–44
overseas, 6, 9–10, 335, 336, 348–49, 350
Irvine, John, 231

"Japan, Inc." view, 359, 367–70, 370–72
Japan Automobile Industry Assoc., 74
Japan-Britain High-Tech Forum (1987),
  227–28, 231
Japan Chemical Fiber Assoc., 188
Japan Commission on Industrial Perfor-
  mance (JCIP), ix, x, xi, 395–408
Japan Development Bank, 228, 322, 326,
  374, 376. *See also* Bank system
  loan portfolio of, 323–25
  structural finance scheme of, 372
Japan Electronic Computer Company
  (JECC), 23
Japanese Exploratory Research for Ad-
  vanced Technology (ERATO) program,
  226, 234, 235, 247
Japan External Trade Organization
  (JETRO), 363
Japan Finance Corporation for Small
  Businesses, 322, 323–24
Japan Industrial Robot Association, 127
Japanity, 227–28, 229, 230–31
Japan Productivity Center, 130, 250, 363
Japan Steel Association, 108, 110
Japan Techno-Economics Society
  (JATES), x, xii, 230, 250
Johnson, Chalmers, 368, 369, 371

Kaizen (accumulation of thorough re-
  forms), 87, 125
Kanban (front line) system, 155, 216,
  217
Kanmin-kyocho hoshiki ("government-
  business cooperation formula"), 371
Kansai Cultural Scholarship and Reseach
  Town, 226
Kato kyoso (tendency toward excessive
  competition), 151
Kawasaki Steel, 110
Keihin region (Tokyo-Yokohama), 136,
  261, 269–70
Keiretsu (conglomerates), 25, 61, 319, 321,
  331, 369
Keisha seisan (priority production sys-
  tem), 322
Kenkyu/gijutsu kaihatsu (research/techno-
  logical development), 167
Kibo (scale), 167
Kimitsu Steel Mill, blast furnaces at, 105–
  106
Kodoka ("upgrading") scheme, 364
Kokusaika (internationalization), 167

Kondo, Jiro, 234
Koseika (individualization), 167

Labor, 200
  abundent *vs.* scarce, 303–306
  demand for, 299–303
  division of, 134–36, 216–17, 265–67, 270
  international distribution of, 8, 82, 298–
    99
  structure of, xiv, 253, 260, 261
Labor force, 4, 73, 93, 136, 273, 292, 293.
  See also Personnel
  in automobile industry, 74, 77, 78, 81–
    83, 86
  changes in, 291, 294–99, 303–309
  in electronics industry, 21, 44
  in fiber industry, 178–82
  and higher education, 276–78, 298
  homogeneous *vs.* heterogeneous, 78,
    291, 304, 305, 306
  in machinery industry, 261, 264–67
  women in, 21, 82, 85–86, 189, 291, 295–
    98
Labor force participation rate, 294, 295–98
Labor productivity index, 76, 301
Labor shortage, 138, 269, 282, 298
  in automobile industry, 71, 74, 77, 78,
    81–86
  in electric appliance industry, 65, 67
  in electronics industry, 19
  in fiber industry, 178–79, 187
  and human capital, 306–309
Labor unions, 193, 199–200, 214
Large-Scale Industrial Technology Research and Development Program, 365
Leadership, 200–202
  discovery-driven, 236–43
  and education, 283–84
Liberalization, 24
  of financial markets, 293, 329
  of trade, 360, 363–64, 383
Living standard, x, 308, 383

Machinery industry, xi, 253, 257–58, 335,
  353, 378
  competition in, 261, 263–64, 266–67, 268
  and direct investments, 352
  earnings of, 354–55
  exports of, 339–40, 355–56
  government financing for, 373–77
  and international development, 350, 351
  labor in, 261, 264–67

plants in, 254, 259, 261–62
production of, 254–55, 268
specialization in, 262–63
structural changes in, 269–70
Machinery Industry Promotion Law, 363
Made in America (MIT, 1989), x, xi
Management, 91–92
  in chemical industry, 141, 153, 161–63, 168
  global, 8–9, 166, 349
  Japanese style of, 13, 189–90, 193, 194, 196, 200–202, 207
  market-driven *vs.* discovery-driven, 230–35, 242–44, 245
  in metals industry, 98, 114, 117, 119
  reform of, 7, 246–47
Manufacturing companies, distribution of *Fortune 500*, 356–57
Manufacturing technologies, 173, 209, 210
  development process of, 211–13
  future of, 220–23
  and job phase-outs, 217, 218–19
  ME technology in, 214–15
Market, Japanese, 6, 9
  distribution structure of, 204–205
  foreign access to, 10, 194
  internationalization of, 164–65
  oligopolistic competition in, 202–204, 206–207
Massachusetts Institute of Technology (MIT), 219–20
Mass production, xiv, 4, 5, 64, 99–100, 115, 216–17
Masumoto, Takeru, 247
Matsushita, Konosuke, 61
Matsushita Electric Industrial Co., Ltd., 51, 58, 62
Meiji period, xiii, 97, 110, 144, 212, 274
  and fiber industry, 173, 174
  light industries during, 292
Metallic materials industry, xi, 119, 253, 350, 377, 378. *See also* Steel industry; Wire rod industry
  copper industry in, 99, 118
  economic crisis in, 97–98
  government financing for, 373–76
  profit reinvestment strategies of, 103–105
"Me-too" syndrome, 140, 154
Microelectronic (ME) technologies, 60, 181–82, 190, 209, 214–15
Microsoft Corp., 30, 32

Mining industry, 118, 373–76, 378, 381, 384
Ministry of Education, Science, and Culture, 44, 275
Ministry of International Trade and Industry (MITI), 21, 24, 146, 164, 230, 231, 237, 368
MITI and the Japanese Miracle (Johnson), 368, 369, 371
Mitsubishi Electric Corp., 51, 58
Mitsubishi Heavy Industries, Ltd., 127
Mitsubishi Petrochemical Co., Ltd., 144, 150, 161
Mitsui Petrochemical Industries, Ltd., 144
Mitsui Toatsu Chemicals, 150
Monopoly, 205, 206–207
Morita, Akio, 65–66
Motorola, Inc., 22, 28
Multimedia industry, 19, 42–43, 69

nae (nurturing) principle, 246
Nakahara, Tsuneo, 228
National Institute of Science and Technology Policy (NISTEP), 219
National Science Foundation (NSF), American, 234
NEC Corp., 22, 23, 24, 28, 29, 34, 237, 242
NIES countries, 30, 52, 56, 69, 171, 179, 190, 314, 353, 354
Nippon Oil, 144
Nippon Steel Corp., 105
Nippon Steel Corporation, 108, 110
Nippon Telegraph and Telephone Corp. (NTT), 21, 25, 28, 29, 33, 111
Nissan Motor Co., Ltd., 74, 75, 87–88
Nixon shocks (1971), 145, 364
Nonmanufacturing industries, growth of, 383–85
North America, 28, 343–44, 346. *See also* United States
"Not invented here" (NIH) view, 244, 246

Odaka, K., 292
Ogura, M., 325
Ohno, Taiichi, 215–16
Oil crises, 99, 110, 229, 311, 312, 335
  and chemical industry, 3, 145, 146
  and electric appliance industry, 59
  and fiber industry, 176, 184, 188
  and fixed investments, 327–28
  and industrial policy, 361
  and labor force, 293, 296

Okazaki, T., 321
Okoshi, Takahiro, 237
Oligopoly
  global, 79, 81, 83–84, 92
  Japanese, 203–204, 206–207
On-the-job training (OJT), 105–108, 278–
  80, 288–89. *See also* Training systems
Optical fibers, 27, 99
Osaka Boseki, Inc., 173

Parallel competition paradigm, 7
Patents, 22, 23
  Japanese chemical firms and, 165–66
  technological, xv, 128
Pension benefits, 297–98
People's Finance Corporation, 322, 374,
  376
Perfect competition model, 203
Performance
  of automobile industry, 72–78, 79
  and international competition, 125
Personnel, xviii, 125, 168. *See also* Em-
  ployees; Workers
  steel industry, 98, 102, 105–108, 113–14,
    117, 119
  training systems for, 105–108, 195, 200,
    292–93
Petrochemical Industry Promotion Pro-
  gram, 363
Petrochemicals industry, 144–47, 148,
  152–53, 155, 157, 166, 168
Pharmaceuticals, 142, 148, 151, 152, 158,
  159, 164
Photographic film, 148, 158, 159, 166
Plants, 9, 261
  number of, 254, 255–57
  small- and medium-sized, 253, 254, 258–
    59, 260, 262–65, 267, 268
Plaza Accords, 197, 255
Pollution, 145–47, 156–57
Population structure, changes in, 295
Prestowitz, Clyde, 369
Prices, 203, 204–205, 384
  in automobile industry, 89–90, 94
  in chemical industry, 158
  in electric appliance industry, 51, 60, 61,
    62, 66–67
  in electronics industry, 31, 37
  in FA industry, 123, 132, 134, 139
  in fiber industry, 171, 188
  in steel industry, 114, 115
Product development, 125, 131, 204

  in automobile industry, 73, 87–88
  steel industry and, 117, 119
Production, 198, 255, 386
  Asian bases of, 253–54
  in automobile industry, 71–73, 78, 79,
    82–83, 84, 85–88, 93–95
  in chemical industry, 158, 164
  in electronics industry, 22–23, 27–28
  in FA industry, 125, 138
  in fiber industry, 171, 176, 177, 178, 180–
    81, 185–86, 188
  in metals industry, 97, 98–101, 103
  quantitative *vs.* qualitative, 309
  rigid systems of, 217–18
  Toyota system of, 95, 215–17
Production, overseas, 83, 197, 353, 355
  chemical industry and, 158–59, 165
  and electric appliance industry, 65
  impetus for, 348–51
  of manufacturing industries, 344–48
Productivity, xix, xviii, 9, 13, 196, 211
  of automobile industry, 76
  and education, 275, 280
  of electric appliance industry, 52–55, 60
  of electronics industry, 19, 20–21, 35–36
  growth per worker of, 301
  market-driven *vs.* discovery-driven, 227–
    28, 237
  measurement of, 130–31
  value-added, 4, 5, 76, 140, 306
  and world resources, 10–11
Profits, 104, 178, 200, 347
  in automobile industry, 79, 92, 93
  in chemical industry, 144, 151, 155, 158,
    167–68
  in electric appliance industry, 62, 63, 66
  in FA industry, 125, 133, 134, 139

Quality, of Japanese products, 4, 23, 31,
  34–37, 60, 73, 182–83, 304, 335

R&D Executive Forum (1993), 250
R&D Program on the Basic Technology
  for Future Industries, 365
Recession, 14, 15, 197, 226, 254, 282
  and automobile industry, 72, 89, 93
  cartels, 153
  chemical industry and, 145, 147
  and electric appliance industry, 52, 65
  and electronics industry, 37
  and employment, 194–95, 198–99
  and steel industry, 99

Reconstruction Finance Corporation, 362
Reconstruction period, industrial policy
    during, 360, 361–62
Recycling, xix, 83, 116, 157
Regulations, 83, 385. *See also* Deregula-
    tion
Research, x, 247, 248
    at Japanese universities, 44, 285–87
    and private industry, 237, 242–43, 244
    styles of, 163, 231, 234, 236
Research and development, xiv–xvi, 98,
    195, 361
    in automobile industry, 83, 92
    in chemical industry, 147, 155, 160–64
    educational system and, 277–78
    in electric appliance industry, 60–61, 63–
        64, 65
    in electronics industry, 12, 13, 43, 44
    in FA industry, 123, 126–29, 137–38
    and industrial policy, 367, 379, 380
    management of, 12–13, 44–45, 225–26,
        228–30, 243–47
    in postwar Japan, 227, 273
    researchers in, 45, 117, 119, 273, 274, 282
    in steel industry, 105–11, 116–19
    user's cost and, 329–30
Research Center for Advanced Sciences
    and Technology (RCAST), 236–37
Research Evaluation Policy Formulation
    Commission, 234
Resource allocation, and industrial pol-
    icy, 367, 370, 374–80
Retirement, 218, 292, 297, 308
Rice crop metaphor, 243
Rice market, 382, 383
RISC processor, 221
Robots, 123, 127, 181, 209, 214. *See also*
    Automation

Sales/service networks, of Japanese com-
    panies, 131–32
San Francisco Peace Treaty, 362–63
Sanyo Electric Co., Ltd., 51, 58
Savings, domestic, and investment
    funds, 313–14, 383
Science and technology. *See also* Technol-
    ogy
    government budget for, 285–87
    higher education in, 273, 274, 277–78
    shift of interest away from, 281–83, 287,
        288
Scientific and Technical Commission, 234

Semiconductor industry, 19, 20, 25, 30,
    38–39, 40–42, 64, 250. *See also* Com-
    puter software industry
    competitiveness of, 21–22, 28–29, 34–35
Senior citizens
    investment activities of, 330
    in labor market, 82, 85–86, 296–98, 307
Seniority system, 4, 193, 194, 198, 199
    limitations of, 202, 284
    wages in, ix, 199, 292, 293
Service industries, workers in, 301
Services, excessive, 5, 132, 155
Sharp Corp., 51, 58
    R&D at, 242–43, 244, 246
Shokusan-kogyo (to increase production),
    360–61
Shop floor, 86, 119, 214–15
    knowledge gained from, 82, 105–108,
        129, 138, 212, 215–20, 221, 280
Showa Denko K. K., 144, 150
Siemens, 29, 34, 242
Small-and medium-sized enterprises
    (SMEs), 253–57, 258–60, 262–65, 376,
        377, 379–80
Small Business Finance Corporation,
    374, 376
Social system, Japanese, and industrial
    development, 4–7, 195
Sony Corp., 58
Southeast Asia, 65, 165, 261. *See also* Asia
    chemical industry and, 143, 151, 166,
        168
South Korea, 21–22, 30, 341
Specialization, 46–47, 140, 253–54, 262–
    63, 266–67
Specific Industries Promotion Bill, 371,
    372
Spinning industry, 179–80, 181, 182, 183,
    185–86. *See also* Fiber industry
Stagnation, in industrial sector, 71–73,
    113–14, 311, 383
Stakeholders, 72, 73, 79, 249
Steel industry, 288. *See also* Metallic mate-
    rials industry; Wire rod industry
    and automobile industry, 110, 111, 112–
        13
    exports of, 98, 110, 113, 339
    and foreign steel corporations, 108, 109,
        110–11
    maturation and, 97, 100, 113–14
    personnel in, 98, 102, 113–14, 117
    production in, 98–101, 103, 115

Steel industry (cont.)
  R&D in, 112–13, 116–19
  training policies in, 105–108, 215
Steel Industry Rationalization Plan, 363
Stockholders, 329
  main banks as, 319
  as stakeholders, 72
Subcontracting, 59, 198, 206
  in FA industry, 124, 134, 135–36
  and large manufacturing companies,
    267–69
  in machinery industry, 253, 262–63, 264–
    65
Subsidiaries, Japanese, 351–53
Sumitomo Chemical Co., Ltd., 144, 150,
  157, 161
Sumitomo Electric Ind., Ltd., 116–19, 228
Sun Micro Systems, 221
Supply, 136
  and perfect competition model, 203
  and technological innovation, 206
Suzuki, Umetaro, 236
Synthetic Fiber Industry Promotion Program, 363
Synthetic fibers, 174, 182–83, 185–86
System fatigue, in manufacturing indus-
  tries, 193, 195, 210, 217–18, 219–20

Taiwan, 102, 341
Takahashi, Kamekichi, 317–18, 320
Takeda Chemical Industries, Ltd., 150,
  161
Target industries view, 359, 370, 372–80
Tariffs, xv, 25, 366
  protection by, 378–79
  and Uruguay Round negotiations, 381–
    82
Tax concession measures, 377, 379
Technicians, skilled, 217, 218–19. See also
  Workers
  and automation, 178–79
  corporate training system and, 273, 278–
    80
Technological development, 266–67, 365
Technological innovation, 222, 231, 306
  and competition, 128, 129, 206–07
  discovery-driven vs. import-driven, 227–
    28
  in electric appliance industry, 60–61
  in electronics industry, 20, 38, 40–41
  market-driven vs. discovery-driven, 234
  and R&D costs, 329–30

in steel industry, 114–15
  in textile industry, 171–72, 180, 190
Technology, xv, 12–13
  adopted, 26, 97, 105, 160–61
  in automobile industry, 83–84, 92
  in chemical industry, 144, 145–46, 153,
    159–60, 165–66
  and corporate decision-making, 201
  in electric appliance industry, 60–61, 63–
    64, 65
  in electronics industry, 19, 24, 25, 26–27,
    30, 32–33, 34, 42, 43
  exported, 128, 165–66
  in FA industry, 124, 126, 137–39
  and job phase-outs, 217, 218–19
  low-volume production, 114–16
  pollution-preventing, 143, 145–47, 157
  scale-up, 210–11
  in steel industry, 99–100, 104, 110–11,
    114–15
  in synthetic fiber industry, 174, 179–84
  transfer of, 7–9, 46, 127, 298–99
Technology, imported, 60, 127–28, 174,
  228–29, 304
  and chemical industry, 145, 165, 166, 168
  and electronics industry, 21
  following World War I, 292–93
  and Japanese manufacturing climate,
    212–13
  R&D and, 225, 230, 231
Temporary Measures Law for Promoting
  Imports and Facilitating Foreign Investments (1992), 366–67
Textile industry, xi, 171. See also Apparel
  industry; Fiber industry
  overseas investments by, 187
  production in, 176, 180–81
  quality in, 182–83
Third world, economic policies and, 381
Tohoku Univ., 249
Tokyo, Univ. of, 219–20, 236–37, 237
Tokyo Institute of Technology, 219–20
Tomonaga, Shinichiro, 236
Toshiba Corp., 22, 24, 28, 51, 58
Toyota Motor Corp., 75, 87–88, 95, 215–
  17, 221
TQC (total quality control), 95, 213
Trade, 79, 201
  free, xiv–xviii, 8, 10, 45, 381, 382, 383
  liberalization of, 360, 363–64, 383
Trade and Foreign Exchange Liberaliza-
  tion Program, 363, 378–79

Trade friction, x, xiii, xiv, xvi, 196–97, 207, 221
  and automobile industry, 81, 93
  and chemical industry, 158
  and electric appliance industry, 65
  electronics industry and, 22, 25, 27, 28, 37
  and international development, 8, 14, 45, 194, 335–36, 341, 352–58
  machinery industry and, 351, 353, 354–56
  and overseas production, 348, 349–51
  steel industry and, 110, 111
Training systems, 44, 105–108, 195, 200, 215, 292–93. See also On-the-job training
Transport, 373–76, 377, 378

Uchihashi, Katsuhito, 78
Uenohara, Michiyuki, xi
Unemployment, x, xiv, xviii, 194–95, 199–200, 303
Union for Research into Technology for the New Computer Series, 24
Unions, Japanese, 4, 77, 199–200
United Kingdom, 102, 260, 276, 341
United States, xiii, xiv, 5–6, 214, 276
  automobile industry in, 76, 81, 84, 90–92
  chemical industry in, 142, 143, 149–51, 154–55, 156, 157, 160, 162, 163, 168
  cost of capital in, 317, 319, 329
  direct investment in, 343, 352
  electric appliance industry in, 57, 61
  electronics industry in, 19, 21, 22, 29, 31, 32, 33–37, 43, 129
  exports of, 335, 336–38, 382
  global presence of, 356–57
  Japanese applications for patents in, 165–66
  and Japanese electronics industry, 22, 25, 27, 28, 37
  overseas production of, 345–46
  plant size in, 259
  product development in, 128, 204
  productivity of, 55, 130–31, 255
  RISC processor in, 221
  steel industry in, 99, 102, 105, 109, 110–11
  and trade with Japan, x, 340–41, 352, 356–58, 382
United States Department of Commerce Report (1972), 368

United States-Japan Framework Talks, 369
Universities, 274, 276. See also Education
  engineering programs at, 110, 113, 212
  impoverishment of, 7, 195, 284–88
  and industrial sector, 25, 108–10, 247–50, 288
  and R&D, 44, 123, 222, 225, 226, 227, 285–87

Value-added production, 4, 5, 76, 148, 198, 306, 386. See also Added value
Value engineering (VE), in automobile industry, 87
van Wolferen, Karel, 369
Virtual corporation, concept of, 249–50
Vision of the Electronics Industry in the 1990s (MITI), 39
Vocational training schools, 276, 278–79
Volvo, 75, 86, 221

Wages, ix, 65, 66, 67, 260, 299, 306
  in fiber industry, 187, 189
  and seniority system, 199, 292, 293
West Germany, 99, 257, 259, 276. See also Germany
Wire rod industry, 99, 111, 116–19
Women, in labor force, 21, 82, 85–86, 189, 291, 295, 296, 297, 298
Worker organizations, as stakeholders, 72
Workers, 15, 77, 82, 200, 202, 218. See also Labor force
  attitudes of, 293–94
  blue-collar, 293, 301, 303, 304
  of future, 306–307
  numbers of per plant, 254, 255–57
  self-employed, 295, 297, 298, 299
  in service industries, 301
  in textile industry, 177, 178–79, 180–82, 184, 188
  in Toyota production system, 215–17
  white-collar, 293, 301, 302, 303, 304, 308
Work ethic, changes in, 308–309
Work hours, 66, 67, 304, 306
  for older people, 307
  shorter, 78, 82, 198, 200, 292, 308
World War II, xiii, 144, 226, 227

Yabushita, Shiro, 319
Yarn industry, 179, 182, 183, 185. See also Fiber industry

Yen, high, x, 14, 97, 293, 335, 342
  and automobile industry, 71, 72–73, 74
  and chemical industry, 154, 158
  and electric appliance industry, 52, 59
  and exports, 338–39
  and fiber industry, 172, 176, 177, 184,
    187–88
  and recession, 196–97
  and steel industry, 99, 114
Yoshikawa, Hiroyuki, xi
Yoshino, N., 325
Youth
  employment trends among, 296, 297
  and science and technology, 281–83
Yukawa, Hideki, 236

Zaibatsu (large family financial com-
    bines), 362